VISUAL QUICKSTART GUIDE

Illustrator 8

FOR MACINTOSH AND WINDOWS

Elaine Weinmann
Peter Lourekas

 **Peachpit Press**

For Alicia and Simona

Visual QuickStart Guide
Illustrator 8 for Macintosh and Windows
Elaine Weinmann and Peter Lourekas

Peachpit Press
1249 Eighth Street
Berkeley, CA 94710
510/524-2178
800/283-9444
510/524-2221 (fax)

Find us on the World Wide Web at: http://www.peachpit.com

Peachpit Press is a division of Addison Wesley Longman

Cover design: The Visual Group
Interior design: Elaine Weinmann
Production: Elaine Weinmann and Peter Lourekas
Illustrations: Elaine Weinmann and Peter Lourekas, except
    as noted

Colophon
This book was created with QuarkXPress 4.0 on a PowerTower Pro 200 and a Power Macintosh 8500. The fonts used are Sabon and Gill Sans from Adobe Systems Inc.

ISBN 0-201-35388-1
9 8 7 6 5 4 3 2 1

Printed and bound in the United States of America

TABLE OF CONTENTS

New or substantially changed features are listed in **boldface**.

Table of Contents

Chapter 5: ## Objects Basics

Daniel Pelavin

Chapter 6: ## Select/Move

Table of Contents

Daniel Pelavin

Chapter 8: Transform

Chapter 9: Fill & Stroke

Table of Contents

Daniel Pelavin

Chapter 13: Style & Edit Type

Chapter 14: Layers

Daniel Pelavin

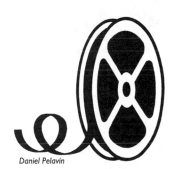

Daniel Pelavin

Chapter 18: **Masks**

Chapter 19: **Graphs**

Table of Contents

Table of Contents

Daniel Pelavin

Table of Contents

ILLUSTRATOR INTERFACE

*This chapter is an introduction to Illustrator's
tools, menus, palettes, and measurement systems.*

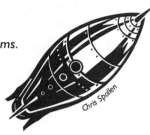

Chris Spollen

Using the Toolbox

TOOLBOX SHORTCUTS

Command-Shift/ Ctrl-Shift double- click any tool	Restore the default display of all tools
Tab	Hide/show all currently open palettes, including the Toolbox
Shift-Tab	Hide/show all currently open palettes except the Toolbox
Caps lock	Turn tool pointer into a crosshair

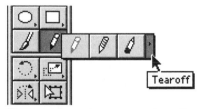

1 *Drag a pop-out menu away from the Toolbox by dragging the tearoff bar.*

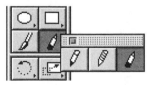

2 *A tearoff toolbar is created.*

Using the Toolbox

The Toolbox contains 51 tools that are used for object creation and modification. If the Toolbox is hidden, choose Window menu > Show Tools to open it. Drag the top bar to move the Toolbox. Click once on a visible tool to select it. Press on a tool with a little triangle to choose a related tool from a pop-out menu. Double-clicking some tools will open an options dialog box for that tool.

To **separate** a pop-out menu from the Toolbox **1**–**2**, release the mouse when it's over the vertical tearoff bar on the far right side of the menu. Move a tearoff toolbar by dragging its top bar. To restore a tearoff toolbar to the Toolbox, click its close box.

To access a tool quickly, use its letter **shortcut** (see the boldface letters on the next two pages). To access a tool that isn't currently visible on the Toolbox, use Shift with the shortcut key (i.e., Shift-L cycles through the Ellipse, Polygon, Star, and Spiral tools).

To turn tool pointers into a **crosshair** for precise positioning, check the Use Precise Cursors box in File menu > Preferences > General. Or press Caps Lock to turn a tool pointer into a crosshair temporarily.

TIP You'll probably want to leave the Disable Warnings box unchecked in File menu > Preferences > General. With this option unchecked, an alert prompt will appear when a tool is being used incorrectly.

The Toolbox

*To access hidden tools on a pop-out menu, press **Shift** and the letter shortcut (i.e. Shift-N cycles through the Pencil, Smooth, and Erase tools).*

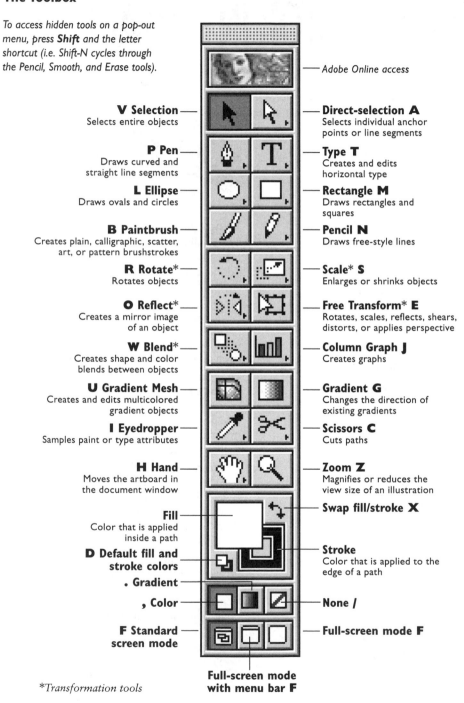

Adobe Online access

V Selection
Selects entire objects

Direct-selection A
Selects individual anchor points or line segments

P Pen
Draws curved and straight line segments

Type T
Creates and edits horizontal type

L Ellipse
Draws ovals and circles

Rectangle M
Draws rectangles and squares

B Paintbrush
Creates plain, calligraphic, scatter, art, or pattern brushstrokes

Pencil N
Draws free-style lines

R Rotate*
Rotates objects

Scale* S
Enlarges or shrinks objects

O Reflect*
Creates a mirror image of an object

Free Transform* E
Rotates, scales, reflects, shears, distorts, or applies perspective

W Blend*
Creates shape and color blends between objects

Column Graph J
Creates graphs

U Gradient Mesh
Creates and edits multicolored gradient objects

Gradient G
Changes the direction of existing gradients

I Eyedropper
Samples paint or type attributes

Scissors C
Cuts paths

H Hand
Moves the artboard in the document window

Zoom Z
Magnifies or reduces the view size of an illustration

Fill
Color that is applied inside a path

Swap fill/stroke X

D Default fill and stroke colors

Stroke
Color that is applied to the edge of a path

. Gradient

, Color

None /

F Standard screen mode

Full-screen mode F

Full-screen mode with menu bar F

*Transformation tools

Toolbox

The tool pop-out menus

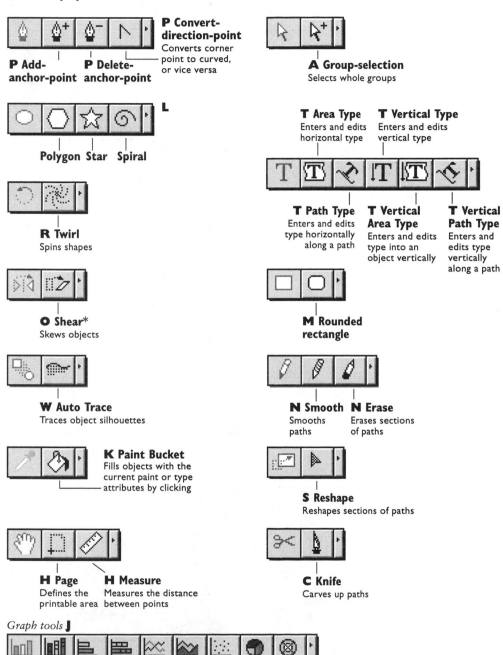

P Convert-direction-point
Converts corner point to curved, or vice versa

P Add-anchor-point

P Delete-anchor-point

L

Polygon Star Spiral

R Twirl
Spins shapes

O Shear*
Skews objects

W Auto Trace
Traces object silhouettes

K Paint Bucket
Fills objects with the current paint or type attributes by clicking

H Page
Defines the printable area

H Measure
Measures the distance between points

A Group-selection
Selects whole groups

T Area Type
Enters and edits horizontal type

T Vertical Type
Enters and edits vertical type

T Path Type
Enters and edits type horizontally along a path

T Vertical Area Type
Enters and edits type into an object vertically

T Vertical Path Type
Enters and edits type vertically along a path

M Rounded rectangle

N Smooth
Smooths paths

N Erase
Erases sections of paths

S Reshape
Reshapes sections of paths

C Knife
Carves up paths

Graph tools **J**

Stacked Column Bar Stacked Bar Line Area Scatter Pie Radar

Toolbox

The Illustrator screen: Macintosh

Illustrator Screen (Macintosh)

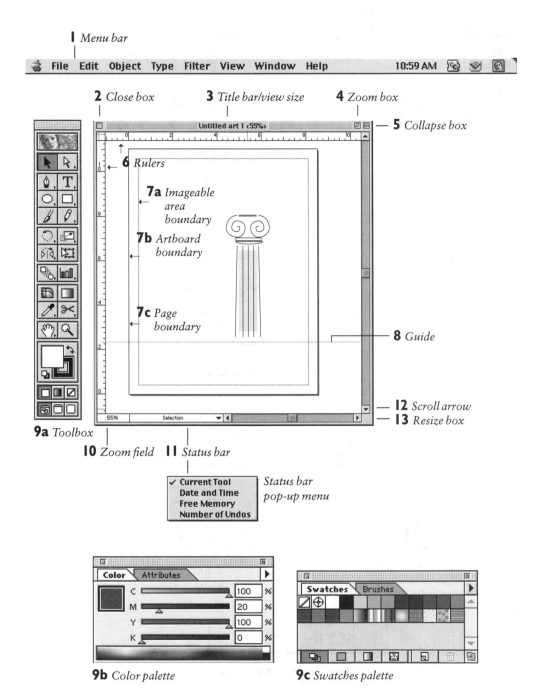

1 *Menu bar*

2 *Close box*   **3** *Title bar/view size*   **4** *Zoom box*

5 *Collapse box*

6 *Rulers*

7a *Imageable area boundary*

7b *Artboard boundary*

7c *Page boundary*

8 *Guide*

12 *Scroll arrow*
13 *Resize box*

9a *Toolbox*

10 *Zoom field*   **11** *Status bar*

Status bar pop-up menu

9b *Color palette*   **9c** *Swatches palette*

Key to the *Illustrator screen: Macintosh*

1 *Menu bar*
Press a menu heading to access dialog boxes, submenus, and commands.

2 *Close box*
To close a document or a palette, click its close box.

3 *Title bar/view size*
Displays the illustration's title and current view percentage.

4 *Zoom box*
Click a document window zoom box to enlarge the window. Click again to restore the window to its previous size. (Click a palette zoom box to shrink the palette or restore it to its previous size.)

5 *Collapse box*
Click the collapse box to shrink the document window to just the title bar. Click the collapse box again to restore the document window to its previous size.

6 *Rulers*
The current position of the pointer is indicated by a marker on the horizontal and vertical rulers. Ruler and dialog box increments can be displayed in a choice of five different measurement units.

7a–c *Imageable area, artboard boundary, and page boundary*
The imageable area within the margin guides is the area that will print on the paper size currently selected in File menu > Page Setup. The artboard is the user-defined work area and the largest possible printable area. The non-printing page boundary matches the current paper size. Objects can be stored in the scratch area (off the artboard), but they won't print.

8 *Guide*
Drag from either ruler to create guides to help you align objects. Guides don't print.

9a–c *Palettes*
Color/Attributes and Swatches/Brushes are four of 19 moveable palettes that open from the Window and Type menus. The Toolbox contains 51 drawing and editing tools and various color controls and screen view mode buttons.

10 *Zoom field*
Enter a new zoom percentage in this field or Control-click in this field and choose a preset zoom percentage from the zoom pop-up menu.

11 *Status bar*
Depending on which category you select from the pop-up menu, the Status bar displays the name of the Current Tool, the current Date and Time from the Macintosh Control Panel, the amount of Free Memory (RAM) available for the currently open file, or the Number of available Undos/Redos. Option-press on the Status bar pop-up menu to learn the National Debt, Shopping Days 'til Christmas, and other vital statistics.

12 *Scroll arrow*
Click the downward-pointing scroll arrow to move the illustration upward in the document window. Click the upward-pointing scroll arrow to move the illustration downward in the document window.

13 *Resize box*
To resize a document window, drag its resize box diagonally.

The Illustrator screen: Windows

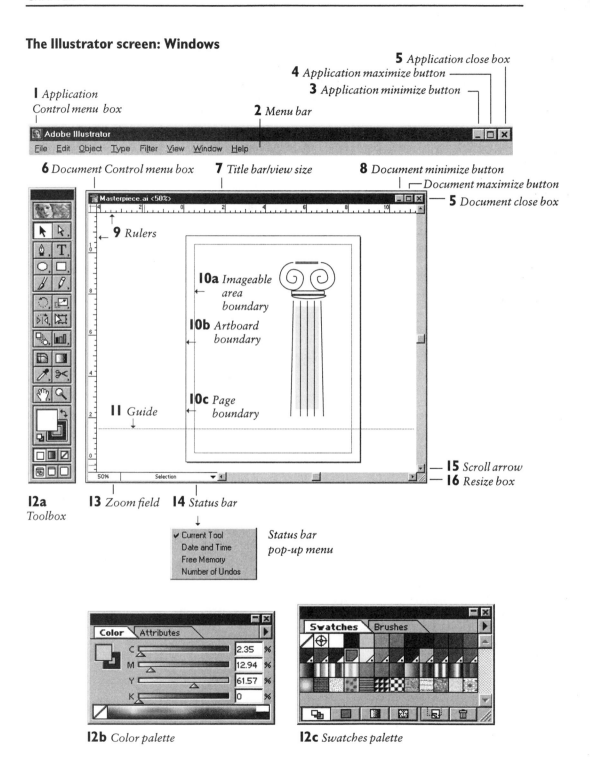

1 *Application Control menu box*

2 *Menu bar*

3 *Application minimize button*

4 *Application maximize button*

5 *Application close box*

6 *Document Control menu box*

7 *Title bar/view size*

8 *Document minimize button*

— *Document maximize button*

5 *Document close box*

9 *Rulers*

10a *Imageable area boundary*

10b *Artboard boundary*

10c *Page boundary*

11 *Guide*

15 *Scroll arrow*

16 *Resize box*

12a *Toolbox*

13 *Zoom field*

14 *Status bar*

Status bar pop-up menu

- ✓ Current Tool
- Date and Time
- Free Memory
- Number of Undos

12b *Color palette*

12c *Swatches palette*

Key to the Illustrator screen: Windows

1 *Application Control menu box*
The Application Control menu box commands are Restore, Move, Size, Minimize, Maximize, and Close.

2 *Menu bar*
Press a menu heading to access dialog boxes, submenus, and commands.

3 *Application minimize button*
Click the Application minimize button to shrink the application to an icon in the Taskbar. Click the icon on the Taskbar to restore the application window to its previous size.

4 *Application (or Document) maximize/ restore button*
Click the Application or Document Restore button to restore that window to its previous size. When a window is at the restored size, the Restore button turns into the Maximize button. Click the Maximize button to enlarge the window.

5 *Close box*
To close a document or a palette, click its close box.

6 *Document Control menu box*
The Document Control menu box commands are Restore, Move, Size, Minimize, Maximize, Close, and Next.

7 *Title bar/view size*
The image's title and view size.

8 *Document minimize button*
Click the Document minimize button to shrink the document to an icon at the bottom left corner of the application window. Click the icon to restore the document to its previous size.

9 *Rulers*
The current position of the pointer is indicated by a marker on the horizontal and vertical rulers. Ruler and dialog box increments can be displayed in a choice of five different measurement units.

10a–c *Imageable area, artboard boundary, and page boundary*
The imageable area within the margin guides is the area that will print on the paper size currently selsected in File menu > Page Setup. The artboard is the user-defined work area and the largest possible printable area. The non-printing page boundary matches the current paper size. Objects can be stored in the scratch area, but they won't print.

11 *Guide*
Drag from either ruler to create guides to help you align objects. Guides don't print.

12a–c *Palettes*
Color/Attributes and Swatches/Brushes are four of 19 moveable palettes that open from the Window and Type menus. The Toolbox contains 51 drawing and editing tools and various color controls and screen view mode buttons.

13 *Zoom field*
Enter a new zoom percentage in this field or Right-click in this field and choose a preset zoom percentage from the pop-up menu.

14 *Status bar*
Depending on which category you select from the pop-up menu, the Status bar displays the name of the Current Tool, the current Date and Time from the computer's internal clock, the amount of Free Memory (RAM) available for the currently open file, or the Number of available Undos/Redos. Alt-press on the Status bar pop-up menu to learn the National Debt, Shopping Days 'til Christmas, and other vital statistics.

15 *Scroll arrow*
Click the downward-pointing scroll arrow to move the illustration upward in the document window. Click the upward-pointing scroll arrow to move the illustration downward in the document window.

16 *Resize box*
To resize a window, press and drag its resize box diagonally.

Mini-glossary

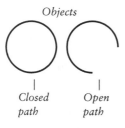

Objects

Closed path   *Open path*

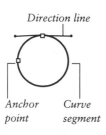

Direction line

Anchor point   *Curve segment*

Straight segment

Selected object

Selected anchor point

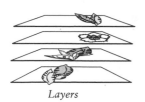

Layers

Path (Or "object") Any individual shape that is created in Illustrator. A path can be open (a line) or closed. Paths are composed of smooth and/or corner anchor points. Smooth anchor points have direction lines. Anchor points and segments can be modified to reshape any path.

Anchor point A corner point or smooth point that joins two segments of a path.

Curve segment The segment between two smooth points or between a corner point and a smooth point.

Straight segment The segment between two corner points.

Direction line Each smooth point has a pair of direction lines. To reshape a curved segment, rotate, lengthen, or shorten a direction line.

Select Only selected objects can be modified. When a whole object is selected, its anchor points are solid (not hollow). The Selection tool is used to select whole objects or groups; the Group-selection tool is used to select nested groups. Use the Direct-selection tool to select individual anchor points or segments.

Layer The positioning of a stack of objects relative to other stacks of objects. An illustration can contain multiple layers, which can be restacked. The most recently created object is automatically placed at the top of its stack within the currently active layer. Multiple objects can be united as a group so they can be moved or modified as a unit. When objects are grouped, they are moved to the layer of the topmost object in the group.

Fill

Stroke

Scatter brushstroke

Linear gradient   *Radial gradient*

Gradient mesh

Transparent

Original objects   *Compound path*

Original objects   *Mask (Preview view)*   *Mask (Artwork view)*

Stroke The color that's applied to the edge (path) of an object.

Fill A color, pattern, or gradient that's applied to the inside of an object.

Brushstroke A calligraphic, art, scatter, or pattern brushstroke that is drawn using the Paintbrush tool or is applied to an existing path.

Gradient fill A graduated blend between two or more colors. A gradient fill can be linear (side to side) or radial (radiating outward from a center point).

Gradient mesh An editable object fill, composed of multicolored gradients along mesh lines, that is created with the Gradient Mesh tool or the Gradient Mesh command.

Compound path Two or more objects that are combined into a single object. Areas where the original objects overlapped become transparent.

Mask An object that trims ("clips") away parts of other objects that extend beyond its border while the mask is in effect. Only parts of objects that are within the confines of a mask object will display and print.

Mini-glossary

The Menus

The Illustrator menus

The File menu

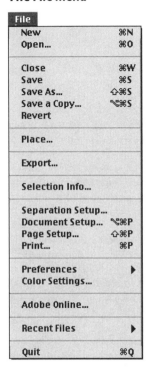

The Edit menu

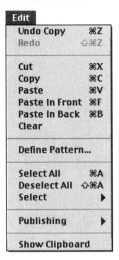

The Object menu

The Type menu

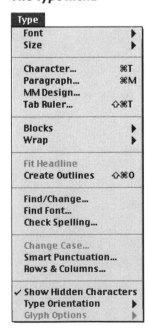

The Filter menu

Filter

Apply Adjust Colors	⌘E
Adjust Colors...	⌥⌘E
Colors	▶
Create	▶
Distort	▶
Pen and Ink	▶
Stylize	▶
Artistic	▶
Blur	▶
Brush Strokes	▶
Distort	▶
Pixelate	▶
Sharpen	▶
Sketch	▶
Stylize	▶
Texture	▶
Video	▶

The View menu

View

Artwork	⌘Y
Preview Selection	⇧⌘Y
Zoom In	⌘+
Zoom Out	⌘-
Fit In Window	⌘0
Actual Size	⌘1
Hide Edges	⌘H
Hide Page Tiling	
Hide Template	⇧⌘W
Hide Rulers	⌘R
Hide Guides	⌘;
✓ Lock Guides	⌥⌘;
Make Guides	⌘5
Release Guides	⌥⌘5
Clear Guides	
Show Grid	⌘"
Snap To Grid	⇧⌘"
✓ Snap To Point	⌥⌘"
Smart Guides	⌘U
New View...	
Edit Views...	

The Cascade, Tile, and Arrange Icons commands are available only in Windows.

The Window menu

Window

New Window
Hide Tools
Show Info
Show Transform
Show Align
Hide Pathfinder
Hide Color
Show Gradient
Hide Stroke
Show Swatches
Swatch Libraries ▶
Hide Brushes
Brush Libraries ▶
Show Links
Hide Layers
Hide Navigator
Show Attributes
Show Actions
✓ Untitled art 1 <50%>

Window

New Window
Cascade
Tile
Arrange Icons
Hide Tools
Hide Info
Show Transform
Show Align
Show Pathfinder
Hide Color
Hide Gradient
Hide Stroke
Hide Swatches
Swatch Libraries ▶
Show Brushes
Brush Libraries ▶
Show Links
Hide Layers
Show Navigator
Show Attributes
Show Actions
Show Transparency
Fillstroke2.ai <112%>
Fillstroke3.ai <112%>
✓ Untitled art 2 <150%>

The Help menu

Help

About Balloon Help...
Show Balloons
Contents...
Index...
Quick Reference...
How to Use Help...

Help

Contents...	F1
Index...	
Quick Reference...	
How to use Help...	
About Illustrator...	
About Plug-ins...	

The Menus

Using dialog boxes

Dialog boxes are like fill-in forms with multiple choices. They are opened from the menu bar or via shortcuts.

Windows: To activate a menu, type Alt-underlined letter, then release Alt and type the underlined letter on the submenu.

Some modifications are made by entering a number in an entry field. Press **Tab** to highlight the next field in a dialog box. Hold down **Shift** and press **Tab** to highlight the previous field. Press on a drop-down menu to choose from more options.

Click **OK** or press **Return/Enter** to accept modifications and exit a dialog box. To cancel a dialog box, click Cancel or press Esc (in Windows, you can also click the close box).

Many Illustrator dialog boxes have a **Preview** option, which, when turned on, will apply the effect while the dialog box is open. Take advantage of this great time-saver. In a dialog box that has sliders (i.e., the raster filters), you can hold down Option/Alt and click Reset to restore the last-applied settings to the dialog box.

Illustrator dialog boxes, like all the other features in the program, function the same way in Macintosh and Windows. The differences in appearance are due to the graphic interface inherent in each operating system.

In Windows, you can type an underlined letter to activate that field (i.e., "U" for "Uniform"). If a field is already highlighted, type Alt plus the underlined letter.

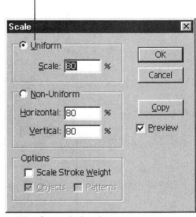

*A **Windows** dialog box.*

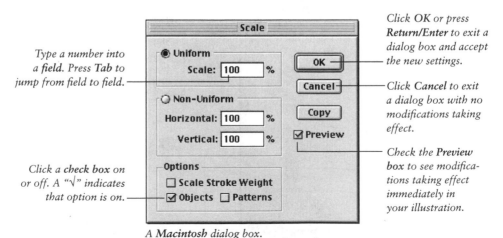

Type a number into a field. Press Tab to jump from field to field.

*Click a **check box** on or off. A "√" indicates that option is on.*

Click OK or press Return/Enter to exit a dialog box and accept the new settings.

Click Cancel to exit a dialog box with no modifications taking effect.

*Check the **Preview** box to see modifications taking effect immediately in your illustration.*

*A **Macintosh** dialog box.*

Using the palettes

There are 19 moveable palettes that are used for creating artwork. To save screen space, the palettes are joined into these default **groups**: Color/Attributes, Stroke/Gradient, Layers/Actions/Links, Character/Paragraph/MM Design, Transform/Align/Pathfinder, Navigator/Info, Swatches/Brushes, Tab Ruler, and Toolbox, but you can compose your own groups.

To **separate** a palette from its group, drag its tab (palette name) away from the group **1**–**2**. To **add** a palette to any group, drag the tab over the group. If you want to gather more palettes together, use as your home base one of the palette group windows that can be resized so the tabs (palette names) will be readable across the top.

To **dock** (hook up) a palette to the bottom of another palette or palette group, drag the tab to the bottom of another palette, and release the mouse when the thick black line appears **3**. To un-dock, drag the palette tab away from the dock group.

Open the Character, Paragraph, MM Design, or Tab Ruler palette from the Type menu. Open all the other palettes from the Window menu. The palette name you choose will appear in front in its group.

To **display** an open palette at the front of its group, click its tab. Most of the palettes have two or more **panels**. Double-click a tab to cycle through the palette configurations: tab only, two option panels, or one option panel. Or to display the full palette, choose Show Options from the palette menu. To shrink a palette to just the tabs, click the palette zoom box (Macintosh) or the mini-mize/maximize box (Windows) in the upper right corner. Click again to restore the palette's previous size.

Press Tab to **hide/show all** currently open palettes, including the Toolbox. Press Shift-Tab to hide/show all open palettes except the Toolbox. Palettes that are open when you quit/exit Illustrator will appear in their same location when you re-launch.

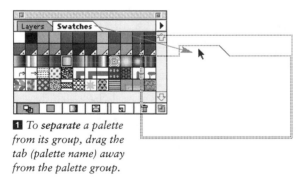

1 *To **separate** a palette from its group, drag the tab (palette name) away from the palette group.*

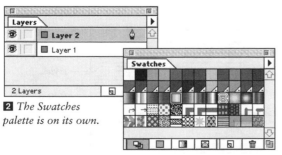

2 *The Swatches palette is on its own.*

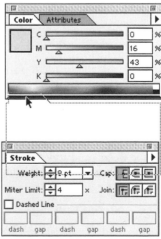

3 *To **dock** palettes together, drag the tab name of one palette to the bottom of another palette, and release the mouse when the thick, black line appears.*

The color controls

The current fill and stroke colors display in color squares on the Toolbox **1** and on the Color palette **2**. The Color palette displays the color model and breakdown of the fill or stroke in the currently selected object or objects, and it's used to mix process colors or adjust global process or spot color tints. The Stroke palette displays the weight and style of the stroke in the currently selected object or objects, and is also used to change those attributes. If no object is selected, then changes made on the Color or Stroke palette will apply to any subsequently-drawn objects.

Color palette

The Color palette is used for mixing, choosing, and switching between the fill and stroke colors. Choose a color model for the palette from the palette menu. You can also Invert the current color or switch to its Complement via the Color palette menu. Quick-select a color, black, white, or None from the color bar on the bottom of the palette. Click the Last Color button if you've clicked None and want to return to the last chosen color.

Whichever box (Fill or Stroke) is currently active (is on top on the Color palette or the Toolbox) will be affected by changes on the Color palette.

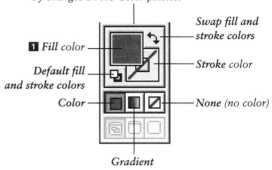

Swap fill and stroke colors

1 *Fill color*

Default fill and stroke colors

Stroke color

Color

None (no color)

Gradient

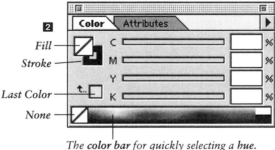

2

Fill

Stroke

Last Color

None

The color bar for quickly selecting a hue.

Stroke palette

The Stroke palette is used for editing the stroke weight and style on the currently selected object, and for creating dashed lines.

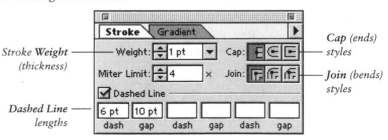

Stroke Weight (thickness)

Cap (ends) styles

Join (bends) styles

Dashed Line lengths

The Swatches palette

Click on a swatch to make that color the current fill or stroke color, depending on which of those color boxes is currently active on the Toolbox or the Color palette. Drag from the current Fill or Stroke color box on the Toolbox or the Color palette to the Swatches palette to save a swatch of that color in the current file. Merge swatches or perform other color-related tasks via the palettte menu.

The Gradient palette

Use the Gradient palette to edit an existing gradient or create a new gradient. Move a color by dragging its square, or click a square and use the Color palette to choose a different color, or click below the Gradient slider to add a new color.

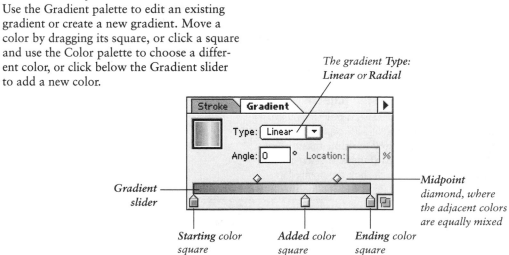

Non-global process color

Global process color

Spot color

Swatch display buttons

All

Colors

Gradients

Patterns

New Swatch

The gradient Type: Linear or Radial

Gradient slider

Midpoint diamond, where the adjacent colors are equally mixed

Starting color square

Added color square

Ending color square

Swatches Palette; Gradient Palette

The Character palette

The Character palette is used to apply type attributes: font, size, leading, baseline shift, vertical scale, horizontal scale, kerning, and tracking. To apply an attribute to currently highlighted text, choose a value from the drop-down menu, or click the up or down arrow, or enter a value in the field and press Return/Enter. The palette is also used for choosing foreign language options.

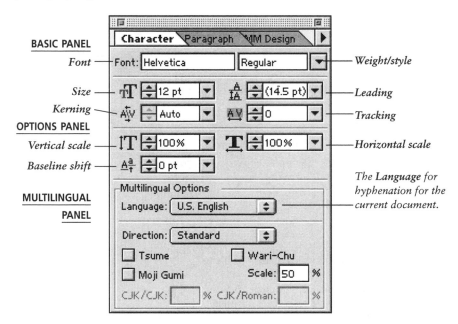

BASIC PANEL

Font — *Font* — *Weight/style*

Size — *Size* — *Leading*

Kerning — *Kerning* — *Tracking*

OPTIONS PANEL

Vertical scale — *Vertical scale* — *Horizontal scale*

Baseline shift — *Baseline shift*

*The **Language** for hyphenation for the current document.*

MULTILINGUAL PANEL

Multiple Masters Design palette

The Multiple Masters Design palette is used to edit the Weight and Width of a multiple master font. Each edited multiple master font is called an instance. Instances are saved with the document for which they are created.

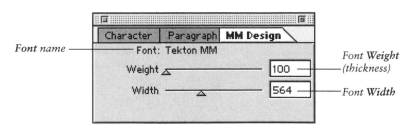

Font name — Font: Tekton MM

Weight ⟶ 100 — *Font **Weight** (thickness)*

Width ⟶ 564 — *Font **Width***

The Paragraph palette

The Paragraph palette is used to apply paragraph-wide specifications, including horizontal alignment, indentation, space before paragraph, word spacing, letter spacing, hyphenation, and hanging punctuation.

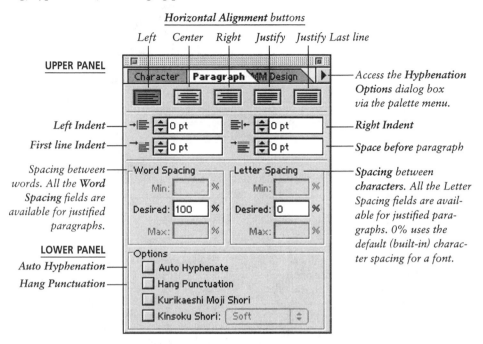

Horizontal Alignment buttons

Left   Center   Right   Justify   Justify Last line

UPPER PANEL

*Access the **Hyphenation Options** dialog box via the palette menu.*

Left Indent

First line Indent

Right Indent

Space before paragraph

*Spacing between words. All the **Word** Spacing fields are available for justified paragraphs.*

Spacing between characters. All the Letter Spacing fields are available for justified paragraphs. 0% uses the default (built-in) character spacing for a font.

LOWER PANEL

Auto Hyphenation

Hang Punctuation

The Tab Ruler palette

The Tab Ruler palette is used to insert or move custom tab markers, which are used to align columns of text.

*The **Snap** function makes a tab marker snap to the nearest ruler tick mark as you insert or drag it. Ruler increments display in the currently chosen ruler units (Document Setup or Preferences).*

Left-, Center-, Right-, and Decimal-Justified buttons

*The **Alignment** box aligns the Tab Ruler with the left edge of the currently selected text.*

*A **left-justified** tab marker*

*A selected **center-justified** tab marker*

Extend Tab ruler box

The Layers palette

The Layers palette is used to add, delete, hide/show, and restack layers in an illustration. You can also use this palette to control which layers are editable or printable, to move an object to a different layer, or to flatten the illustration into one layer. Choose Small Palette Rows from the palette menu to squeeze more layer names onto the palette.

The currently highlighted (active) layer

*The eye icon signifies that this layer is currently **displayed**.*

*The **pencil** icon with a slash through it signifies that this layer is **locked** (uneditable).*

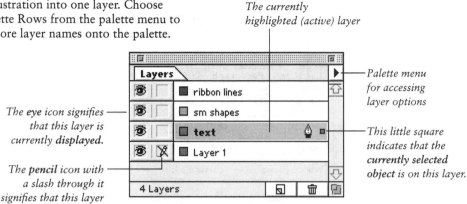

Palette menu for accessing layer options

*This little square indicates that the **currently selected object** is on this layer.*

The Info palette

If no object is selected in the current document, the Info palette shows the horizontal and vertical location of the pointer on the illustration, as in the palette pictured at right. If an object is selected, the palette displays the location of the object on the page and the object's width and height. If a type tool and type are selected, the palette displays type specifications. The Info palette automatically opens when the Measure tool is used, and displays the distance and angle calculated by that tool.

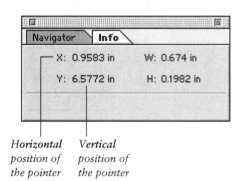

Horizontal position of the pointer   *Vertical position of the pointer*

The Attributes palette

The Attributes palette is used to specify overprint options for an object, show or hide an object's center point, reverse an object's fill in a compound path, or change an object's output resolution.

In the URL field, you can enter a Web address for an object if you're designating it as a button on an imagemap. Click Launch Browser to launch an installed Web browser.

*Reverse Path Direction **Off** and Reverse Path Direction **On** buttons switch a shape's fill between color and transparency in a compound path.*

Don't Show Center

Show Center

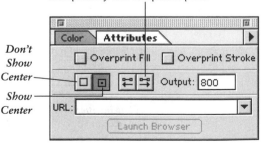

The Align palette

The Align palette is used to align or distribute two or more objects along their centers or along their top, left, or bottom edges, or to equalize (distribute) the space between three or more objects.

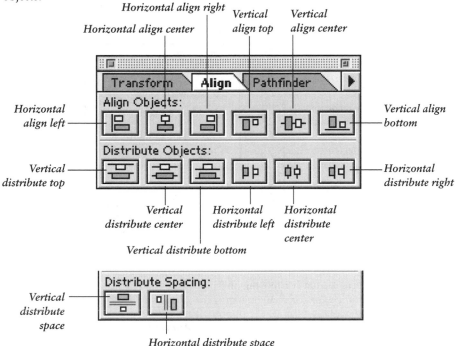

Horizontal align right

Horizontal align center

Vertical align top

Vertical align center

Horizontal align left

Vertical align bottom

Vertical distribute top

Horizontal distribute right

Vertical distribute center

Horizontal distribute left

Horizontal distribute center

Vertical distribute bottom

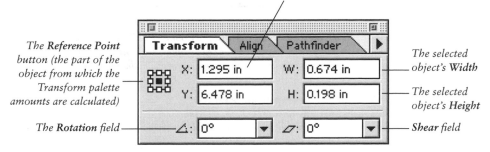

Vertical distribute space

Horizontal distribute space

The Transform palette

The Transform palette displays location, width, and height information for a selected object. The palette is also used to move, resize, rotate, or shear a selected object or objects.

The x and y axes location of the currently selected object. Enter new values to move the object.

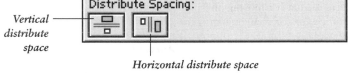

The Reference Point button (the part of the object from which the Transform palette amounts are calculated)

The selected object's Width

The selected object's Height

The Rotation field

Shear field

Actions palette

The Actions palette is an automation tool. You record a series of commands or steps as you create or edit an illustration, and then replay those commands on any file to create or edit objects. The Actions palette can also be used to create and access shortcuts.

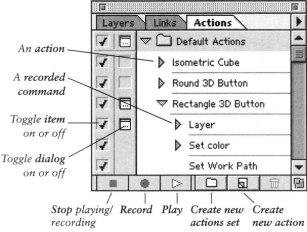

An *action*

A *recorded command*

*Toggle **item** on or off*

*Toggle **dialog** on or off*

Stop playing/ recording   Record   Play   Create new actions set   Create new action

Navigator palette

The Navigator palette is used for moving an illustration in its window or for changing an illustration's view size.

Artboard   View box

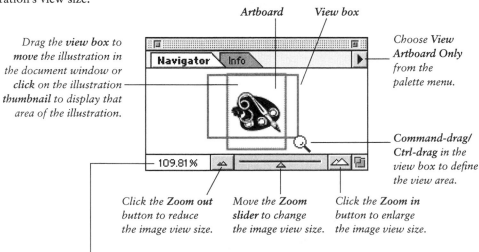

*Drag the **view box** to move the illustration in the document window or click on the illustration thumbnail to display that area of the illustration.*

*Choose **View Artboard Only** from the palette menu.*

Command-drag/ Ctrl-drag in the view box to define the view area.

*Click the **Zoom out** button to reduce the image view size.*

*Move the **Zoom** slider to change the image view size.*

*Click the **Zoom in** button to enlarge the image view size.*

*Enter the desired **zoom percentage** between 3.13% and 6400%, then press Return/Enter. To zoom to a percentage and keep the field highlighted, press Shift-Return/Shift-Enter.*

The Links palette

A linked image is an image that is placed into an Ilustrator file without being embedded into that file. The Links palette lets you keep track of and update linked images, modify a linked image in its original application, and convert a linked image to an embedded image.

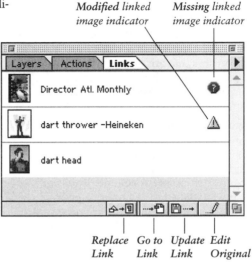

Modified linked image indicator   *Missing* linked image indicator

Replace Link   *Go to Link*   *Update Link*   *Edit Original*

The Pathfinder palette

The Pathfinder palette is used for executing the Pathfinder commands, which combine two or more objects into either a new closed object or a compound path. (The Pathfinders were accessed via the Object menu in Illustrator version 7).

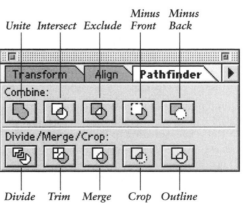

Unite   Intersect   Exclude   Minus Front   Minus Back

Divide   Trim   Merge   Crop   Outline

(To access these buttons, choose Show Options from the palette menu.)

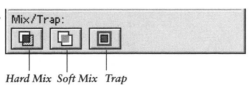

Hard Mix   Soft Mix   Trap

Brushes Palette; Multiple Undos

Brushes palette

The four varieties of brushes on the Brushes palette—calligraphic, scatter, art, and pattern—are used to apply brushstrokes to paths. There are two basic ways to apply brushstrokes. You can either choose the Paintbrush tool and a brush and then draw a shape, or you can apply a brushstroke to an existing path that was drawn using any tool. The brushes that are currently on the Brushes palette save with the document. To personalize your brushstrokes, you can create your own brushes.

To change the contour of a brushstroke, you can use any tool or command that you'd normally use to reshape a path (i.e., Erase, Reshape, Pencil, Smooth, Add-anchor-point, Convert-direction-point). If you modify a brush that was applied to any existing paths in a document, you'll be given the option via an alert dialog box to reapply the revised brush to those paths.

Multiple undos

To undo an operation, choose Edit menu > Undo (Command-Z/Ctrl-Z). To undo the second-to-last operation, choose Edit menu > Undo again, and so on. To reverse an undo, choose Edit > Redo (Command-Shift-Z/ Ctrl-Shift-Z). Or Control-click/Right-click on the artboard and choose either command from the context menu **1**. You can undo or redo after saving your document, but not after you close and reopen it.

The minimum number of undos that can be performed depends on the current Minimum Undo Levels setting in File menu > Preferences > Units & Undo. You can undo up to 200 operations, depending on currently available memory. If Illustrator requires additional RAM to perform illustration edits, the specified number of undos will be reduced to the minimum.

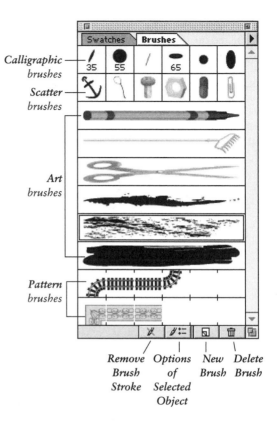

Calligraphic brushes

Scatter brushes

Art brushes

Pattern brushes

Remove Brush Stroke — *Options of Selected Object* — *New Brush* — *Delete Brush*

1 *Control-click/Right-click on the artboard and choose Undo [command name] or Redo from the context menu.*

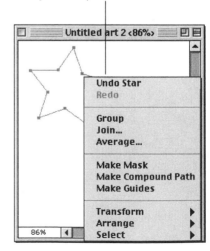

DIVISION THE EASY WAY

Let's say you want to reduce an object's width by 25%. Select the object, highlight the **entire** W field on the Transform palette, type "75%", then press Return/Enter. The width will be reduced to three-quarters of its current value (i.e., 4p becomes 3p). You could also click to the right of the current entry, type an asterisk (*), type a percentage, and press Return/Enter.

SYMBOLS YOU CAN USE		POINTS 'N' PICAS
Unit	**Symbol**	12 pts = 1 pica
Picas	**p**	6 picas = 1 inch
Points	**pt**	
Inches	**"** or **in**	
Millimeters	**mm**	
Centimeters	**cm**	
Q (a type unit)	**q**	

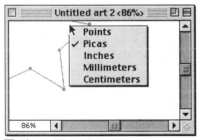

1 *Choose Units via a context menu...*

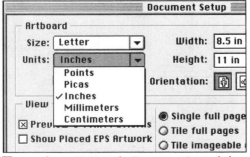

2 *...or choose Units in the Document Setup dialog.*

Measuring up

The current ruler units are used in most palettes and dialog box entry fields, and of course on the rulers. You can choose a unit of measure for an individual document (instructions below) that differs from the default unit of measure that is currently chosen for the application in File menu > Preferences > Units & Undo.

You can enter numbers in dialog boxes or on palettes in any of the units of measure used in Illustrator, regardless of the default general units. If you enter a number in a unit of measure other than the default units, the number will be translated into the default units when you press Tab or Return/Enter. If you enter the symbol for subtraction (-), addition (+), multiplication (*), or division (/) after the current value in any field, Illustrator will do the math for you automatically.

TIP To enter a combination of picas and points, separate the two numbers by a "p". For example, 4p2 equals four picas plus 2 points, or 50 pt. Be sure to highlight the entire entry field first.

Follow the instructions below to change the ruler units for the current document only. Choose a unit of measure for the current *and* future documents in File menu > Preferences > Units & Undo.

To change the units for the current document:

Control-click/Right-click on either ruler in the illustration window (or in the spot where the rulers would display, if they were visible) and choose a unit from the context menu **1**.
or
Choose File menu > Document Setup (Command-Option-P/Ctrl-Alt-P); choose Units: Points, Picas, Inches, Millimeters, or Centimeters **2**; then click OK.

TIP The larger the view size, the finer the ruler increments. The current location of the pointer is indicated by a dotted line on both rulers.

Units of Measure

Context-sensitive menus

Call us efficiency experts or call us lazy, but we think context-sensitive menus are the greatest thing since sliced bread. They allow you to choose a command from an on-screen menu without having to mouse to the menu bar or even to a palette. To open a context menu, Control-click (Macintosh) or Right-click (Windows) on the artboard.

Context menu offerings change depending on which tool is selected and whether any objects are selected in your illustration **1**–**4**. Not all of the commands that appear on a context menu may be applicable to or available for the currently selected objects.

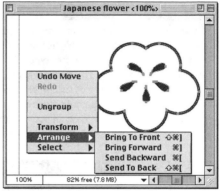

1 *A **group** of objects is selected.*

2 ***Nothing** is selected.*

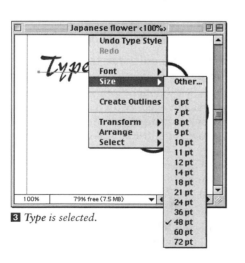

3 *Type is selected.*

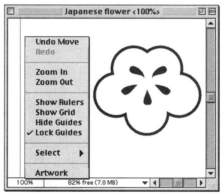

4 *Two paths are selected.*

HOW ILLUSTRATOR WORKS 2

In this chapter you will learn the basic differences between object-oriented and bitmap applications and you'll get a broad overview of how objects are created and modified in Illustrator.

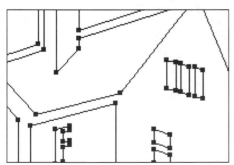

1 *An object-oriented graphic.*

2 *A closeup of the same object-oriented graphic in **Artwork** view, showing selected line segments and anchor points.*

Vectors and rasters

There are two main types of picture-making applications: bitmap (or "raster") and object-oriented (or "vector"), and it's important to know their strengths and weaknesses. Bitmap programs are ideal for creating soft, painterly effects; object-oriented programs are ideal for creating sharp, smooth-edged layered images, like logos, and for creating typographic designs.

Some bitmap applications—like Painter— also have some built-in vector capabilities. In Illustrator, you can **rasterize** a vector image— convert an object-oriented image into a bitmap image. And you can also place or open a bitmap image into an Illustrator document.

Drawings created in an **object-oriented** program like Adobe Illustrator or Macromedia FreeHand are composed of separate, distinct objects or groups of objects that are positioned on one or more **layers**. Objects are drawn using free-style or precise drawing tools, and are mathematically defined. An object drawn in Illustrator can be recolored, resized, and reshaped without diminishing its sharpness or smoothness, and it can be moved easily without disturbing any other objects. An object in an object-oriented drawing will look smooth and sharp regardless of the size at which it is displayed or printed **1**–**2**.

Object-oriented files are usually relatively small in storage size, so you can save multiple versions of a file without filling up valuable hard drive space. And object-oriented drawings are resolution independent, which means the higher the resolution of the printer, the sharper and finer the printed image will be.

An image created in a **bitmap** program, like Photoshop, on the other hand, is composed of a single layer of tiny squares on a grid, called pixels. One pixel layer can be arranged above or below another pixel layer. If you paint on a bitmap image, you'll recolor just that area of pixels, not whole, independent objects. If you zoom way in on a bitmap image, you'll see a checkerboard of tiny squares. Bitmap files tend to be quite large, and the printout quality of a bitmap image is dependent on the resolution of the image. On the other hand, bitmap programs are ideal for creating subtle color gradations, digital paintings, montages, or photorealistic images, and for editing photographs 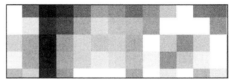–.

1 *A bitmap graphic.*

2 *Extreme closeup of a bitmap, showing the individual pixels that make up the image.*

Your Illustrator images will mostly consist of vector shapes, though you can place or open a raster image in Illustrator and perform some operations on it.

How objects are made

In Illustrator, the key building blocks that you will be using to compose an illustration are Bézier objects, type, and placed bitmap images. Bézier objects are composed of **anchor points** connected by **curved** or **straight segments 3**. The edge of an object is called its **path.** A path can be open (with two endpoints) or closed and continuous. You can close an open path by joining its endpoints or open a closed path using the Scissors tool.

Some Illustrator tools—like the Rectangle, Ellipse, Polygon, and Star—produce complete, closed paths simply by clicking on the artboard. The number and position of the anchor points on these paths is determined automatically.

Other tools—like the Pencil and Pen—produce open *or* closed paths by clicking or dragging with the mouse. The **Pencil** tool creates open or closed freeform lines. The **Paintbrush** tool can be used with its four categories of brushes to create **calligraphic, scatter, art,** or **pattern** brushstrokes. You can use Illustrator's brushes or create your own. And using Illustrator's most versatile tool of all—

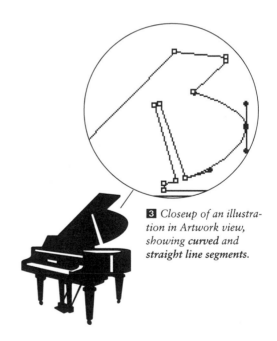
3 *Closeup of an illustration in Artwork view, showing curved and straight line segments.*

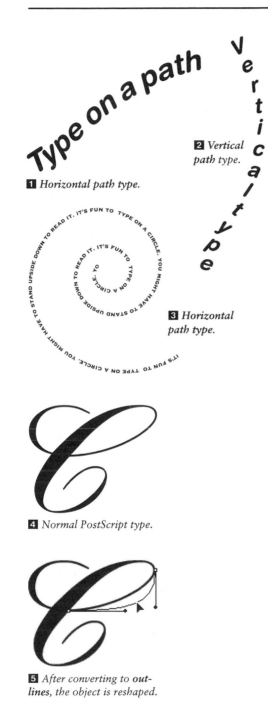

1 *Horizontal path type.*

2 *Vertical path type.*

3 *Horizontal path type.*

4 *Normal PostScript type.*

5 *After converting to outlines, the object is reshaped.*

the **Pen**—you can create as many corner or curve anchor points as you need to form an object of any shape.

If you want to use a scanned image as a starting point, you can place it onto a **template layer** in an Illustrator file, and then trace it manually with the Pen tool or trace it automatically using the **Auto Trace** tool.

The **Layers** palette's role is to help you keep track of the various elements in an illustration. This palette is used to restack objects and to toggle locking, displaying, and printing on or off for individual layers.

Adding words

Illustrator has six tools for creating PostScript **type**, and a smorgasbord of features with which type can be styled and formatted. Type can be free floating (point type), it can flow along the edge of an object (path type) **1**–**3**, or it can fill the inside of an object of any shape (area type). Depending on which tool is used to create it, type can flow and read vertically or horizontally. It can be repositioned, edited, restyled, recolored, or transformed. And if your text is too long to fit inside one object, it can be linked so it flows into another object.

You can also convert type characters into graphic objects, called **outlines**, which can be reshaped or modified like any other Illustrator object **4**–**5**. This is how letter shapes can be personalized.

How objects are modified

An object must be **selected** before it can be modified, and there are three tools that do the job: Selection, Direct-selection, and Group-selection.

An object can be modified using menu commands, filters, dialog boxes, palettes, and tools. There are 51 (yes, 51) tools and 18 movable palettes (Toolbox, Actions, Align, Attributes, Color, Character, Gradient, Info, Layers, Links, MM Design, Navigator, Paragraph, Pathfinder, Stroke, Swatches, Tab Ruler, and Transform). If you need fast access, leave most of the palettes open while you work. To save screen space, you can dock them together in groups and shrink down the ones you use infrequently.

How everything shapes up

An object's path can be reshaped by moving its anchor points or segments or by converting its curve anchor points into corner anchor points (or vice versa). A curve segment can be reshaped by rotating, lengthening, or shortening its direction lines. Because a path can be reshaped easily, you can draw a simple shape first and then develop it into a more complicated form later on **1**. We'll show you how to do this.

Some tools are specifically designed for modifying paths, such as the **Add-anchor-point** tool, which adds points to a path; the **Delete-anchor-point** tool, which deletes points from a path; the **Scissors** tool, which splits a path; and the **Convert-direction-point** tool, which converts corner points into curve points, and vice versa.

Some tools are used like sculptors' tools to change the contour of an object. The **Knife** tool carves out sections of an object. The **Smooth** tool removes points to create smoother curves. The **Erase** tool removes whole chunks of a path. And the **Pencil** or **Reshape** tool reshapes an object when it's dragged along the object's edge.

There are two categories of **filters** in Illustrator. The vector filters randomly distort an object's shape or modify its color. The bitmap filters add artistic, painterly touches or textures to a rasterized object or a placed bitmap image.

The **Pathfinder** commands, applied via the Pathfinder palette, combine overlapping objects, divide areas where objects overlap into separate objects, or apply color to areas where objects overlap—and produce a new object in the process **2**–**3**.

Other modifications can be made using the **transformation** tools. The **Scale** tool enlarges or reduces an object's size; the **Rotate** tool rotates an object; the **Reflect** tool creates a mirror image of an object; the **Shear** tool slants an object; and the **Blend** tool transforms

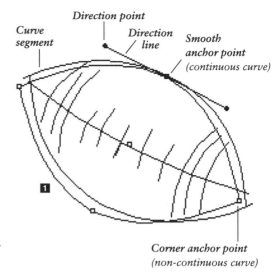

Direction point
Curve segment
Direction line
Smooth anchor point (continuous curve)
1
Corner anchor point (non-continuous curve)

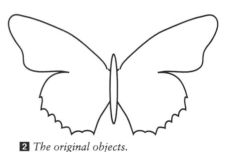

2 *The original objects.*

3 *After clicking the **Unite** button on the **Pathfinder** palette, the individual shapes are combined into a single shape.*

1 *The original formation.*

2 *After applying the Transform Each command.*

3 *Blends in Illustrator are **live**, which means they're editable.*

4 *Illustrator's **gradient mesh** features can be used to create lush photorealistic, naturalistic, or painterly imagery.*

one object into another object by creating a series of transitional shapes. Multiple transformations can be performed at once using the **Free Transform** tool, the **Transform Each** command **1**–**2**, or the **Transform** palette.

Still other Illustrator commands combine individual objects into more complex configurations. The **Compound Path** command, for example, "cuts" a hole through an object to reveal underlying shapes. Or you can use an object as a **mask** to hide parts of other objects that extend beyond its edges.

And don't fret about making a mistake: Illustrator has a **multiple-undo** capability. If you *want* to repeat a series of operations, on the other hand, use the **Actions** palette.

Filling and stroking

You can **fill** the inside of an open or closed object with a **flat color**, a **gradient** (a smooth gradation of two or more colors), or a **pattern** of repeating tiles. Patterns and gradients can be produced right in Illustrator. And you can **stroke** the edge of an object with a flat color in a solid or dashed style. If you have a painter's touch, you'll enjoy Illustrator's live, editable **blends 3** and its **gradient mesh** features, which create multicolored, editable gradient mesh objects **4**.

A stroke or fill color can be a color from a matching system, like PANTONE, or a CMYK, HSB, or RGB color that you mix yourself. In Illustrator, you can mix, apply, and save colors in true RGB or CMYK color mode. This means that a color will be consistent for its model—whether it's a CMYK color being color managed for color separation, an RGB color being color managed for display on screen, or a spot color being converted to a process color.

On the screen

You can draw an illustration by eye or you can use any of Illustrator's precision tools to help you work more exactly: **Smart Guides**, **rulers**, **guides**, **grids**, the **Measure** tool, the **Move** dialog box, and the **Align** palette.

You can change the **view size** of an illustration as you work to facilitate editing and

How Illustrator Works

reduce eyestrain. You can **Zoom in** to work on a small detail or **Zoom out** to see how the drawing looks as a whole. Illustrator does everything but squint for you. If a drawing is at a large view size, you can move it around in its window using the **Hand** tool or the **Navigator** palette.

An illustration can be displayed and edited in **Preview** view , in which all the fill and stroke colors are displayed. Or to speed up editing and screen redraw and to make it easier to select anchor points, you can display your illustration in **Artwork** view , where objects are displayed as wireframe outlines. In **Preview Selection** view, you can selectively preview individual objects.

You may already be familiar with **tool tips**, the on-screen prompter, which you can use to remind yourself of a tool name or shortcut. The even more useful on-screen helpers are **context-sensitive menus**, from which you can choose most of Illustrator's commands.

When all is said and done

There are many options for outputting your Illustrator artwork. It can be **color separated** right from Illustrator or printed on any PostScript output device (e.g., laser printer or imagesetter). If you want to **export** an Illustrator file to a page layout application, like PageMaker or QuarkXPress, or to an image editing application, like Photoshop, you can save it in an assortment of file formats, including EPS, TIFF, and WMF/EMF.

And last but not least, for **on-screen** output, you can use an Illustrator file in a multimedia program (e.g., Director, Premiere, After Effects). You can save it in the GIF or JPEG file format, export it, if you like, to Adobe's ImageReady to refine its appearance or file size, and then display it on a World Wide Web page. Or you can assign a URL to an Illustrator object to create an imagemap GIF, and export the file for use as a clickable element on a Web page.

1 *Preview view.*

2 *Artwork view.*

HOW TO USE THIS BOOK

If Illustrator is brand new to you, we recommend that you read Chapter 1 to familiarize yourself with the basic application features (if you snuck past it, go back now). Read Chapter 3 to learn how to open and save documents, and read Chapter 4 to learn how to navigate around your document. Then proceed to Chapter 5, where you'll learn how to draw basic shapes, and so on, up to the power and precision tool features in the later chapters. Happy illustrating!

STARTUP 3

In this chapter you will learn how to launch Illustrator, create a new illustration, define the working and printable areas of a document, save an illustration in various file formats, open an existing illustration, place a file from another application into Illustrator, use the Links palette to manage linked images, close an illustration, and quit/exit Illustrator.

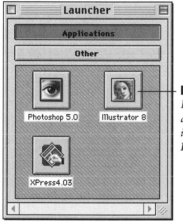

1 *Click the Illustrator application icon on the Launcher.*

To launch Illustrator (Macintosh):

Open the Adobe Illustrator 8 folder on the desktop, then double-click the Illustrator 8 application icon.

or

Click the Illustrator application icon on the Launcher. **1**

or

Double-click an Illustrator file icon. **2**

TIP If you launch Illustrator by clicking the application icon, a new, untitled document window will appear automatically. This window will close and be deleted automatically if you haven't created any artwork in it and you open another file.

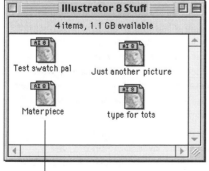

2 *Or double-click an Illustrator file icon.*

To launch Illustrator (Windows):

Open the Adobe Illustrator folder in My Computer, then double-click the Illustrator application icon.

or

Double-click an Illustrator file icon .

or

Click the Start button on the Taskbar, choose Programs, choose Adobe, choose Illustrator 8.0, then click Adobe Illustrator 8.0 **2**.

TIP If you launch Illustrator by choosing or clicking the application icon, a new untitled document window will appear automatically.

1 *Double-click an Illustrator file icon.*

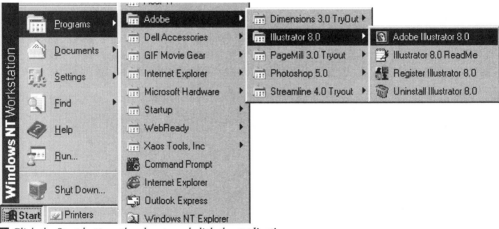

2 *Click the Start button, then locate and click the application.*

To create a new document:

When you launch Illustrator using any method other than by clicking an existing file icon, a new document window will open automatically. If Illustrator is already open and you want to create a new document, choose File menu > New (Command-N/Ctrl-N).

EASIER TO TRACE

You'll learn more about tracing on pages 99–102, but here's a sneak preview. To trace over a bitmap image, create or open an Illustrator document, then use File menu > Place to import a TIFF, PICT, or EPS with the Template box checked. Then, on another layer, use the Pen, Pencil, or Auto Trace tool to draw path shapes above the placed image.

To convert an existing layer into a template layer, click the layer name on the Layers palette, then choose Template from the Layers palette menu. All objects on a template layer are dimmed and uneditable.

Launch Illustrator (Windows)

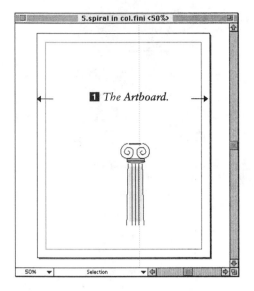

1 *The Artboard.*

*In the Document Setup dialog box, choose a preset Artboard Size, or enter custom **Width and Height** values, or check the Use **Page Setup/Use Print Setup** box to use the Paper size currently chosen in the Page Setup/Print Setup dialog box.*

In the center of every Illustrator document is a non-movable artboard work area that represents the maximum printable size of the illustration **1**. The default artboard area is 8½ inches wide by 11 inches high. You can specify whether the artboard will contain one printable page or facing printable pages. Or you can tile (subdivide) an oversized illustration into a grid so it can be printed in sections on standard-size paper.

Note: The Scale of the printable page is specified in File menu > Page Setup/Print Setup.

To change the artboard dimensions:

1. Choose File menu > Document Setup (Command-Option-P/Ctrl-Alt-P).

2. Choose a preset size from the Artboard: Size drop-down menu **2**.
or
Enter numbers in the Width and Height fields. The maximum work area is 227 by 227 inches.
or
Check the Use Page Setup/Use Print Setup box to have the Artboard dimensions conform to the Paper size currently selected in Page Setup/Print Setup. Click Page Setup/Print Setup to view those settings. Choosing a size other than the current Page Setup/Print Setup size automatically unchecks the Use Page Setup/Print Setup box.

3. Click OK (Return/Enter).

TIP Objects placed outside the artboard will be saved with the illustration, but they won't print.

Note: If the Page Setup/Print Setup Scale percentage is other than 100%, the page size and artboard will resize and the illustration will print proportionately smaller or larger. If the Use Page Setup/Use Print Setup box is unchecked in the Document Setup dialog box, the artboard will match the Artboard: Size option, but the Page boundary will match the current Page Setup/Print Setup size. If Use Page Setup/Use Print Setup is checked, the artboard dimensions can only match the Page Setup/Print Setup printout size.

You can switch the printable area of an illustration from a vertical (portrait) to a landscape orientation. Then you'll need to make the artboard conform to the new orientation.

To create a landscape page:

1. Choose File menu > Document Setup (Command-Option-P/Ctrl-Alt-P).

2. *Macintosh:* Click Page Setup, then choose Page Attributes from the topmost drop-down menu.

   Windows: Click Print Setup.

3. Click the landscape Orientation icon **1**.

4. Click OK (Return/Enter).

5. Click OK (Return/Enter) again to close the Document Setup dialog box **2**.

TIP Drag with the Page tool (H or Shift-H) if you want to reposition the printable area on the artboard **3**. Double-click the Page tool to reset the printable area to its default position.

TIP Double-click the Hand tool to display the entire artboard in the document window.

To create a landscape artboard:

1. Choose File menu > Document Setup.

2. Click the landscape Orientation icon, if it isn't already highlighted.

3. Click OK (Return/Enter). (See the tips above).

4. If the entire page isn't visible on the artboard **4**, reopen Document Setup and enter new Width and Height values to enlarge the artboard to accommodate the new orientation. And remember, objects outside the artboard area won't print.

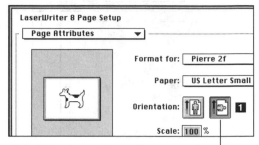

Click the landscape **Orientation** icon in the Page Setup dialog box (Macintosh).

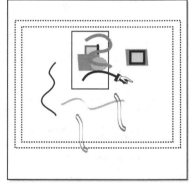

2 The printable page in landscape Orientation.

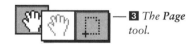

3 The Page tool.

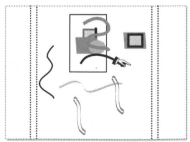

4 The artboard in landscape Orientation. The printable page doesn't extend beyond the artboard.

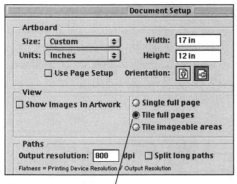

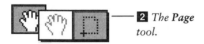

1 *Click the Tile full pages button in the Document Setup dialog box.*

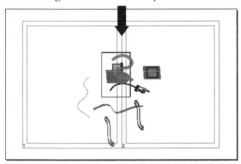

2 *The Page tool.*

Parts of objects that fall within this "gutter" area will not print.

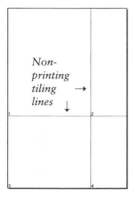

3 *The artboard divided into two pages.*

Non-printing tiling lines →
↓

4 *An oversized illustration tiled into sections for printing (see page 308).*

By default, a new document contains a single page, but you can turn it into a multi-page document. If you turn on the Tile full pages option, as many full page borders as can fit in the current size of the artboard will be drawn. Changing the artboard size will then increase or decrease the number of page borders.

To divide the artboard into multiple pages:

1. Choose View menu > Fit In Window (Command-0/Ctrl-0).

2. Choose File menu > Document Setup.

3. Enter a new Width that's at least double the existing single-page width.

4. Click the View: "Tile full pages" button **1**.

5. Click OK (Return/Enter).

6. *Optional:* Choose the Page tool (H or Shift-H) **2**, then click near the left edge of the artboard. New page borders will be drawn **3**. (If the tile lines aren't showing, choose View menu > Show Page Tiling.)

TIP You can also tile full pages in landscape mode by clicking the landscape Orientation icon in the Document Setup dialog box and in the Page Setup/Print Setup dialog box and choosing Artboard Size: Tabloid. Then, if necessary, click with the Page tool near the top or bottom of the artboard to cause the new page borders to be drawn.

TIP To tile an entire artboard page into the printer's paper size, create an artboard size that's large enough to hold several print paper sizes, and then click "Tile imageable areas" in the Document Setup dialog box **4**.

TIP If you're going to need trim, crop, or registration marks, make the artboard larger than the page.

Divide the Artboard

A file saved in the native Illustrator format will be smaller in file size than the same file saved in the EPS format. However, if you want to open an Illustrator file in any application that doesn't read native Illustrator files, you must save it in the Illustrator EPS format (instructions on the next page) or in another file format that your target application can read (see pages 37–40).

To save a new illustration in the native Illustrator format:

1. Choose File menu > Save (Command-S/ Ctrl-S).

2. Enter a name in the "Save this document as" field (Mac) **1** or File Name field (Win) **2**.

3. *Mac:* Click Desktop.

4. Highlight a drive, then click Open.

5. *Mac:* Highlight a folder in which to save the file, then click Open. Or, to create a new folder, choose a location in which to save the new folder, click New, enter a name for the folder, then click Create.

   Win: Use the Save in pop-up menu to navigate to the folder in which you want to save the file.

6. Leave the Format (Macintosh) or Save as Type (Windows) as Illustrator, and click Save (Return/Enter).

7. Click a Compatibility option **3**. If you choose an earlier version, some elements of your illustration (such as gradient meshes) may be altered if the file is reopened later in Illustrator 8.

8. *Optional:* Check the Include Placed Files box to save a copy of any placed files within the illustration.

9. Click OK (Return/Enter).

The prior version of a file is overwritten when the Save command is executed. Don't be shy—save frequently! And back up!

To save an existing file:

Choose File menu > Save (Command-S/ Ctrl-S).

Save a New Document: Illustrator Format

THE SAVE SHORTCUTS

	Macintosh	Windows
Save	Command-S	Ctrl-S
Save As	Command-Shift-S	Ctrl-Shift-S
Save a Copy	Command-Option-S	Ctrl-Alt-S

1 *Macintosh: Enter a name in the Save this document as field, click Desktop, open a drive and a folder, then click Save.*

2 *Windows Save dialog box for Illustrator.*

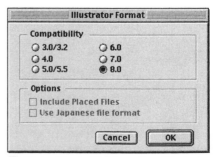

3 *Click a Compatibility option (Illustrator version) and other Options, if applicable, in the Illustrator Format dialog box.*

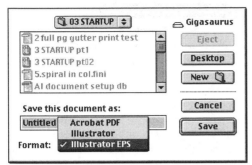

1 *Choose Format: Illustrator EPS in the Save or Save As dialog box.*

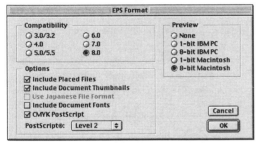

2 *Click a Compatibility option (Illustrator version), a Preview option, and other Options, if applicable, in the EPS Format dialog box.*

INCLUDE PLACED FILES?

If you check the Include Placed Files box in the EPS Format dialog box, and you print, from another program (i.e., QuarkXPress or PageMaker), an Illustrator file containing a linked, placed EPS image, you won't need the original EPS image. You will still need the original EPS image to print the file from Illustrator, though.

If your Illustrator file contains linked, placed images and you *don't* check the Include Placed Files option when saving, you'll get a second chance to save with placed files, because an alert box will open. Just say yes.

A file in the native Illustrator format has no preview option, and it can be opened and modified only in Illustrator or Photoshop. To import an Illustrator file into a page layout, word processing, or other drawing application, save it in the Illustrator EPS format. Other file formats for other applications are discussed on pages 39–40.

To save an illustration as an EPS:

1. Follow steps 1–5 on the previous page. If the file has already been saved, choose File menu > Save As or Save a Copy for Step 1 (see the sidebar on the next page).

2. Choose Format (Macintosh) or Save as Type (Windows) Illustrator EPS **1**.

3. Click Save (Return/Enter).

4. Click a **Compatibility** option **2**. If you choose an earlier version, some elements in your illustration may be altered. Only version 8 preserves gradient meshes.

5. Click a Preview option:
   None to save the illustration with no preview. The EPS won't display on screen in any other application, but it will print.

   1-bit IBM PC or **1-bit Macintosh** to save the illustration with a black-and-white preview.

   8-bit IBM PC or **8-bit Macintosh** to save the illustration with a color preview. This option produces the largest file storage size.

   Note: Regardless of which preview option you choose, color information will be saved with the file and the illustration will print normally from Illustrator or any other application into which it's imported.

6. *Optional steps:*
   Check the **Include Placed Files** box to save a copy of any linked, placed files with the illustration (see the sidebar).

   Check the **Include Document Thumbnails** box to save a thumbnail with the file for previewing in Illustrator's Open dialog box.

(Continued on the following page)

Save an Illustration as an EPS

Check the **Include Document Fonts** box to save any fonts used in the document as a part of the document. Only individual characters used in the font are saved, not the whole character set. Included fonts will show and print on any system, even where they aren't installed. Be sure to check this option if your Illustrator file contains type and you're going to import it into a layout application.

7. Check the **CMYK PostScript** box to convert any RGB color fills or strokes on Illustrator paths into CMYK equivalents.

8. Choose a **PostScript** level that conforms to your printing device from the drop-down menu. Level 2 or 3 are the preferred choices, with Level 3 being the best option for printing gradient meshes. Level 1 produces a significantly larger file size. If you are saving an Illustrator EPS file that contains gradient meshes and you will be placing that EPS file back into Illustrator, choose PostScript Level 1.

9. Click OK (Return/Enter). If you didn't check the Include Place Files box and your file contains placed, linked images, an alert box will appear. Click "Save with placed files" or "Save without placed files."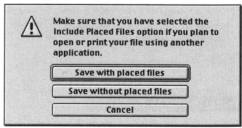

   Note: You'll get a warning prompt if you save an EPS file that contains a placed, drag-and-dropped, or rasterized RGB image , whether or not you check the CMYK PostScript option (this option is designed to convert RGB objects to CMYK for improved printing). RGB color objects are saved as RGB in an Illustrator EPS file and will separate correctly from Illustrator. An image that is drag-copied from Photoshop to Illustrator is automatically converted to RGB. To prevent this mode change, save the file in Photoshop in CMYK Color mode and in the TIFF or EPS format, then place it into Illustrator.

To revert to the last saved version:

1. Choose File menu > Revert.

2. Click Revert.

You can use the Save As or Save a Copy command to save an existing file in a different format (i.e., Illustrator, Illustrator EPS, or Acrobat PDF) or to convert a file to an earlier Illustrator version. Use **Save As** to save the illustration under a new name and continue working on the new version while preserving the original on disk. Use **Save a Copy** to do just the opposite—save the current version as a new file to disk and continue working on the original.

If you save an illustration in an earlier version of Illustrator, but it was created using features that are not present in that earlier version, the illustration may be altered or information may be deleted from it to make it compatible with the earlier version. For example, a gradient fill or gradient mesh may be converted into a blend, or vertical type will become horizontal type. The earlier the Illustrator version, the more the illustration could change.

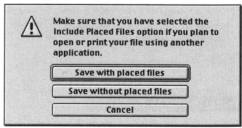

1 *This prompt will appear if you didn't check the Include Placed Files box in the EPS Format dialog box and your file contains placed, linked images. Here's your second chance to include those placed files.*

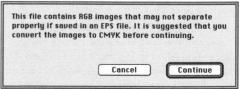

2 *This prompt will appear if you save, as EPS, an Illustrator file that contains RGB images from other applications or objects with applied RGB colors that were rasterized in Illustrator.*

Revert to Last Saved Version

REOPENING A PDF

Blend, gradient, or brushstroke objects will be included in an Illustrator file that is saved as a PDF. *However,* if such a file is reopened in Illustrator, these objects will be converted into expanded objects.

When saving as PDF, if the Compress Text and Line Art option is checked (the default) in the Compression part of the PDF Format dialog box, then earlier versions of Illustrator will not be able to open that saved PDF file.

You can save an Illustrator file that contains a linked image as a PDF file. When that PDF file is reopened into Illustrator, the linked image will be converted into an embedded image.

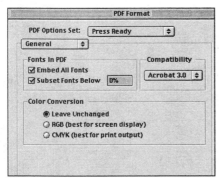

1 *General options for the Press Ready PDF Options Set.*

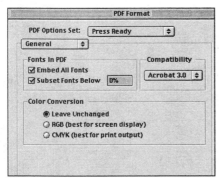

2 *Compression options for the Press Ready PDF Options Set.*

Use PDF (Portable Document Format) to transfer an Illustrator file to another application or another computer platform that reads PostScript-based Acrobat PDF files or to save your Illustrator file for display on the World Wide Web. The PDF format preserves groups, text, and layering information, and saves RGB colors as RGB and CMYK colors as CMYK. A file in PDF format can also be viewed in Acrobat Reader or edited using Acrobat Exchange.

You can open one page of a multi-page PDF file in Illustrator, edit any vector graphics or bitmap images on the page, and then resave the page in PDF format. If you save an Illustrator file as PDF and then reopen or place it in Illustrator, you'll still be able to edit individual objects as you normally would, with the exception of gradient fills. (As a workaround, you can expand a gradient fill into separate objects, and then edit the individual objects.)

To save a file as an Acrobat PDF:

1. Choose File menu > Save, Save As, or Save a Copy.

2. Enter a name in the "Save this document as" field, choose a location in which to save the file, choose Acrobat PDF from the Format (Macintosh) or Save as Type (Windows) drop-down menu, then click Save.

3. When you choose a **PDF Options Set**, the dialog box reconfigures automatically.

Press Ready for high-end printing. All fonts are automatically embedded, and compression is set to JPEG, maximum quality. Custom color and high-end image options are preserved. This set produces maximum image quality, but the resulting file size is the largest of the options sets.

Print Quality for low-end printing (ink jet, laser printers, or laser copiers). All CMYK color information is included and fonts are embedded. No high-end image options are used, so the file size is smaller than the Press Ready option produces.

(Continued on the following page)

Save as Acrobat PDF

Web Ready for on-screen display output. Images are converted to RGB color, fonts are not embedded, and image resolution is 72 ppi. The resulting file size will be the smallest possible.

Note: If you want to manually change any of the preset settings, proceed with the remaining steps. If you're satisfied with the current settings, skip to step 8.

4. Choose **General** from the second drop-down menu.

5. Check **Embed All Fonts** to have all fonts used in the file embedded in the file.

Check **Subset Fonts Below** and enter a value in the % field to determine how many glyphs (characters used in the document) from the font's character set will be embedded. The higher the percentage, the more glyphs will be embedded. *Note:* Adobe recommends not choosing the Subset Fonts Below option for TrueType fonts. If you do so, those fonts will be substituted if the PDF file is reopened in Illustrator.

6. Choose Acrobat 3 format (or Acrobat 4 when that version is released) from the **Compatibility** drop-down menu.

7. Choose a **Color Conversion** method: Unchanged to leave colors in their current modes; RGB to convert colors in vector objects to RGB color mode (suitable for on-screen output); or CMYK to convert colors to CMYK color mode for print output.

8. Choose **Compression** from the second drop-down menu. The compression options will update for the chosen PDF options set. If you want to change any settings, refer to page 4 of the Adobe Illustrator 8 Read Me, otherwise, leave them as is.

9. Click OK (Return/Enter).

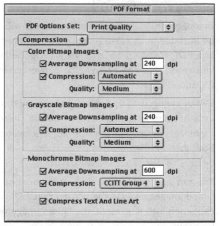

3 *Compression* options for the *Print Quality PDF Options Set.*

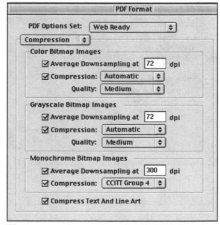

4 *Compression* options for the *Web Ready PDF Options Set.*

Native formats: Illustrator versions 1.0 through 8.0 (.ai).

Raster (bitmap) formats: Filmstrip, Kodak PhotoCD, and PixelPaint.

Vector formats: CMX, CGM, and CorelDRAW up to version 7.

FORMATS YOU CAN OPEN OR PLACE IN ILLUSTRATOR

Native formats: EPS (.eps), PDF (.pdf).

Raster (bitmap) formats: EPS, Amiga IFF, BMP, GIF89a, JPEG, PCX, PNG, Photoshop (layers are flattened!), PICT, Pixar, DXF, TGA, and TIFF.

Graphics (vector) formats: FreeHand up to version 8, DXF, WMF/EMF, and Macintosh PICT (from DeltaGraph or a CAD program).

Text file formats: Plain text (ASCII), MS RTF, MS Word (up to 6.0/95), and WordPerfect DOS or Windows.

Note: Before importing a FreeHand or CorelDRAW file, see the Illustrator ReadMe file to learn about some limitations.

WATCH YOUR DOWNSAMPLING

A TIFF that you drag-and-drop into Illustrator or a PICT that you drag-and-drop, open, or place into Illustrator will downsample to 72 ppi, which is an acceptable resolution for a multimedia or Web project, but not for printing. To acquire a high resolution image for a print project, use Illustrator's Place command to place an EPS or TIFF, or use the Open command.

Acquiring images in Illustrator

You can use Illustrator to open or import objects or images in a variety of file formats, which means you can work with imagery that was originally created in another application. Methods for acquiring an image from another application include the Open command, the Place command, and the drag-and-drop method. The method you choose to use depends on which file formats are available for saving the file in its original application and how you intend to use the imagery in Illustrator.

When you open a document from another drawing (vector) application using the **Open** command, a new Illustrator file is created, and the acquired objects can be manipulated using any Illustrator tool, command, or filter. If you open a document from a bitmap-based program like Photoshop using the Open command, the image won't convert into workable paths; it will stay in its outlined box.

The **Place** command inserts imagery or text into an existing Illustrator document. EPS and TIFF are the best formats for saving a file for placing into Illustrator, because in these formats, the color, detail, and resolution of the original image are preserved. If you place a layered image from Photoshop, it will appear on one layer (flattened) in Illustrator. If you want to **trace** an image, check Template in the Place dialog box.

If you **drag-and-drop** a Photoshop selection or layer into Illustrator, it will appear in a bounding box.

A bitmap image that is acquired in Illustrator via the Open, Place, or drag-and-drop method can be moved, placed on a different layer, masked, modified using any transformation tool, or modified using any color or raster (bitmap) filter.

TIP If you reduce the scale of an opened or placed TIFF or EPS image, the resolution of that image will increase, respectively. Conversely, if you enlarge such an image, its resolution will decrease.

A list of file formats that can be opened in Illustrator appears on the previous page.

To open a file from within Illustrator:

1. Choose File menu > Open (Command-O/Ctrl-O).

2. Check the Show Preview box to display a thumbnail of the illustration, if it contains a preview that Illustrator can display.

3. *Macintosh:* Check the Show All Files box to list all file formats. Otherwise, only files in the formats Illustrator can read will appear on the list.

    Windows: Filter out files by choosing from the Format drop-down menu, or choose All Formats to display files of all formats. The default setting is *.ai.

4. Locate and highlight a file name, then click Open (Return/Enter) **1**.
    or
    Double-click a file name.

    Note: If you get a warning prompt about a linked file, see page 44.

5. If you're opening a multi-page PDF, another dialog box will open **2**. Click an arrow to locate the desired page (or click the "1 of [ ]" button, enter the desired page, then click OK), then click OK.

TIP When opening an EPS file in Illustrator:

Any fonts used in the file must be installed in your system in order to print properly.

If the EPS file contains a clipping path, use the Selection tool to select both the image box and the clipping path. Use the Direct-selection tool to select only the image box or the clipping path, or to reshape the path.

If Illustrator can't parse (embed) the EPS, you'll get a warning prompt. Stop the opening operation, resave the EPS in its original application as a PostScript Level 1 file, and then reopen it in Illustrator.

EASY REOPEN

From the File menu > **Recent Files** submenu, you can choose from a list of up to 10 of the most recently opened files.

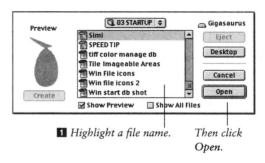

1 *Highlight a file name.*   *Then click Open.*

2 *Choose the page you want to open in a **multi-page** PDF.*

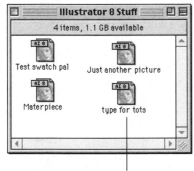

1 *Double-clicking an existing Illustrator file icon will cause the application to launch, if it isn't already open.*

2 *Double-click a bitmap or vector file.*

REPLACE ONE PLACED IMAGE WITH ANOTHER

Check the **Replace** box before you click Place. Any transformations that were made to the original placed image will be applied automatically to the newly placed one.

To open a file from the Macintosh Finder or Windows Explorer:

Double-click an Illustrator file icon in the window. Illustrator will launch if it is not already open **1**.

A placed image can be moved, moved to a different layer, masked, transformed, or modified using any raster filter. A list of file formats that can be placed into Illustrator is on page 41.

To place an image from another application into an Illustrator document:

1. Open an Illustrator file.
2. Choose File menu > Place.
3. Locate and highlight the name of the file that you want to place, then click Place.
   or
   Double-click a file name **2**.
4. Check the Link box to place only a screen version of an image into Illustrator (the image must reside on your hard disk). The actual, original image will remain separate from the Illustrator file at its original resolution. If you modify and resave a linked image in its original application, it will automatically update in the Illustrator document (see pages 45–46).
   or
   Uncheck the Link box to embed (parse) the actual image into the Illustrator file. This increases a file's storage size. You can edit the bounding box of and apply color filters to an embedded EPS or PDF.
5. *Optional:* Check the Template box if you want the placed image to appear as a dimmed image on its own template layer.
6. Click Place (Return/Enter).

TIP When placing an EPS file, any fonts that are used in the file must be installed in your system in order to print properly.

TIP If you place an EPS file with a clipping path into Illustrator, the area around the path will be transparent, and it will remain transparent even if you move it, transform it, or apply a bitmap filter to it.

Open a File; Place an Image into Illustrator

If a placed image was saved in its original application with a preview that Illustrator recognizes, it will render fully in Preview view, whether or not the "Show Images in Artwork" box is checked in Document Setup. If you place an image that *doesn't* contain a preview that Illustrator recognizes, the image will display as an empty outlined box with an "x" through it in either view. Follow these instructions to have images display in black-and-white in their outlined box in Artwork view.

To display a placed image in Artwork view:

1. Choose File menu > Document Setup.

2. Check the View: Show Images in Artwork box **1**–**4**.

3. Click OK (Return/Enter).

Reopening a file that contains linked images

If the actual linked image is moved from its original location after the file into which it was placed was last saved, you will be prompted to re-link the image when you reopen the Illustrator file. Click **Replace 5**, relocate the same file or a different file, then click Replace.

If you click **Ignore**, the linked image will not display, but a question mark icon will display for the file on the Links palette, and its bounding box will still be visible in the Illustrator file in Artwork view. To completely break the link and prevent any alert prompts from appearing, delete this bounding box and save the file. You'll never need to re-link a Macintosh PICT, because such images are embedded automatically.

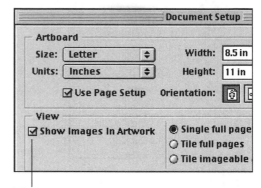

1 *Check the Show Images in Artwork box in the Document Setup dialog box.*

2 *Placed image, Artwork view.*

3 *Placed image, Artwork view, Show Images in Artwork box checked.*

4 *Linked, placed image selected, Preview view. Notice the "X" across the outline box, designating this image as linked.*

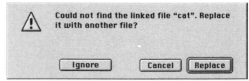

5 *If a linked file was **moved** to another folder or is otherwise **missing**, Illustrator will alert you with this dialog box when you open the illustration. To reestablish the link, click **Replace**, then locate the file.*

Modified linked   Missing linked
image indicator.   image indicator.

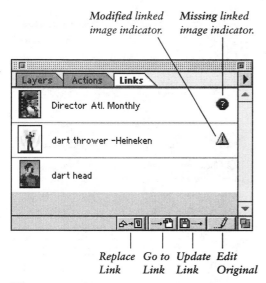

Replace   Go to   Update   Edit
Link   Link   Link   Original

1 *The Links palette lets you keep track of linked images, link to new files, and convert linked images into embedded ones. It's especially useful if you plan to send complex Illustrator files to a print shop.*

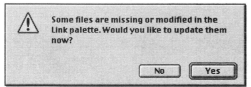

2 *This prompt will appear if you edit a link in its original application via the Edit Original button.*

The Links palette

To keep file sizes down, you can link any imported EPS, GIF, JPEG, or TIFF image to an Illustrator file rather than embed it within the file. A copy of the image will act as a placeholder in your Illustrator document, but the actual image will remain separate from the Illustrator file. If you revise a linked image via the Edit Original button, the image will update in the Illustrator document.

To link a file, use the File menu > Place command, and make sure the Link box has a check mark. Instructions for placing and linking images are on page 43.

Illustrator's Links palette helps you and your service bureau or print shop keep track of linked files. It lists all the linked and embedded files in your Illustrator document and puts a number of useful controls at your fingertips **1**. To view the Links palette, choose Window menu > Show Links.

To edit a linked image in its original application:

1. Click on the name of the image on the Links palette list.

2. Click the Edit Original button at the bottom of the palette.
   or
   Choose Edit Original from the Links palette menu.

   The application in which the linked image was created will launch if it isn't already open, and the image will open.

3. Make your edits, save the file, and then return to Illustrator. When the warning prompt appears, click Yes **2**. The linked image will update.

   Note: In our testing in Windows, the correct application didn't always open when these steps were followed. Oh well.

The Links palette; Edit a Linked Image

45

If you replace one linked image with another, any transformations that were applied to the original image, such as scaling or rotating, will be applied to the new image.

To replace one linked image with another:

1. On the Links palette, click the name of the file that you want to replace **1**.

2. Click the Replace Link button at the bottom of the Links palette.
   or
   Choose Replace from the Links palette menu.

3. Locate the replacement file, then click Place **2**.

TIP To replace a linked image another way, click on the existing image in the document window, choose File menu > Place, check the Replace box, locate the replacement image, then click Place.

When you locate a linked image, it becomes selected in the document window.

To locate a linked image in an Illustrator file:

1. Open the illustration that contains the linked image.

2. Click the name of the linked image on the Links palette list.

3. Click the Go to Link (second) button at the bottom of the palette.
   or
   Choose Go to Link from the Links palette menu.

To view file information for a linked image:

1. Double-click the file name on the Links palette. A dialog box with the image's file format, location, size, modifications, and transform information will appear **3**.

2. Click OK (Return/Enter).

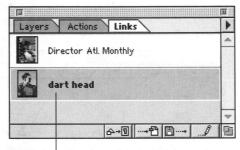

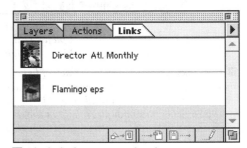

1 *Click on the name of the linked image that you want to replace, then click the Replace Link (first) button.*

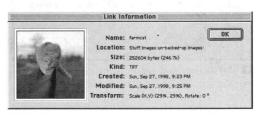

2 *The linked image is replaced.*

3 *The **Link Information** dialog shows the linked image's file format, location, size, and modifications.*

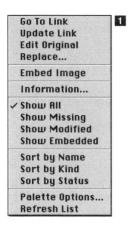

Embedded image icon.

2 *The Links palette, Show All and Sort by Status display options chosen.*

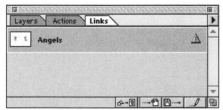

3 *The Links palette, Show Modified display option. Only modified, linked images are listed.*

To choose Links palette display options:

To change the **size** of the **thumbnail** images that are displayed in the Links palette, choose **Palette Options** from the Links palette menu, click the preferred size, then click OK. To display just the file icon without a thumbnail, click None.

To change the **order** of links on the palette, from the Links palette menu choose **Sort by Name** (alphabetical order), **Sort by Kind** (file format) or **Sort by Status** (missing, then modified, then embedded, then fully linked) **1**–**2**. To sort only selected links, first click, then Shift-click consecutive names or Command-click/Ctrl-click non-consecutive names.

To control which **type** of links display on the palette, choose **Show All, Show Missing, Show Modified,** or **Show Embedded** from the Links palette menu **3**.

An exclamation mark icon appearing to the right of a link on the Links palette list indicates that the original file has been modified and the link is outdated. Use the Update Link button to update it.

Note: If you edit a linked image via the Edit Original button, you won't need to update it this way—you'll get a warning prompt to update it automatically. You can't update a missing linked image (indicated by a question mark); you'll have to replace it instead (see page 46).

To update a modified linked image:

1. Click on the name of the modified image on the Links palette list.
2. Click the Update Link (third) button at the bottom of the palette.
   or
   Choose Update Link from the Links palette menu.

   Note: To refresh the thumbnails and image names on the Links palette, choose Refresh List from the palette menu.

Links Palette Display Options; Update Linked Image

To convert a linked image to an embedded image:

1. On the Links palette list, click the name of the image that you want to embed.

2. Choose Embed Image from the Links palette menu.

Note: You can't un-embed an embedded image. You *can* use the Replace command on the Links palette menu to replace an embedded image with a linked image.

To close a file:

Macintosh: Click the close box in the upper left corner of the document window (Command-W).

Windows: Click the close box in the upper right corner of the document window (Ctrl-W).

If you attempt to close a picture that was modified since it was last saved, a warning prompt will appear **1**. You can close the file without saving (click Don't Save), save the file (click Save), or cancel the close operation (click Cancel).

TIP Hold down Option/Alt and choose Close (or Option/Alt click the close box) to close all open files.

To quit/exit Illustrator:

Macintosh: Choose File menu > Quit (Command-Q).

Windows: Choose File menu > Exit (Ctrl-Q).

All open Illustrator files will close. If changes were made to any open files since they were last saved, a warning prompt will appear. Save the file(s) or quit/exit without saving them.

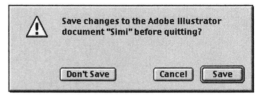

1 *If you try to close a picture that was modified since it was last saved, this prompt will appear.*

In this chapter you will learn how to change view sizes, change views (Preview or Artwork), create custom view settings, move an illustration in its window, change screen display modes, and display the same illustration in two windows.

To use the Navigator palette to change the view size of an illustration:

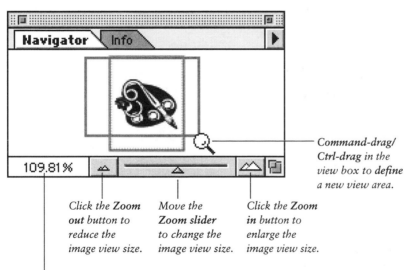

Command-drag/ Ctrl-drag in the view box to define a new view area.

*Click the **Zoom out** button to reduce the image view size.*

*Move the **Zoom slider** to change the image view size.*

*Click the **Zoom in** button to enlarge the image view size.*

*Enter the desired **zoom percentage** between 3.13% and 6400%, then press Return/Enter. To zoom to a percentage and keep the field highlighted, press Shift-Return/Shift-Enter.*

TIP You can also change the view size by double-clicking the zoom field in the lower left corner of the document/ program window, typing the desired zoom percentage (up to 6400%), and then pressing Return/Enter.

TIP To separate the Navigator from its palette group, drag its tab name.

To move the illustration in its window using the Navigator palette:

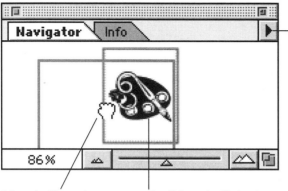

*Choose **View Artboard Only** from the palette menu to have the palette display only objects on the artboard. This is like a quick print preview.*

*Move the illustration in its window by dragging the **view box**.*

*Or **click** on the illustration **thumbnail** to display that area of the illustration.*

TIP To change the color of the view box frame from its default red, choose Palette Options from the Navigator palette menu, then choose a preset color from the Color drop-down menu or double-click the color swatch and choose a color from the Color Picker.

TIP The proportions of the view box match the proportions of the document window.

TIP The Navigator palette will display multiple pages, if any, and tiling of the imageable area.

TIP To stop a slow screen redraw on Macintosh, press Command-. (period). On Windows, press Esc. The display will change to Artwork view. Choose View menu > Preview (Command-Y/Ctrl-Y) to restart the redraw.

Navigator Palette

1 *Make sure no objects are selected, then Control-click/ Right-click on an image and choose Zoom In or Zoom Out from the context menu.*

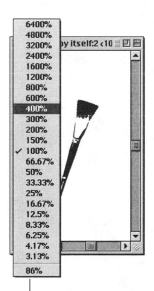

2 *Control-click/Right-click in the Zoom field in the lower left corner of the document/ program window and choose a **preset percentage** from the context menu.*

Within the document window, you can display the entire artboard or an enlarged detail of an illustration, or any preset view size in between. The display size (3.13%–6400%) is indicated as a percentage on the title bar and in the lower left corner of the document/program window. 100% is actual size. An illustration's display size has no bearing on its printout size.

To choose a preset view size:

Choose View menu > Zoom In (Command-+/Ctrl-+). Repeat to magnify further.
or
Choose View menu > Zoom Out (Command--/Ctrl--). Repeat, if desired.
or
Make sure no objects are selected, Control-click/Right-click on the image, then choose Zoom In or Zoom Out from the context menu **1**.
or
Control-click/Right-click in the zoom field in the lower left corner of the document/ program window and choose a preset percentage from the context menu **2**.
or
Double-click in the Zoom field in the lower-left corner of the document/program window, type in the desired magnification, then press Return/Enter.

TIP Choose View menu > Fit in Window (Command-0/Ctrl-0) or double-click the Hand tool to display the entire artboard in the document window.

TIP To exit the Zoom field without changing the current value, press Tab.

Choose a Preset View Size

To change the view size using the Zoom tool:

1. Choose the Zoom tool (Z) **1**.

2. Click on the illustration in the center of the area that you want to enlarge or drag a marquee across an area to magnify that area **2**–**3**. The smaller the marquee, the greater the degree of magnification.

   or

   Option-click/Alt-click on the illustration to reduce the view size.

   or

   Drag a marquee, then, without releasing the mouse, press and hold down Spacebar, move the marquee over the area you want to magnify, then release the mouse.

TIP Double-click the Zoom tool to display an illustration at Actual Size (100%). Or, choose View menu > Actual Size (Command-1/Ctrl-1).

If you double-click the Zoom tool when your illustration is in a small view size, the white area around the artboard may appear in the document window instead of the illustration. Use the Navigator palette to reposition the illustration in the document window.

TIP You can click to change the view size while the screen is redrawing.

This is the method to master for speedy picture editing.

To change the view size using the keyboard:

To magnify the illustration with any tool other than Zoom selected, Command-Spacebar-click/Ctrl-Spacebar-click or -drag in the document window.

or

To reduce the display size, Command-Option-Spacebar-click/Ctrl-Alt-Spacebar-click.

1 *the Zoom tool.*

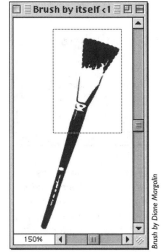

2 *Drag with the Zoom tool.*

3 *The view is enlarged.*

An illustration can be displayed and edited in any of these three views: Preview, Artwork, or Preview Selection. In all three views, the other View menu commands—Hide/Show Page Tiling, Edges, Guides, and Grid—are accessible, and any selection tool can be used.

To change the view:

From the View menu, toggle between...

Preview (Command-Y/Ctrl-Y) to display all the objects with their fill and stroke colors, as well as all placed images.

or

Artwork (Command-Y/Ctrl-Y) to display all the objects as wire frames with no fill or stroke colors. The screen redraws more quickly in Artwork view.

Or make sure no objects are selected, then Control-click/Right-click and choose Artwork or Preview from the context menu.

Choose **Preview Selection** (Command-Shift-Y/ Ctrl-Shift-Y) to display any currently selected object or objects in Preview view and all non-selected objects in Artwork view. To preview an object, click on it with any selection tool. To turn this option off, choose Artwork view.

TIP Use the Layers palette to choose a view for an individual layer (see page 222).

TIP The display of placed images is discussed on page 44.

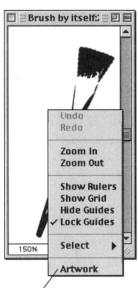

1 *Make sure no objects are selected, then choose Artwork (or Preview) from the context menu.*

2 *Preview view.*

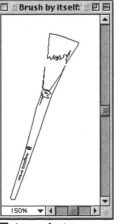

3 *Artwork view.*

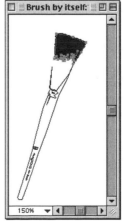

4 *Preview Selection view.*

Change the View (Artwork or Preview)

You can define and save up to 25 custom view settings that you can switch to quickly using an assigned shortcut, and you can specify whether your illustration will be in Preview view or Artwork view for each setting that you define.

To define a custom view setting:

1. Display your illustration at the desired view size and choose scroll bar positions.
2. Put your illustration into Preview or Artwork view (Command-Y/Ctrl-Y).
3. Choose View menu > New View.
4. Enter a name for the new view in the Name field, as in "40% view" 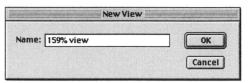.
5. Click OK (Return/Enter).

To choose a custom view setting:

Choose the view name from the bottom of the View menu .

or

Hold down Command-Option-Shift/ Ctrl-Alt-Shift and press the number that was assigned automatically to the view setting. The shortcut will be listed next to the view name under the View menu.

TIP You can switch views at any time. For example, if you choose a custom view setting for which you chose Artwork view but you want to display your illustration in Preview view, choose View menu > Preview.

To rename or delete a custom view setting:

1. Choose View menu > Edit Views.
2. Click on the name of the view you want to change .
3. Type a new name in the Name field.
   or
   Click Delete to delete the view setting.
4. Click OK (Return/Enter). The View menu will update to reflect your changes.

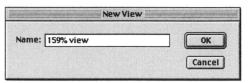

1 *Enter a Name for the view setting in the New View dialog box.*

2 *Choose a custom view setting from the bottom of the View menu.*

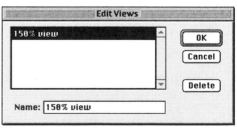

3 *In the Edit Views dialog box, highlight a view, then change the Name or click Delete.*

1 *Hand tool.*

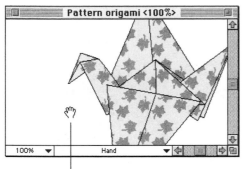

2 *Spacebar-drag in the document window to move the illustration.*

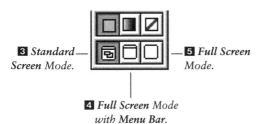

3 *Standard Screen Mode.* **5** *Full Screen Mode.*

4 *Full Screen Mode with Menu Bar.*

To move an illustration in its window:

Click the up or down scroll arrow.

or

Choose the Hand tool **1** (or hold down Spacebar to turn any other tool into the Hand tool temporarily), then drag the illustration to the desired position **2**.

TIP Double-click the Hand tool to fit the entire artboard in the document window.

To change the screen display mode:

Click the Standard Screen Mode button at the bottom of the Toolbox **3** to display the image, menu bar, and scroll bars in the document window. This is the default mode.

or

Click the Full Screen Mode with Menu Bar (second) button **4** to display the image and the menu bar, but no scroll bars. The area around the image will be white.

or

Click the Full Screen Mode button **5** to display the image, but no menu bar or scroll bars. The area around the image will be white.

TIP Press "F" to cycle through the three modes.

TIP Press Tab to hide (or show) all currently open palettes, including the Toolbox; press Shift-Tab to hide (or show) all the palettes except the Toolbox.

Move Illustration in its Window; Screen Modes

The number of Illustrator documents that can be open at a time is limited only by the amount of RAM (Random Access Memory) currently available to Illustrator. Open windows are listed under and can be activated via the Window menu **1**.

You can open the same illustration in two windows, one in a large view size, such as 200%, to edit small details, and the other in a smaller view size so you can see the whole illustration. In one window you could hide individual layers or display individual layers in Artwork view and in another window you could Preview all the layers together.

Note: The illustration in the window for which Preview view is selected will redraw each time you modify the illustration in the window for which Artwork view is selected, which means you won't save processing or redraw time when you work in the Artwork window.

To display an illustration in two windows:

1. Open an illustration.

2. Choose Window menu > New Window. A new window of the same size will appear on top of the first window, and with the same title followed by ":2" **2**.

3. *Macintosh:* Reposition the new window by dragging its title bar so the original and new windows are side by side, and resize one or both windows.

   Windows: Choose any of these Window menu commands: Cascade to arrange the currently open illustrations in a stair-step configuration; Tile to tile open windows side by side; or Arrange Icons to move the minimized windows to the bottom of the application window.

   TIP If you save the file, close both windows, and then later reopen the file, both windows will reopen.

The currently open documents.

1 *The Window menu.*

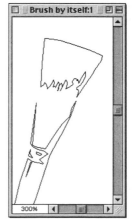

2 *One illustration displayed in **two windows**.*

OBJECTS BASICS 5

An path, or object, is a shape that is composed of anchor points connected by straight and/or curved line segments. A path can be open or closed. Rectangles and ovals are closed paths because they have no endpoints. A line is an open path. As you'll learn in Chapter 7, any path can be reshaped.

In this chapter you will learn how to delete objects; draw rectangles and ovals; round the corners of any existing path; draw in a freehand style using the Pencil tool; add to a line; and use the Polygon, Spiral, and Star tools to create simple geometric shapes.

Once you've learned the basics in this chapter, check out these related chapters:

Daniel Pelavin

Artist and designer Danny Pelavin builds crisp, effective images from geometric shapes.

You'll be creating lots of different shapes in this chapter, and your artboard may start to get crowded with junk. To remove an object that you've just created, Undo (Command-Z/Ctrl-Z). To remove an object that's been lying around, follow these instructions.

To delete one object:

1. Choose the Selection tool (V),  then select the object.
2. Press Delete/Backspace or Del or choose Edit menu > Clear or Cut.

TIP If you're using the Direct-selection tool and only some of the object's points are selected, press Delete twice.

To delete a bunch of objects:

1. Marquee the objects you want to remove using the Selection tool (V) or use any of the other methods for selecting multiple objects that are described in the next chapter.
2. Press Delete/Backspace or Del.

To create a rectangle or an ellipse by dragging:

I. Choose the Rectangle (M or Shift-M)  or Ellipse tool (L or Shift-L) .

2. Press and drag diagonally **3**. As you drag, you'll see a wire frame representation of the rectangle or oval. When you release the mouse, the rectangle or oval will be selected, and it will be colored with the current fill and stroke settings (Preview view).

TIP To create a series of perfectly-aligned, equal-size rectangles, create and select a rectangle, then use Type menu > Rows & Columns (see page 202).

To create a rectangle or an ellipse by specifying dimensions:

I. Choose the Rectangle (M or Shift-M)  or Ellipse tool (L or Shift-L) .

2. Click on the artboard where you want the object to appear.

3. In the Rectangle or Ellipse dialog box, enter dimensions in the Width and Height fields **4**. To create a circle or a square, enter a number in the Width field, then click the word Height (or vice versa)—the value in one field will copy into the other field.

4. Click OK (Return/Enter).

TIP Values in dialog boxes are displayed in the unit of measure that is currently selected in File menu > Preferences > Units & Undo (General drop-down menu) for the application as a whole. A different Units setting in File menu > Document Setup for an individual document will supercede the Units & Undo setting.

Draw a rectangle or oval from its center	Option-drag/Alt-drag
Move a rectangle or ellipse as you draw it	Spacebar-drag
Draw a square with the Rectangle tool or a circle with the Ellipse tool	Shift-drag

QUICK RECOLOR

You'll learn all about Illustrator's fill and stroke controls in Chapter 9, but here's a sneak preview. Select an object, activate the Fill or Stroke box (square) on the Toolbox or the Color palette, then click a swatch on the Swatches palette or click on the color bar on the Color palette.

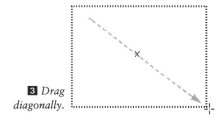

1 *Rectangle tool.*

2 *Ellipse tool.*

3 *Drag diagonally.*

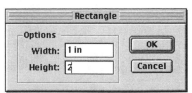

4 *Enter **Width** and **Height** dimensions in the **Rectangle** (or Ellipse) dialog box. The dimensions of the last-drawn object will display when the dialog box opens.*

1 *Rounded Rectangle tool.*

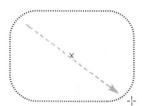

2 *Drag diagonally.*

3 *The rectangle is automatically painted with the current fill and stroke settings.*

Chris Spollen

A great use of rounded rectangles!

4 *Top row: the original objects; second row: after applying the Round Corners filter (30pt).*

To create a rounded rectangle:

1. Choose the Rounded Rectangle tool (M or Shift-M) **1**.

2. Drag diagonally. As you drag, you'll see a wireframe representation of the rounded rectangle **2**. When you release the mouse, the rounded rectangle will be selected and colored with the current fill and stroke settings (Preview view) **3**.

   Note: Keep the mouse down as you draw the rectangle and press or hold down the up arrow to make the corners rounder or the down arrow to make them more square.

TIP To draw a rectangle of a specific size, choose the Rounded Rectangle tool, click on the artboard, then enter Width, Height, and Corner Radius values.

TIP The current Corner Radius value in File menu > Preferences > General, which controls how curved the corners of a rectangle will be, is entered automatically in the Corner Radius field in the Rectangle dialog box, and vice versa.

To round the corners of an existing object:

1. Select the object.

2. Choose Filter menu > Stylize > Round Corners.

3. Enter a Radius value (the radius of the curve, in points).

4. Click OK (Return/Enter) **4**.

Create a Rounded Rectangle

59

1 *Pencil tool.*

Lines drawn with the Pencil tool look hand drawn or quickly sketched. Use the Pencil tool for freehand drawing, but not to create straight lines—that's not what it was designed for. If you need to draw straight lines and smooth curves, use the Pen tool.

Note: The Pencil tool performs two distinctly different functions. If you drag over an empty area of the artboard with the Pencil, you'll create a new, open path. If you drag along the edge of a selected path (open or closed), the Pencil will reshape the path (see page 81).

To draw using the Pencil tool:

1. Choose the Pencil tool (N or Shift-N) **1**.

2. Click the Stroke color box on the Color palette ▣, then choose a stroke color. And choose stroke attributes from the Stroke palette. (See Chapter 9.)

3. Click the Fill Color box ■ and the None button ⊘ on the Color palette so the curves on the path won't fill in.

4. Draw a line. A dotted line will appear as you draw. When you release the mouse, the line will be colored with the current fill and stroke settings and its anchor points will be selected (Preview view) **2**. In Artwork view, you'll see only a wireframe representation of the line **3**.

   Note: To create a closed path with the Pencil tool, hold down Option/Alt before you release the mouse.

TIP Read about the Pencil tool settings on the next page.

2 *Blue-footed booby, drawn with the **Pencil** tool.*

Diane Margolin

To close an existing Pencil line:

1. Choose the Selection tool (V) **1**.

2. Select the line.

3. Click the Unite (first) button on the Pathfinder palette 🔲.

3 *The booby in Artwork view.*

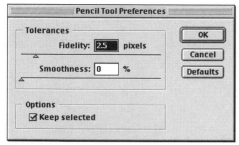

1 Choose **Fidelity** and **Smoothness** values in the Pencil Tool Preferences dialog box.

2 A line drawn with a **high** Fidelity value.

3 A line drawn with a **low** Fidelity value.

Diane Margolin

If you change the Fidelity and Smoothness settings for the Pencil tool, which control the number of anchor points and the size of curve segments the tool produces, only subsequently drawn lines will be affected, not existing lines.

To choose Pencil tool settings:

1. Double-click the Pencil tool (or press "N" to choose the tool, then press Return/Enter).

2. Choose a Fidelity value (0.5–20). The lower the Fidelity, the more closely the line will follow the movement of the mouse and the greater the number of anchor points will be created. The higher the Fidelity, the smoother the path.

3. Choose a Smoothness value (0–100). The higher the Smoothness, the smoother the curves; the lower the smoothness, the more bends and twists in the path.

4. Check the "Keep selected" box to keep a Pencil path selected after it's created. Turn this option on if you often like to add to an existing path after it's drawn.

5. Click OK (Return/Enter).

TIP Click Defaults to reset the Pencil tool to its default preferences.

TIP To smooth a path, use the Smooth tool (see page 82).

Pencil Tool Settings

Note: You can use the Pencil tool on any open path—not just on a path that's drawn with the Pencil tool.

To add to a line:

1. Choose the Selection tool (V), and select the line.

2. Choose the Pencil tool (N).

3. Position the pointer *directly* over either end of the line, and draw an addition to the line **1**. When you release the mouse, the path will remain selected and the addition will be connected to the existing line **2**.

TIP If the new and existing lines did not connect, delete the new line and try again. Or select an endpoint on each line using the Direct-selection tool, then choose Item menu > Paths > Join to join them with a segment.

Using the Polygon, Spiral, or Star tool, you can easily create geometric objects with sides of equal length without having to draw with the mouse. The current fill and stroke settings are automatically applied to objects that are produced using these tools.

To create a polygon by clicking:

1. Choose the Polygon tool (L or Shift-L) **3**.

2. Click where you want the center of the polygon to be.

3. Enter a value in the Radius field (the distance from the center of the object to the corner points) **4**.

4. Choose a number of Sides for the polygon by clicking the up or down arrow or by entering a number between 3 and 1000. The sides will be of equal length.

5. Click OK (Return/Enter) **5**.

1 *Continue-a-line pointer.*

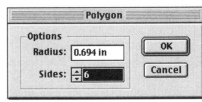

2 *An extension is added to the line.*

3 *Polygon tool. Star tool. Spiral tool.*

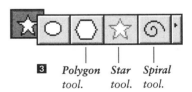

4 *In the Polygon dialog box, choose a Radius distance and a number of Sides.*

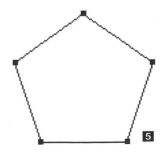

1 *The Polygon tool.*

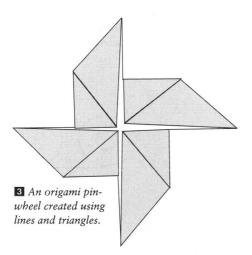

2 *A polygon.*

3 *An origami pinwheel created using lines and triangles.*

To create a polygon by dragging:

1. Choose the Polygon tool (L or Shift-L) **1**.

2. Drag on the artboard, starting from where you want the center of the polygon to be **2**–**3**.

   While dragging, do any of the following:

   Drag away from or towards the center to increase or decrease the size of the polygon, respectively.

   Drag in a circular fashion to rotate the polygon.

   Hold down Shift while dragging to constrain the bottom side of the polygon to the horizontal axis.

   With the mouse still held down, press or hold down the up or down arrow key to add or delete sides from the polygon, respectively.

   Hold down Spacebar and move the polygon.

3. When you release the mouse, the polygon will be selected and it will be colored with the current fill and stroke settings.

Daniel Pelavin

Create a Polygon

63

To create a spiral by clicking:

1. Choose the Spiral tool (L or Shift-L) .

2. Click where you want the center of the spiral to be.

3. Enter a number in the Radius field (the distance from the center of the spiral to the outermost point) **2**.

4. Enter a percentage (5–150) in the Decay field to specify how tightly the spiral will wind.

5. Choose a number of Segments for the spiral (the number of quarter revolutions around the center point) by clicking the up or down arrow or by entering a number.

6. Click a Style button (the direction the spiral will wind from the center point).

7. Click OK (Return/Enter) **3**.

8. Apply a stroke color to the spiral (see pages 122–126).

To create a spiral by dragging:

1. Choose the Spiral tool (L or Shift-L).

2. Drag on the artboard, starting from where you want the center of the spiral to be.

3. While dragging, do any of the following:

   Drag away from or towards the center to increase or decrease the size of the spiral, respectively.

   Hold down Option/Alt while dragging to add or delete segments from the center of the spiral as you change its size.

   Drag in a circular fashion to rotate the spiral.

   Hold down Shift while dragging to constrain the rotation of the entire spiral to an increment of 45°.

   With the mouse still held down, press or hold down the up or down arrow key to add to or delete segments from the center of the spiral, respectively.

   Hold down Spacebar while dragging to move the spiral.

1 *The* **Spiral** *tool.*

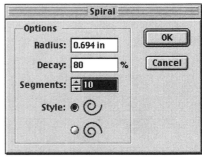

2 *In the* **Spiral** *dialog box, enter numbers in the* **Radius** *and* **Decay** *fields, choose a number of* **Segments**, *and click a* **Style** *button.*

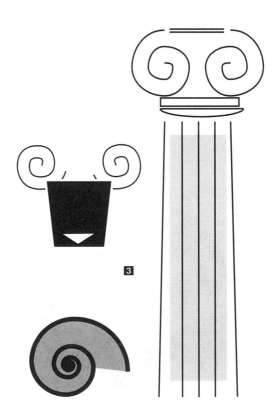

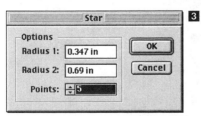

1 *A spiral.*

After applying Filter menu > Distort > Punk and Bloat (Bloat 15%)...

...and then reversing the fill and stroke colors.

2 *The Star tool.*

Hold down Command/Ctrl and drag away from/towards the center to control how tightly the spiral winds (the Decay value).

4. When you release the mouse, the spiral will be selected and it will be colored with the current fill and stroke colors **1**.

To create a star by clicking:

1. Choose the Star tool (L or Shift-L) **2**.

2. Click where you want the center of the star to be.

3. Enter a number in the Radius 1 and Radius 2 fields. Whichever value is higher will become the distance from the center of the star to its points. The lower value will become the distance from the center of the star to the angles where the arms meet **3**. The greater the difference between the Radius 1 and Radius 2 values, the thinner will be the arms of the star.

4. Choose a number of Points for the star by clicking the up or down arrow or entering a number between 3 and 1000.

5. Click OK (Return/Enter) **4**.

TIP You can use the Rotate tool to rotate the completed star.

(After putting circles on top of the points and then clicking the Unite button on the Pathfinder palette to join the shapes.)

4 *Classic, five-point star.*

Create a Star

To create a star by dragging:

1. Choose the Star tool (L or Shift-L).

2. Drag on the artboard, starting from where you want the center of the star to be.

   While dragging, do any of the following:

   Drag away from or towards the center to increase or decrease the size of the star, respectively.

   Drag in a circular fashion to rotate the star.

   Hold down Shift while dragging to constrain one or two points to the horizontal axis.

   With the mouse still held down, press the up or down arrow key to add or delete points from the star, respectively.

   Hold down Spacebar while dragging to move the star.

   Hold down Option/Alt to make shoulders (opposite segments) parallel .

   Hold down Command/Ctrl and drag away from/towards the center to increase/decrease the length of the arms of the star, while keeping the inner radius points constant.

3. When you release the mouse, the star will be selected and it will be colored with the current fill and stroke settings.

TIP Hold down "~" while dragging with the Star or Polygon tool to create progressively larger copies of the shape 2. Drag quickly. Apply a stroke color to distinguish the different shapes. Use the Twirl tool to twirl the shapes around their center 3.

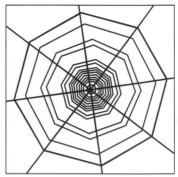

2 *Multiple polygons drawn with the Polygon tool with "~" held down.*

3 *Stars created by dragging with the Star tool with "~" held down, and then twirled using the Twirl filter.*

SELECT/MOVE 6

In Chapter 5 you learned how to create various objects. In later chapters you will learn many methods for modifying objects, such as reshaping, recoloring, and transforming. An object must be selected before it can be modified, however, so selecting objects is an essential Illustrator skill to learn. In this chapter you will learn how to use the selection tools and commands to highlight objects for modification. You'll also learn how to hide an object's anchor points and direction lines, how to hide, lock, or deselect whole objects, how to copy or move objects within the same file or between files, how to use Smart Guides to align objects, and how to offset a copy of a path.

If you like to move or position objects by entering values or measuring distances, after you learn the fundamental techniques in this chapter, read Chapter 20, Precision Tools. To select objects by color, see page 70.

The three selection tools

The **Selection (V)** tool is used to select all the anchor points on a path. If you click on the edge (or the fill*) of an object with the Selection tool, you will select all the points on that object.

The **Direct-selection (A or Shift-A)** tool is used to select one or more individual anchor points or segments of a path. If you click on a curve segment with the Direct-selection tool, that segment's direction lines and anchor points will become visible. (Straight line segments don't have direction lines—they only have anchor points.) If you click on the fill* of an object in Preview view using this tool, you will select all the points on the object.

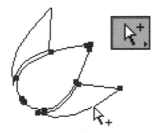

The **Group Selection (A or Shift-A)** tool can be used to select all the anchor points on a path, but its primary use is to select groups nested inside larger groups. Click once to select an object; click twice to select that object's group; click three times to select the next group that was added to the larger group, and so on.

*If the Use Area Select option is turned on in File menu > Preferences > General.

To select an object or objects:

1. Choose the Selection tool (V) or Group Selection tool (A or Shift-A) .

2. Click on the path (the object's edge) **3**.
   or
   Click on the center point of the path, if it's visible.
   or
   If the path has a fill, your illustration is in Preview view, and the Use Area Select option is on (see the sidebar at right), click on the path's fill.
   or
   Position the pointer outside the path(s) you want to select, then drag a marquee across all or part of it **4**. The whole path will be selected, even if you only marquee a portion of it.

3. *Optional:* Shift-click to select additional objects or deselect any selected paths individually.

TIP Hold down Option/Alt to use the Group Selection tool while the Direct-selection tool is chosen, and vice versa.

USING AREA SELECT

If the Use Area Select box is checked in File menu > Preferences > General, you can click on an object's fill when your illustration is in Preview view to select the entire path. If the Use Area Select box is unchecked or the path has no fill, you must click on the edge of the path to select it. If your illustration is in Preview Selection view, you must click on a center point or the edge of an object to select it, regardless of the Use Area Select setting. ("Fill" and "Stroke" are defined in Chapter 9.)

1 *Selection tool.*

2 *Group Selection tool.*

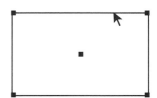

3 *Using the Selection tool to select a path and all its anchor points.*

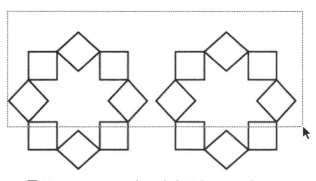

4 *Marqueeing two paths with the Selection tool.*

Select Objects

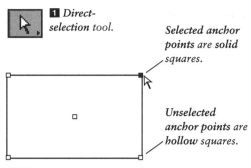

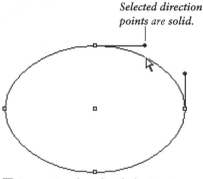

1 *Direct-selection* tool.

Selected anchor points are solid squares.

Unselected anchor points are hollow squares.

2 *One anchor point selected with the Direct-selection tool (Artwork view).*

Selected direction points are solid.

3 *A segment selected with the Direct-selection tool.*

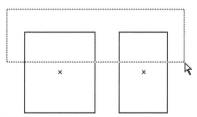

4 *A marquee selection being made with the Direct-selection tool.*

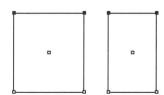

5 *Only the anchor points that fall within the marquee are selected.*

To select anchor points or segments:

1. Choose the Direct-selection tool (A or Shift-A) **1**.

2. Click on the path (the object's edge). If you click on a curve segment of the path, the direction lines for that segment will become visible.

or

If the object isn't already selected, click on the object's edge. Then click on an anchor point **2**–**3**.

or

Position the pointer outside the object or objects whose points you want to select, then drag a marquee across them (a dotted marquee will define the area as you drag over it). Only the anchor points you marquee will be selected **4**–**5**.

3. *Optional:* Shift-click to select additional anchor points or segments or deselect selected anchor points or segments individually.

TIP Hold down Command/Ctrl to use the last highlighted selection tool while a non-selection tool is highlighted. With Command/Ctrl held down, you can click to select or deselect an object.

TIP If you select or move a curve segment without moving its corresponding anchor points, you will reshape the curve and the anchor points will remain stationary. You'll learn more about reshaping curves in the next chapter.

To select all the objects in an illustration:

Choose Edit menu > Select All (Command-A/Ctrl-A). All unlocked objects in your illustration will be selected, wherever they are—on the artboard or the scratch area. Any objects on a hidden layer (eye icon turned off) will not be selected.

Select Anchor Points or Segments; Select All

Use the Select commands to select objects with characteristics similar to a currently selected object. Each command is named for the attributes it searches for.

To select using a command:

1. Choose any selection tool.
2. Click on an object that contains the characteristics you want to search for in other objects.
3. From the Select submenu under the Edit menu 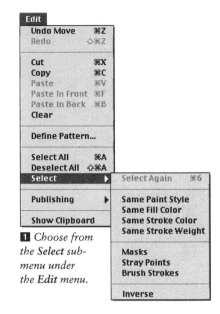, choose:

    Same Paint Style (fill and stroke color and stroke weight) to search for all paint attributes.

    Same Fill Color to search only for fill attributes.

    Same Stroke Color to search only for stroke attributes.

    Same Stroke Weight to search only for strokes of the same weight.

    Masks to select masking objects. This command is useful because the edges of a masking object display in Preview view only when the object is selected.

    Stray Points to select single points that are not part of any paths, so they can be deleted easily.

    Brush Strokes to search for brushstrokes on objects.

    Inverse to select all the currently deselected objects and deselect all the currently selected objects.
    or
    Control-click/Right-click, then choose Select > First Object Above, Next Object Above, Next Object Below, or Last Object Below . This works only if you click in the spot where the object you want to select is located, and if that object has a fill color, or if the pointer is directly over the lower object's path.

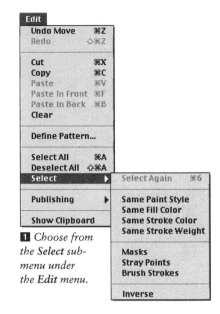

1 *Choose from the Select submenu under the Edit menu.*

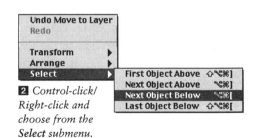

2 *Control-click/ Right-click and choose from the Select submenu.*

To prevent an object from being modified, you must deselect it.

To deselect an object or objects:

1. Choose a selection tool.

2. Click outside the selected object or objects.
   or
   Choose Edit menu > Deselect All (Command-Shift-A/Ctrl-Shift-A).

TIP To deselect an individual object within a multiple selection, Shift-click on it or Shift-drag over it using the Selection tool. If only some of the object's anchor points are selected, you'll have to click twice.

TIP To deselect all selected objects and select all unselected objects, choose Edit menu > Select > Inverse.

Choose the Hide Edges command to hide an object's anchor points and direction lines while still keeping the object selected and editable. Hide edges if you want to see how different stroke attributes look on an object in Preview view or hide distracting points when you're working in Artwork view.

To hide the anchor points and segments of an object or objects:

1. Select the object or objects.

2. Choose View menu > Hide Edges (Command-H/Ctrl-H). To redisplay the anchor points and segments, choose View menu > Show Edges.

To hide/show an object's center point:

1. Open the Attributes palette.

2. If the Show Center point options aren't visible on the palette, choose Show All from the palette menu.

3. Click the Show Center Point button **1** or the Hide Center Point button **2**.

4. Click OK (Return/Enter).

TIP To hide the bounding box for all the objects in a file, choose File menu > Preferences > General, and uncheck Use Bounding Box **3**–**4**.

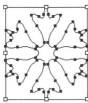

1 *Center point showing.*

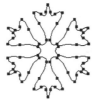

2 *Center point hidden.*

3 *Bounding box on.*

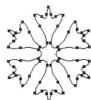

4 *Bounding box off.*

Deselect Object; Hide Edges; Hide Center Point

The Hide Selection command can help you isolate objects to work on. If your illustration is complex, you'll find this command to be particularly useful both for selecting the objects you *do* want to work on more easily and to speed up screen redraw. Hidden objects are invisible in both Artwork and Preview views, and will not print. If you close and reopen the file, any previously hidden objects will redisplay.

To hide an object:

1. Select the object or objects to be hidden.

2. Choose Object menu > Hide Selection (Command-3/Ctrl-3).
   or
   To hide all *unselected* objects, hold down Option/Alt and choose Object menu > Hide Selection.

TIP Individual hidden objects cannot be selectively redisplayed. To redisplay *all* hidden objects, choose Object menu > Show All (Command-Option-3/Ctrl-Alt-3). You can use the Layers palette to hide or lock all the objects on a layer (see page 221).

A locked object cannot be selected or modified. If you close and reopen the file, locked objects remain locked.

To lock an object:

1. Select the object or objects to be locked.

2. Choose Object menu > Lock (Command-2/Ctrl-2).
   or
   To lock all *unselected* objects, hold down Option/Alt and choose Object menu > Lock.

TIP Locked objects can't be unlocked individually. To unlock all locked objects, choose Object menu > Unlock All (Command-Option-2/Ctrl-Alt-2). The newly unlocked objects will be selected; any previously selected, unlocked objects will be deselected.

TIP To lock a whole layer, use the Layers palette.

LOCK/HIDE TIPS

You can't lock or hide *part* of an object or a path.

To unlock or show only *one of several* locked or hidden objects, choose Unlock All or Show All from the Object menu, choose the Selection tool, Shift-click on the object you want to unlock or show, then choose Lock or Hide Selection for the remaining selected objects.

If you lock or hide an object in a *group* and you want to unlock or show just that object and leave any other non-grouped objects locked or hidden, select the group using the Selection or Group Selection tool, then hold down Option/Alt and Shift and choose Unlock All or Show All from the Object menu.

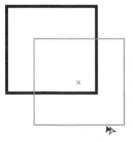 **1** *Selection* tool.

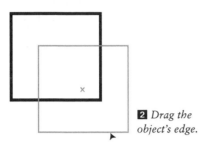

2 *Drag the object's edge.*

3 *To copy an object, hold down Option/Alt and drag the object. Note the double arrowhead pointer.*

To move an object by dragging:

1. Choose the Selection tool (V) **1**.

2. If your illustration is in Artwork view, drag the object's edge **2**.

or

If your illustration is in Preview view, drag the object's edge. Or drag the object's fill if the Use Area Select option is on in File menu > Preferences > General. This can also be done with the Direct-selection tool.

TIP Press any arrow key to move a selected object the current Keyboard Increment: Cursor Key value from File menu > Preferences > General. The default is 1 point. Precise methods for moving and aligning objects, such as the Move dialog box and the Transform palette, are covered in Chapter 20, Precision Tools.

TIP If View menu > Snap to Point is on, the part of an object that is directly underneath the pointer will snap to the nearest guide if it comes within two pixels of that guide (the pointer will turn white when it's over the guide). If you drag an anchor point using the Direct-selection tool, you can snap it to a point on another object.

TIP Hold down Shift while dragging to constrain the movement to a multiple of 45°.

To drag-copy an object:

1. Choose the Selection tool.

2. Option-drag/Alt-drag the fill or the edge of the object you want to copy (the pointer will turn into a double arrowhead) **3**. If the bounding box feature is on, don't drag a bounding box handle.

3. Release the mouse, then release Option/Alt. A copy of the object will appear in the new location.

TIP To create additional copies of the object, choose Object menu > Transform > Transform Again (Command-D/Ctrl-D) any number of times.

Note: You can drag-and-drop objects between Illustrator documents or between drag-aware applications. The drag-and-drop method (instructions on the next page) uses fewer steps than does using the Clipboard.

If you select an object or group and then choose the Cut or Copy command, that object or group is placed onto the Clipboard, a temporary storage area in memory. The previous contents of the Clipboard are replaced each time you choose Cut or Copy.

The Paste command places the current Clipboard contents in the center of the currently active document window. The same Clipboard contents can be pasted an unlimited number of times.

To move an object or a group from one document to another:

1. Open both documents.

2. Choose the Selection tool (V), and click on the object or group.

3. Choose Edit menu > Cut (Command-X/ Ctrl-X). The object or group will be removed from the current document.
   or
   To move a copy of the object or group, choose Edit menu > Copy (Command-C/ Ctrl-C).

4. Click in the destination document.

5. *Optional:* Select an object to paste in front of or behind.

6. Choose Edit menu > Paste (Command-V/ Ctrl-V). Or, if you've selected an object in the destination document, choose Edit menu > Paste in Front or Paste in Back.

TIP You can place an Illustrator object into a document in another Adobe PostScript application via the Clipboard. *Macintosh:* If you copy and paste an object from Illustrator into Photoshop, a Paste dialog box will open ■. Click Paste As Pixels (check or uncheck the Anti-Alias box) or click Paste As Paths.

Note: To copy or paste a gradient mesh object from Illustrator 8 into Photoshop 5, rasterize it first.

MOVING GROUPED OBJECTS

If you copy an object in a group by dragging (start dragging with the Direct-selection tool, then continue dragging with Option/Alt held down), the copy will be *part of* that group. If you use the Clipboard to copy and paste an object in a group, the object will paste *outside* the group. The Group command is discussed on page 212.

■ *This dialog box will open if you paste from Illustrator into Photoshop.*

(sidebar, left margin) **Move an Object to a Different Document**

DRAG TO THE DESKTOP

If you drag an Illustrator object to the Desktop, a Picture Clipping file will be created in PICT format on Macintosh. This intermediary file can then be dragged into any drag aware application.

Note: Currently, Windows does not support this drag feature.

DRAG-AND-DROP A RASTERIZED OBJECT WITHOUT A MASK?

If you drag-and-drop a rasterized object (created without a mask), from Illustrator to Photoshop, the bounding area (background) of the object in Photoshop will become opaque white and will block pixels below it. To make the non-pixel layer areas transparent, use Photoshop's Magic Wand tool to select the white background on that object's layer, then press Delete.

To drag-and-drop an object (Illustrator-to-Illustrator or between Photoshop and Illustrator):

1. Select the object you want to drag-and-drop in an Illustrator or Photoshop document.

2. Open the Illustrator or Photoshop document to which you want to copy the object.

3. Drag the object into the destination document window, and presto, a copy of the object will appear in the new location. In Photoshop, the object will become pixels on a new layer.

TIP Hold down Command/Ctrl when dragging a path object from Illustrator to preserve the object as a path in Photoshop.

TIP Hold down Shift after you start dragging into Photoshop to position the resulting pixels in the middle of the Photoshop document window.

TIP If you drag-and-drop from Photoshop to Illustrator via Photoshop's Move tool, the image will drop as an RGB PICT, 72 ppi. If you're going to print the image, use the following method instead: Convert the file to CMYK Color mode, save the Photoshop file as a TIFF or EPS, and then use the Place or Open command in Illustrator to acquire it.

TIP Drag-and-drop does not use the Clipboard, so whatever is currently on the Clipboard is preserved.

Note: To drag-and-drop a gradient mesh object from Illustrator 8 into Photoshop 5, rasterize it first.

Drag-and-Drop

Smart guides are temporary guides that appear when you draw, move, duplicate, or transform an object. They are designed to help you align objects with one another or along a particular axis. And Smart Guides have magnetism: Drag an object near one, and the pointer will snap to it.

To turn smart guides on or off, choose View menu > Smart Guides (Command-U/Ctrl-U). Smart guides settings are chosen in Edit menu > Preferences > Smart Guides **1** (see page 303). You'll understand smart guides pretty quickly once you start working with them—they're easier done than said.

You can start by using Smart Guides to move an object along an axis or align one object with points on another object. Here's how that works:

To use smart guides to align objects:

1. Make sure View menu > Smart Guides (Command-U/Ctrl-U) is turned on (has a check mark). And make sure View menu > Snap to Grid is turned off (if Snap to Grid is on, you won't see the smart guides).

2. Choose the Selection tool (V).

3. Make sure Text Label Hints and Object Highlighting are turned on in Edit menu > Preferences > Smart Guides. (The Construction Guides and Transform Tools options are discussed on page 303.)

4. Start dragging an object. Smart Guide angle line guides will appear as you move the object (the angle is relative to the location from which you started dragging). Release the mouse any time the word "on" appears, and the object will be positioned along that angle **2**. You don't need to hold down Shift to constrain the movement!

   or

   First move the pointer, mouse button up, over an anchor or center point of an unselected object to which you want to align the object you're moving. Since Object Highlighting is turned on in Smart Guides Preferences, the outline of that

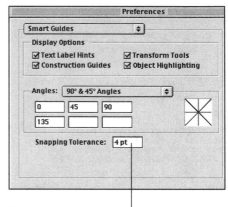

1 *The Snapping Tolerance is the distance within which the pointer must be from an object for the snap function to work.*

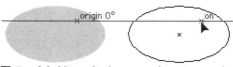

2 *Text label hints display as an object is moved along the horizontal axis.*

3 *The edge of the object highlights as the pointer is moved over it (button up).*

Smart Guides

INTERESTING ANGLE

You can specify the angle for smart guides in Edit menu > Preferences > Smart Guides. You can choose a predefined Angles set or you can enter your own angles. If you switch from Custom Angles to a predefined set and then switch back to Custom Angles at a later time, the last-used custom settings will be restored.

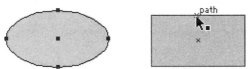

4 *First the mouse (button up) is moved over the unselected rectangle. The word "path" appears as the mouse is moved over the edge of the rectangle.*

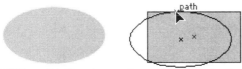

5 *Then the ellipse is moved over the rectangle. As the mouse is dragged over the rectangle's path, the word "path" displays again. This tells you that that portion of the selected object is over the path of the unselected object.*

6 *First the mouse (button up) is moved over an anchor point of the unselected rectangle.*

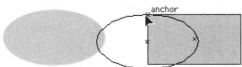

7 *Then the ellipse is dragged by an anchor point and is aligned to an anchor point (as revealed by the word "anchor") on the rectangle.*

object will be highlighted **3**, and the word **path** will appear when the pointer is over the edge of the path **4**. Then start dragging the second object, position the pointer over the edge of the unselected path to which you're aligning the second object, and release the mouse when the word "path" appears **5**.

or

First move the pointer, mouse button up, over an anchor point on the unselected object to which you want to align the current, selected object **6**. Then start dragging the selected object, position the pointer over the point on the path to which you want to align, and release the mouse when the word **anchor** appears **7**.

Note: You could also align a path of one object to an anchor point on another object or an anchor point of one object to the path of another object.

TIP You can't lock smart guides—they vanish as quickly as they appear. To create guides that stay on screen, drag from the horizontal or vertical ruler.

TIP Smart Guides are the same color as the current Guides color, which is chosen in File menu > Preferences > Guides & Grid.

The Offset Path command copies a path and offsets the copy around or inside the original path by a specified distance. The copy is also reshaped automatically so it fits nicely around the original path.

Note: Try using this command on a path that has a stroke, but no fill.

To offset a copy of a path:

1. Select an object **1**.

2. Choose Object menu > Path > Offset Path.

3. In the Offset field, enter the distance you want the offset path to be from the original path **2**. Be sure your Offset value is larger than the stroke weight of the original path so the original and offset paths won't overlap each other.

4. Choose a Joins (bend) style: Round (semicircular), Miter (pointed), or Bevel (square-cornered).

5. *Optional:* Enter a different Miter Limit for the maximum amount the offset path's line weight (as measured from the inside to the outside of the corner point) can be enlarged before the miter join becomes a bevel join. The Miter limit value times the stroke weight value equals the maximum inner-to-outer corner measurement. Use a high Miter Limit to create long, pointy corners; use a low Miter limit to create bevel join corners.

6. Click OK (Return/Enter) **3**–**6**. The offset paths will be closed paths, separate from the original path.

Offset a Copy of a Path

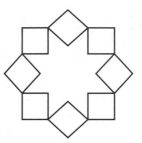

1 *The original path.*

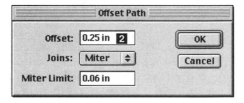

3 *After applying the Offset Path command.*

4 *After recoloring the objects.*

5 *The original path.* **6** *With an **offset path**.*

RESHAPE 7

In Chapter 5 you learned how to draw closed and open paths without thinking about their individual components. In this important chapter, you will learn how to reshape paths using the nuts and bolts that paths are composed of: direction lines, direction points, anchor points, and segments. Once you learn how to alter the profile of an object by changing the number, position, or type of anchor points on its path, you'll be able to create just about any shape imaginable.

You will learn how to move anchor points, direction lines, or path segments to reshape a path; how to use the Pencil, Smooth, Erase, or Reshape tool to quickly reshape part of a path; how to convert a corner anchor point into a curve anchor point (or vice versa) to reshape the segments that it connects; and how to add or delete anchor points. You will also learn how to split a path; how to average anchor points; how to join endpoints; how to combine paths using the Unite command; how to carve away parts of a path using the Knife tool; how to make cutout shapes using the Slice command; and how to trace a placed image automatically or manually. Also included in this chapter are three practice exercises.

The path building blocks

Paths are composed of curved and/or straight segments. A curve consists of two anchor points connected by a curve segment, with at least one direction point and one direction line attached to each anchor point. When an anchor point connects a curve and a straight line segment, it has one common direction line. When an anchor point connects two curve segments, it has a pair of direction lines.

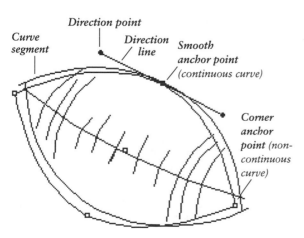

Curve segment · Direction point · Direction line · Smooth anchor point (continuous curve) · Corner anchor point (non-continuous curve)

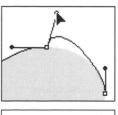

The **angle** of a direction line affects the **slope** of the curve into the anchor point.

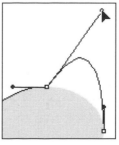

The **length** of a direction line affects the **height** of the curve.

If you move an anchor point, the segments that are connected to it will reshape. If you move a curve segment, the connecting anchor points will remain stationary. If you move a straight line segment, connecting anchor points *will* move.

To move an anchor point or a segment:

1. Choose the Direct-selection tool (A or Shift-A) **1**.

2. Drag an anchor point **2** or drag a segment **3**. You can use Smart Guides for precise positioning (Command-U/Ctrl-U).

TIP Shift-drag to constrain the movement of an anchor point to multiples of 45°.

TIP If all the anchor points on a path are selected, you will not be able to move an individual point or segment. Deselect the object, then reselect an individual point.

TIP To select more than one anchor point at a time, Shift-click them or drag a marquee around them.

In the instructions above, you learned that you can drag a curve segment or an anchor point to reshape a curve. A more precise way to reshape a curve is to lengthen, shorten, or change the angle of its direction lines.

To reshape a curve segment:

1. Choose the Direct-selection tool.

2. Click on an anchor point **4**.

3. Drag a direction point (the end of the direction line) toward or away from the anchor point **5**.
   or
   Rotate the direction point around the anchor point. The anchor point will remain selected when you release the mouse.

TIP Direction line antennae on a smooth curve always move in tandem. They'll stay in a straight line even if the curve segment or anchor point they are connected to is moved.

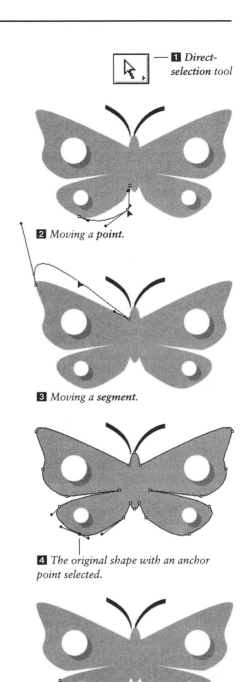

1 *Direct-selection* tool

2 *Moving a* ***point***.

3 *Moving a* ***segment***.

4 *The original shape with an anchor point selected.*

5 *A* ***direction point*** *is dragged away from its anchor point.*

 — **1** *Pencil tool*

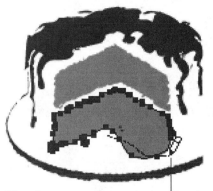

2 *Reshaping a path using the **Pencil** tool.*

Diane Margolin

3 *The path is reshaped.*

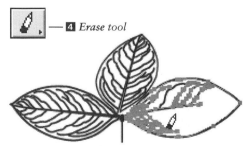 — **4** *Erase tool*

6 *Using the **Erase** tool.*

In addition to being used to draw freehand shapes, the Pencil tool also has a quick-'n'-easy reshape function.

To reshape a path using the Pencil tool:

1. Choose the Pencil tool (N or Shift-N) **1**.

2. Command-click/Ctrl-click on a path to select it.

3. Position the pointer directly over the path edge, then start dragging **2**. End up over another edge of the path. The path will reshape instantly **3**.

TIP To create an addition to a line using the Pencil, start dragging from an endpoint.

To erase part of a path using the Erase tool:

1. Choose the Erase tool (N or Shift-N) **4**

2. Command-click/Ctrl-click to select an object or objects (not a gradient mesh or a text path).

3. Position the eraser (black) part of the pointer directly over the edge of a path, drag across the area that you want to remove, and end up with the eraser on another edge. If you erase on a closed path, you'll end up with an open path. If you erase on an open path, you'll end up with two separate paths. You can also remove lines using this tool **5**–**7**.

5 *The original objects.*

7 *Some points are erased.*

Reshape using the Pencil; Erase

To smooth part of an existing path:

1. Choose the Selection tool, and select a path. The path can be open or closed.
2. Choose the Smooth tool (N or Shift-N) **1**. Or choose the Pencil tool and press Option/Alt to access the Smooth tool temporarily.
3. Drag along the path. The bumps on the path will be smoothed out **2**–**4**. Some anchor points may be removed in order to do so. Now read about the Smooth tool preferences, which affects how drastically a path is reshaped using this tool.

To choose settings for the Smooth tool:

1. Double-click the Smooth tool **1**.
2. Choose a Fidelity value (0.5–20) **4**. The higher the Fidelity, the greater the number of anchor points removed.
3. Choose a Smoothness value (0–100). The higher the Smoothness, logically, the greater the amount of smoothing; the lower the smoothness, the less drastic the reshaping.
4. Check the "Keep selected" option to keep a path selected after using the Smooth tool.
5. Click OK to accept the current settings and close the dialog box.

TIP Click Default to reset the preferences to their defaults.

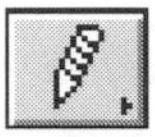

1 *Smooth tool*

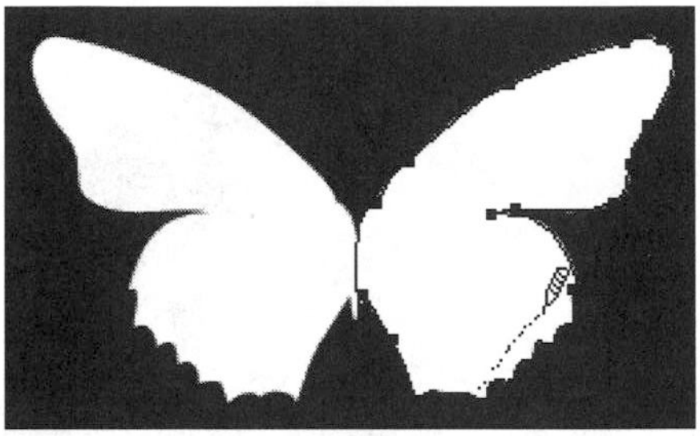

2 *Using the* ***Smooth*** *tool.*

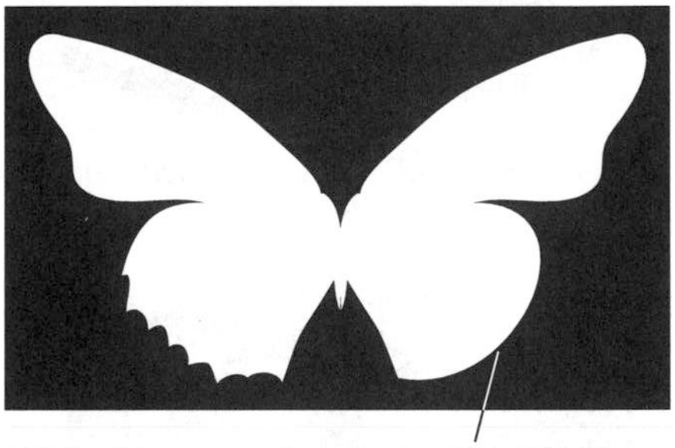

3 *The Smooth tool used with* ***high Fidelity*** *and* ***Smoothness*** *settings.*

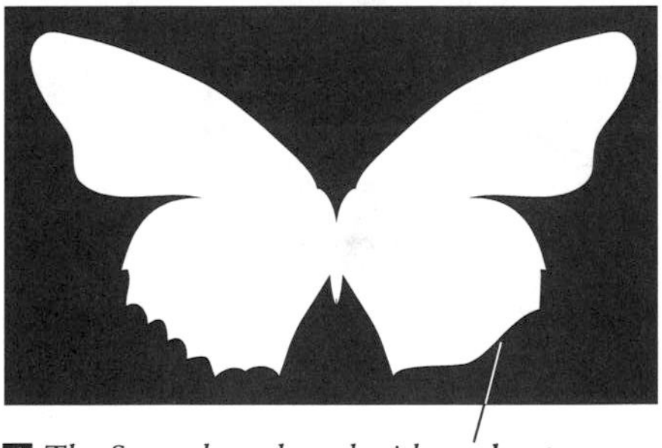

4 *The Smooth tool used with* ***moderate Fidelity*** *and* ***Smoothness*** *settings.*

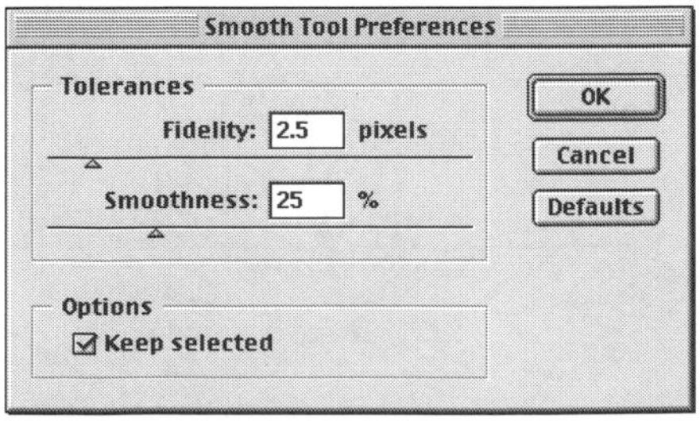

5 *Smooth Tool Preferences.*

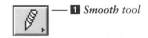

1 *Convert-direction-point tool.*

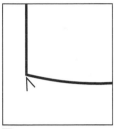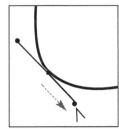

2 *To convert a corner point into a curve point, press with the Convert-direction-point tool on the anchor point...*

3 *...then drag away from the point.*

To convert a corner anchor point into a curve anchor point:

1. Choose the Selection or Direct-selection tool.

2. Click on the edge of the object.

3. Choose the Convert-direction-point tool (P or Shift-P) **1**.
or
Choose the Pen tool and hold down Option/Alt.

4. Press on an anchor point **2**, then drag away from it **3**. Direction lines will appear as you drag. The further you drag, the rounder the curve will become.

5. *Optional:* To further modify the curve, choose the Direct-selection tool, then drag the anchor point or a direction line **4**.

Note: If the new curve segment twists around the anchor point as you drag, keep the mouse button down, rotate the direction line back around the anchor point to undo the twist, then continue to drag in the new direction **5**.

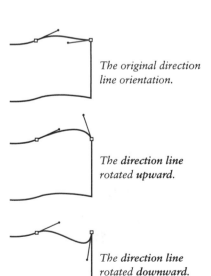

The original direction line orientation.

*The **direction line** rotated **upward**.*

*The **direction line** rotated **downward**.*

4

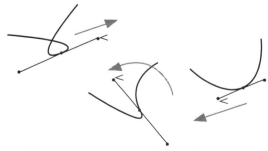

5 *If the curve twists around the anchor point, rotate the direction line to un-twist it.*

Convert a Corner Point into a Curve Point

To convert a curve anchor point into a corner anchor point:

1. Choose the Selection tool (V) or Direct-selection tool (A or Shift-A).

2. Click on the edge of the object to display its anchor points.

3. Choose the Convert-direction-point tool (P or Shift-P).
   or
   Choose the Pen tool and hold down Option/Alt.

4. Click on a curve anchor point—don't drag! Its direction lines will be deleted **1**–**2**.

The direction lines in a pinched curve rotate independently of each other—they don't stay in a straight line.

To pinch a curve inward:

1. Choose the Direct-selection tool (A or Shift-A).

2. Click on the edge of an object to display its anchor points, then click on a point **3**.

3. Choose the Convert-direction-point tool (P or Shift-P).
   or
   Choose the Pen tool and hold down Option/Alt.

4. Drag a direction point at the end of one of the direction lines. The curve segment will reshape as you drag **4**.

5. Choose the Direct-selection tool.

6. Click on the anchor point, then drag the other direction line for that anchor point **5**.

TIP To revert an independent-rotating direction line pair back to its previous straight-line alignment and produce a smooth, un-pinched curve segment, choose the Convert-direction-point tool, then click on and drag away from the anchor point.

1 *Click with the Convert-direction-point tool on a curve point...*

2 *...to convert it into a corner point.*

3 *A point is selected on an object.*

4 *A direction line is moved independently using the Convert-direction-point tool.*

5 *The second direction line is moved.*

1 *Add-anchor-point tool. Press "P" to cycle through the pen tools.*

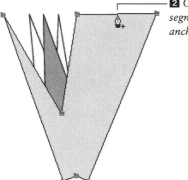

2 *Click on a segment to add an anchor point...*

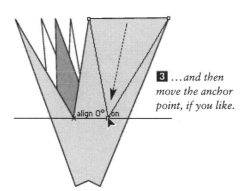

3 *...and then move the anchor point, if you like.*

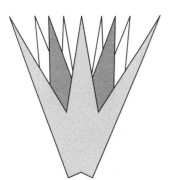

Another way to reshape a path is to manually add or delete anchor points from it. Adding or deleting points from a path will not split or open it.

Note: If you want to use the Pen tool to add points to a path, make sure the Disable Auto Add/Delete box is unchecked in File menu > Preferences > General. Then all you have to do is click on a segment to add a point to it.

To add anchor points to a path manually:

1. Choose the Selection tool, and select an object.

2. Choose the Add-anchor-point tool **1**.
   or
   Choose the Pen tool (P or Shift-P).

3. Click on the edge of the object. A new, selected anchor point will appear **2**. Repeat, if desired, to add more points.

   Note: An anchor point added to a curve segment will be a curve point with direction lines. An anchor point added to a straight segment will be a corner point.

4. *Optional:* Use the Direct-selection tool to move the new anchor point **3**.

TIP Hold down Shift to disable the add/delete function of the Pen tool. Release Shift before releasing the mouse button.

TIP If you don't click precisely on a path segment, a warning prompt may appear. Click OK, then try again.

TIP Hold down Option/Alt to use the Delete-anchor-point tool when the Add-anchor-point tool is selected, and vice versa.

It's difficult to produce a smooth curve if you place anchor points at the top...

It's better to place anchor points at the ends of a curve.

Add Anchor Points to a Path

The Add Anchor Points command inserts one anchor point midway between every two existing anchor points.

To add anchor points to a path using a command :

1. Select an object or objects.

2. Choose Object menu > Path > Add Anchor Points –. Repeat, if desired. To display the new anchor points, click on the object with the Direct-selection tool.

1 *The original object.*

2 *After adding anchor points to the original object and then applying the Punk and Bloat filter (Punk 70%).*

3 *After adding more anchor points and then applying the Punk and Bloat filter (Bloat 70%).*

Diane Margolin

Note: If you want to use the Pen tool to delete points from a path, make sure the Disable Auto Add/Delete box is unchecked in File menu > Preferences > General. Then all you have to do is click on a point to delete it.

To delete anchor points from a path:

1. Choose the Selection tool.

2. Select an object.

3. Choose the Delete-anchor-point tool **4**.
   or
   Choose the Pen tool (P or Shift-P).

4. Click on an anchor point. The point will be deleted and an adjacent point will become selected **5**. Repeat to delete other anchor points, if desired.

TIP Hold down Shift to disable the add/delete function of the Pen tool. Release Shift before releasing the mouse button.

TIP If you don't click precisely on an anchor point, a warning prompt may appear. Click OK, then try again.

4 *Delete-anchor-point tool*

5 *Click on an anchor point with the Delete-anchor-point tool.*

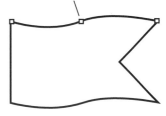

Scissors tool.

 *Click with the Scissors tool on a path.*

 *Move the new endpoint.*

Fill   Stroke

No stroke between the endpoints.

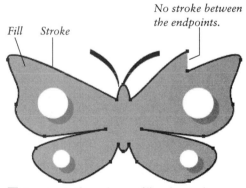

An open path can have a fill and a stroke.

Using the Scissors tool, an open path can be split into two paths or a closed path can be opened. A path can be split at an anchor point or in the middle of a segment.

To split a path:

1. Choose any selection tool.
2. Click on an object to display its anchor points.
3. Choose the Scissors tool (C or Shift-C) **1**.
4. Click on the object's path **2**. If you click once on a **closed** path, it will turn into a single, open path. If you click in **two** different spots on a closed path, the object will be split into two open paths. If you click once on an **open** path, it will split into two paths.

   If you click on a **segment**, two new endpoints will appear, one on top of the other. If you click on an anchor **point**, a new anchor point will appear on top of the existing one. One of the new endpoints will be selected.

To move the new endpoints apart:

5. Choose the Direct-selection tool.
6. Drag the selected point away to reveal the endpoint underneath it **3**.

TIP You can apply a fill color to an open path. If you apply a stroke color, you will be able to see where the missing segment is **4**.

TIP You can split a closed path with text inside it (area text), but you can't split an open path that has text on it or inside it.

Split a Path

The Average command reshapes one or more paths by precisely realigning their endpoints or anchor points along the horizontal and/or vertical axis.

To average anchor points:

1. Choose the Direct-selection tool.

2. Shift-click or marquee two or more anchor points **1**. You might want to zoom in on the objects so you can clearly see the selected points.

3. Choose Object menu > Path > Average (Command-Option-J/Ctrl-Alt-J).
   or
   Control-click/Right-click on the artboard and choose Average from the context menu.

4. Click **Horizontal** to align the points along the horizontal (x) axis **2**. Points will actually move vertically.
   or
   Click **Vertical** to align the points along the vertical (y) axis. Points will actually move horizontally.
   or
   Click **Both** to overlap the points along both the horizontal and vertical axes. Choose this option if you want to join them later into one point (instructions on the following page).

5. Click OK (Return/Enter) **3**.

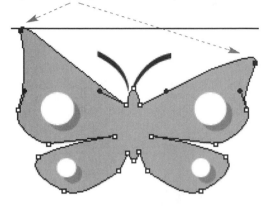

1 *Two anchor points are selected.*

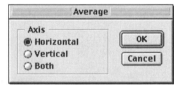

2 *Click an Axis button in the Average dialog box.*

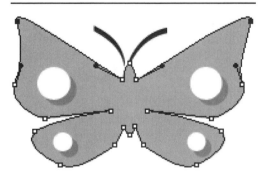

3 *After averaging the selected points, Axis: Horizontal. The points now align horizontally.*

To average and **join** two selected endpoints using one keystroke: Command-Option-Shift-J/ Ctrl-Alt-Shift-J. *Note:* To undo this, use the Undo command twice!

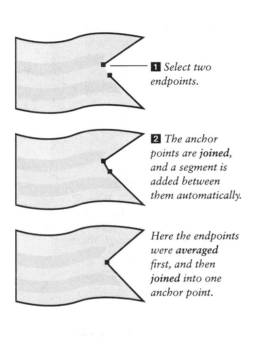

1 *Select two endpoints.*

2 *The anchor points are joined, and a segment is added between them automatically.*

Here the endpoints were averaged first, and then joined into one anchor point.

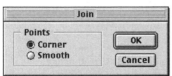

3 *Click Points: Corner or Smooth in the Join dialog box.*

If you align two endpoints on top of each other and then execute the Join command with the endpoints selected, they will combine into one anchor point. If the endpoints are not on top of each other, a new straight line segment will be created between them. The Join command will not add direction lines to the new anchor point. The endpoints you join can be on separate open paths or one open path.

To join two endpoints:

1. Choose the Direct-selection tool.

2. *Optional:* If you want to combine two endpoints into one, move one endpoint on top of the other manually and marquee them to select them both, or use the Average command (Axis: Both) to align them (instructions are on the previous page).

3. Shift-click or marquee two endpoints **1**.

4. Choose Object menu > Path > Join (Command-J/Ctrl-J) or Control-click/ Right-click on the artboard and choose Join from the context menu.

   If the endpoints are not on top of each other, the Join command will connect them with a straight line segment **2**. If the endpoints are aligned on top of each other and are both selected (marquee them, if necessary), the Join dialog box will open **3**. In the Join dialog box:

   Click **Corner** to join corner points into one corner point with no direction lines or to connect two curve points (or a corner point and a curve point) into one curve point with independent-moving direction lines. This is the default setting.
   or
   Click **Smooth** to connect two curve points into a curve point with direction lines that move in tandem.

5. Click OK (Return/Enter).

Join Endpoints

The Pathfinder commands combine multiple objects into one new object. Here's an introduction to one of the most straightforward and useful ones: The Unite command. (More about the Pathfinders in Chapter 15.)

To combine two or more objects into one using the Unite command:

1. Position two or more objects so they overlap **1**.

2. Choose any Selection tool.

3. Marquee at least some portion of all the objects.

4. On the Pathfinder palette, click the Unite button. The individual objects will combine into one closed object **2**–**6**, and will be colored with the topmost object's paint attributes.

TIP If you apply a stroke color to the new object, you will see that the previously overlapping segments were removed.

TIP You can use the new closed object as a masking object. (You could not have created a single mask with the original objects before they were united.)

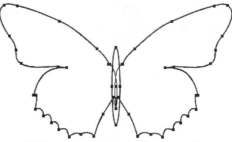

1 *Two or more objects are arranged so they overlap, and then they're selected.*

2 *After clicking the Unite button on the Pathfinder palette, the individual shapes are combined into a single shape.*

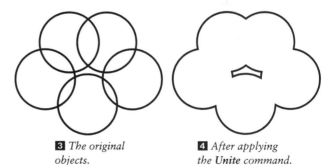

3 *The original objects.*

4 *After applying the Unite command.*

5 *The original objects.*

6 *After applying the Unite command.*

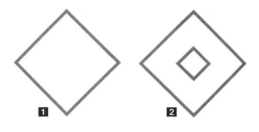

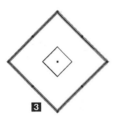

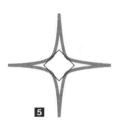

Exercise

Change a square into a star

1. Choose the Rectangle tool (M or Shift-M). Set up the Color palette to have a fill of None and a stroke of 2 points (see Chapter 9).

2. Click on the artboard.

3. In the Rectangle dialog box, enter 2″ in the Width field, click the word Height, then click OK.

4. Double-click the Rotate tool, enter 45 in the Angle field, then click OK **1**.

5. Double-click the Scale tool, enter 30 in the Uniform Scale field, then click Copy **2**.

6. Choose View menu > Make Guides to turn the small diamond into a guide.

7. Select the large diamond shape. Choose Object menu > Path > Add Anchor Points **3**.

8. Choose the Direct-selection tool. Deselect, then click on the edge of the diamond.

9. Drag each of the new midpoints inward until it touches the guide shape. Use Smart Guides to drag on a 45° angle **4**.

10. Choose the Convert-direction-point tool, and drag each of the inner midpoints to create a curve. Drag clockwise and drag along the edge of the guide shape **5**.

11. Choose the Ellipse tool, position the cursor over the center point of the star shape, then Option-Shift-drag/Alt-Shift-drag until the circle touches the curves of the star.

12. Fill the circle with white, stroke of None. Apply a black fill and a gray stroke to the star shape **6**.

13. *Optional:* Select the circle. Choose the Scale tool. Start dragging, hold down Option-Shift/Alt-Shift, and continue to drag until the copy of the circle touches the outer tips of the star. Fill the large circle with None, and apply a 2-point stroke **7**.

Using the Reshape tool, you can quickly reshape part of a path simply by dragging the path's edge—that portion will reshape smoothly. Use this tool to stretch or add a twist or bend to any part of an existing path.

To use the Reshape tool:

1. Click on the edge of a path using the Direct-selection tool. Only one point or segment should be selected.

2. Choose the Reshape tool on the Scale tool pop-out menu (S or Shift-S) **1**.

3. Drag any visible point. A square border will display around the point when you release the mouse.
   or
   Drag any segment of the path. A new square border point will be created.
   or
   Try this: Shift-click multiple points on the path using the Reshape tool (squares will display around these points), then drag. For smooth reshaping, leave at least one point on the path unselected (with no square around it) to act as an anchor for the shape **2**–**3**. Or, choose the Reshape tool, marquee the points you want to reshape, then drag the points (this may not work).

TIP Choose Edit menu > Undo to undo the last Reshape. Undo will also automatically select the whole shape. Before continuing to work with the Reshape tool, you must deselect the shape, and then click again on the edge of the shape with the Direct-selection tool.

TIP To reshape multiple paths at the same time, leave at least one point on each path unselected by the Reshape tool (with no square around it) to act as an anchor. For fun, try this on a series of lines.

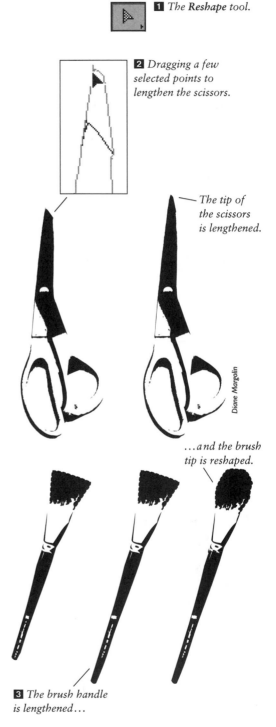

1 *The Reshape tool.*

2 *Dragging a few selected points to lengthen the scissors.*

The tip of the scissors is lengthened.

Diane Margolin

…and the brush tip is reshaped.

3 *The brush handle is lengthened…*

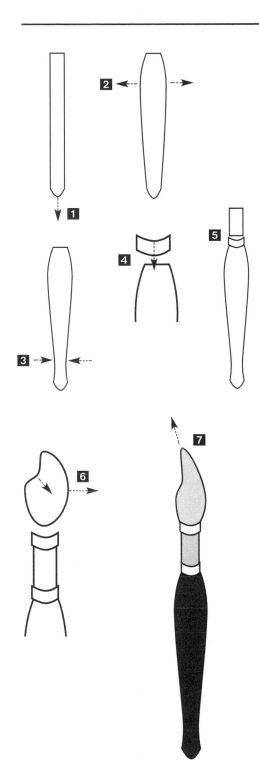

Exercise
Draw a paintbrush using the Reshape tool

1. Using the Rectangle tool, draw a narrow vertical rectangle, white fill, black stroke.

2. Choose the Direct-selection tool (A or Shift-A), deselect the shape, then click on the edge of the path.

3. Choose the Reshape tool (S or Shift-S), then drag downward from the middle of the bottom segment **1**.

4. Drag the upper middle of the right vertical segment slightly outward and drag the upper middle of the left vertical segment outward the same distance **2**.

5. Drag each side of the bottom vertical segments inward to pinch the stem **3**.

6. Draw a small horizontal rectangle. Then choose the Direct-selection tool, deselect the rectangle, and click on the path.

7. Choose the Reshape tool again, click the middle of the top segment, Shift-click the middle of the bottom segment, then drag downward **4**.

8. Choose the Selection tool (V), place the rectangle over the top of the brush stem, scale it to fit, and fill it with white.

9. Draw a vertical rectangle above the horizontal rectangle in a slightly narrower width. Choose Object menu > Arrange > Send to Back **5**.

10. Option-Shift/Alt-Shift drag the horizontal rectangle upward. Move the copy to the top of the vertical rectangle.

11. Using the Ellipse tool, draw an oval for brush tip. Choose the Direct-selection tool, deselect the oval, then click on the edge of the path.

12. Choose the Reshape tool, drag the right middle point outward, drag the upper left segment inward **6**, and drag the top point upward to lengthen the tip **7**.

13. Position the brush tip shape over the brush stem, then choose Object menu > Arrange > Send to Back.

The Knife tool reshapes paths like a carving knife, and is a wonderful tool for artists who have a freehand drawing style.

Note: The Knife tool works only on a closed path—not on an open path.

To cut an object into separate shapes:

1. Choose the Knife tool from the Scissors tool pop-out menu (C or Shift-C) .

2. Starting from outside the object, drag completely across an object to divide it, or end up outside the object again to carve off a piece of it –**4**. Option-drag/Alt-drag to cut in a straight line.

TIP Choose Object menu > Group to group the newly separated shapes together, and then use the Direct-selection tool if you need to select separate shapes within the group.

TIP If you drag the Knife tool completely inside the object (and not outside-to-inside the object), the resulting shape will be a compound. The line you created using the Knife will be like a tear in the object. To open up the tear, use the Direct-selection tool to select it, then pull on its direction lines or segments.

1 *Knife tool.*

2 *The original mother and child elephants.*

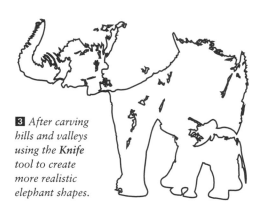
3 *After carving hills and valleys using the **Knife** tool to create more realistic elephant shapes.*

4 *The final image, after applying a black fill.*

Diane Margolin

Knife Tool

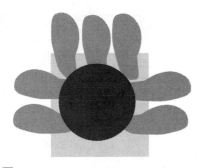

1 *The black circle is the cutting object.*

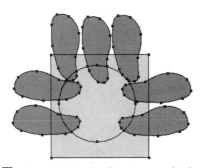

2 *After applying the **Slice** command. The objects are shown selected.*

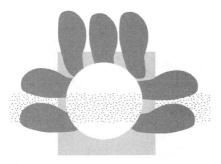

3 *After **deleting** the inner part of each petal and the center of the gray rectangle. We placed a pattern behind all the objects so you can see that the slicing circle produced a cutout.*

The Slice command uses an object like a cookie cutter to cut the objects underneath it, and then deletes the cutting object.

To cut objects using the Slice command:

1. Create or select an object to be used as the cutting shape. The Slice command will cause this object to be deleted, so make a copy of it now if you want to preserve it.

2. Place the cutting object on top of the objects you want to cut **1**.

3. Make sure no other objects are selected except the cutting object.

4. Choose Object menu > Path > Slice. The topmost shape (cutting object) will be deleted automatically and the underlying objects will be cut where they meet the edge of the cutting object **2**–**3**.

TIP To prevent an object from being affected, put it on a separate layer and hide or lock that layer.

Some Illustrator filters can be used to explode a simple shape into a more complex one. The Zig Zag filter, for example, adds anchor points to a path or line and then moves those points to produce waves or zigzags. (Read more about filters in Chapter 17.)

To apply the Zig Zag filter:

1. Select a path.

2. Choose Filter menu > Distort (upper part of the menu) > Zig Zag.

3. Check the Preview box **1**.

4. Click Points: Smooth to make curvy waves or click Corner to create sharp-cornered zigzags.

5. Choose an Amount for the distance the added anchor points will move.

6. Choose a number of Ridges for the number of anchor points to be added between existing points. If you enter a number, press Tab to preview.

7. Click OK (Return/Enter).

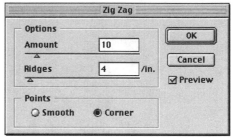

1 *In the* **Zig Zag** *dialog box, click the Preview box, click Points:* **Smooth** *or* **Corner,** *and choose an* **Amount** *and number of* **Ridges.**

The original line.

Amount 48, Ridges 12, Corner.

Amount 48, Ridges 7, Smooth.

The original star.

The original oval.

Amount 24, Ridges 20, Corner.

Amount 45, Ridges 4, Smooth.

The original star.

Amount 17, Ridges 20, Smooth.

Zigzag Filter

If you apply a Pathfinder command to an open path, the path is closed automatically. You may want to apply the Outline Path command first (instructions on this page) to close the path yourself. Another reason to convert a line or a stroke into a closed path is so it can be filled with a gradient or a pattern.

Note: The Outline Path command produces the most predictable results when it's applied to an object that has wide curves. It may produce odd corner shapes if it's applied to an object that has sharp corners. You can use the Unite button on the Pathfinder palette to eliminate the resulting odd corner shapes.

To turn a stroke or an open path into a closed, filled object:

1. Select an object that has a stroke color **1**.

2. Choose Object menu > Path > Outline Path. The width of the new filled object will be the same thickness as the original stroke **2**.

TIP If you apply the Outline Path command to a closed path to which fill and stroke colors have been applied, you'll end up with two separate objects: a fill object and a compound stroke object.

1 *Select an object with a stroked path. To produce the button shown below, a gradient fill and a stroke were applied to the object before applying the* **Outline Path** *command.*

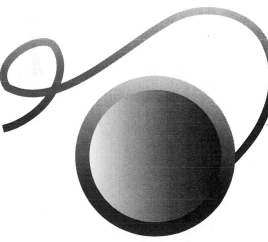

The thread was created using the Pencil tool. The **Outline Path** *command was applied to it, and then it was also filled with a gradient.*

2 *The* **Outline Path** *command converted the stroke into a compound path. To produce this button, the compound path (outer ring) was selected with the Selection tool and a gradient fill was applied to it. Then the Gradient tool was dragged across it to make it contrast with the gradient fill in the inner circle. To modify the gradient in the inner circle, the compound would have to be released and only the inner circle selected.*

Exercise
Create a light bulb

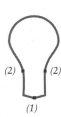

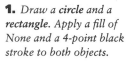

1. *Draw a **circle** and a **rectangle**. Apply a fill of None and a 4-point black stroke to both objects.*

2. *Select the bottom point of the circle with the **Direct-selection** tool, and drag the point downward. Select **both** objects using the Selection tool.*

3. *Click the **Unite** button on the Pathfinder palette. Use the **Add-anchor-point** tool to add a point on the bottom segment (1), then use the **Direct-selection** tool to drag it downward. Rotate the direction lines upward for the points where the curve meets the straight line segment (2). Use Smart Guides for this.*

4. *Choose Object menu > Path > **Outline Path**.*

5. *Create a rounded rectangle or an oval that's wider than the base of the bulb. Rotate it using the **Rotation** tool. Choose the Selection tool, and Option-Shift/Alt–Shift drag two copies downward.*

6. *Fill the ovals, and position them on the bottom of the bulb.*

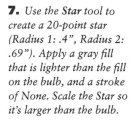

7. *Use the **Star** tool to create a 20-point star (Radius 1: .4", Radius 2: .69"). Apply a gray fill that is lighter than the fill on the bulb, and a stroke of None. Scale the Star so it's larger than the bulb.*

8. *Position the star over the bulb. Select the Star, then Command-click/Right-click on the artboard and choose Arrange > **Send to Back**.*

9. *Shift-select the bulb (the star and bulb should be selected), then click the **Divide** button on the Pathfinder palette to divide the star. Use the Direct-selection tool to select the part of the star inside the bulb, then delete it.*

10. *Use the **Pencil** tool to draw a filament line inside the bulb. Apply a fill of None and a black stroke to the filament.*

11. *A variation: Before clicking the **Divide** button (step 9), apply Filter menu > Distort > **Roughen** to the star (Size: 2, Detail: 3–6).*

1 *The placed artwork in the document window. When placing an EPS for tracing, do not link the file, as this will produce an inferior screen image.*

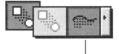

2 *Auto Trace tool.*

3 *After tracing the outer path. Apply a fill of None to prevent the new tracing shapes from blocking out the placed image.*

4 *The outer and inner paths traced.*

5 *The final objects after applying black and white fills.*

The Auto Trace tool automatically traces a path over any image that's opened via the File menu > Place command. A flaw of this tool is that it can create extraneous anchor points or place points in inappropriate locations, so autotraced shapes usually need to be cleaned up—points removed, etc. The Auto Trace tool works best on simple, high contrast artwork, or if you're deliberately looking for a rough, hand-drawn look. Photographs, on the other hand, are best traced manually using the Pen or Pencil tool.

The exactness with which the Autotrace tool traces a path is controlled by the Auto Trace Options settings in File menu > Preferences > Type & Auto Tracing. The higher the Auto Trace Tolerance (0–10 pt), the less precisely an object will be traced, and the fewer anchor points will be created. The Tracing Gap (0–2 pt) is the minimum width a gap in linework must be in order to be traced. A high Tracing Gap setting may result in the creation of a lot of extraneous points.

Note: Adobe's Streamline program traces more accurately and offers more options than Illustrator's Auto Trace tool. You can also color-adjust a bitmap image in Streamline before using the program to trace it.

To use the Auto Trace tool:

1. Open a file, then choose File menu > Place.

2. Locate and highlight a PICT, TIFF, EPS, or other bitmap file, check the Template box, then click Place **1**. (You can also create a template layer later via the Layers palette.)

3. Create or click on an editable layer.

4. *Optional:* Choose a fill of None and a black stroke.

5. Choose the Auto Trace tool on the Blend tool pop-out menu (W or Shift-W) **2**.

6. Click on areas or edges of the placed image or drag the Auto Trace tool over the area to be traced. The shape will be traced automatically **3**–**4**. Experiment!

7. Fill the traced shapes, as desired **5**.

To trace letters manually:

The Auto Trace tool traces quickly and is useful if the feel of the relatively coarse rendering it produces is appropriate for your particular project. If you need to create smoother shapes, you can either refine the Auto Trace tool paths or trace the template manually . What follows is a description of how you can use Illustrator to produce your own letterforms.

1. *Scan the artwork*

To make sure the baseline of your letterwork squares with the horizontal guides in Illustrator, trim the edge of your drawing parallel to the baseline, then slide it against the glass frame of the scanner. Scan your artwork at a resolution between 72 and 150 ppi. Save it as a PICT, TIFF or EPS. Even at 300% view, you will see only a minor difference in crispness between a placed 72-ppi PICT and a placed, non-linked, 250-ppi EPS.

2. *Trace manually*

Place an image in an Illustrator file via File menu > Place, the Template box checked .

Use the Pen tool to trace the upright letters. In the illustration at right, anchor points were placed on the topmost, bottommost, leftmost, and rightmost parts of the curve . Most round shapes can be created with as few as four anchor points. Hold down Shift to draw out the direction lines horizontally or vertically.

To create the inclined letter shown in , a line was drawn following the inclination of a stem (in this case the lower case "t"), and then it was copied and converted into a guide for positioning the direction lines (View menu > Make Guides). The direction lines of the leftmost and rightmost points were extended to align with the guides.

Here's an alternate method: Use the Measure tool to measure the inclination of a letter, note that angle on the Info palette, choose File menu > Preferences > Smart Guides, and enter that angle into the first blank field in the Angles area. Smart Guides will display on that angle as you drag with the Pen tool.

A closeup of the placed artwork.

Peter Fahrni

1 *A closeup of an Auto Trace of the letters. Note the non-systematic distribution of anchor points and direction lines.*

2 *A closeup of the placed artwork.*

3 *The letters drawn manually (the artwork is hidden). All the direction lines are horizontal or on the same diagonal.*

Manual Trace

3. *Fine tune the flow of curves*

Select an anchor point, then move it by pressing the arrow keys. The length and the angle of the direction lines won't change. Select a curve segment, and press the arrow keys to adjust its shape. The length, but not the angle, of the direction lines will change.

The manually traced "B" consisted of two closed, crisscrossing paths **1**. The Unite command was applied to combine the two paths into one **2**–**3**.

1 *The hand-drawn "B."*

2 *The final "B" after applying the Unite command.*

Peter Fahrni

3 *The letters* **Auto Traced***, shown here for comparison.*

A comparison between an Auto Traced character and an Adobe font character

Placed artwork in Illustrator.

The character Auto Traced.

A character in the Goudy 100 Adobe PostScript font, created as type in Illustrator.

Using the Pen or Pencil tool, you can manually trace over any placed image. When you manually trace an image, you can organize and simplify path shapes as well as control their stacking order. If you like, you can even place different path shapes on different layers as you trace.

To manually trace over a placed image:

1. Create or open an an Illustrator document, then choose File menu > Place .

2. Locate and highlight the image you want to trace, check the Template box, then click Place (Return/Enter). The image will appear dimmed on its own uneditable layer.

3. Create or click on a different layer.

4. Choose the Pen (P or Shift-P) or Pencil (N or Shift-N) tool.

5. Trace the placed image .

TIP If you're using the Pencil tool, double-click the tool to change its Tolerance: Fidelity or Smoothness settings.

TIP You can transform a placed image before you trace it.

1 *A placed image.*

2 *After **tracing** the image using the Pen tool, filling and stroking the paths with various shades of black, and applying the Roughen filter with low Size and Detail settings to give the path strokes a more handmade appearance.*

TRANSFORM 8

This chapter covers methods for transforming an object, including the five individual transformation tools (Rotate, Scale, Reflect, Shear, and Blend), the Free Transform tool, the bounding box, and the Transform Each command. The Transform palette is discussed on page 285, the Move command on page 283.

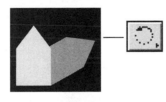

The **Rotate** tool rotates an object around its center or around another specified point.

The **Scale** tool enlarges or reduces the size of an object proportionally or non-proportionally.

The **Reflect** tool creates a mirror image of an object across a specified axis.

The **Shear** tool slants an object on a specified angle.

The **Free Transform** tool can be used to distort or apply perspective, in addition to rotate, scale, reflect, and shear.

The **Blend** tool transforms one object into another by creating a multi-step color and shape progression between them.

Using the transformation tools

The Rotate, Scale, Reflect, and Shear tools transform objects from a user-defined point of origin.

Dialog box method

Select the whole object, and double-click the Rotate, Scale, Reflect, or Shear tool to open the tool's dialog box or Control-click/ Right-click in the document window and choose from the Transform submenu on the context menu 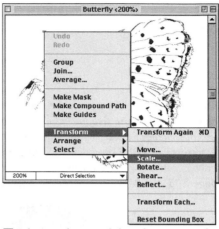. The default point of origin at the object's center will now be visible. Check the Preview box in the tool dialog box, enter numbers (press Tab to preview), then click OK or click Copy.

To use a point of origin other than the object's center, select the object, choose a transform tool, then Option-click/Alt-click on or near the object to establish a new point of origin. A dialog box will open.

Dragging method

Select the whole object; choose the Rotate, Scale, Reflect, Shear, or Free Transform tool; position the pointer outside the object; then drag.

TIP Once the point of origin is established, for finer control position the pointer (arrow-head) far from the point of origin before dragging. You can use Smart Guides (Command-U/Ctrl-U) for positioning.

To use a point of origin other than the object's center 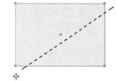, select the object, choose an individual transform tool (not the Free Transform tool), and click another location to establish a new point of origin . Reposition the mouse , then drag to complete the transformation 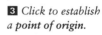. The point of origin can be dragged to a different location.

Hold down Option/Alt while dragging with an individual transform tool to transform a copy of the original (release the mouse first).

To transform an object using its bounding box, see page 111.

Repeating a transformation

Once you have performed a transformation on an object (other than a blend), you can

1 Select an object, and then choose a transform command from the **Transform** submenu on the context menu.

2 Point of origin indicator.

3 Click to establish a point of origin.

4 Reposition the mouse.

5 Drag to transform.

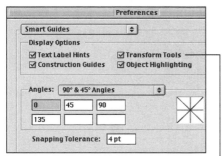

1 *Check the **Transform Tools** box in the Smart Guides Preferences dialog box.*

2 *Using Smart Guides with the **Reflect** tool.*

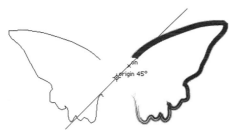

3 *Using Smart Guides with the **Scale** tool.*

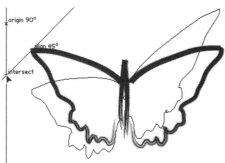

4 *Using Smart Guides with the **Shear** tool.*

repeat the transformation using the same values by choosing Object menu > Transform > **Transform Again** (Command-D/Ctrl-D). If you make a copy of an object while transforming it and then apply Transform Again, a new copy will be transformed.

Transforming fill patterns

If you transform an object that contains a pattern fill, you can transform the pattern when you transform the object by checking the Patterns box in the transformation tool dialog box or by checking the Transform Pattern Tiles box in File menu > Preferences > General (Command-K/Ctrl-K). Checking or unchecking this option in one location automatically resets it in the other locations.

To transform a pattern but not the object, uncheck the Objects box in the transformation tool's dialog box. Or, choose an individual transformation tool, click to position the point of origin, then hold down "~" and drag. This doesn't work with the Free Transform tool.

To use smart guides as you rotate, scale, or shear an object:

1. Choose File menu > Preferences > Smart Guides, and make sure the Transform Tools box has a check mark **1**. You can choose a different Angles set or enter custom angles, if you like.

2. Make sure View menu > Smart Guides is turned on (has a check mark).

3. Choose the Selection (V) tool, and select the object to be transformed.

4. Choose any individual transform tool except the Free Transform tool.

5. As you drag the mouse to transform the object, Smart Guides will appear temporarily **2**–**4**. Move the pointer along a Smart Guide to transform along that axis.

To rotate an object using a dialog box:

1. Select an object (or objects) using the Selection tool **1**.

2. Double-click the Rotate tool if you want to rotate the object around its center **2**.
   or
   Choose the Rotate tool, then Option/Alt click near the object to establish a new point of origin.

3. Check the Preview box.

4. Enter a positive Angle (then press Tab) to rotate the object counterclockwise or a negative Angle to rotate the object clockwise (-360–360) **3**.

5. *Optional:* If the object contains a pattern fill and you check the Patterns box, the pattern will rotate with the object. (This option can also be turned on or off via the Transform Pattern Tiles box in File menu > Preferences > General.)

6. Click Copy to rotate a copy of the original (not the original object) and close the dialog box.
   or
   Click OK (Return/Enter) **4**–**6**.

To rotate an object by dragging:

1. Select an object (or objects) using the Selection tool **1**.

2. Choose the Rotate tool (R or Shift-R) **2**.

3. Drag around the object to use the object's center as the point of origin.
   or
   Click to establish a new point of origin (the pointer will turn into an arrowhead), reposition the mouse as far from the origin as possible, then drag to rotate the object.

   Note: Start dragging, then press Option/Alt to rotate a copy of the object (release the mouse before you release Option/Alt).

   Note: Hold down Shift while dragging to rotate in 45° increments. Release the mouse before you release Shift.

2 *Rotate tool.*

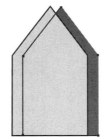

1 *The shadow object is selected.*

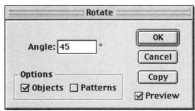

3 *Enter an Angle in the Rotate dialog box. Click Copy to rotate a copy of the object.*

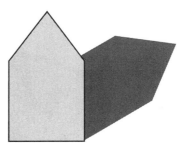

4 *The shadow was rotated –60°, and then moved.*

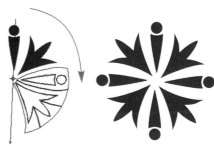

5 *An object is copy-rotated.* **6** *And then the Transform Again command is applied twice (Command-D/Ctrl-D).*

Rotate

1 *Scale tool.*

2 *The Scale dialog box.*

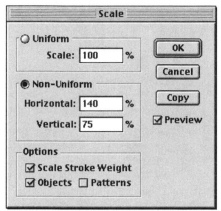

3 *The original object.*

4 *The object scaled Uniformly, Patterns box checked.*

5 *The original object scaled Non-uniformly, Patterns box checked.*

6 *The original object scaled Non-uniformly, Patterns box unchecked.*

To scale an object using a dialog box:

1. Select an object (or objects) using the Selection tool.

2. To scale the object from its center, double-click the Scale tool **1**.
   or
   Choose the Scale tool, then Option/Alt click near the object to establish a new point of origin.

3. Check the Preview box.

4. To scale the object proportionally, click Uniform, then enter a percentage in the Scale field (press Tab) **2**.
   or
   To scale the object non-proportionally, click Non-Uniform, then enter a percentage in the Horizontal and Vertical fields (press Tab).

   Note: Enter 100 to leave a dimension unchanged.

5. *Optional:* Check the Scale Stroke Weight box to also scale the stroke thickness by the same percentage. This option can also be turned on in File menu > Preferences > General.

6. *Optional:* Check the Patterns box if the object contains a pattern fill and you want the pattern to scale with the object.

7. Click Copy to scale a copy of the original (not the original object) and close the dialog box.
   or
   Click OK (Return/Enter) **3**–**6**.

Scale

To scale an object by dragging:

1. Select an object (or objects) using the Selection tool.

2. Choose the Scale tool (S or Shift-S).

3. To scale from the object's center, drag (without clicking first) away from or toward the object.

   or

   Click near the object to establish a point of origin (the pointer will turn into an arrowhead), reposition the mouse 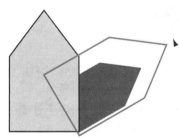, then drag away from the object to enlarge it or drag toward the object to shrink it .

   Note: Option-drag/Alt-drag to scale a **copy** of the object .

   Note: Shift-drag diagonally to scale the object **proportionally**. Release the mouse before you release Shift.

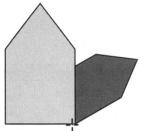

1 *Click to establish a point of origin.*

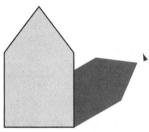

2 *Reposition the mouse,...*

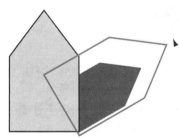

3 *...then drag away from the object.*

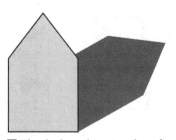

4 *The shadow object is **enlarged**.*

Scale

1 *Reflect tool.*

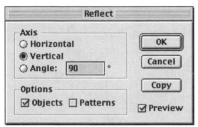

2 *In the Reflect dialog box, click* **Horizontal** *or* **Vertical**, *or enter a number in the* **Angle** *field.*

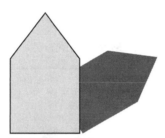

3 *The original objects.*

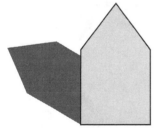

4 *The shadow reflected across the* **Vertical Axis** *at the default angle of 90°.*

DEFAULT ANGLE

The default Horizontal angle is 0°, the default Vertical angle is 90°. The default starting point for measuring the degree of an angle is the horizontal *(x)* axis (the 3 o'clock position).

To reflect (flip) an object using a dialog box:

1. Select an object (or objects) using the Selection tool.

2. To reflect from the object's center, double-click the Reflect tool **1**.
or
Choose the Reflect tool, then Option/Alt click near the object to establish a new point of origin.

3. Check the Preview box.

4. Click Axis: Horizontal or Vertical (the axis the mirror image will flip across) **2**.
or
Enter a number between 360 and –360 in the Angle field (press Tab). Enter a positive number to rotate the object counterclockwise or a negative number to rotate the object clockwise. The angle is measured from the horizontal *(x)* axis.

5. *Optional:* Check the Patterns box if the object contains a pattern fill and you want the pattern to reflect with the object.

6. Click Copy to reflect a copy of the original (not the original object) and close the dialog box.
or
Click OK (Return/Enter) **3**–**4**.

To reflect an object by dragging:

1. Select the object (or objects) using the Selection tool.

2. Choose the Reflect tool (O or Shift-O) **1**.

3. Click near the object to establish a new point of origin (the pointer will turn into an arrowhead), reposition the mouse, then drag horizontally or vertically towards, or rotate around, the point of origin. The object will flip across the axis you create by dragging.

Note: Option-drag/Alt-drag to reflect a copy of the object **4**.

Note: Shift-drag to reflect the object along a multiple of 45°. Release the mouse first.

Reflect

To shear (slant) an object using a dialog box:

1. Select an object (or objects) using the Selection tool **1**.
2. To shear the object from its center, double-click the Shear tool **2**.
   or
   Choose the Shear tool, then Option-click/Alt-click near the object to establish a new point of origin.
3. Check the Preview box.
4. Enter a number between 360 and –360 in the Shear Angle field (press Tab) **3**.
5. Click Axis: Horizontal or Vertical (the axis along which the object will be sheared) **4**.
   or
   Click Axis: Angle, then enter a number in the Angle field (press Tab). The angle will be calculated clockwise relative to the horizontal *(x)* axis **5**.
6. *Optional:* Check the Patterns box to shear a pattern fill with the object.
7. Click Copy to shear a copy of the original (not the original object) and close the dialog box.
   or
   Click OK (Return/Enter).

To shear an object by dragging:

1. Select an object (or objects) using the Selection tool.
2. Choose the Shear tool (O or Shift-O) **2**.
3. To slant from the object's center, without clicking first, position the pointer outside the object, then drag away from the object.
   or
   Click near the object to establish a new point of origin, reposition the mouse, then drag.

   Note: Option-drag/Alt-drag to shear a copy of the object. To shear the object to a multiple of 45°, start dragging, then hold down Shift. Release the mouse button first.

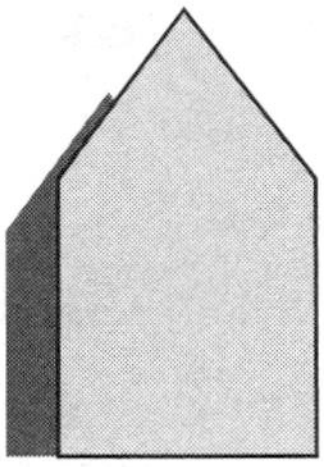

1 *The shadow object is selected.*

2 *Shear tool*

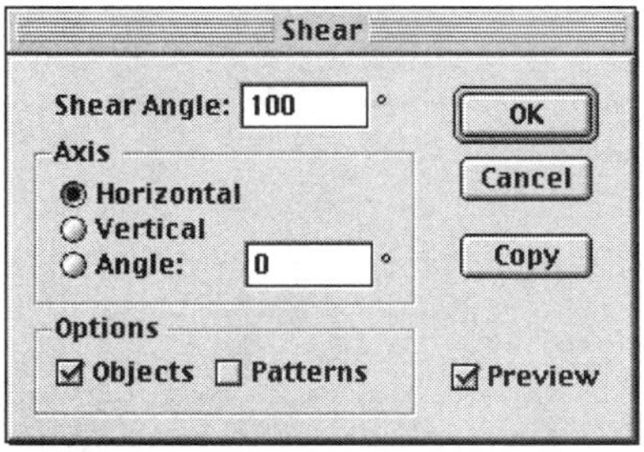

3 *In the* ***Shear*** *dialog box, enter a* ***Shear Angle****, then click an* ***Axis*** *button.*

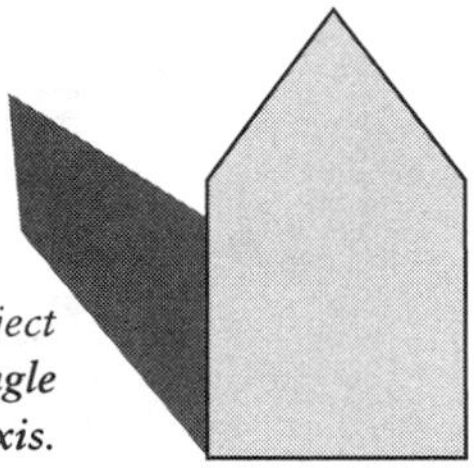

4 *The shadow object sheared at a –35°* ***Angle*** *on the* ***Horizontal Axis****.*

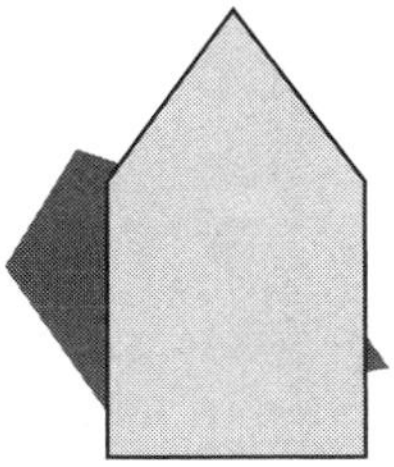

5 *The shadow object sheared at a –35°* ***Angle*** *on a 35°* ***Axis Angle****.*

GET THE NUMBERS

If you transform an object manually by dragging and then double-click the tool you just used for the transformation, the values used for that transformation will display in the dialog box.

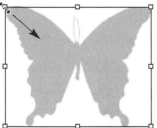

1 *Option-drag/Alt-drag to scale a path from its center.*

2 *The path is scaled down.*

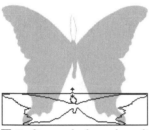

3 *To flip a path, drag a bounding box handle all the way across it.*

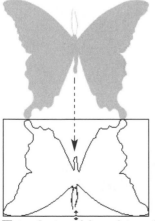

4 *A reflection of the path is made.*

Note: There is no moveable point of origin for a transformation when the bounding box method is used.

To transform an object using its bounding box:

1. Turn on the Use Bounding box option in File menu > Preferences > General.

2. Choose the Selection tool, and select an object (or objects). A rectangular box with eight handles will surround the object. The handles and box will be drawn in the color of the currently active layer.

3. To **scale** the object, drag a corner handle to resize along two axes or drag a center handle to resize along one axis. Shift-drag to resize proportionally. Hold down Option/Alt to scale from the object's center **1**–**2**.
   or
   To create a **reflection** (mirror image) of the object, drag a center handle all the way across it.
   or
   To **flip** the object, drag a corner handle all the way across the object or Shift-drag a center handle to reflect and flip **3**–**4**. Option-drag/Alt-drag to reflect or flip from the object's center.

TIP If all of an object's anchor points are selected and then the Selection tool is chosen, the bounding box will appear automatically.

TIP If you rotate a box using either the Rotate tool or the Free Transform tool, the bounding box edges no longer align with the *x/y* axes of the page. To reset the bounding box to align with the page, choose Object menu > Transform > Reset Bounding Box or Control-click/Right-click and choose Transform > Reset Bounding Box from the context menu. *Note:* This command changes the orientation of the bounding box only—not the orientation of the object.

Transform using Bounding Box

The Free Transform tool performs all the transformations of the individual tools, plus distort and perspective.

Note: The Free Transform tool always works from the center of the object or objects. This point of origin is not moveable.

To use the Free Transform tool:

1. Select an object(s) or group.

2. Choose the Free Transform tool (E) **1**.

3. To **scale**, in two dimensions, drag a corner handle. Shift-drag to resize proportionally. Option-drag/Alt-drag to resize the object from its center. Or to resize the object in one dimension, drag a center handle.

   To **rotate**, position the pointer outside the object, then drag in a circular motion. Shift-drag to rotate in 45° increments.

   To **shear**, drag a center point then hold down Command/Ctrl and continue to drag **2**–**3**. To shear in 45° increments, drag a center point, then hold down Command-Shift/Ctrl-Shift and continue to drag. To shear along the *x* or *y* axis from the object's center, drag, then hold down Command-Option-Shift/Ctrl-Alt-Shift and continue to drag.

   To **reflect**, drag a center point all the way across the object. To flip the object, drag a corner point all the way across it. To reflect or flip from the object's center, Alt-drag/Option-drag a center or corner point. Include the Shift key to reflect and flip proportionally.

   To **distort**, drag a corner (not a side) point, then hold down Command/Ctrl and continue to drag **4**–**5**. *Note:* You can't distort type or a brushstroke.

   To apply **perspective**, drag a corner point, then hold down Command-Option-Shift/Ctrl-Alt-Shift and continue to drag **6**–**7**. The perspective will occur along the *x* or *y* axis, depending on which direction you drag. *Note:* You can't apply perspective to type or a brushstroke.

1 *Free Transform tool.*

2 *Shear.*

3 *The **sheared** object.*

4 *Distort.*　　**5** *The **distorted** object.*

6 *Perspective.*

7 *The object with applied **perspective**.*

The original formation.

*The formation rotated 15° via the **Rotate** tool.*

*The formation rotated 15° via the **Transform Each** command (Random box unchecked).*

1 *The **Transform Each** command vs. the **Rotate** tool.*

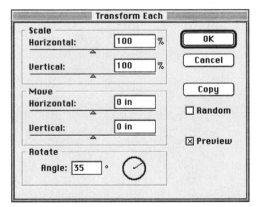

2 *The **Transform Each** dialog box.*

The Transform Each command modifies one or more selected objects relative to their *individual* center points (even if the objects are grouped). The transformation tools, by contrast, transform multiple objects relative to a single, *common* center point **1**. To make your illustration look less regular and more hand drawn, apply the Transform Each command to multiple objects with the Random box checked.

To apply multiple transformation commands at once:

1. Select one or more objects.

2. Choose Object menu > Transform > Transform Each.
   or
   Control-click/Right-click and choose Transform > Transform Each.

3. Check the Preview box, and move the dialog box out of the way, if necessary.

   Perform any or all of steps 4–7 **2**:

4. Move the Horizontal or Vertical Scale slider (or enter a percentage and press Tab) to change the object's horizontal and/or vertical dimensions. Objects are scaled horizontally or vertically from their center points.

5. Choose a higher or lower Horizontal Move amount to move the object to the right or left, or a higher or lower Vertical Move amount to move the object up or down, respectively.

6. Enter a number in the Rotate Angle field and press Tab, or rotate the dial.

7. Check the Random box to have Illustrator apply random transformations within the range of the slider values you've chosen for Scale, Move, or Rotate. For example, at a Rotate Angle of 35°, a different angle between 0° and 35° will be used for each selected object.

8. Click OK (Return/Enter).

(See the illustrations on the following page.)

Transform Each

The original objects.

*After applying **Transform Each** (**Horizontal Scale** 120, **Vertical Scale** 80, **Horizontal Move** 13, **Vertical Move** –13, and **Rotate** 17°—non-matching Horizontal and Vertical Scale values).*

Blends are live!

Both the Blend tool and the Make Blend command create a multi-step color and shape progression between two or more objects. Using the Blend tool, you control which parts of the objects are calculated for the blend, whereas the Make Blend command controls this function automatically.

If you reshape, recolor, or reposition any of the individual objects in a blend or reshape, reposition, or transform the overall blend shape, the blend will update automatically. You can also alter the appearance of an existing blend by reshaping the straight path (spine) that the Blend tool or command creates using any path editing tool, or by selecting the blend and changing the number of steps or other options in the Blend Options dialog box.

Note: The objects you use for a blend can have non-matching shapes and different fill and stroke attributes. They can contain gradients or other blends, but not gradient meshes or brushstrokes. You can blend two open paths or two closed paths, but you can't blend between an open and a closed path.

To blend only colors between objects—not shapes—use a Blend filter (see page 143).

PROCESS OR SPOT?

If one of the original blend objects contains a process color and the other object contains a spot color, the transition objects will be painted with process colors. If you blend two tints of the same spot color, the transition objects will be painted with graduated tints of that color. To blend between a spot color and white, apply 0% of the spot color to the white object.

Blends are Live

1 *The original objects.*

2 *After choosing Object menu > Blends > Make, with Spacing: Smooth Color chosen in the Blend Options dialog box (see the following page).*

3 *After choosing Object menu > Blends > Make, with Spacing: Specified Steps (7) chosen in the Blend Options dialog box (see the following page).*

To blend between objects using the Make Blend command:

1. Position two or more open paths or two or more closed paths (or even groups), allowing room for the transition shapes that will be created between them, and select the objects using the Selection tool **1**.

2. Choose Object menu > Blends > Make (Command-Option-B/Ctrl-Alt-B) **2**–**3**.

3. To change the appearance of the blend, read the instructions on the next two pages.

TIP If you don't like the blend, use the Undo command or release the blend (instructions below).

To release a blend:

1. Select the blend.

2. Choose Object menu > Blends > Release (Command-Option-Shift-B/Ctrl-Alt-Shift-B). The original objects and the *path* created by the blend will remain; the transition objects will be deleted.

Blend Command; Release Blend

Note: If you change the Blend Options settings, any currently selected blends update automatically, and the new settings also affect any subsequently created blends.

To choose or change blend options:

1. Double-click the Blend tool **1**.
   or
   Select an existing blend and choose Object menu > Blends > Blend Options.

2. Check the Preview box to preview changes on any currently selected blends.

3. Choose an option from the Spacing drop-down menu **2**:

   Smooth Color to have Illustrator automatically calculate the necessary number of blend steps (transition shapes) to produce smooth, non-banding color transitions **3**. This option may take a moment to preview on existing objects.

   Specified Steps, and enter the desired number of transition steps in the blend (press Tab to preview). Use this option if you want to create distinct, discernible transition shapes **4**.

   Specified Distance to enter the desired distance between the transition shapes in the blend. The Specified Distance has no effect on the overall length of the blend.

4. Click the **Align to Page** Orientation (first) button to keep the blend objects perpendicular to the page (horizontal axis) **5**.
   or
   Click the **Align to Path** Orientation (second) button to keep the blend objects perpendicular to the blend path **6**. (To place blend objects on a user-drawn spine, see page 119.)

5. Click OK (Enter/Return).

1 *Blend tool.*

2 *Choose **Spacing** and **Orientation** options for existing and future blends in the **Blend Options** dialog box.*

3 *Spacing: **Smooth Color**.*

4 *Spacing: **Specified Steps** (7).*

5 *Orientation: **Align to Page**.*

6 *Orientation: **Align to Path**.*

Blend Options

For a Smooth Color blend, Illustrator automatically calculates the number of steps needed to produce a smooth blend based on the difference in CMYK color-component percentages between the blend objects (i.e., changes in the percentage of Magenta between each object), and based the assumption that the blend will be output on a high-resolution device (1200 dpi or higher). To specify the number of steps for a blend, enter the desired number (1 to 1000) in the Blend Options dialog box in the Spacing drop-down menu: Specified Steps field. Banding is more likely to occur in a color blend if it spans a wide distance (more than seven inches). For better results, use Adobe Photoshop to create a wide color blend, then place it into Illustrator.

To reverse the overlapping order of objects in a blend:

1. Select the blend ■.

2. Choose Object menu > Blends > Reverse Front to Back ■. The original and transition blend objects will now be in their reverse overlapping order (i.e., what was originally the backmost object will now be the frontmost object, and vice versa).

To reverse the transition order of objects in a blend:

1. Select the blend ■.

2. Choose Object menu > Blends > Reverse Spine. The blend objects will swap positions ■.

TIP To modify blend colors, use Filter menu > Colors > Adjust Colors or Direct-select any of the original blend objects and recolor them.

■ *The original blend.*

■ *After applying the **Reverse Front to Back** command.*

■ *Figure ■ after applying the **Reverse Spine** command.*

Reverse Front to Back; Reverse Spine

To blend objects using the Blend tool:

1. Position two or more different-shaped open paths or two or more closed paths, allowing room for the transition shapes that will be created between them. You can apply different colors or gradients to the objects.

2. Choose the Blend tool (W or Shift-W) .

3. Click on the fill area of the first object (but not on the center point). Illustrator will determine which anchor points to use for the blend.
   or
   Click on an anchor point on the first object **2**. The little square on the Blend tool pointer will turn from hollow to filled when it's over an anchor point.

4. Click on the fill or on an anchor point on the next object **3**. For the smoothest shape transitions, click on corresponding points on all the objects (e.g., the top left corner point of all the objects; not the top left corner point of one object and the lower right corner point of another object). If you click on an open path, click on an endpoint. The blend will appear **4**–**5**.

   Repeat this step for any other objects that you want to include in the blend. The blend will update automatically!

5. To change the appearance of the blend, (e.g., you want Smooth Color instead of Specified Steps) see page 116.

TIP If you don't like the blend, use the Undo command or choose Object menu > Blends > Release (Command-Option-Shift-B/Ctrl-Alt-Shift-B).

TIP If the original objects contain different pattern fills, the transition shapes will be filled automatically with the pattern fill from the topmost object.

TIP Apply a stroke color to the original objects if you want the transition shapes to be clearly delineated.

TIP See the "Blends are live" sidebar on the next page.

1 *Blend tool.*

2 *Click on the fill or an anchor point of one object.*

3 *Then click on the fill or an anchor point of another object.*

4 *The blend appears.*

5 *This is what happens if you click on non-corresponding points.*

1 *Select a user-drawn path and a blend.*

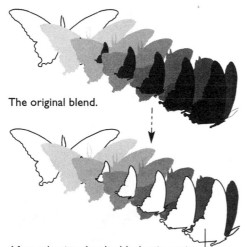

2 *After choosing* **Replace Spine,** *the blend flows along the path.*

To apply an existing blend to a path:

1. Create a blend, then draw a separate path along which you want the blend to flow. The path you draw can be closed or open. If it's closed, the blend will wrap around the object as best as it can.

2. Choose the Selection tool, then select both the blend and the path **1**.

3. Choose Object menu > Blends > Replace Spine. The blend will now follow along the user-drawn path **2**.

TIP If you release the blend from a user-drawn path (Object menu > Blends > Release), the path will be retained, but it won't have a stroke. You can locate the path in Artwork view or using Smart Guides (Object Highlighting).

TIP To change the orientation of the blend objects, select the blend, choose Object menu > Blends > Blend Options, and click the non-highlighted Orientation button (see **5** and **6** on page 116).

BLENDS ARE LIVE

The original blend.

After selecting the the black wing using the Direct-selection tool and **recoloring** it. The blend updates automatically.

You can also try recoloring a blend using a filter on the Filter menu > **Colors** submenu. Or **transform** it using an individual transform tool or the Free Transform tool.

The original blend after **Option-dragging/ Alt-dragging** the white butterfly shape downward from the upper left corner.

Apply a Blend to a Path

Use a blend to create a 3-D effect:

1. Select an object , and apply a fill color and a stroke of None.

2. Double-click the Scale tool.

3. Click Uniform, enter a number between 60 and 80 in the Scale field, then click Copy.

4. With the copy still selected, choose a lighter or darker variation of the original fill color (or black or white) **2**. (For a process color, you can Shift-drag a process color slider on the Color palette to lighten or darken the color.)

5. Choose the Selection tool, and marquee both objects. Make sure the smaller object is in front of the larger object before blending so you'll be able to see the blend.

6. Choose Object menu > Blends > Make (Command-Option-B/Ctrl-Alt-B) **3**–**4**. If the resulting blend doesn't look smooth, select it, double-click the Blend tool, choose Smooth Color from the Spacing drop-down menu, then click OK.

TIP You can modify either blend object at any time. Select the object using the Direct-selection tool, and then reposition or recolor it. You can resize the selected object using the Free Transform or the Scale tool. The blend will redraw automatically.

TIP A simlar effect can be achieved using Object menu > Create Gradient Mesh and choosing Appearance: To Center. Or to create a 3-D surface-modeling effect the old-fashioned way, create a line in the desired shape, copy it to a new location, reshape the copy, if desired, and recolor it. Make sure the Smooth Color option is chosen in the Blend Options dialog box, then create the blend using the Make Blend command or the Blend tool.

1 *The original object.*

2 *A reduced-size copy of the object is created, and a darker fill color is applied.*

3 *The two objects are blended together.*

4 *Here's another variation.*

FILL & STROKE | 9

In this chapter you will learn to fill the inside or stroke the edge
of an object with a color, shade, or pattern, and choose stroke
attributes like dashes and joins. You'll learn how to mix a process
color; save a color as a swatch; copy swatches from another
library or document; and edit, replace, delete, move, and duplicate swatches. You'll learn to convert a process color into a spot
color (or vice versa); colorize a TIFF; globally replace or edit a
color; merge swatches; apply fill and stroke colors simultaneously
using the Paint Bucket; and sample colors from any window using
the Eyedropper. You'll also learn to invert, adjust, convert, and
saturate/desaturate colors, and blend fill colors between objects.
Finally, you'll learn how to create and modify fill patterns. For
gradients, see Chapter 16. For path patterns, see Chapter 10.

Fills and strokes

The flat color, pattern, or gradient that's
applied to the inside of a closed or open
shape is called the **fill**. The color or brushstroke that's applied to the edge of a closed
or open path is called the **stroke**. A stroke
can be solid or dashed, and it can have an
applied brushstroke, but not a gradient.

Colors and patterns are applied using the
Color or Swatches palette, buttons on the
Toolbox, or the Paint Bucket tool. The Stroke
palette is also used to apply characteristics
such as stroke thickness (weight) and style
(dashed, solid). You can store any color, pattern, or gradient on the Swatches palette for
later use. The color attributes of a selected
object are displayed on the Toolbox and
the Color palette. The current fill and stroke
colors are automatically applied to any new
object you create.

Note: Before you start working with color,
you should calibrate your monitor (see pages
324–326). Then, for the instructions in this
chapter, open the Color, Stroke, and Swatches
palettes. And of course work with your illustration in Preview view so you can see colors
on screen as you apply them.

Chris Spollen

121

Here's a quick-and-dirty method for applying color, just to get you started. The beauty of this method is that you don't need to choose any particular tool or select anything in your document. Try this method, then keep on reading—there's a lot more to this chapter!

QuickStart drag-color:

Click the Fill **1** or Stroke **2** box on the Toolbox or the Color palette, click a color on the spectrum bar on the Color palette **4**, then drag from the active box right over an object's fill or stroke—whichever element you want to recolor. The object doesn't have to be selected.

TIP You could also drag from the Color box on the Gradient palette or drag a swatch from the Swatches palette **6**.

To apply a fill or stroke of black or white:

1. Select an object.
2. Click the Fill or Stroke box on the Color palette **1**–**2**, then click the white or black selector at the right end of the spectrum bar on the Color palette **5** or click the white or black swatch on the Swatches palette **6**.
   or
   To apply a white fill *and* a black stroke, click the Default Colors button (D) on the Toolbox **3**.

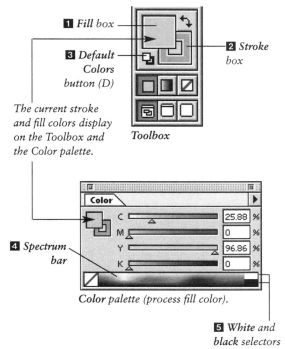

1 *Fill box*

3 *Default Colors button (D)*

2 *Stroke box*

The current stroke and fill colors display on the Toolbox and the Color palette.

Toolbox

4 *Spectrum bar*

Color palette (process fill color).

5 *White and black selectors*

White swatch *Black swatch*

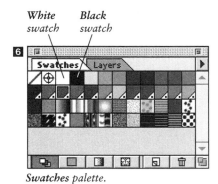

Swatches palette.

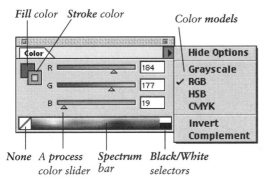

Fill color *Stroke color* *Color models*

None *A process color slider* *Spectrum bar* *Black/White selectors*

1 *Color palette.*

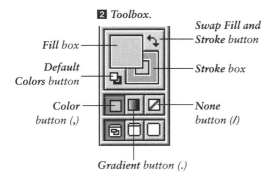

2 *Toolbox.*

Fill box *Swap Fill and Stroke button*

Default Colors button *Stroke box*

Color button (,) *None button (/)*

Gradient button (.)

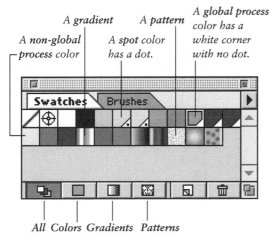

A gradient *A pattern* *A global process color has a white corner with no dot.*

A non-global process color *A spot color has a dot.*

All *Colors* *Gradients* *Patterns*

3 *The Swatches palette.*

The palettes you'll use for coloring

Color palette

The Color palette is used to mix and choose solid colors. The color boxes on the Color palette display the current fill and stroke colors of the currently or last-selected object or objects **1**. The palette options change depending on whether the Grayscale, RGB, HSB, or CMYK color model is chosen from the palette menu. You can click a color on the spectrum bar or mix a process color using exact percentages.

Toolbox

The Fill and Stroke boxes on the Toolbox display the attributes of the currently or last-selected object, as well as any changes you make to the current fill or stroke color via the Color or Swatches palette **2**. The Color or Gradient button is used to quickly switch between the last-chosen solid color or gradient.

Swatches palette

The Swatches palette contains process color (RGB, HSB, or CMYK), spot color, pattern, and gradient swatches **3**. You can append additional swatches from other libraries (e.g., PANTONE). If you click a swatch, that color will appear on the current Fill or Stroke box (whichever is currently active) on the Toolbox and on the Color palette, and it will apply immediately to all currently selected objects. If a selected object contains a color or colors from the Swatches palette, those swatches will be highlighted on the palette.

A default set of process color, spot color, pattern, and gradient swatches is supplied with Illustrator. You can also create your own swatches, which will save with the document in which they're created.

Using the None button

The None button is located on the Color palette, the Swatches palettes, and the Toolbox. Select an object and then click this button to remove any fill or stroke color, depending on which color box is currently active on the Color palette or the Toolbox.

Color Palette; Toolbox; Swatches Palette

The basic coloring steps

Open these four palettes: Toolbox, Color, Swatches, and Stroke.

- Select the objects whose color attributes you want to change.

- Make sure the box for the attribute that you want to change is active on the Color palette or the Toolbox—Fill or Stroke. Press "X" to toggle between the two.

- To choose a solid color, choose a color model from the Color palette menu, then click on the Spectrum bar on the Color palette or choose specific color percentages.
  or
  Click a swatch on the Swatches palette to assign a saved color or pattern to a selected object. (You can also drag a swatch over an unselected object.)

- Adjust the line Weight and other stroke attributes using the Stroke palette.

- To save the current color, follow the instructions below. *Note:* Swatches that are stored on the Swatches palette are saved with the current document, but not with the application as a whole.

To save the current fill or stroke color as a new swatch:

Drag the Fill or Stroke box from the Color palette or the Toolbox to an empty area of the Swatches palette to make it the last swatch **1** or release the mouse between two colors to insert the new color between them.
or
Make sure the Fill or Stroke button is active on the Color palette—whichever you want to save as a swatch—then click the New Swatch button on the Swatches palette **2**.
or
To choose options for the new swatch as you save it, Option-click/Alt-click the New Swatch button, enter a Swatch Name, choose a Color Type (Process Color or Spot Color), check or uncheck the Non-Global box, choose a Color Mode, then click OK.

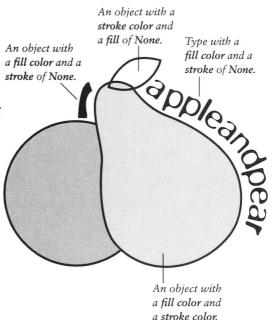

An object with a stroke color and a fill of None.

An object with a fill color and a stroke of None.

Type with a fill color and a stroke of None.

An object with a fill color and a stroke color.

TIP *Command-drag/Ctrl-drag to convert a process color into a spot color.*

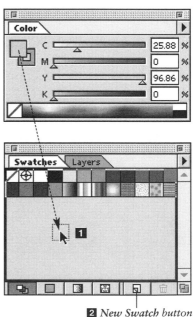

2 *New Swatch button*

Illustrator's Color Settings command works with the system's color management software to ensure more accurate color matching between the on-screen display of CMYK and RGB colors and the printed version of those colors. This command utilizes monitor and printer device profiles and output intents, all chosen by the user, to better translate color between particular devices. However, the profiles won't produce a perfectly reliable on-screen proof.

For a print job, you shouldn't mix process colors or choose spot colors (e.g., PANTONE) based on how they look on the screen, because screen colors don't look like printed colors. Instead, use matching system books to choose spot colors, or mix process colors, and be sure to run a color proof (or two or three) of your document.

1 *The Registration color appears on all plates when a file is color separated.*

Non-global process colors have a white triangle with no dot in the lower right corner.

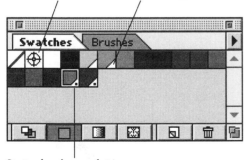

Spot colors have a dot in the lower right corner.

What's the difference between a spot and a process color?

Note: If you create images only for on-screen display, use the RGB color model when you mix colors, and skip all this stuff.

A **spot** color appears on its own plate after color separation. It can be a color that you mix yourself or a pre-mixed color from a matching system, like PANTONE. If you mix your own spot color, to ensure that it separates onto its own plate, double-click the swatch for the color on the Swatches palette, choose Color Type: **Spot Color**, then click OK. You can use spot colors exclusively if your illustration doesn't contain any continuous-tone (raster) images.

TIP You can achieve a pleasing range of tints using a black plate and a single spot color plate by varying the tint percentages of that spot color throughout your illustration.

A **process** color, on the other hand, is printed from four plates, one each for Cyan (C), Magenta (M), Yellow (Y), and Black (K). You can enter process color percentages yourself or you can choose a pre-mixed process color from a matching system, like TRUMATCH, FOCOLTONE, or PANTONE Process. Process printing *must* be used for any document that contains continuous-tone images. Budget permitting, spot color plates can be added on top of a four-color process job.

Note: Normally, Illustrator converts all spot colors into process colors when they are color separated. To make your spot colors separate to their own plates—which is what they *should* do—uncheck the **Convert to Process** box in File menu > Separation Setup.

TIP To display the process color breakdown of a spot color, double-click the spot color swatch.

TIP The Registration color is used for crop marks and the like **1**. To change the Registration color (let's say your illustration is very dark and you need white Registration marks), double-click the swatch and adjust the sliders.

To apply a fill and/or stroke to a path while or after you draw it:

1. Select an existing object (not all the anchor points need to be solid).
   or
   Choose the tool with which you want to draw a new object.

2. Click the Fill **1** or Stroke **2** box on the Color palette. To toggle between these two boxes, press "X".

3. Click a color or pattern swatch on the Swatches palette. If you chose a spot color swatch or a global process color swatch, you can move the Tint (T) slider on the Color palette or click or drag inside the Tint Ramp bar to adjust the percentage of that color **3**.
   or
   Choose a color model from the Color palette menu and choose color percentages (instructions on the next page).

   To choose a color from a matching system (e.g., PANTONE), see page 129.

4. If you're applying a stroke color, define stroke attributes using the Stroke palette (see page 130).

5. If you didn't select an existing object for step 1, now you're ready to draw it. It will reflect the current Color and Stroke palette settings.

TIP You can fill an object with any of the patterns that are supplied with Illustrator or you can create and use your own patterns (see pages 144–146). Patterns tile upward and rightward from the ruler origin. Don't apply a path pattern as a fill—it won't look right.

TIP A gradient cannot be applied as a stroke. For a workaround, see page 97.

TIP To define a color as process or spot, double-click the swatch on the Swatches palette, choose Color Type: Spot Color or Process Color, decide whether the process color will be global or Non-Global, choose a Color Mode, then click OK.

GLOBAL OR NON-GLOBAL?

If a process color is global (the Non-Global box is unchecked for that color in the Swatch Options dialog box) and you modify that color, it will update on all objects to which it was previously applied. If you modify a non-global color (Non-Global box checked), that color will update only on currently selected objects.

1 *Fill box*

2 *Stroke box*   *Tint slider*

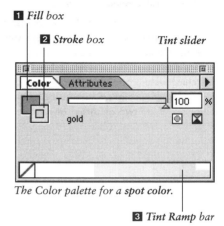

The Color palette for a spot color.

3 *Tint Ramp bar*

Fill color box   *Stroke color box*

1 *Color models*

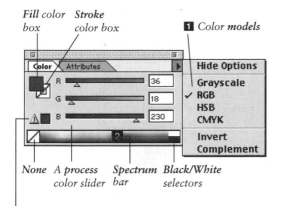

None   *A process color slider*   *Spectrum bar*   *Black/White selectors*

3 *An exclamation point will appear if you mix a color that's out of the printable CMYK gamut.*

If the fill or stroke colors differ among currently selected objects, a question mark will appear in the corresponding Fill or Stroke box on the Color palette and the Toolbox, but you can go ahead and apply a new fill and/or stroke color to all the selected objects.

Follow these instructions to mix your own process color. *Note:* To apply a color from a color matching system, like TRUMATCH or FOCOLTONE, see page 129.

To mix a process color:

1. *Optional:* If you want to recolor an existing object or objects, select them now, and click the Fill or Stroke box on the Color palette (X). Otherwise, make sure no objects are selected.

2. Choose a color model from the Color palette menu **1**:

   Choose Grayscale to remove color from any selected objects or to choose a gray shade.

   Choose RGB to mix colors for output on a monitor—video or Web graphics.

   Choose HSB to individually adjust a color's hue, saturation, or brightness.

   Choose CMYK to create process colors for output on a four-color press.

3. Click a color on the spectrum bar at the bottom of the Color palette **2**.
   and/or
   Move the sliders to adjust the individual color percentages.

   Note: If an exclamation point appears below the Color boxes on the Color palette **3**, you have mixed an RGB or HSB color that has no CMYK equivalent, which means it isn't printable on a four-color press. If you click the exclamation point, Illustrator will substitute the closest CMYK (printable) equivalent.

4. *Optional:* To save the newly mixed color as a swatch, see page 124.

TIP Premixed swatches and colors that are applied to objects remain associated with their color model. If you click on a swatch or on an object to which a color is applied, the Color palette will reset to reflect that color's model.

 TIP Hold down Option/Alt and drag on the spectrum bar to modify the stroke while the Fill box is active, or vice versa.

Mix a Process Color

Color Editing Shortcuts

Color editing shortcuts

- Shift-click the spectrum bar on the Color palette to cycle through the color **models**. You can also convert the current color by choosing a different color model from the palette menu. To convert the colors on selected objects, choose Filter menu > Colors > Convert to CMYK, or Convert to Grayscale, or Convert to RGB. If a color has been saved as a swatch, the swatch itself won't change.

- Press "X" to toggle between the Fill and Stroke boxes on the Toolbox and the Color palette.

- To make the fill color the **same** as the stroke color, or vice versa, drag one box over the other on the Toolbox or the Color palette.

- If you've chosen a fill or stroke of None for a path and then want to restore the last-applied colors to the path, click the Last Color button on the Color palette **1**.

- Choose Complement from the Color palette menu to convert the current color into its **complementary** color **2**. This won't change the color model.

- Shift-drag any RGB or CMYK slider on the Color palette to change that color's strength—the other sliders will readjust automatically.

- To select multiple objects with the same paint attributes, see page 141.

The Color, Gradient, and None buttons

Click the Color, Gradient, or None button on the Toolbox to change the current fill color (if the Fill box is active) to a solid color, a gradient, or a fill of none, respectively, or to change the current stroke to a solid color or none. The Color button displays the last chosen solid color; the Gradient button displays the last chosen gradient. If an object is selected, it will be recolored (or its color removed) when you click a different button. If you click the Color button on the Toolbox, the Color palette and any other palettes that are grouped with or docked to the Color palette will display.

Click the Swap Fill and Stroke button to switch the fill and stroke colors.

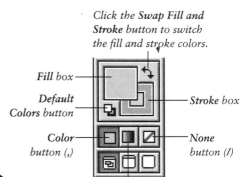

Fill box

Default Colors button

Stroke box

Color button (,)

None button (/)

Gradient button (.)

1 *Last Color button.*

2 *Complementary colors are opposite each other on the color wheel.*

APPLY COLOR THE SPEED-DEMON WAY

These are the shortcuts for activating the Color, Gradient, and None buttons:

Color , (comma)

Gradient . (period)

None / (slash)

The comma, period, and slash keys appear next to each other on the keyboard, which makes them easy to remember. Let's say the Fill box on the Toolbox happens to be selected and you want to remove a stroke from a selected object. Press "X", then "/", then "X" again. No mousing around.

QUICK-APPEND

Apply a color to a path directly by clicking a swatch on a swatch library palette. It will be added automatically to the current document's Swatches palette (except for a color from the Macintosh or Windows System or Web library).

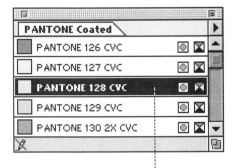

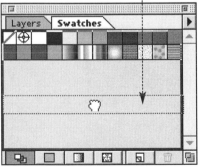

1 *Dragging a spot color from a* swatch library *to the current document.*

OOPS!

Did you apply a Web or System palette color to an object and forget to copy it to the Swatches palette before closing the swatch library palette from which it originated? Not to worry. Select the object, then drag the Fill or Stroke box from the Color palette to the Swatches palette.

In order to apply colors from a matching system, like the PANTONE, FOCOLTONE, TOYO, TRUMATCH, or DIC (Diccolor), or from the Web palette, you must open the swatch library that contains those swatches and then drag a swatch onto the main Swatches palette. The name of the newly opened library will appear as a new tab on a separate palette.

Note: The Web palette contains the 216 Web-safe RGB colors commonly used by Web browsers.

To add matching system or Web colors to the Swatches palette:

1. Display the Swatches palette.
2. Choose a matching color system name from the Window menu > Swatch Libraries submenu.
3. Click the tab for the desired color system, if it isn't already displayed.
4. Locate the desired color on the newly opened swatch library palette (scroll downward or expand the palette, if necessary), and drag it onto the document's Swatches palette **1**.
   or
   Click a swatch (or swatches) on the swatch library palette, then choose Add to Swatches from the swatch library palette menu. The new color will be added to the current document's Swatches palette.

   Note: To add multiple swatches at a time, before dragging, Command-click/Ctrl-click them individually. Or click, then Shift-click a contiguous series of them.

TIP You can't modify swatches on a swatch library palette (note the non-edit icon in lower left corner of palette)—the Swatch Options dialog box won't be available. You *can* edit any swatch once it's saved to a document's Swatches palette.

TIP If you open more than one swatch library palette and then you want to close one of them, drag its tab out of the palette and then click that palette's close box.

You can change a stroke's color, weight (thickness), and style (dashed or solid, rounded or sharp corners, flat or rounded ends).

To change the width of a stroke:

1. Select an object or objects.

2. On the Stroke palette:

    Enter a width in the Weight field (0–1000 pt) 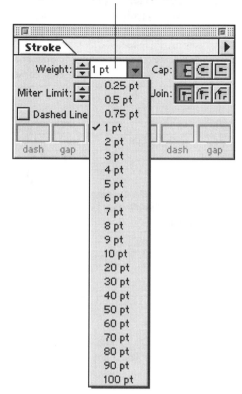.

    or

    Choose a preset weight from the Weight drop-down menu.

    or

    Click the up or down arrow on the palette to change the current stroke weight one unit at a time. Or click in the Weight field, then press the up or down arrow on the keyboard.

    The stroke will be balanced on the path: Half the stroke width on one side of the path, the other half on the other side of the path **2**.

TIP Don't apply a large stroke weight to small type—it will distort the letterforms.

TIP You can enter a number in inches (in), millimeters (mm), centimeters (cm), or picas (p) in the stroke Weight field. The value will convert to the Stroke unit currently chosen in File menu > Preferences > Units & Undo.

1 *To change a stroke's thickness, enter a value in the stroke* **Weight** *field, or click the up or down arrow, or choose from the drop-down menu.*

The path.

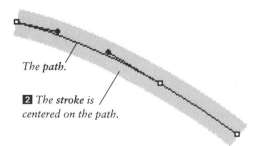

2 *The stroke is centered on the path.*

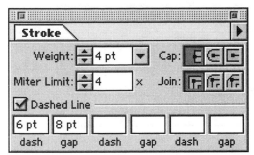

1 *Stroke palette settings for a **dashed line** with a 6-pt. dash **length** and an 8-pt. **gap** between dashes.*

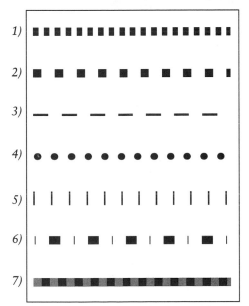

A variety of dashed lines (the first Cap button was chosen for all except #4):

1) *stroke 6, dash 4, gap 4.*

2) *stroke 6, dash 6, gap 10.*

3) *stroke 1.5, dash 11, gap 10.*

4) *stroke 5, dash 0, gap 12 (round cap).*

5) *stroke 10, dash 1, gap 12.*

6) *stroke 6, dash 0, gap 10, dash 8, gap 10.*

7) *stroke 6, dash 6, gap 6 (pasted in front of a 6-point gray stroked line).*

To create a dashed stroke:

1. Select an object, and make sure it has a stroke color and a weight above zero.

2. If the Stroke palette options aren't fully displayed, choose Show Options from the palette menu.

3. Click a Cap button for the dash shape **1**.

4. Click the Dashed Line box.

5. Enter a number in the first dash field (the length of the first dash, in points), then press Tab to proceed to the next field.

6. Enter an amount in the first gap field (the length of the first gap after the first dash), then press Tab to proceed to the next field or press Return/Enter to exit the palette.

7. *Optional:* To create dashes of varying lengths, enter different amounts in the other dash fields. If you enter an amount only in the first dash field, that amount will apply to all the other dashes.

8. *Optional:* Enter different amounts in the other gap fields to create gaps of varying lengths. If you enter an amount only in the first gap field, that amount will apply to all the gaps.

TIP To create a dotted line, click the second Cap button, enter 0 for the Dash value, and enter a Gap value that is greater than or equal to the stroke Weight.

TIP You can enter a value in inches (in), millimeters (mm), centimeters (cm), or picas (p) in the dash or gap fields. That number will be translated automatically into the current units.

TIP The default first dash unit is 1 pica (12 pt). Any user-defined values will remain in effect until you change them or quit/exit Illustrator.

Create a Dashed Stroke

To modify stroke caps and/or joins:

1. Select an object, and make sure it has a stroke color and weight.

2. If the Stroke palette options aren't fully displayed, choose Show Options from the palette menu.

3. To modify the endpoints of a solid line or all the dashes in a dashed line:

   Click the left **Cap** button **1** to create square-cornered ends in which the stroke stops at the endpoints, or to create square-cornered dashes. Use this option if you need to align your paths very precisely.

   Click the middle **Cap** button to create semicircular ends or semicircle-ended dashes.

   Click the right **Cap** button to create square-cornered ends in which the stroke extends beyond the endpoints or to create rectangular dashes.

4. To modify the line bends:

   Click the left **Join** button to produce pointed bends (miter joins) **2**.

   Click the middle **Join** button to produce semicircular bends (round joins).

   Click the right **Join** button to produce square-cornered bends (bevel joins). The miter limit is discussed on page 78.

To create arrowheads:

1. Select an open path.

2. Choose Filter menu > Stylize > Add Arrowheads.

3. Click the left or right arrow to choose from the various head and tail designs **3**.

4. Choose a location for the arrowhead (Start, End, or Both Ends) from the Arrowhead at drop-down menu.

5. *Optional:* Resize the arrowhead by entering a different Scale percentage. This is the easiest way to scale an arrowhead.

6. Click OK (Return/Enter). The arrowhead can be reshaped like any other path. There's no one-step way to remove it.

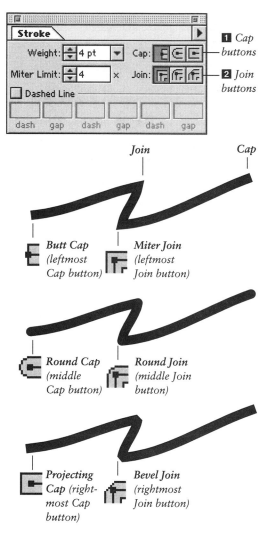

1 *Cap buttons*

2 *Join buttons*

Butt Cap (leftmost Cap button)   *Miter Join (leftmost Join button)*

Round Cap (middle Cap button)   *Round Join (middle Join button)*

Projecting Cap (rightmost Cap button)   *Bevel Join (rightmost Join button)*

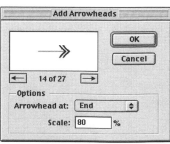

3 *Choose a style, a location (Start, End, or Both Ends), and a Scale in the Add Arrowheads dialog box.*

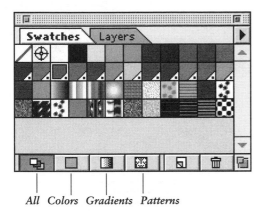

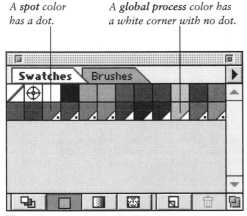

All   Colors   Gradients   Patterns

1 *The Swatches palette display options.*

A *spot color*
has a dot.

A *global process color* has
a white corner with no dot.

2 *Color swatches only displayed.*

The color model icons

Global   *CMYK*
process color   *color*
Spot color

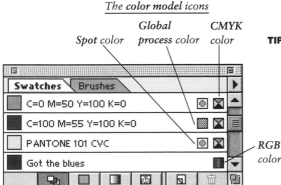

*RGB
color*

3 *The swatches displayed by Name.*

You can control whether the Swatches palette displays all types of swatches or only certain categories of swatches, and whether the swatches are large or small.

To choose swatch display options:

1. Click a display button at the bottom of the Swatches palette to control which category of swatches is displayed **1**: Show All, for all types (colors, gradients, and patterns); Show Color, for solid process and spot colors only **2**; Show Gradient, for gradients only; or Show Pattern, for patterns only.

2. Choose a display mode for that category of swatches from the palette menu: Name **3**, Small Swatch, or Large Swatch

   TIP Choose Large Swatch for patterns.

   Note: In Name view, the RGB, HSB, or CMYK breakdown will be displayed for any process color that doesn't have a name. The palette also displays an icon for the color's color model in Name view.

3. Choose Sort by Name from the palette menu to sort the swatches alphabetically by name.
   or
   Choose Sort by Kind to sort swatches into color, then gradient, then pattern groups (use when all the categories of swatches are displayed).

   TIP To choose a swatch by typing, choose Sort By Name from the palette menu, Command-Option-click/Ctrl-Alt-click on the palette, then start typing. Click the swatch name or press Return/Enter to apply the swatch and exit the palette.

   TIP Hold down Option/Alt as you choose Name, Small Swatch, or Large Swatch from the palette menu to force all the other categories of swatches to display the same way.

Whatever swatches are on the Swatches palette will save with the current file.

To load swatches from another Illustrator file:

1. Choose Window menu > Swatch Libraries > Other Library.

2. Locate the Illustrator file from which you want to copy the swatches (the file shouldn't be open), then click Select.

3. Drag an individual swatch from the newly opened swatch palette into the current document's Swatches palette **1**. Or to add multiple swatches at a time, first Command/Ctrl click them individually or click, then Shift-click a contiguous series of them.
   or
   Choose Add to Swatches from the secondary swatch palette's option menu. The new color will be added to the current document's Swatches palette.

TIP Look for patterns in the Illustrator 8 > Other Libraries > Pattern Samples folder or in the Illustrator Extras folder on the Illustrator 8.0 CD-ROM.

There's no simple way to restore the Swatches palette to its default state. You have to manually drag swatches from the Default palette.

To restore default swatches to the current Swatches palette:

1. *Optional:* If you want to completely clear the current document's Swatches palette, drag all the swatches except None and Registration to the Delete button.

2. Choose Window menu > Swatch Libraries > Default.

3. On the Default Swatches palette, select the swatches you want to restore to your document (Shift-click or Command/Ctrl click to select multiple swatches).

4. Drag those swatches to the current document's Swatches palette.
   or
   Choose Add to Swatches from the Default palette's option menu.

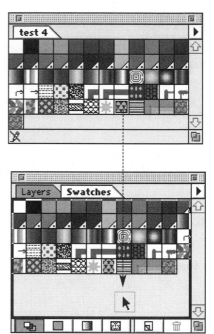

1 *Moving a swatch from a **library** to the Swatches palette.*

SWATCHES AT LAUNCHTIME

If you want to control which colors appear on the Swatches palette when the application is launched, create a custom startup file that contains those colors (see page 297).

If you turn on the Persistent command from a swatch library palette menu, that swatch library palette will reopen automatically when you re-launch Illustrator, with the same tab in front.

If you delete a color, gradient, or pattern swatch that was applied to an object in the current file, you can retrieve it by selecting the object and then dragging the Fill box from the Toolbox or the Color palette onto the Swatches palette.

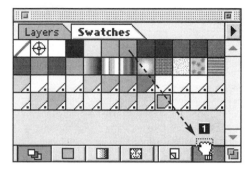

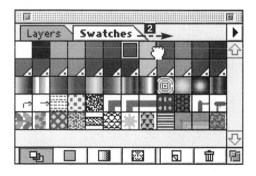

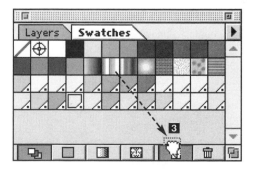

To delete a swatch or swatches:

Select a swatch (then, if desired, Shift-click the last swatch in a series of contiguous swatches, or Command-click/Ctrl-click to select additional swatches). Then click the Delete button on the Swatches palette; or choose Delete Swatch from the palette menu and click Yes; or Option-click/Alt-click the Delete button.

or

Drag the swatch(es) you want to delete over the Delete button **1**.

TIP Choose Undo to restore the deleted swatch.

TIP To select only swatches that are *not* currently applied to objects in your document, choose Select All Unused from the palette menu. To limit the selection to a particular category (i.e. patterns or gradients), make sure only those swatches are displayed on the palette before choosing Select All Unused.

To move a swatch or swatches:

Drag a swatch to a new location on the palette **2**. A dark vertical line will show the swatch location as you drag it. (To select multiple swatches, click a swatch, then Shift-click the last swatch in a series of contiguous swatches, or Command-click/Ctrl-click to select individual swatches.)

To duplicate a swatch:

Select the swatch you want to duplicate, then choose Duplicate Swatch from the palette menu or click the New Swatch button.

or

Drag the swatch to be duplicated over the New Swatch button **3**. The duplicate swatch will appear at the bottom of the palette.

TIP If no swatch is selected and you click the New Swatch button, a new swatch will be created for the current fill or stroke color.

TIP Option-drag/Alt-drag one swatch over another to replace the existing swatch with the one you're dragging.

Delete, Move, Duplicate Swatches

To convert a process color into a spot color or vice versa:

1. Mix a color on the Color palette.
or
Select the object that contains the color you want to convert.

2. If the color isn't already on the Swatches palette, drag the Fill or Stroke box from the Color palette or the Toolbox onto the Swatches palette.

3. Double-click the swatch to open the Swatch Options dialog box.

4. Choose Color Type: Spot Color or Process Color ❶, and rename the color, if you like.

5. Choose whether a process color will be global (unchecked) or Non-Global (checked). If you edit a global process color that has been applied to objects in a document, the color will update on those objects.

6. Choose a Color Mode.

7. Click OK (Return/Enter).

TIP By default, spot colors are converted to process colors during color separation. To prevent this conversion, choose File menu > Separation Setup and uncheck the Convert to Process box.

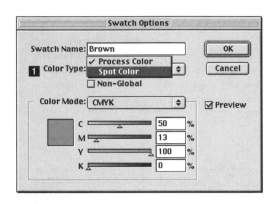

A 1-bit TIFF or Photoshop image that is opened or placed in Illustrator (not drag-and-dropped) can be colorized via the Color palette. Black areas in the TIFF will recolor; white areas will remain transparent.

To colorize a 1-bit TIFF image:

1. Use File menu > Open or Place to open a 1-bit TIFF image in Illustrator. The image can be linked or embedded.

2. Select the TIFF image.

3. Apply a fill color.

TIP To make transparent areas in a 1-bit TIFF look as if they're colorized, create an object with the desired background color and send it behind the TIFF.

TRANSPARENCY IN ILLUSTRATOR!

Do you covet FreeHand's transparency capabilities? Covet no longer. You can make objects transparent in Illustrator 8 using Hot Door Software's inexpensive Hot Door Transparency 1.0 extension, which is available for Macintosh and Windows. Hot Door Inc., Grass Valley, CA; 530-274-0626 or 888-236-9540; or www.hotdoor.com.

Hot Door Transparency 1.0 makes the fill of any closed object transparent (less than full opacity). It cannot be used on a compound path (i.e., outlined letters with inner shapes), a stroke, a gradient, or a bitmap image. Feature options are chosen from a Hot Door palette from within Illustrator and a slider is used to control the amount of transparency. *Note:* If you export an Illustrator file that contains semi-transparent objects as EPS, the transparent objects will be expanded into individual shapes and masks.

CHANGE WITHOUT CHANGING

If you want to globally change a color without changing the swatch from which it originated, use an Edit menu > Select submenu command to select all the objects that contain that color (see page 141), then choose a new swatch or mix a new color for those selected objects.

If you replace a spot or global process color swatch with a different swatch, that color (or tint of that color) will automatically update in *all* the objects to which it has already been applied, whether or not those objects are selected. The object's original tint value will be preserved. If you replace a non-global process color swatch, only currently *selected* object or objects containing that color will be recolored.

To replace a color globally:

On the Color palette, mix a new color (not merely a tint variation of the global process or spot color that you want to replace). Then Option-drag/Alt-drag the Fill or Stroke box from the Color palette over the swatch on the Swatches palette that you want to replace.
or
To edit a gradient swatch, use the Gradient palette (see page 234). To edit a pattern swatch, follow the instructions on page 145.
or
Option-drag/Alt-drag one swatch over another swatch. Use this method to replace one PANTONE color with another.

The new color will replace the old in all objects to which the original swatch was applied.

Follow these instructions to edit—not replace—a color.

To edit a color globally:

1. Double-click a global process or spot color swatch on the Swatches palette.

2. Modify the color using the Color Type menu, the Color Mode menu, or by moving the sliders, and then click OK (Return/Enter). The color will update in all objects to which it was previously applied. Individual tint variations will be preserved.

Swatch conflicts

If you copy or drag-and-drop an object to another document, that object's colors will appear as swatches on the target document's Swatches palette. If a swatch color on a copied object contains the same name, but different color percentages, as an existing global process or spot color swatch in the target document, the Swatch Conflict dialog box will open 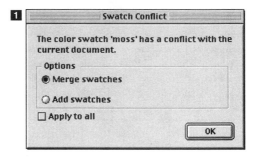.

If you click **Merge swatches**, the existing swatch in the target document will be applied to the copied objects. If you click **Add swatches**, the new swatch will be added to the Swatches palette in the target document and the copied objects will be unchanged.

Check the **Apply to all** box to have the current Options setting apply to any other name conflicts that crop up for other objects being copied. This will prevent the alert dialog from opening repeatedly if more than one name conflict crops up.

Normally, if there are two colors that have the same color breakdown, but different names, Illustrator color separates each of those colors to a separate sheet of film. You can use the Merge Swatches command to selectively merge colors into one swatch.

To merge spot color swatches:

1. Select the swatches on the Swatches palette that you want to merge. Click, then Shift-click to select contiguous swatches or Command-click/Ctrl-click to select individual swatches 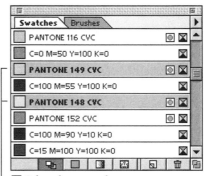. The **first** swatch you select will replace all the other selected swatches, so strategize as you do this.

2. Choose Merge Swatches from the Swatches palette menu 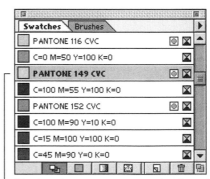. If any of the merged swatches were applied to objects in the file, those objects will be recolored with the first swatch you selected.

1 Select the spot colors you want to merge.

3 After choosing **Merge Swatches** from the palette menu, the swatches are merged into the first-selected swatch.

Paint Bucket tool.

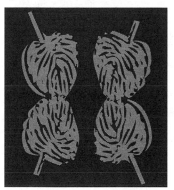

2 *The original illustration.*

Diane Margolin

3 *After using the Paint Bucket to apply a white fill and a dashed stroke to the leaves on the left side.*

If you click with the Paint Bucket tool on an object, that object will be filled *and* stroked using the current Color and Stroke palette settings. Neither palette needs to be displayed for you to use the Paint Bucket.

To use the Paint Bucket tool:

1. With no objects selected, choose the Paint Bucket tool (K) **1**.

2. Choose fill and stroke colors from the Color or Swatches palette.
   or
   Option-click/Alt-click on a color any-where in any open Illustrator window (this is a temporary Eyedropper).

3. Choose a stroke weight, and choose other stroke options, if desired.

4. Click on an object (the object does not have to be selected). The object will become colored with the current Color and Stroke palette attributes **2**–**3**. For an object without a fill color, or if you're working in Artwork view, position the black spill of the Paint Bucket pointer on the path outline before clicking.

Use the Paint Bucket/Eyedropper dialog box to change the default attributes for either or both tools.

To choose paint attributes the Paint Bucket applies or the Eyedropper picks up:

1. Double-click the Paint Bucket or Eyedropper tool.

2. Click check box options on or off **4**.

3. Click OK (Return/Enter).

Paint Bucket and Eyedropper Tools

Paint Bucket/Eyedropper Options

Paint Bucket Applies:	Eyedropper Picks Up:
▽ ☑ Fill	▽ ☑ Fill
☑ Color	☑ Color
☑ Overprint	☑ Overprint
▽ ☑ Stroke	▽ ☑ Stroke
☑ Color	☑ Color
☑ Overprint	☑ Overprint
☑ Weight	☑ Weight
☑ Cap	☑ Cap
☑ Join	☑ Join
☑ Miter Limit	☑ Miter Limit
☑ Dash Pattern	☑ Dash Pattern
▷ ☑ Character	▷ ☑ Character
▷ ☑ Paragraph	▷ ☑ Paragraph

4 *Paint Bucket/Eyedropper Options.*

If you click on a path or a placed image with the Eyedropper tool, it will sample the object's paint attributes, display them on the Toolbox and the Color and Stroke palettes, and apply them to any currently selected objects.

To use the Eyedropper tool:

1. *Optional:* Select an object or objects if you want to recolor them immediately with the attributes you pick up with the Eyedropper.

2. Choose the Eyedropper tool (I) .

3. Click on an object in any open Illustrator window that contains the color(s) you want to sample. The object doesn't have to be selected. You can also drag from the Illustrator document window into any location on your screen—in another application or on the Desktop.

   If you selected any objects (step 1), they will take on the paint attributes of the object you click on.

   TIP Hold down Option/Alt to use the Paint Bucket tool while the Eyedropper is selected, or vice versa.

   TIP To preserve the sampled color to use again, drag the Fill or Stroke box from the Toolbox or the Color palette onto the Swatches palette.

   TIP Shift-click a color on an unselected object with the Eyedropper to copy that color to only the fill or stroke (whichever box is currently active on the Color palette) of any selected objects.

Both conversion methods in these instructions convert colors into their opposites.

To invert colors:

1. Select the object or objects whose colors you want to invert.

2. Choose Filter menu > Colors > Invert Colors **2**–**3**. This filter converts *only non-global process* colors. It will not convert spot colors, global process colors, gradients, or patterns.
   or

GRAB A COLOR FROM ANOTHER APPLICATION

Open the application from which you want to sample colors. If that application's color palette stays open even if the application isn't currently active (as in Director), open that as well.

Move the window or palette that you want to sample from over to one side of the screen and move the Illustrator document window so that you can see the other application window behind it. Choose the Eyedropper tool, drag from the Illustrator document window over a color in another application window (the color will appear on Illustrator's Toolbox and Color palette), then save the color as a swatch. Repeat for other colors.

 1 *Eyedropper tool.*

2 *The original image.*

3 *The colors **inverted**.*

To invert only the object's *fill* or *stroke* color, click either box on the Color palette, then choose Invert from the Color palette menu. This command will convert *any* kind of solid color—spot, global process, or non-global process.

To select objects with the same paint attributes for recoloring:

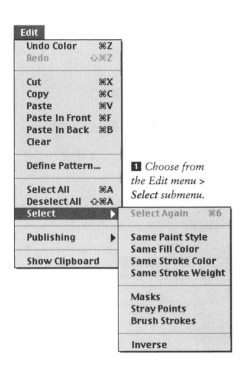

1 *Choose from the Edit menu > Select submenu.*

1. Select an object whose paint attributes you want to replace (fill color, stroke color, stroke weight).
   or
   With no object selected, choose the attributes that you want to search for from the Swatches palette, the Color palette, or the Stroke palette.

2. Choose Edit menu > Select > Same Paint Style, or Same Fill Color, or Same Stroke Color, or Same Stroke Weight to select objects with the same paint attributes as you chose in the previous step **1**. All objects with those paint attributes will now be selected.

3. With the objects still selected, mix a new color using the Color palette.
   or
   Click a new swatch on the Swatches palette.
   or
   Choose a new Weight or other attributes from the Stroke palette.

TIP The Select menu > Same Fill Color command selects all objects that contain the same spot color, regardless of any differences in tint strength among those objects.

TIP To globally change a spot color or a global process color by replacing its swatch, see page 137.

Select Objects with Same Attributes

Use the Adjust Colors filter to adjust color percentages or convert color modes in one or more selected objects, including text objects (but not gradients or patterns).

To adjust or convert colors:

1. Select the object or objects whose colors you want to adjust or convert.

2. Choose Filter menu > Colors > Adjust Colors.

3. Check the Preview box to preview color adjustments in your illustration while the dialog box is open 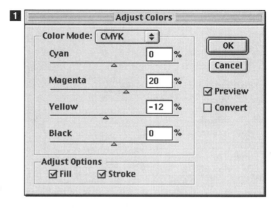.

4. Check the Adjust Options: Fill and/or Stroke box to adjust one or both of those attributes.

5. The sliders will reflect the color mode of the currently selected object or objects. If the selected objects' colors are in more than one mode, the sliders will display in the first mode that's present, in the following order: Global mode, then CMYK mode, then RGB mode, then Grayscale mode. Move the sliders or enter new percentages in the fields. Only colors in that mode will be adjusted. After you adjust colors in one mode, you can choose another mode and adjust other colors.
or
To convert all the currently selected objects to the same color mode, check the Convert box, choose a Color Mode, then move the sliders.

6. Click OK (Return/Enter).

To convert an object's colors to a different mode:

1. Select the object or objects whose colors you want to convert.

2. Choose Filter menu > Colors > Convert to CMYK, or Convert to Grayscale, or Convert to RGB.

TIP To convert a swatch, see page 136.

PATHFINDERS FOR RECOLORING

You can use the Hard Mix or Soft Mix command on the Pathfinders palette to change colors in overlapping paths (see page 230).

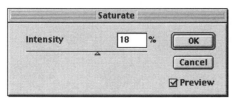

1 *Change a color's **Intensity** in the **Saturate** dialog box.*

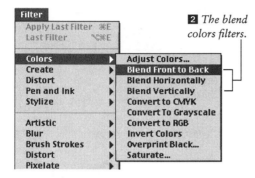

2 *The blend colors filters.*

3 *The original image.*

4 *After applying the **Blend Horizontally** filter.*

The Saturate filter deepens or fades colors in selected objects by a specified percentage.

To saturate or desaturate colors:

1. Select the object(s) whose colors you want to saturate or desaturate.

2. Choose Filter menu > Colors > Saturate.

3. Check the Preview box to preview color changes in your illustration.

4. Move the Intensity slider or enter a percentage for the amount you want to intensify or fade the color or colors **1**. A 100% tint cannot be further saturated.

5. Click OK (Return/Enter).

To blend fill colors between objects:

1. Select three or more objects.

   Note: The two objects that are farthest apart (or frontmost and backmost) cannot contain gradients, patterns, global colors, or different spot colors. The frontmost and backmost objects can contain different tints of the same spot color. Objects with a fill of None won't be recolored.

2. From the Colors submenu under the Filter menu **2**, choose:

   Blend Front to Back to create a blend using the fill colors of the frontmost and backmost objects as the starting and ending colors. Objects will stay on their respective layers.

   Blend Horizontally to create a color blend using the fill colors of the leftmost and rightmost objects as the starting and ending colors **3**–**4**.

   Blend Vertically to create a color blend using the fill colors of the topmost and bottommost objects as the starting and ending colors.

   Any selected objects that are stacked between the frontmost and backmost objects (or positioned between the leftmost and rightmost or topmost and bottommost objects) will be assigned intermediate blend colors.

To create a fill pattern:

1. Draw an object or objects to be used as the pattern 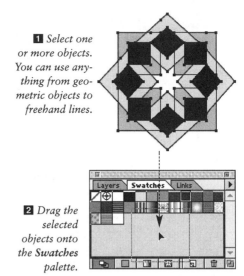. They may not contain a gradient, gradient mesh, mask, pattern, brushstroke, or EPS file. Simple shapes are least likely to cause a printing error.

2. *Strictly optional:* Apply Filter > Distort > Roughen at a low setting to make the pattern shapes look more hand drawn.

3. Marquee all the objects with the Selection tool (V).

4. Choose Edit menu > Define Pattern.
   or
   Drag the selection onto the Swatches palette , deselect the objects, then double-click the new swatch.

5. Type a name in the Swatch Name field.

6. Click OK (Return/Enter) .

You can use a rectangle to control the amount of white space around a pattern or to crop parts of the objects that you want to eliminate from the pattern.

To use a rectangle to define a fill pattern:

1. Draw objects to be used as the pattern.

2. Choose the Rectangle tool (M or Shift-M).

3. Drag a rectangle or Shift-drag a half-inch to one-inch square around the objects (use the Info palette to check the dimensions). Fit the rectangle closely around the objects if you don't want any blank space to be part of the pattern (use Smart Guides to assist you) 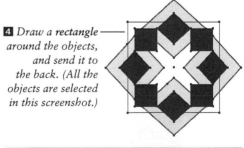. If the pattern is complex, make the rectangle small to crop the objects to facilitate printing.

4. Choose Object menu > Arrange > Send to Back. The rectangle must be behind the pattern objects.

5. Apply a fill and stroke of None to the rectangle if you don't want it to become part of the pattern. Apply a fill color to the rectangle if you want it to become the background color in the pattern.

6. Follow steps 3–6 in the previous set of instructions 5.

1 *Select one or more objects. You can use anything from geometric objects to freehand lines.*

2 *Drag the selected objects onto the **Swatches** palette.*

3 *An object is **filled** with the new pattern.*

4 *Draw a rectangle around the objects, and send it to the back. (All the objects are selected in this screenshot.)*

5 *An object is **filled** with the new pattern.*

Create a Fill Pattern

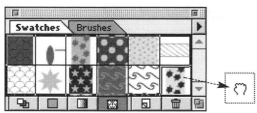

1 *Drag the pattern you want to modify out of the Swatches palette.*

3 *The pattern is **modified**, and then it's selected and dragged back over the original swatch.*

2 *The original pattern swatch.*

You can modify any pattern, including any pattern that's supplied with Illustrator. To change an existing pattern, first its swatch must be dragged back into a document.

To modify a fill pattern:

1. Display a blank area in your document window, then drag the pattern swatch out of the Swatches palette **1**. The pattern is now a group with a bounding rectangle (with a fill and stroke of None) added behind it **2**.

2. Modify the pattern objects. Use the Direct-selection tool (A) to select the individual components **3**.

3. Choose the Selection tool (V).

4. Click on any of the pattern objects to select the whole group.

5. Option-drag/Alt-drag the selected pattern shapes over the original pattern swatch. Objects already filled with the pattern in the file will update automatically.

   Note: If you decide instead that you *don't* want to save over the original pattern, drag the selection onto the Swatches palette without holding down Option/Alt. (Double-click the new swatch to rename it.) A new swatch will be created—the original swatch won't change.

   TIP Read about transforming patterns on page 105.

The modified pattern.

Note: To create a pattern that repeats seamlessly, see the Illustrator User Guide.

To create a geometric fill pattern:

1. Create a symmetrical arrangement of geometric objects **1**–**2**. You can use the Rectangle, Ellipse, Polygon, Spiral, or Star tool to create objects easily. To copy an object, Option-drag/Alt-drag it using a selection tool. Also hold down Shift to constrain the movement horizontally or vertically. Position objects so they abut each other. You can show the grid or turn on and use Smart Guides to help you align the objects (see page 76).

2. *Optional:* Apply different fill colors to add variety to the pattern.

3. Choose the Rectangle tool.

4. Choose a fill and stroke of None, then carefully draw a rectangle around the objects. Make sure the symmetry is preserved **3**. In order to produce a perfect repetitive pattern fill, align the rectangle with the edges of the geometric shapes.

5. With the rectangle still selected, choose Object menu > Arrange > Send to Back.

6. Marquee all the objects with the Selection tool (V), drag the selection onto the Swatches palette, and use it as a fill in any object **4**.

TIP To see see a sneak preview of what the pattern tile will look like, bring the rectangle that you created for step 4 to the front, then click the Crop command on the Pathfinder palette.

To expand a pattern fill into individual objects:

1. Select an object with a pattern fill **5**–**6**.

2. Choose Object menu > Expand.

3. Check the Fill box, then click OK **7**. The pattern fill will be divided into the original shapes that made up the pattern tile, and these shapes will be inside a mask. You can now release the mask, alter the mask shape, or delete it.

To reposition the pattern fill in an object without moving the object itself, hold down "~" and drag inside it with the Selection tool.

1 *Draw geometric objects.*

2 *Copy the object(s) and arrange the copies symmetrically.*

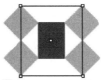

3 *Draw a rectangle and position it so it will create symmetry in the pattern tile.*

4 *The **geometric** pattern fill.*

5 *The original pattern.*

6 *A detail of the pattern expanded (Artwork view).*

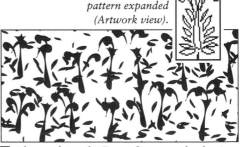

7 *After applying the **Expand** command, releasing the mask, and applying the **Transform Each** command (moved .3" horizontally and -.3" vertically, rotated 17°, Random).*

Diane Margolin

BRUSHES 10

In this chapter you will learn about Illustrator's four types of brushes: calligraphic, scatter, art, and pattern. You will learn how to create and edit custom brushes; how to add, modify, or remove brushstrokes from existing paths; how to open or create other brush libraries; and how to duplicate, move, or delete brushes from the Brushes palette.

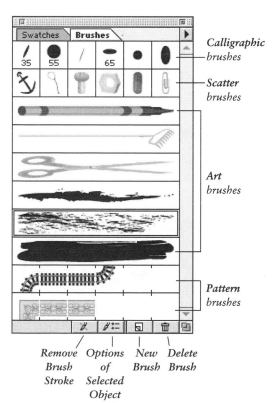

Calligraphic brushes

Scatter brushes

Art brushes

Pattern brushes

Remove Brush Stroke   *Options of Selected Object*   *New Brush*   *Delete Brush*

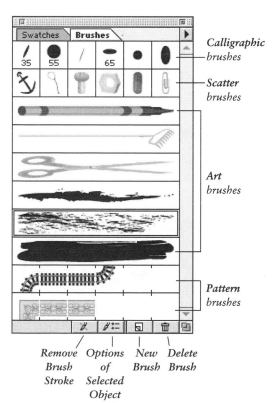

The Brushes

Illustrator's brushes are an illustrator's dream. They combine the ability to draw variable, freehand brushstrokes or apply a pattern or objects to a path with all the advantages of vector graphics—small file sizes, resizability, and crisp output.

There are two ways to work with the brushes: Choose the Paintbrush tool and a brush and draw a shape right off the bat with a brushstroke built in or apply a brushstroke to an existing path.

To change the contour of a brushstroke, you can use any tool or command you'd normally use to reshape a path (Reshape, Pencil, Smooth, Erase, Add-anchor-point, Convert-anchor-point, etc.).

The brushes come in four flavors: scatter, calligraphic, art, and pattern, and they are stored on and accessed from the Brushes palette. The brushes that are currently on the Brushes palette save with the document. If you modify a brush that was applied to any existing paths in a document, you'll be given the option via an alert box to update those paths with the revised brush. You can also create your own brushes.

As a first introduction to the brushes, grab the Paintbrush tool, click on a default brush on the Brushes palette, and draw (see the instructions on the following page).

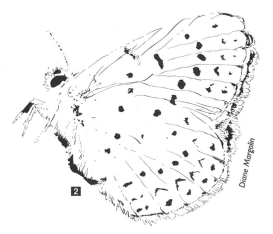

1 *Paintbrush tool.*

Note: The Paintbrush tool reacts to pressure—if you use a stylus and a pressure-sensitive tablet, the harder you press on the tablet, the wider the shape.

To draw with the Paintbrush tool:

1. Choose the Paintbrush tool (B) **1**, and choose a fill of None.

2. Click a brush type on the Brushes palette: calligraphic, scatter, art, or pattern (Window menu > Show Brushes).

3. Draw with the Paintbrush tool to create an open path shape **2**–**3**.

TIP A path created with the Paintbrush tool can be reshaped with the Pencil or Direct-selection tool.

TIP Choose Edit menu > Select > Brush Strokes to select all the brushstrokes in an illustration.

Settings you choose for the Paintbrush affect only future—not existing—brushstrokes. You'll learn how to choose options for individual brushes later on in this chapter.

To choose settings for the Paintbrush:

1. Double-click the Paintbrush tool (or choose the tool and press Return/Enter).

2. Choose a Fidelity value (0.5–20) **4**. A Fidelity value below 5 will produce a path very close to the way you drag the tool. A high setting will produce a smoother path with fewer anchor points that only approximates the path you drag.

3. Choose a Smoothness value (0–100) for the amount of curvature the tool creates in the path. The higher the Smoothness, the fewer the irregularities in the path.

4. *Optional:* Check the "Fill new brush strokes" box if you want new paths to be filled with the current fill color.

5. *Optional:* Check the Keep Selected box to keep the newly drawn path selected.

6. Click OK (Return/Enter).

TIP Click Default to reset the Paintbrush preferences to their defaults.

3 *Simple strokes drawn with Illustrator's default "Marker" art brush.*

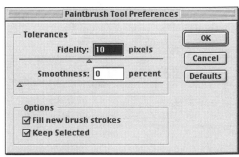

4 *Choose settings for the Paintbrush in its Preferences dialog box.*

1 *Select a path.*

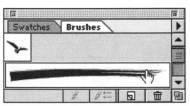

2 *Click a brush on the **Brushes** palette.*

3 *A **calligraphic** brushstroke is applied.*

4 *An **art** brushstroke.*

5 *A **scatter** brushstroke.*

6 *Another **scatter** brushstroke (made from five birds).*

7 *A **pattern** brushstroke.*

To apply a brushstroke to an existing path:

1. Choose Window menu > Show Brushes, if the palette is not already displayed.

2. Click a brush on the brushes palette, then drag the selected brush onto an existing path (the path need not be selected first). Release the mouse when the hand pointer is directly over the edge of the object.
   or
   Select a path of any kind (except a type path) **1**, then click a brush on the Brushes palette **2**–**7**.

   Note: To create or modify a brush, see the instructions for the individual brush types starting on page 154.

▸ **TIP** You *can't* apply a brushstroke to a type path, but you *can* convert type into outlines and then apply a brushstroke to the outlines.

*For a **scatter** brush, you have the option, via the Brush Options dialog, to make the **size, spacing, scatter,** and **rotation** variables more or less **random**.*

Apply a Brushstroke to an Existing Path

Add Brushes

After opening another brush library, you can apply a brush from that library directly to a path or you can move select brushes to the current document's Brushes palette. You can modify any brush from any library.

To add brushes from other libraries:

1. Choose a library from the Window menu > Brush Libraries submenu.
   or
   To open a library that is not in the Brush Libraries folder, choose Window menu > Other Library, locate and highlight a custom library, then click Select.

2. Drag a brush from the library palette onto an object in your document (you don't have to select the object). The brush-stroke will appear on the object and the brush will appear on the Brushes palette.
   or
   Drag a brush from the library palette onto the Brushes palette. To drag multiple brushes, Shift-click or Command-click/Ctrl-click them first 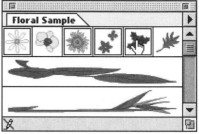–.
   or
   Select one or more brushes, then choose Add to Brushes from the library palette menu.

TIP To delete brushes from the Brushes palette, see page 157.

TIP To close a library palette, click its close box. You can drag a palette tab into another palette group. To close one palette, drag its tab out of the palette grouping, then click its close box.

TIP If you choose Persistent from a brush library palette menu, that palette will open automatically when you re-launch Illustrator.

1 *To append multiple brushes, first **Shift-click** or **Command-click/Ctrl-click** them.*

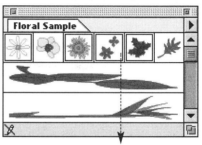

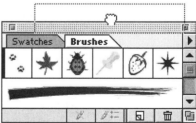

2 *Drag the selected brushes to the Brushes palette.*

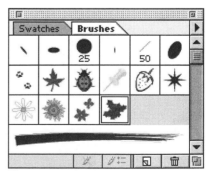

3 *The brushes appear on the current document's **Brushes** palette.*

1 *The original object with a **brushstroke**.*

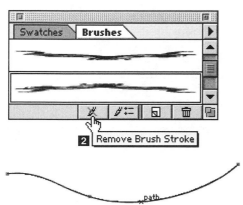

2 Remove Brush Stroke

3 *The brushstroke is **removed** from the object.*

4 *The original **brushstroke** on an object.*

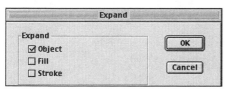

5 *Check only the **Object** or **Stroke** box in the **Expand** dialog box.*

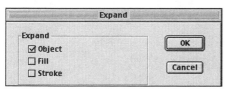

6 *The brushstroke is now an object, **separate** from the original path (they were ungrouped and moved away from each other for this illustration).*

To remove a brushstroke from an object:

1. Select the object or objects from which you want to remove the brushstroke **1**.
2. Click the Remove Brush Stroke button on the Brushes palette **2**–**3**.

If you expand a brushstroke, it is converted into an ordinary object. If you then change the original brush, you won't have the option to update the brushstroke on the object.

To expand a brushstroke:

1. Select the brushstroked object **4**.
2. Choose Object menu > Expand.
3. Check the Object or Stroke option and uncheck the Fill option **5**.
4. Click OK (Return/Enter). The brushstroke is now a separate object or objects **6**. Choose Object menu > Ungroup to separate the brushstroke object from the original path.

Remove Brushstroke; Expand Brushstroke

To choose brush display options:

With the **View By Name** option unchecked on the Brushes palette menu, you'll see only a thumbnail for each brush 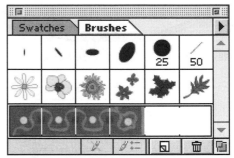. With the View By Name option checked, for each brush there will be a smaller thumbnail, the brush name, and an icon for the brush type (calligraphic, scatter, art, pattern) **2**.

To control which **brush types** (categories) display on the palette, choose a brush type from the palette menu to check or uncheck that option. A brush type that has no check mark will not display on the palette.

You can **drag** a brush to a different spot on the Brushes palette within its category. To move multiple brushes, select them first (Shift-click or Command-click/Ctrl-click).

Scatter objects are placed evenly or randomly along the contour of a path. Any Illustrator object or text outline can be made into a scatter brush. A gradient, gradient mesh object, or mask *cannot* be made into a scatter brush. A compound path *can* be made into a scatter brush.

To create or modify a scatter brush:

1. To create a new brush, select an object or objects **3**, click the New Brush button on the Brushes palette 🖫, click New Scatter Brush, then click OK.
   or
   To modify an existing brush, double-click the brush on the Brushes palette. Or click a brush, then choose Brush Options from the palette menu.

2. Enter a new name or modify the existing name (**4**, next page).

3. For an existing brush, check the Preview box. Changes will preview on any paths to which the brush is currently applied.

4. Each of the four brush properties (Size, Spacing, Scatter, and Rotation) can be set to the Fixed, Random, or Pressure variation via the drop-down menu next to each option. Choose **Fixed** to use a single, fixed value.

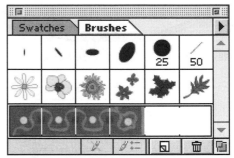

1 *With the* **View By Name** *option* **unchecked** *on the Brushes palette menu.*

2 *With the* **View By Name** *option* **checked** *on the Brushes palette menu.*

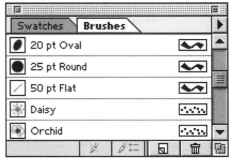

3 *The original objects.*

Brush Display Options; Create, Modify Scatter Brush

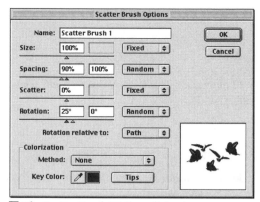

4 *The Scatter Brush Options dialog box.*

5 *The new scatter brush applied to a path.*

6 *The same scatter brush after moving the Size sliders apart (Random setting).*

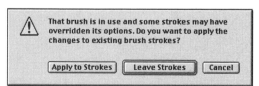

7 *This prompt will appear if you modify a brush that is currently applied to objects in the file.*

Choose **Random,** then move the sliders (or enter different values into the left and right fields) to define a range within which that property value can vary.

Choose **Pressure** and move the sliders (or enter different values in the left and right fields) to define a range within which that property can respond to stylus pressure. A light pressure will produce a brush property based on the minimum property value (left field); a heavy pressure will produce a brush property based on the maximum property value (right field). Pressure will be available only if you're using a graphics tablet.

Size controls the size of the scatter objects.

Spacing controls the spacing between the scatter objects.

Scatter controls the distance of the objects from either side of the path. When Scatter is set to Fixed, a positive value places all the objects on one side of the path; a negative value places all the objects on the opposite side of the path. The further the Scatter value is from 0%, the greater the distance from the path.

Rotation adjusts the amount objects rotate relative to the page or the path. Choose **Page** or **Path** from the **Rotation relative to** drop-down menu for the axis the rotation will be based on.

5. For the Colorization options, see the sidebar on page 157.

6. Click OK or press Return/Enter **5**–**6**. If the brush was already applied to existing paths in the document, an alert box will appear. Click Apply to Strokes to change the existing strokes or click Leave Strokes to leave existing strokes unchanged **7**.

TIP You'll find scatter brushes in the Animal Sample, Arrow Sample, Floral Sample, and Object Sample libraries.

TIP Shift-drag a slider to move its counterpart gradually along with it. Option-drag/

(Continued on the following page)

Alt-drag a slider to move it in the direction opposite to its counterpart's motion.

TIP To make the scatter objects' orientation along a path uniform, set Scatter and Rotation to Fixed, set Scatter to 0°, and choose Rotation relative to: Path **8**–**9**.

TIP Make type into outlines before trying to drag it into the Brushes palette.

The calligraphic brushes create strokes that vary in thickness as you draw, like traditional calligraphy media.

To create or modify a calligraphic brush:

1. To create a new calligraphic brush, click the New Brush button on the Brushes palette ▣, click New Calligraphic Brush, then click OK.
   or
   To modify an existing brush **1**, double-click the brush on the Brushes palette **2**.

2. Enter a new name or modify the existing name **3**.

3. To preview an existing brush, check the Preview box. Changes will preview immediately on any paths to which the calligraphic brush is currently applied. Changes also update in the preview area of the dialog box.

4. The Angle, Roundness, and Diameter can be set to the Fixed, or Random, or Pressure variation via the drop-down menu next to each option.

   Choose **Fixed** to keep the value constant.

   Choose **Random** and move the Variation slider to define a range within which the specific brush attribute value can vary. A stroke can range between the set value (for angle, roundness, or diameter) plus or minus the Variation value (e.g., a 50° angle with a Random Variation value of 10 could have an angle anywhere between 40° and 60°).

   Choose **Pressure** and move the Variation slider to define a range within which the

8 *Illustrator's default "Fish" scatter brush applied to a path.*

9 *After choosing the Fixed option for Scatter and Rotation and setting Scatter to 0%.*

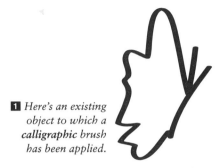

1 *Here's an existing object to which a* **calligraphic** *brush has been applied.*

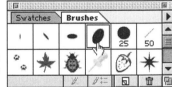

2 *Double-click a brush on the Brushes palette.*

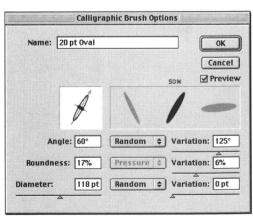

3 *Modify the brush via the* **Calligraphic Brush Options** *dialog box.*

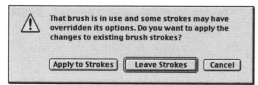

That brush is in use and some strokes may have overridden its options. Do you want to apply the changes to existing brush strokes?

Apply to Strokes | Leave Strokes | Cancel

4 *If you modify a brush that has been applied to objects in the file, this prompt will appear.*

5 *The Angle and Diameter were set to Random in the Calligraphic Brush Options dialog and Apply to Strokes was clicked when the prompt appeared. The brushstrokes* **update** *on the object.*

specific brush attribute value can respond to pressure from a stylus (available only with a graphics tablet). A light pressure will produce a brush attribute based on the set value for angle, roundness, or diameter minus the Variation value. A heavy pressure will produce a brush attribute based on the set value plus the Variation value.

5. Enter a value in the **Angle** field or drag the gray arrowhead in the preview box. The angle controls the thickness of the horizontals and verticals in the stroke. A 0° angle will produce a thin horizontal stroke and a thick vertical stroke. A 90° angle will produce the opposite effect. Other angles will produce different effects.

6. Enter a **Roundness** value or reshape the tip by dragging either black dot inward or outward on the ellipse.

7. Enter a value in the **Diameter** field or drag the slider for the size of the brush.

8. Click OK (Return/Enter). If the brush was already applied to existing paths in the document, an alert dialog will appear **4**. Click Apply to Strokes to update the existing strokes with the revised brush or click Leave Strokes to leave existing strokes unchanged **5**.

Create or Modify Calligraphic Brush

An art brush can be made from one or more objects, including a compound path, but not a gradient, gradient mesh, or mask. When it's applied to a path, an art brushstroke follows the shape of the path. If you reshape the path, the art brushstroke will stretch or bend to conform to the new path contour.

To create or modify an art brush:

1. To create a new brush, select one or more objects **1**, drag the object(s) onto the Brushes palette **2**, click New Art Brush **3**, then click OK (Return/Enter).
or
To modify an existing brush, double-click that brush on the Brushes palette. Or choose an art brush, then choose Brush Options from the palette menu.

2. For a new brush, enter a Name **4**.

3. For an existing brush, check the Preview box. Changes will preview immediately on any existing paths to which the art brush is currently applied.

4. Click a Direction button to control the orientation of the object on the path. The object will be drawn in the direction the arrow is pointing. The Direction will be more distinct for objects with a distinct directional orientation, like text outlines, or a vase or a leaf.

5. Enter a Size: Width to scale the art brush. Check Proportional to preserve the original object's proportions.

6. *Optional:* Check Flip Along to reverse the object on the path (left to right). Check Flip Across to reverse the object across the path (up and down).

7. Choose a Colorization option (see the sidebar on the next page).

8. Click OK (Return/Enter) **5**.

TIP You'll find art brushes in Illustrator's Animal Sample, Arrow Sample, Artistic Sample, Floral Sample, and Object Sample libraries.

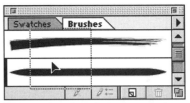

1 *To create a new art brush, select an object or objects. These objects are text outlines.*

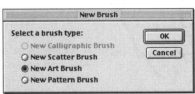

2 *Drag the selected objects onto the Brushes palette.*

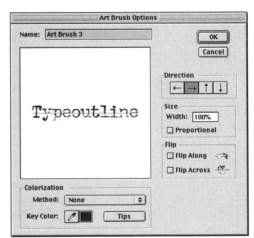

3 *Click New Art Brush.*

4 *Enter a Name for a new brush; change any of the settings to modify an existing brush.*

5 *The new art brush is applied to a path.*

156

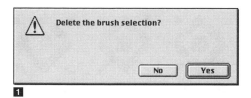

1

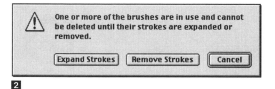

2

THE COLORIZATION OPTIONS

From the Colorization drop-down menu (unavailable for a calligraphic brush), choose:

None to leave the colors unchanged.

Tints to change black areas in the brushstroke to the stroke color at 100% and non-black areas to tints of the current stroke color. White areas stay white.

Tints and Shades to change non-black or white colors in the brushstroke to tints of the current stroke color. Black and white areas don't change.

Hue Shift to apply the current stroke color to areas containing the most frequently used color on the object (the Key Color) and to change other colors in the brushstroke to related hues.

If you're editing the brush itself (not a brush-stroke), you can click the **Key Color** eyedropper and then click on a color in the preview area of the dialog box to change the Key Color.

Click **Tips** to read more **3**.

3 Click Tips in the Stroke Options dialog box to read these Colorization Tips.

To delete a brush from the Brushes palette:

1. Click the brush you want to delete.

2. Choose Delete Brush from the palette menu or click the Delete Brush button on the palette, then click Yes **1**.
or
Drag the selected brush over the Delete Brush button.
or
Option-click/Alt-click the Delete Brush button.

Note: If the brush is currently applied to any objects in the current document, an alert dialog will appear **2**. Click Expand Strokes to turn those brushstrokes into non-brushstroke objects or click Remove Strokes to remove them from the objects.

TIP Choose Undo to restore the brush to the palette.

TIP To delete all the brushes that are not being used in a file, choose Select All Unused from the Brushes palette menu, then use any method in step 2, above, to delete the selected brushes.

TIP To restore a saved brush that you may have inadvertently deleted, choose the library that the brush is stored in from the Window menu > Brush Libraries submenu, then drag the brush from the library palette to the Brushes palette.

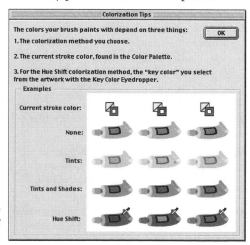

Delete a Brush

The pattern brush renders patterns along the edge of a closed or open path, and can be used to create custom frames, borders, or other decorative shapes. You can use up to five different-shaped tile pieces when you create a path pattern: a Side tile, an Outer Corner tile, an Inner Corner tile, a Start tile, and End tile. Each type of tile adapts to fit its assigned location on the path. Here's how to design your own tiles.

To create tiles for a pattern brush:

1. Draw closed path shapes for the side pattern tile. Try to limit the tile to about an inch wide—two inches at the most. You can resize it later via the Pattern Brush Options dialog box.

2. Since a pattern brush places side tiles perpendicular to the path, you should rotate any design that is taller than it is wide. To do this, choose the Selection tool, select the shapes for the side tile, double-click the Rotate tool, enter an Angle of 90°, then click OK.

3. Draw separate shapes for the corner, start, and end tiles , if necessary, to complete the design. Corner tiles should be square, and they should be the same height as the rotated side tile.

4. Choose the Selection tool, then select one of the tile shapes.

5. Drag the selection onto the Swatches palette , then deselect the tile shape.

6. Double-click the new swatch. Enter a name in the Swatch Name field. Type words like "side," "outer," "start," and "end" after the tile name to help you remember the tile's placement. Click OK (Return/Enter) 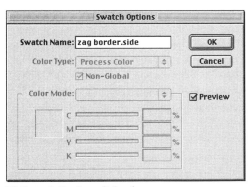.

7. Repeat steps 4 through 6 for the other tile shapes.

8. Follow the steps on the next page to make the new tiles that are now on the Swatches palette into a pattern brush (, next page).

TIP You don't *have* to use a bounding rectangle behind the shapes when you a create

1 *Start tile*   *Side tile*   *Outer Corner tile*

End tile

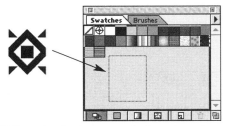

2 *Drag the tile shape onto the Swatches palette.*

3 *Swatch Options dialog box.*

4 *The pattern tiles made into a pattern brush and then applied to a path.*

Tile buttons

Side Outer corner Inner corner Start End

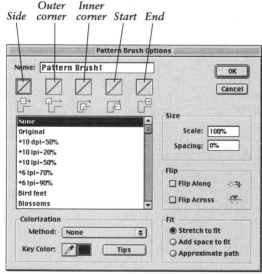

1 *The **Pattern Brush Options** dialog box.*

pattern brush tile, but you *can* do so if it helps you fit the tiles together. Apply a fill and stroke of None to the rectangle, and make sure none of the pattern shapes extend beyond it. The rectangle won't act as a cropping device as it would in a pattern fill.

TIP When they're applied to a path, corner tiles will be rotated 90° for each corner of the path, starting from the upper left corner.

TIP Apply spot fill and stroke colors to the tile shapes, and name the colors appropriately so they can be readily associated with the tile. The tiles can then be recolored easily by changing the spot colors.

TIP To make geometric shapes look more hand drawn, before making shapes into a pattern brush, apply Filter menu > Distort > Roughen at a low setting.

To create a pattern brush:

1. Create tiles for the pattern brush (instructions start on the previous page).

2. Click the New Brush button on the Brushes palette ⬚, click New Pattern Brush, then click OK.

3. Enter a Name.

4. Click a tile button (along the top) to assign the pattern to that part of a path, then click a pattern name on the scroll list **1**. (The scroll list displays the tiles that are currently on the Swatches palette.) Repeat for the other tile buttons, if desired.

    Use the icons under the buttons to distinguish one type of tile from another. To assign no pattern for a position on the path, choose None. For a round object, you'll need to assign only a side tile.

5. Click OK (Return/Enter). Apply the brush to a path, and then modify the path, or modify the brush by following the steps on the next page.

(Continued on the following page)

TIP If you reshape a path that has a pattern brushstroke, the pattern will reshape along with the path. Corner and side tiles will be added or removed as needed.

TIP Illustrator's Border Sample library contains pattern brushes, and additional pattern brushes can be found in the Goodies folder on the Adobe Illustrator 8.0 CD-ROM.

To modify a pattern brush:

1. Double-click the pattern brush you want to modify.
   or
   Click a pattern brush, then choose Brush Options from the palette menu.

2. Check the Preview box. Changes will preview on any existing paths to which the pattern is currently applied.

3. To change tiles, click a **tile button**, then click a pattern name on the scroll list 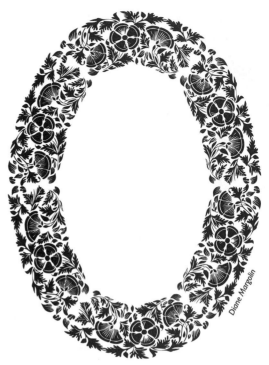. Repeat for the other tile buttons, if desired. Use the icons under the buttons to distinguish one type of tile from another. To assign no pattern for a position on the path, choose None. For a round object, you need to assign only one tile.

4. Do any of the following:

   Enter a new Size: **Scale** percentage for the pattern tile.

   To add blank space between pattern tiles, enter an amount in the Size: **Spacing** field.

   To alter the pattern tile's orientation on the path, check the **Flip Along** and/or **Flip Across** box. Be sure to preview this—you may not like the results.

   In the Fit area, click **Stretch to fit** to have Illustrator shorten or lengthen the tiles, where necessary, to fit on the path. Click **Add space to fit** to have Illustrator add blank space between tiles, where necessary, to fit the pattern along the path, factoring in the Spacing amount, if one was entered. Choose this option if you want the original path's stroke color (or

Modify a Pattern Brush

A *pattern* brushstroke.

Diane Margolin

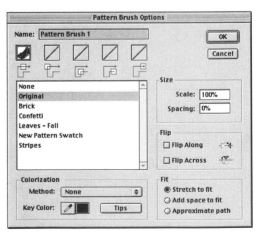

1 *Reassign different tiles and choose other options in the* **Pattern Brush Options** *dialog.*

To create this pattern, Diane Margolin turned on the "Stretch to fit" option, and used Side, Outer Corner, and Inner Corner tile shapes.

Diane Margolin

subsequently applied fill color) to show through blank spaces in the pattern.

For a rectangular path, if you click **Approximate path**, the pattern tiles will be applied slightly inside or outside the path, rather than centered on the path, in order to produce even tiling.

5. For the **Colorization** option, see the sidebar on page 157.

6. Click OK (Return/Enter). If the pattern brush is currently applied to a path or paths in the file, an alert dialog will appear. Click Apply to Strokes to update the existing strokes or click Leave Strokes to leave them unchanged.

In addition to editing a brush via its Options dialog, you can also edit a brush by reshaping or recoloring it manually.

To edit a scatter, art, or pattern brush manually:

1. Drag the brush from the Brushes palette onto a blank area of the artboard (**1**–**2**, next page).

2. Deselect the brush objects.

3. To recolor or transform the entire brush, select it using the Selection tool (**3**, next page). To recolor or transform individual objects within the brush or individual pattern brush tiles, select them using the Direct-selection tool.

4. For a **scatter** or **art** brush, choose the Selection tool (V), and select the modified brush object or objects. Start dragging the objects onto the Brushes palette, hold down Option/Alt when you pass over the Brushes palette, then release the mouse when the pointer is over the original brush icon and it is highlighted. To save over the original brush, leave the name as is. To make the revised brush into a new brush, in addition to the original, enter a new name. Click OK (Return/ Enter).

(Continued on the following page)

For a **pattern** brush:

Drag each revised tile individually onto the Swatches palette, and then deselect all the tiles on the artboard.

Double-click each new swatch on the Swatches palette, enter an appropriate name, then click OK.

Double-click the original pattern brush on the Brushes palette, reassign the new tiles to the appropriate tile buttons (see page 159), then click OK. If the brush is currently applied to paths in the document, an alert dialog will appear. Click Apply to Strokes to update those paths with the revised brush or click Leave Strokes to leave the existing brushstrokes unchanged **4**–**5**.

or

Start dragging the new pattern tile shape, hold down Option/Alt as you pass over the Brushes palette, and release the mouse when the new tile is over a specific tile slot to replace only that highlighted tile. The Pattern Brush Options dialog box will open with the new tile in the chosen tile position. Click OK.

TIP The tile slots for a pattern brush on the Brushes palette are arranged, from left to right, in the following order: outer corner, side, inner corner, start, and end.

To create a new brush library:

1. Create brushes in an Illustrator file or move them to the current document's Brushes palette from other libraries.

2. Choose File menu > Save, and save the file in the Adobe Illustrator 8 > Brush Libraries folder. Use an appropriate name for the type of brushes.

3. Re-launch Illustrator. The new library will appear on the Window menu > Brush Libraries submenu.

1 *The original pattern brushstroke.*

2 *Drag the brush onto the artboard.*

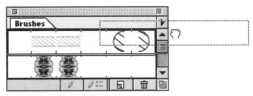

3 *Edit the pat-* **4** *The brush updates on the*
tern manually. *Brushes palette.*

5 *The edited pattern brushstroke.*

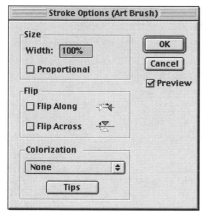

1 *Select an object or objects to which a brush has been applied.*

2 *Stroke Options for an art brush.*

3 *The **brushstroke** is altered on the **object** using the options shown in Figure **2**.*

If you edit a brush, you can't selectively choose which objects to which that brush has been applied will update to reflect the changes. Follow these instructions if you want to modify a brushstroke on a selected object or objects without editing the brush itself.

To change the stroke options for an individual object:

1. Select one or more objects to which the *same* brush is currently applied **1**.

2. If you want to recolor the brushstroke, choose a stroke color now.

3. Click the Options of Selected Object button on the Brushes palette ⟦🖊⟧.

4. Check the Preview box **2** (and **4**–**5**, next page).

5. For a scatter brushstroke, follow step 4 starting on page 152.

   For a calligraphic brushstroke, follow steps 4–7 starting on page 154.

   For an art brushstroke, follow steps 5–6 on page 156.

   For a pattern brushstroke, follow step 4 starting on page 160.

6. From the **Colorization** drop-down menu (this is *not* available for calligraphic brushes), choose:

   None to leave the colors unchanged.

   Tints to change black areas in the brushstroke to the stroke color at 100% and non-black areas to tints of the current stroke color. White areas stay white.

   Tints and Shades to change non-black or white colors in the brushstroke to tints of the current stroke color. Black and white areas stay as they are.

   Hue Shift to apply the current stroke color to areas containing the most frequently used color on the object (the Key Color) and to change other colors in the brushstroke to related hues.

   Note: If you're editing the brush itself (not a brushstroke), you can click the

(Continued on the following page)

Change Stroke for Individual Object; Duplicate Brush

Key Color eyedropper and then click on a color in the brush or pattern tile preview area of the dialog box to change the Key Color.

7. *Optional:* Click Tips to see an illustration of the Colorization options.

8. Click OK (Return/Enter) (**3**, previous page). Only the selected object will change; the brush itself on the Brushes palette will not change.

TIP To restore the original brushstroke to the object, select the object, click a different brush on the Brushes palette, then click back on the original brush.

TIP If you've used the Options of Selected Object option to customize a brushstroke on a selected object and you now want to apply a different art brush with those new options to the same object, Option-click/Alt-click a different brush. Huh?

Here's a way to create a variation on an existing brush—a slimmer or fatter version, for example.

To duplicate a brush:

1. Click the brush you want to duplicate.

2. Choose Duplicate Brush from the palette menu.
   or
   Drag the selected brush over the New Brush button 🗐 **6**–**7**.

   The word "copy" will be appended to name of the brush. To modify the brush, see the individual instructions for that brush type elsewhere in this chapter.

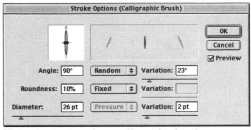

4 *Stroke Options* for a *calligraphic* brush.

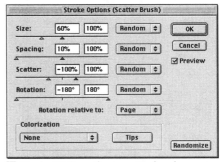

5 *Stroke Options* for a *scatter* brush.

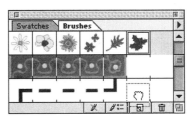

6 To *duplicate* a brush, drag it over the *New Brush* button.

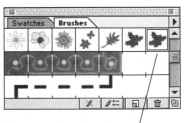

7 The duplicate brush appears next to the original brush.

PEN 11

Mastering the Pen tool—Illustrator's most difficult tool—requires patience and practice. Once you become comfortable creating Pen tool paths, read Chapter 7 to learn how to reshape them. If you find the Pen tool too difficult to use, remember that you can always transform a simple shape into a complex shape using the point and path editing tools or simply draw a free-hand shape using the Pencil or Paintbrush tool. Simpler methods for creating shapes are covered in Chapter 5.

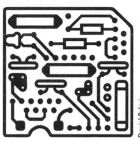

Daniel Pelavin

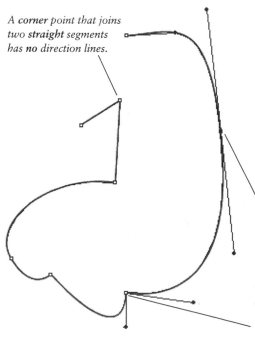
*A **corner** point that joins two **straight** segments has **no** direction lines.*

*A **smooth** point has a pair of direction lines that move in **tandem**.*

*A **corner** point that joins two curved seg-ments has independent-moving direction lines.*

Pen Tool

What the Pen tool does

The Pen tool creates precise curved and straight line segments connected by anchor points. If you click with the Pen tool, you will create corner points and straight line segments with *no* direction lines. If you drag with the Pen tool, you will create smooth curve points and curve segments *with* direction lines. The distance and direction in which you drag the mouse determine the shape of the curve segment.

In the instructions on the following pages, you'll learn how to draw straight sides, continuous curves, and non-continuous curves using the Pen tool. Once you master these three types of path shapes and start using the Pen tool as an illustrator, you'll naturally combine all three techniques without really thinking about it.

Click with the Pen tool to create an open or closed straight-sided polygon.

To draw a straight-sided object using the Pen tool:

1. If a color is selected for the Fill box on the Color palette (not None), the Pen path will be filled as soon as three points are created (you'll see this only in Preview view, of course). To create segments that appear as lines only, choose a stroke color and a fill of None now (or at any time while you're drawing the path).

2. Choose the Pen tool (P or Shift-P) .

3. Click to create an anchor point.

4. Click to create a second anchor point. A straight line segment will connect the two points.

5. Click to create additional anchor points. They will be also connected by straight line segments.

6. To complete the shape as an **open** path:

   Click the Pen tool or any other tool on the Toolbox.
   or
   Hold down Command/Ctrl and click outside the new shape to deselect it.
   or
   Choose Edit menu > Deselect All (Command-Shift-A/Ctrl-Shift-A).

   To complete the shape as a **closed** path, position the Pen pointer over the starting point (a small circle will appear next to the pointer), and click on it 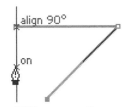.

TIP Hold down Shift while clicking with the Pen tool to constrain a segment to a multiple of 45°.

TIP Use smart guides to help you align points and segments (see page 76) 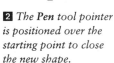.

1 *Pen tool.*

2 *The Pen tool pointer is positioned over the starting point to close the new shape.*

3 *You can use Smart Guides to align points as you create them.*

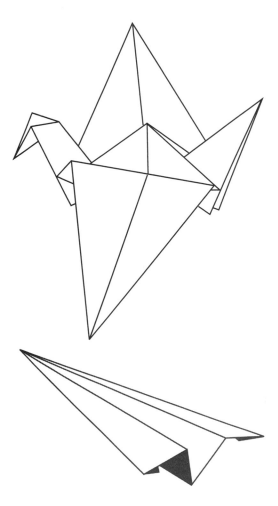

Draw a Straight-Sided Object

1 *Drag to create the first anchor point.*

2 *Release and reposition the mouse, then drag in the direction you wish the curve to follow.*

3 *Continue to reposition and drag the mouse.*

4 *Continue to reposition and drag.*

Follow these instructions to create continuous curves, which consist of smooth anchor points connected by smooth curve segments, each with a pair of direction lines that move in tandem. The longer the direction lines, the steeper or wider the curve. You can practice drawing curves by tracing over a placed image that contains curve shapes or by converting curved objects into guides and then tracing over the guide lines.

To draw continuous curves using the Pen tool:

1. Choose the Pen tool. *Optional:* Turn on Smart Guides (Command-U/Ctrl-U).

2. Drag to create the first anchor point **1**. The angle of the pair of direction lines that you create will be determined by the direction you drag.

3. **Release** the mouse, **move** it away from the last anchor point, then drag in the direction in which you want the curve to follow to create a second anchor point **2**. A curve segment will connect the first and second anchor points, and a second pair of direction lines will be created. The shape of the curve segment will be defined by the length and direction you drag the mouse. Remember, you can always reshape the curves later (see Chapter 7).

4. Drag to create additional anchor points and direction lines **3**–**4**. The points will be connected by curve segments.

(Continued on the following page)

Draw Continuous Curves

5. To complete the object as an **open** path:

Choose a different tool.

or

Click a selection tool (or hold down Command/Ctrl), then click away from the new object to deselect it.

or

Choose Edit menu > Deselect All (Command-Shift-A/Ctrl-Shift-A).

To complete the object as a **closed** path, position the Pen pointer over the starting point (a small loop will appear next to the pointer), drag, then release the mouse.

TIP The fewer the anchor points, the smoother the shape. Too many anchor points will produce bumpy curves.

TIP Hold down Command/Ctrl to use the Selection tool or Direct-selection tool (whichever was last highlighted) while the Pen tool is selected.

ADJUST AS YOU GO

If the last-created anchor point was a curve point and you want to convert it into a corner point, click on it with the Pen tool, move the mouse, and continue to draw. One direction line will disappear.

If the last-created anchor point was a corner point and you want to convert it into a curve point, position the Pen tool pointer over it, then drag. A direction line will appear.

To move an anchor point as it's being created, keep the mouse button down, hold down Spacebar, and drag the point.

GET SMART WITH YOUR PEN

As a path is drawn with the Pen tool, if you first move the pointer over unselected points to which you want to align, Smart Guide angle lines will appear for those points as you click or drag to produce new points. And when you create a new point, the Smart Guides will match the angle of the direction lines for that point.

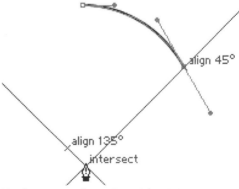

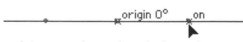

*With **Smart Guides** on, draw the first anchor point (and its direction lines).*

*To align new anchor points with existing, unse-lected anchor points using Smart Guides, first, with the mouse button **up**, move the pointer over the **unselected** points to which you want to align. Then click or drag to create the new point(s).*

1 *Drag to create the first anchor point.*

2 *Release the mouse, reposition it, then drag to create a second anchor point.*

3 *Hold down Option/Alt and drag from the last anchor point in the direction you want the new curve to follow. The direction lines are on the same side of the curve segment.*

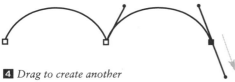

4 *Drag to create another anchor point, and so on.*

You can use the Pen tool to create corner points that join non-continuous curves, which are segments that curve on only one side of an anchor point. (Segments curve on both sides of a smooth anchor point.) If you move one direction line from a corner point, only the curve on that side of the point will reshape. Smooth points and corner points can be combined in the same path, of course. You can convert smooth points into corner points (or vice versa) as you draw them (instructions on this page) or after you draw them (instructions on the next page).

To convert smooth points into corner points as you draw them:

1. Choose the Pen tool (P or Shift-P).
2. Drag to create the first anchor point **1**.
3. **Release** the mouse, **move** it away from the last anchor point, then drag to create a second anchor point **2**. A curve segment will connect the first and second anchor points, and a second pair of direction lines will be created. The shape of the curve segment will be determined by the length and direction you drag.
4. Option-drag/Alt-drag from the last anchor point to create a new independent-moving direction line. Drag in the direction in which you want the curve to follow **3**.
   or
   Click on the last anchor point to remove one of the direction lines from that point.
5. Repeat the previous two steps to draw a series of anchor points and curves **4**.

Convert Points as You Draw Them

Follow these instructions to convert points on an existing, completed path.

To convert points in an existing object:

1. Choose the Direct-selection tool (A or Shift-A).

2. Click on the path, then click on the anchor point that you want to convert.

3. Choose the Convert-direction-point tool (P or Shift-P) .

4. Drag new direction lines from a corner point to convert it into a smooth point 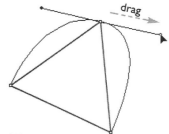.
   or
   To convert a smooth point into a corner point with a non-continuous curve, rotate a direction line from the anchor point so it forms a "V" shape with the other direction line **4**.
   or
   Click on a smooth point to convert it into a corner point with no direction lines **5**–**6**.

5. Repeat the previous step to convert other anchor points.

1 *Direct-selection tool.*

2 *Convert-direction-point tool.*

3 *Converting a corner point into a smooth point.*

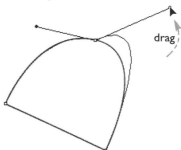

4 *Converting a smooth point into a corner point (non-continuous curve).*

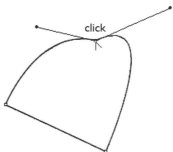

5 *Converting a non-continuous curve into a corner point with no direction lines.*

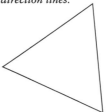

6 *Back to the original triangle.*

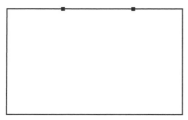

1 *Click to add two anchor points at the ⅓ points along the rectangle's top segment.*

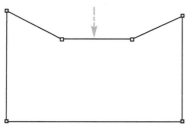

2 *Drag the segment between the new points downward.*

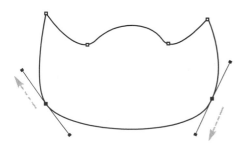

3 *With the Convert-direction-point tool, drag to convert each new point into a curve point.*

Exercise

Convert a rectangle into a costume mask

The outer mask shape

1. Draw a rectangle with a fill of None and a 1-point black stroke.

2. Choose the Add-anchor-point tool.

3. Click to add two anchor points at the ⅓ points along the rectangle's top segment **1**.

4. Choose the Direct-selection tool, then drag the segment between the new points downward **2**.

5. Choose the Convert-direction-point tool. Drag the new point on the left upward and to the right to convert it into a smooth point, and drag the new point on the right point downward and to the right **3**.

6. Convert the rectangle's bottommost corner points into curve points by dragging the left corner point upward and to the left and dragging the right corner point downward and to the left **4**.

7. Choose the Add-anchor-point tool, then click to create a point in the center of the rectangle's bottom segment.

8. Choose the Direct-selection tool, click on the new center point, then drag it upward slightly **5**.

(Continued on the following page)

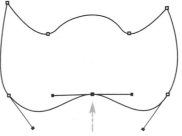

4 *Using the Convert-direction-point tool, drag to convert the rectangle's bottom corner points into curve points.*

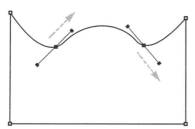

5 *Use the Add-anchor-point tool to create a point in the center of the rectangle's bottom segment. Click on, then drag that new center point upward using the Direct-selection tool.*

Exercise: Rectangle into Costume Mask

The eye holes

1. Choose the Ellipse tool, then draw a small ellipse for an eye hole .

2. Choose the Direct-selection tool. Deselect, click on the leftmost anchor point of the ellipse, then drag it upward to form an eye shape .

3. Click on the bottommost anchor point of the ellipse, then drag the left handle of that point to the left to widen the bottom segment **3**.

4. Click on the top middle point of the ellipse, then drag the right handle of that point upward and to the right to widen the top right segment **4**.

5. Choose the Selection tool, then drag the eye hole shape over the left side of the mask shape.

6. Choose the Reflect tool.

7. Option-click/Alt-click in the center of the mask shape. In the dialog box, check the Preview box, click Vertical, enter 90° in the Angle field, press Tab to force a preview, if desired, then click Copy. Use the Selection tool to reposition the new eye hole, if necessary .

8. Use the Selection tool to marquee all three shapes, and fill the shapes with a color. Leave them selected.

9. Choose Object menu > Compound Paths > Make (Command-8/Ctrl-8). The eye holes will now cut through the mask shape **6**.

1 *Create a small ellipse for the eye holes.*

2 *With the Direct-selection tool, click on the left point of the ellipse, then drag upward.*

3 *Click on the bottom point of the ellipse, then drag the left handle of that point to the left.*

4 *Click on the top point of the ellipse, then drag the right handle of that point upward and to the right.*

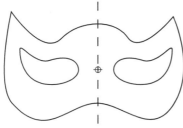

5 *To create the second eye hole, Option-click/Alt-click in the center of the mask shape with the Reflect tool. Check Preview, click Vertical, enter 90° in the Angle field, then click Copy.*

6 *All the shapes are selected and made into a compound. A fill is applied to the compound shape. (The gray rectangle behind reveals the transparency in the compound.)*

CREATE TYPE 12

This chapter is an introduction to Illustrator's impressive type creation tools. You will learn how to create type that stands by itself, and how to enter type inside an object or along a path. You'll also learn how to import type from another application, link type, copy type or a type object, and convert type into graphic outlines.

Typographic attributes are modified using the Character, Paragraph, and MM (Multiple Master) Design palettes, which are covered in the next chapter, along with methods for selecting type.

There are three horizontal type tools: The Type tool, the Area Type tool, and the Path Type tool. Each of these tools has a counterpart for creating vertical type: The Vertical Type tool, the Vertical Area Type tool, and the Vertical Path Type tool. Some of these tools' functions overlap, but each of them has unique characteristics for producing a particular kind of type object.

The **Type** tool creates a free-floating block of type, called **point** type, that is not associated with a path. You can also draw a rectangle with it and enter type inside the rectangle; you can use it to enter type along the edge of an open path; and you can use it to enter type inside a closed path. It's the most versatile of the type tools.

The **Area Type** tool creates type *inside* an open or closed path. Lines of type created with the Area Type tool automatically wrap inside the path.

The **Path Type** tool creates a line of type along the outside *edge* of an open or closed path.

The **Vertical Type** tool has the same function as the Type tool, except that it creates vertical type.

The **Vertical Area Type** tool creates vertical type *inside* an open or closed path. Vertical type reads from *right to left,* making it useful for typesetting text in languages that read in that direction.

The **Vertical Path Type** tool creates vertical type along the outside *edge* of an open or closed path.

A few things to know about fonts

Some fonts, such as Helvetica, Courier, and Times, are automatically installed in the System Folder > Application Support > Adobe > Fonts > Reqrd > Base folder (Mac), or Program Files > Common Files > Adobe > Fonts > Reqrd > Base (Win). Only Adobe products can access and utilize this folder.

Illustrator no longer uses Adobe Type Manager (ATM) to perform type rasterization and font management. These functions are performed internally within Illustrator. You still need to have the printer fonts for a type-face in a location that Illustrator can find in order to print the typeface from Illustrator.

If you open a file containing type that's styled in a font that is installed but unavailable to the System, an alert box message will tell you that a substitute font will be used for the missing one. If you subsequently activate that font for the System, the font will reappear on Illustrator's font list and the type should display correctly. If it doesn't, choose View menu > Artwork and then Preview to force the screen to redraw. Illustrator 8 supports ATM 4.0 Deluxe's activation and deactivation of fonts, but not TrueType fonts on Win 95 or NT 4.0 (see the Illustrator Read Me file).

Point type stands by itself—it's neither inside an object nor along a path. Use this tool to set a type block like a picture caption or a pull quote that doesn't need to be aligned with any neighboring type blocks.

To create point type:

1. Choose the Type or Vertical Type tool .

2. Click on a blank area of the artboard where you want the type to start (not on an object). A flashing insertion marker will appear.

3. Enter type. Press Return/Enter when you want to start a new line **2**.

4. Choose a selection tool and click away from the type block to deselect it.
   or
   Click the Type tool again to complete the type block and start a new one.

CHOOSE TYPE ATTRIBUTES FIRST?

If you like to choose character and paragraph attributes before you create type, use the Character and Paragraph palettes. They're discussed in depth in the next chapter.

RECOLOR AFTER?

When type is entered inside an object or on a path, the object becomes filled and stroked with None. You can then apply fill and/or stroke colors to the type object—just deselect then reselect it with the Direct-selection tool (select only the edge). To recolor the type itself, first select it using a type tool or a selection tool (type selection methods are discussed in the next chapter).

Illustrator's type tool lineup on the pop-out menu.

1 *Type tool.*

Vertical Type tool.

'It spoils people's clothes to squeeze under a gate; the proper way to get in, is to climb down a pear tree.'

Beatrix Potter

2 *Point type created using the Type tool.*

Once you place type inside or along a graphic object, it becomes a type object, and it can only be converted back into a graphic object via the Undo command. To preserve the original graphic object, Option-drag/Alt-drag it to copy it, then convert the copy into a type path. You can't enter type into a compound path, a mask object, a gradient mesh object, or a blend, and you can't make a compound path from a type object. If you create type on a brushstroke path, the brushstroke will be removed.

'It spoils people's clothes to squeeze under a gate; the proper way to get in, is to climb down a pear tree.'

1 *Drag with the* **Type** *tool to create a rectangle, then enter type. To see the edges of the rectangle, go to Artwork view or use Smart Guides (Object Highlighting).*

2 *Drag with the* **Vertical Type** *tool, then enter type. Type flows from top to bottom and from right to left.*

C
l
i
m
B

d
o
w
N

a
p
e
a
R

T
r
e
E

.
.
.

'It spoils
people's
clothes to
squeeze
under a
gate; the
proper
way to
get in,
is to climb
down a
pear tree.'

3 *The type rectangle is reshaped using the Direct-selection tool.*

Use this method if you want to define the shape of the type container before creating the type. To enter type in a non-rectangular shape, see page 179.

To create a type rectangle:

1. Choose the Type or Vertical Type tool (T or Shift-T).

2. Drag to create a rectangle. When you release the mouse, a flashing insertion marker will appear in the upper left corner if you're using the Type tool or in the upper right corner if you're using the Vertical Type tool.

3. Enter type. Press Return/Enter only when you need to create a new paragraph. The type will automatically conform to the shape of the rectangle **1**–**2**.

4. Choose a selection tool and click away from the type block to deselect it.
   or
   To keep the type tool selected so as to create another, separate type rectangle, press Command/Ctrl (to temporarily access the last-used selection tool) and click away from the type block to deselect it. Release Command/Ctrl, then click again to start the new type block. (You could also click the Type tool again to complete the type object.)

   Note: If the overflow symbol appears (tiny cross in a tiny square) and you want to reveal the hidden type, you can reshape the rectangle using the Direct-selection tool (deselect it first). Use Smart Guides (with Object Highlighting) or choose Artwork view to locate the rectangle. The type will reflow to fit the new shape **3**. Another option is to spill the overflow type into another object via linking (see page 177).

 TIP To turn a path created with the Rectangle tool into a type rectangle, click on the edge of the path with either Type or Area Type tool, then enter type.

Create a Type Rectangle

You can import text into a type rectangle or any other type shape from another application, such as Microsoft Word, WordPerfect, SimpleText (Mac), or WordPad (Windows).

Note: You can also import text with no object selected using File menu > Open (creates a new document) or using File menu > Place (appears in the current document). The text will appear in a new type object, complete with paragraph breaks. (It may default to Courier.)

To import type into an object from another application:

1. Choose the Type or Vertical Type tool, then drag to create a type rectangle.
   or
   Choose the Area Type or Vertical Area Type tool , then click on the edge of a graphic object to create a flashing insertion marker .

2. Choose File menu > Place.

3. Highlight the name of the text file you want to import.

4. Click Place. The text file will flow into the object, with the same paragraph breaks, but not necessarily the same line breaks 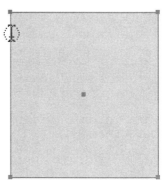. (It may default to Courier.)

TIP If you click with the Type tool in a blank area rather than drag to create a rectangle, the placed type will stretch across the entire artboard.

TIP Some type styling may be lost if you open or place an MS Word file. The MS RTF format, on the other hand, preserves most type styling.

TIP To export text, see page 200.

IMPORTING TEXT IN EPS FORMAT

Create and style your type in a layout program, and then save the file in EPS format. If you then open the EPS file using Illustrator's Open command, you'll be able to manipulate it as you would any type in Illustrator. Beware, though; a new point type block will be created for each word in the imported text, and they may be grouped.

---

1 *Area Type tool.*

Vertical Area Type tool.

2 *An object will lose its fill and stroke colors immediately if you click on its edge with the Area Type tool.*

Here was peace. She pulled in her horizon like a great fishnet. Pulled it from around the waist of the world and draped it over her shoulder.

Zora Neale Hurston

3 *Type appears inside the path.*

Taking Stock, *Nancy Stahl*

Context Magazine, *Nancy Stahl*

Puck, *Nancy Stahl*

Co-ed, *Nancy Stahl*

Flamingo, *Nancy Stahl*

Fisherman, *Si Huynh*

Book cover, *Daniel Pelavin*

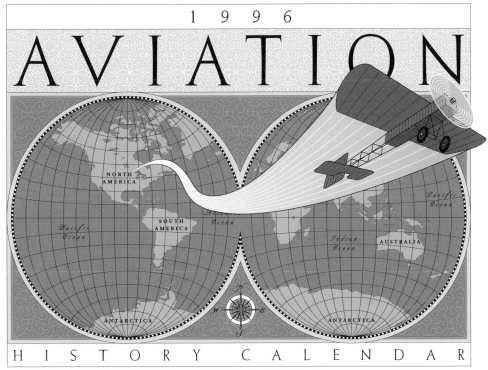

Aviation Calendar, *Rich Stromwal*

Travel The World, *Si Huynh*

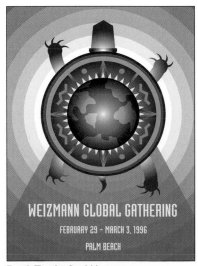

Earth Turtle, *Brad Hamann*

El Mundo, *Jose Ortega*

Groups, *David Flaherty*

Globe, *Mike Quon*

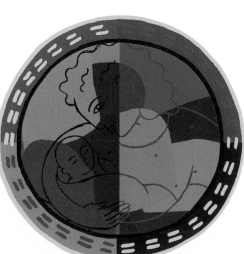

Woman and Child, *Jose Ortega*

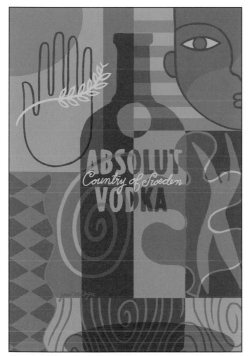

Absolut Blue, *Jose Ortega*

Absolut Citron, *Jose Ortega*

"MTA Mural: *People, Jose Ortega"*

PeopleSoft Users Conference cover, *Ron Chan*

New Asteroid, *Brad Hamann*

High Tech Tools, *Brad Hamann*

Kimona Lisa, *Brad Hamann*

Gorious Vase,
Carol Pulitzer

Caviars, Smoked Salmon, Fine Cheeses, Spanish Saffron
French Butter, For Parties, Gifts, and Self Indulgence

False China, *Carol Pulitzer*

Derain, *Carol Pulitzer*

Robot Factory, *Chris Spollen*

Director, Suburban Characters, *Nancy Stahl*

1 *Rectangle tool.*

Here was peace. She pulled in her horizon like a great fish-net. Pulled it from around the waist of the world and draped it over

*The **overflow** symbol.*

2 *Create a new rectangle with the Rectangle tool.*

Here was peace. She pulled in her horizon like a great fish-net. Pulled it from around the waist of the world and draped it over

her shoulder. So much of life in its meshes! She called in her soul to come and see.

3 *The objects are **linked**, and the overflow type spills from the first object into the second object.*

If your type overfloweth

If a type rectangle isn't *quite* large enough to display all the type inside it, you can enlarge it to reveal the hidden type. Click on the type block with the Selection tool, then drag a bounding box handle. Or select only the rectangle—not the type—with the Direct-selection tool (turn on Smart Guides with Object Highlighting or go to Artwork view to locate the rectangle), then drag a segment.

Another way to deal with overflow type that was created using either of the Type or Area Type tools is to spill it into a rectangular object (instructions on this page) or spill it into a non-rectangular object (instructions on the next page).

To link overflow type from one rectangular type object to another:

1. Choose the Rectangle tool **1**.
2. Drag diagonally to create a new rectangle **2**.
3. Choose any selection tool.
4. Shift-click or marquee the original type rectangle and the new, empty rectangle.
5. Choose Type menu > Blocks > Link. Overflow type from the first rectangle will flow into the new rectangle **3**.

TIP To add a type object to the end of a chain, use a selection tool to select the object you want to add and the object that you want to link it to, then choose Type menu > Blocks > Link.

To unlink two or more type objects:

1. Choose the Selection tool and click on one of the objects (all the linked objects will become selected).
2. Choose Type menu > Blocks > Unlink. All the objects will unlink; the type in each object will be separate and unlinked. *Note:* To rejoin the type, cut and paste it back into the original object using a type tool.

Link Type; Unlink Type

To remove one type object from a chain and keep the text stream intact:

1. Choose the Direct-selection (A or Shift-A).

2. Click on the edge of the type object to be removed.

3. Press Delete/Backspace twice. The type will reflow into the remaining objects. *Note:* To display the overflow symbol, select the remaining type.

To link overflow type to a copy of an existing non-rectangular object:

1. Turn on Smart Guides (Command-U/ Ctrl-U) or display your illustration in Artwork view (Command-Y/Ctrl-Y toggles Preview and Artwork views).

2. Choose the Direct-selection tool .

3. Click away from the type object to deselect it.

4. Click on the edge of the type object. The type should not be underlined after you click. Don't move the mouse yet!

5. Option-drag/Alt-drag a copy of the type object away from the original object. Option-Shift-drag/Alt-Shift-drag to constrain the movement to a multiple of 45°. Release the mouse, then release Option/ Alt (and Shift, if used). The overflow type will appear inside the new object **2**.

6. *Optional:* Choose Object menu > Transform > Transform Again (Command-D/Ctrl-D) to create additional linked boxes.

TIP If both the type and the type object are selected when you drag, a copy of the object *and* the type will be created, but it will not be linked to the first object.

TIP To change the order in which type flows from one object to another, change an objects' stacking order: Control-click/ Right-click and choose Arrange > Bring to Front, Send to Back, Bring Forward, or Send Backward.

TIP To create columns and rows of type, see page 202.

1 *Direct-selection tool.*

The kiss of memory made pictures of love and light against the wall. Here was peace.

She pulled in her horizon like a great fish-net. Pulled it from around the waist of the world and

2 *Overflow type from the first object appears in a **linked copy** of that object. (A paragraph indent was applied to the type to move it away from the edge of the objects.)*

Area Type tool.

 Vertical Area Type tool.

This is text in a copy of a light bulb shape. You can use the Area-Type tool to place type into any shape you can create. When fitting type into a round shape, place small words at the top and the bottom. This is text in a copy of a light bulb shape.

2 *Area type.*

The kiss of memory made pictures of love and light against the wall. Here was peace. She pulled in her horizon like a great fish-net. Pulled it from around the waist of the world and draped it over her shoulder. So much of life in its meshes! She called in her soul to come and see.
ZORA NEALE HURSTON

3 *Type in a circle.*

Use the Area Type or Vertical Area Type tool to place type inside a rectangle or an irregularly shaped path, or on an open path. The object you use will turn into a type path.

To enter type inside an object:

1. Choose either Area Type tool **1** if the object is an open or closed path, or choose either Type tool if the object is a closed path.

2. Click on the edge of the object. You must click precisely on the edge of the path. A flashing insertion marker will appear, and any fill or stroke on the object will be removed.

3. Enter type. It will stay inside the object and conform to its shape **2**–**3**. Vertical area type flows from top to bottom and from right to left. The smaller the type, the more snugly it will fit inside the shape. Justify it to make it hug both sides of the object, and turn on hyphenation.
   or
   Import text using File menu > Place (see page 176).

4. Choose a selection tool and click away from the type object to deselect it.
   or
   To keep the type tool selected so as to enter type in another object, press Command/Ctrl to temporarily access the last-used selection tool and click away from the type block to deselect it, then release Command/Ctrl and click on the next type object. You could also click again on the type tool you used to complete the type object.

TIP With any type tool selected, you can press Shift to toggle between the vertical or horizontal equivalent of that tool.

To switch type between horizontal and vertical:

1. Choose the Selection tool.

2. Click on a type block.

3. Choose Type menu > Type Orientation > Vertical or Horizontal.

Use the Path Type tool to place type on the inside or outside edge of a path. Type cannot be placed on both sides of the same path, but it can be moved from one side to the other after it's created. Only one line of type can be created per path.

To place type on an object's path:

1. Choose the Type, Path Type, Vertical Type, or Vertical Path Type tool 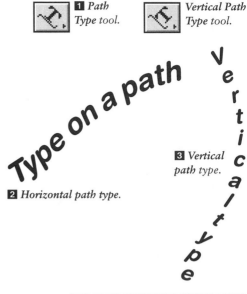.

2. Click on the top or bottom edge of the object. A flashing insertion marker will appear.

3. Enter type. Don't press Return/Enter. The type will appear along the edge of the object, and the object's fill and stroke will revert to None ❷–❸.

4. Choose a selection tool and click away from the type object to deselect it.
   or
   Click the type tool again if you want to enter type into a new type block.

To adjust the position of type on a path:

1. Choose the Selection or Direct-selection tool.

2. Click on the type.

3. Drag the I-beam to the left or the right along the edge of the path.
   or
   To flip the type to the other side of the path, move the I-beam inside the path or double-click the bottom of the I-beam.
   or
   To shift *all* the characters slightly toward or away from the center of the path, but keep their orientation, choose the Selection tool and click on or marquee the path. To shift *some* but not all of the characters, choose any type tool, and highlight the desired characters. Then choose a new number in the baseline shift area of the Character palette ❹–❻. (If the baseline shift field isn't visible, choose Show Options from the palette menu.)

❶ *Path Type tool.*

❸ *Vertical Path Type tool.*

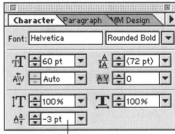

❸ *Vertical path type.*

❷ *Horizontal path type.*

❹ *The baseline shift field on the Character palette.*

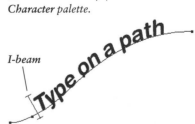

I-beam

❺ *Path type—normal baseline position.*

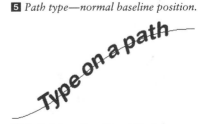

❻ *Path type—Baseline shifted downward.*

ITALICS INTO PHOTOSHOP

If you copy or drag-and-drop italic type characters in some fonts into Photoshop, part of the rightmost character may be cropped. To prevent this from happening, convert the characters into outlines before copying them.

To test whether an italic character will copy properly, select the character with any Type tool. Any portion of the character that extends beyond the highlight will be cropped.

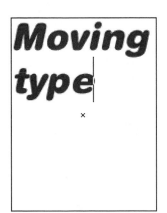

1 *Point type is **highlighted** and put on the Clipboard via the Cut command.*

2 *Then it's **pasted** into a rectangle.*

To copy or move type with or without its object, use the Clipboard, a temporary storage area in memory. The Clipboard commands are Cut, Copy, and Paste. You could also use the drag-and-drop method to move a type object (see page 75).

To copy type and its object between Illustrator documents or between Illustrator and Photoshop:

1. Choose the Selection tool.

2. Click on the edge of the object, on the type, or on the baseline of the type you want to copy.

3. Choose Edit menu > Copy (Command-C/Ctrl-C).

4. Click in another Illustrator document window, then choose Edit menu > Paste (Command-V/Ctrl-V). The type and its object will appear.
or
Click in a Photoshop document window, choose Edit menu > Paste, click Paste As Pixels, then click OK. The type and its object will appear on a new layer.

To move type from one object to another:

1. Choose any type tool.

2. Highlight the type (or a portion of the type) you want to move **1**.

3. Choose Edit menu > Cut (Command-X/Ctrl-X). When type is cut from a path, the path still remains a type object.

4. Click within a type block or in a type object to create a flashing insertion marker.

5. Choose Edit menu > Paste **2**.

The Create Outlines command converts each letter into a separate graphic object. As outlines, the paths can be reshaped, transformed, used in a compound or as a mask, or filled with a gradient, gradient mesh, or pattern—like any non-type object. Once type is converted into outlines, unless you Undo immediately, they can't be converted back into type again, nor can you change their font.

To create type outlines:

1. Create type using any type tool. *All* the characters in the type object or on the path are going to convert into outlines.

2. Choose the Selection tool.

3. If the type isn't already selected, click right on it or click on its baseline.

4. Choose Type menu > Create Outlines (Command-Shift-O/Ctrl-Shift-O) **1**–**3**.
   or
   Control-click/Right-click and choose Create Outlines from the context menu.

   The characters' original fill and stroke attributes will be preserved, but the path object will be deleted.

TIP To create accurate outlines, the Type 1 font (screen font and printer outlines) or TrueType font for the typeface you are using must be installed in your system or in Adobe's Font folder (see page 174). Otherwise, Illustrator will use a substitute font to recreate the missing font and the outlines for it.

TIP Group multiple outline paths together (Object menu > Group) to make it easier to select and move them.

TIP If the original character had an interior counter—as in an "A" or a "P"—the individual components (outside and inside shapes) will become a compound path after the Create Outlines conversion. If you want to divide the inside and outside parts of the type outline into separate objects, choose Object menu > Compound Paths > Release. To reassemble the components, select them both, then choose Object menu > Compound Paths > Make (see page 224).

The Create Outlines command is most suitable for creating logos or other large characters that require reshaping. And the printer fonts are not required in order to print such type outlines properly from another application. *However,* small type (i.e., body type) shouldn't be made into outlines, because the Create Outlines command removes the hinting information that is designed to preserve character shapes during printing. Outline "characters" are also slightly heavier than their pre-outline counterparts, and thus less legible, particularly if a stroke is applied to them.

1 *The original type.*

2 *The type converted into outlines (Artwork view).*

3 *The same outline type in Preview view.*

Type Outlines

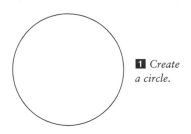

 *Create a circle.*

 — **2** *Path Type tool*

3 *Create path type on the top of the circle. The circle will have a stroke of None. (This is Artwork view.)*

4 *Option-drag/ Alt-drag the type I-beam to the bottom of the circle.*

5 *Select the type on the bottom of the circle, and type the words that you want to appear on the bottom.*

Putting type on both sides of a circle, and having all of it read vertically, requires creating two circles.

Exercise

Type on a circle

Type on the top

1. Open the Character and Color palettes.

2. Choose File menu > Preferences > Units & Undo, then choose General: Inches.

3. Choose the Ellipse tool (L or Shift-L), then click on the artboard (don't drag).

4. Enter "3" in the Width field, click the word "Height," then click OK **1**.

5. On the Character palette, enter 24 in the Size field and choose a font.

6. Choose the Path Type tool (T or Shift-T) **2**.

7. Click on the top of the circle, then type the text that you want to appear on the top of the circle ("TYPE ON THE TOP," in our example) **3**.

8. Choose the Selection tool, then drag the I–beam to the left to reposition the type.

Type on the bottom

1. Option-drag/Alt-drag the I-beam into the circle and position the type copy on the inside bottom of the circle **4**.

2. Choose Path Type tool (T or Shift-T) and click on the bottom type.

3. Select the type on the bottom using the Path Type tool, type the words that you want to appear there **5**, then reselect the type.

4. On the Character palette, enter a negative value in the baseline shift field to

(Continued on the following page)

Type on a Circle

move the type downward (the appropriate amount will depend on the typeface and type size) . Try around -15 or -20 first. Then deselect the type.

5. Choose the Selection tool (V), then reposition the bottom type as necessary, but don't drag it outside the circle.

6. Marquee the two circles.

7. If the type needs recoloring, apply a fill color and a stroke of None to each type block.

   Note: Make sure the Type Area Select box is checked in File menu > Preferences > Type & Auto Tracing to make it easier to select the type.

8. Choose Object menu > Group (Command-G/Ctrl-G) . To recolor either circle, use the Direct-selection tool.

TIP Set the baseline shift field back to zero (with no type selected) to prevent the negative baseline shift value from being applied to any subsequently-created type.

6 *Baseline shift the path type on the bottom of the circle downward, and center it on the circle.*

7 *The final type. The circles still have a stroke of None.*

In this chapter you will learn how to select type and apply character-based typographic attributes using the Character palette (font, size, leading, kerning, tracking, baseline shift, and horizontal and vertical scaling) and how to apply paragraph-based attributes using the Paragraph palette (alignment, indentation, inter-paragraph spacing, and word and letter spacing).

You'll learn to use Illustrator's word processing features to check spelling, export text, find and replace fonts or text, create text rows and columns, apply professional typesetter's marks, auto hyphenate, apply tabs, change case, and hang punctuation. And finally, you'll learn how to sample and apply type attributes using the Eyedropper tool, wrap text around an object, create shadow type, and create slanted type.

Before you can modify type, you must select it. If you use the **Selection** tool, both the type and its object will be selected **1**. If you use the **Direct-selection** tool, you can select the type object alone or the type object *and* the type **2**. If you use a **type** tool to select type, only the type itself will be selected, not the type object **3**.

Select Type

If we
shadows
have
offended,
Think but
this—
and all is
mended—

If we
shadows
have
offended,
Think but
this —
and all is
mended—

If we
shadows
have
offended,
Think but
this —
and all is
mended—

William Shakespeare

1 *Type and type object selected with the* **Selection** *tool.*

2 *Type object selected with the* **Direct-selection** *tool.*

3 *Type (but not its object) selected with the* **Type** *tool.*

Note: Use this selection method if you want to move, transform, restyle, or recolor a *whole type block*. To reshape or recolor a type *object*, use the first selection method on the next page. To edit type or to restyle or recolor *part* of a type *block*, use the second selection method on the next page.

To select type and its object:

1. Choose the Selection tool ▮.

2. Turn on Smart Guides (Command-U/ Ctrl-U), with Object Highlighting (File menu > Preferences > Smart Guides).

3. With the Type Area Select box checked in File menu > Preferences > Type & Auto Tracing, click on the type. Or click inside the type object if the object has a fill.
   or
   In Artwork view, click on the edge of the type object. In Preview view, click on the Smart Guide (Object Highlighting).
   or
   To select point type, click on the little "x" preceding the first character ▮. The "x" is always visible in Artwork view; in Preview view, the "x" is a Smart Guide.
   or
   Click on the baseline of any character ▮.

   If you select point type (type that's created by clicking, then entering text with the Type or Vertical Type tool), the type will have a solid anchor point before the first character and each line will be underlined. The bounding box will also display, if that option is turned on in File menu > Preferences > General.

TIP To modify the paint attributes of type, use the Color palette (see Chapter 9).

TIP To move, scale, rotate, shear, or reflect type, use a command on the Object menu > Transform submenu or use a transform tool.

Double-click on a type block with any selection tool—the Type tool will select automatically.

 ▮ *Selection tool.*

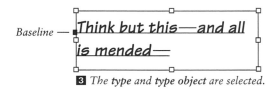

ₓThink but this—and all is mended—

▮ *For **point type** in **Artwork** view, click on the "**x**." Or click on the type itself if Type Area Select is turned on.*

Baseline — *Think but this—and all is mended—*

▮ *The type and type object are selected.*

1 *Direct-selection tool.*

Think but this—and all is mended—

2 *Only the **type object** is selected; the type is not.*

Think but this—
and all is mended— ◄---

3 *The **type object** is reshaped.*

ₓMy line drawing is the purest and most direct translation of my emotion.

Henri Matisse

4 *Two words are selected.*

Use this selection method if you want to reshape a type object (and thus reflow the type) or recolor a type object.

To select a type object but not the type:

1. Choose the Direct-selection tool **1**.

2. Click on the edge of the type object **2**–**3**. Use Smart Guides (Object Highlighting) to assist you, or go to Artwork view. Now, modifications you make will only affect the type object, and not the type.

Use this selection method if you want to edit all or a portion of a type block, or change its character, paragraph, or paint attributes.

To select type but not its object:

1. Choose any type tool.

2. Drag horizontally (for horizontal type) with the I-beam pointer to select and highlight a word or a line of type **4**.
   or
   Drag vertically (for horizontal type) to select lines of type.
   or
   Double-click to select a word.
   or
   Triple-click to select a paragraph.
   or
   Click in the text block, then choose Edit menu > Select All (Command-A/Ctrl-A) to select all the type in the block or on the path, including any type to which it is linked.
   or
   Click to start the selection, then Shift-click where you want the selection to end. (You can also Shift-click to extend a selection.)

3. After modifying the type, click anywhere on the type block to deselect it and keep the flashing insertion marker in the type block for further editing.
   or
   Choose a selection tool and click away from the type object to deselect it.

TIP To select vertical type, with any type tool, drag vertically to select a line or drag horizontally to select lines.

Select Type

The type palettes

Press **Tab** to apply a value in a highlighted field on a palette and move to the next field on that palette. Press **Return/Enter** to apply a value and exit the palette. Press **Shift-Return/Shift-Enter** to apply a value and keep the field highlighted.

Character palette

Use the Character palette (Command-T/Ctrl-T) to modify font, type size, leading, kerning, and tracking values in one or more highlighted text characters . Choose Show Options from the palette menu to expand the palette for baseline shift, and horizontal and vertical scale adjustments.

1 *The Character palette.*

Paragraph palette

Use the Paragraph palette (Command-M/Ctrl-M) to modify paragraph-wide attributes, such as alignment and indentation **2**. Choose Show Options from the palette menu to expand the palette for word spacing, letter spacing, auto hyphenation, hanging punctuation, and East Asian font options.

To change the paragraph attributes of *all* the text in a type object or on a path, select the object or path with the Selection tool. To isolate a paragraph or series of paragraphs, select just those paragraphs with a type tool.

Note: A paragraph is created when the Return/Enter key is pressed within a type block. Choose Type menu > Show Hidden Characters to reveal symbols for line breaks and spaces.

TIP The font, size, and tracking values of selected type display on, but can't be changed using, the Info palette (Window menu > Show Info) **3**.

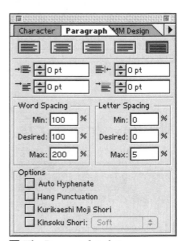

2 *The Paragraph palette.*

MM Design palette

Use the **Multiple Master** Palette to modify the weight and width of characters in a multiple master (MM) font **4**. Choose Type menu > MM Design when text in a MM font is highlighted. The axes that can be adjusted vary depending on the MM font. Multiple Master fonts are useful if you require a type style that's slightly slimmer or heavier than an existing style.

3 *The Info palette.*

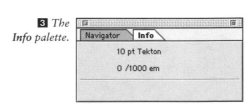

4 *The MM Design palette.*

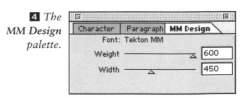

 **1** *The Type tool.*

2 *Select the type you want to modify.*

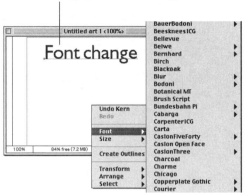

3 *Then choose a font from the context menu.*

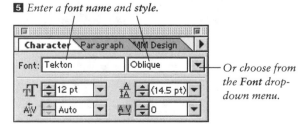

4 *The font is changed from Gill Sans Bold to Bodoni Poster.*

You can, of course, choose a font before entering your text—just skip the type selection step.

To choose a font:

1. Choose any type tool **1**, then select the type you want to modify **2**.
   or
   Choose the Selection tool, then click on the type object.

2. Control-click/Right-click on the type and choose a font from the Font submenu on the context menu **3**–**4**.
   or
   On the Character palette, choose a font from the Font drop-down menu, and choose from a submenu if the font name has an arrowhead next to it. Or type the name of a font and the name of a style in the Font fields, then press Return/Enter. You need only enter the first few letters of the font name or style—the name or style with the closest spelling match will appear in the field **5**. For the Roman or Regular style of a font, type only the font name (not the style), then press Return/Enter.

TIP You can also choose from the Type menu > Font submenu.

TIP Press Command-Option-Shift-M/Ctrl-Alt-Shift-M to quickly highlight the Font field on the Character palette. The palette will open, if it isn't open already.

Choose a Font

5 *Enter a font name and style.*

Character	Paragraph	M Design
Font: Tekton	Oblique	

Or choose from the Font drop-down menu.

The Character palette.

189

To resize type:

1. Choose any type tool, then select the type you want to modify.
   or
   Choose the Selection tool, then click on the type object.

2. *On the Character palette:*

   Enter a point size in the Size field (.1–1296), then press Return/Enter to apply, or press Tab to apply the value and highlight the next field 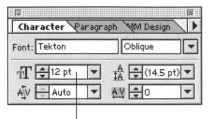–**2**. You don't need to reenter the unit of measure. *Note:* If the type you have selected contains more than one point size, the Size field will be blank. Entering a size now will change all selected type to the new size.
   or
   Choose a preset size from the Size drop-down menu or click the up or down arrow. Or click in the Size field, then press the up or down arrow on the keyboard.
   or
   To resize type via the keyboard, hold down Command-Shift/Ctrl-Shift and press ">" to enlarge or "<" to reduce. The increment the type resizes each time you use this shortcut is specified in the Size/Leading field in File menu > Preferences > Type & Auto Tracing. Two points is the default increment.

   To choose a size via the context menu:
   Control-click/Right-click on the type and choose a preset size from the context menu. Choosing Other from the context menu highlights the size field on the Character palette.

   TIP If you use the Undo command while entering a value on the Character palette, that field will stay highlighted.

   TIP Other methods for resizing type: Choose a preset size from the Type menu > Size submenu. Or select the point or path type using the Selection tool, then drag a bounding box handle (hold down Shift to scale uniformly). Or scale type and its object using the Scale tool.

1 *On the* ***Character*** *palette, enter a number in the* ***Size*** *field, or choose a preset size from the drop-down menu.*

Origami
Origami

2 *Type enlarged.*

FITTING TYPE TO ITS CONTAINER

To track horizontal or vertical type outward to the edges of a text rectangle or type container, choose any type tool, highlight a one-line paragraph, then choose Type menu > Fit Headline **3**–**4**. When the Fit Headline command is applied to a Multiple Master font, both the weight and tracking of the text are adjusted.

3 *The original, selected characters.*

Fit Headline

4 *After applying the* ***Fit Headline*** *command.*

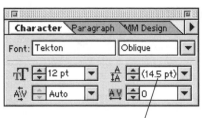

1 *On the* **Character** *palette, enter the desired leading in points in the* **Leading** *field, or choose Auto or a preset leading amount from the drop-down menu.*

ACT III

Scene I

The Wood. The QUEEN OF FAIRIES *lying asleep.*

Enter QUINCE, SNUG, BOTTOM, FLUTE, SNOUT, *and* STARVELING.

Bot. Are we all met?

Quin. Pat, pat; and here is a marvellous convenient place for our rehearsal. This green plot shall be our stage, this hawthorn brake our tiring-house; and we will do it in action, as we will do it before the duke.

2

Loose **leading** *(8-point type; 12 point leading)*

ACT III

Scene I

The Wood. The QUEEN OF FAIRIES *lying asleep.*

Enter QUINCE, SNUG, BOTTOM, FLUTE, SNOUT, *and* STARVELING.

Bot. Are we all met?
Quin. Pat, pat; and here is a marvellous convenient place for our rehearsal. This green plot shall be our stage, this hawthorn brake our tiring-house; and we will do it in action, as we will do it before the duke.

3

Tight **leading** *(8-point type; 8.75 point leading)*

Leading is the distance from baseline to baseline between lines of type, and it is traditionally measured in points. Each line of type in a block can have a different leading amount. (To add space between paragraphs, follow the instructions on page 196.)

To change leading:

1. *Select the type you want to modify:*

Click anywhere in a type block with the Selection tool to change the leading of the entire block.

or

Highlight an entire paragraph with a type tool (triple-click anywhere in the paragraph) to change the leading of all the lines in that paragraph.

or

Highlight an entire line with a type tool (including the space at the end, if there is one) to change the leading of only that line.

2. *On the Character palette:*

Enter a number in the Leading field, then press Return/Enter or Tab to apply **1**–**3**.

or

Choose a preset leading amount from the Leading drop-down menu or click the up or down arrow.

or

Choose Auto from the drop-down menu to set the leading to 120% of the largest type size on each line.

or

To make the leading value match the point size, double-click the leading button.

TIP Option-press/Alt-press the up arrow on the keyboard to decrease leading in selected horizontal text or the down arrow to increase leading. The increment leading changes each time you use this shortcut is specified in the Size/Leading field in File menu > Preferences > Type & Auto Tracing.

Leading

Kerning is the adjustment of the space between *two adjacent* characters. All fonts have kerning pairs built into them, and body text sizes usually don't require manual kerning. Words or phrases set in larger sizes, on the other hand, like headlines or logos, usually require careful manual kerning to add or remove awkward spacing between character pairs. To kern a pair of characters, the cursor must be inserted between them.

Tracking is the simultaneous adjustment of the space between *three or more* characters. It's normally applied to a range of type—a paragraph or a line. To track type, first highlight the range of type you want to track using a type tool, or select an entire type block with a selection tool.

To kern or track type:

1. Choose a type tool, then click to create an insertion point between the two characters you want to kern or highlight the range of text you want to track.
   or
   To track all the type in an object, choose the Selection tool, then click on the object.

2. In the Kerning or Tracking field on the Character palette, enter a positive number to add space between characters or a negative number to remove space, then press Return/Enter or Tab to apply **1**–**4**.
   or
   Choose a preset kerning or tracking amount from the drop-down menu or click the up or down arrow.
   or
   Hold down Option/Alt and press the right arrow on the keyboard to add space between letters or the left arrow to remove space between letters. The amount of space that is added or removed each time you press an arrow is specified in the Tracking field in File menu > Preferences > Type & Auto Tracing. Add Command/Ctrl to the shortcut to track in larger increments.
   or
   Use this shortcut: Command-Shift-[or]/ Ctrl-Shift-[or].

SPACING OUT

- To adjust the overall word or letter spacing in a text block, use the Word Spacing and Letter Spacing fields on the Paragraph palette (see page 196).

- Every font has built-in kerning pairs for improved inter-character spacing. To enable this feature, select the text you want to affect, then choose Auto from the Kerning drop-down menu on the Character palette (see the Figure **1** below). But do this before manual kerning. Choose or enter 0 to turn this feature off.

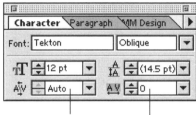

1 *Kerning field and drop-down menu.* *Tracking field and drop-down menu.*

2 *Normal type.*

3 *Space added between the first two characters (kerning).*

4 *Space removed between the last five characters (kerning or tracking).*

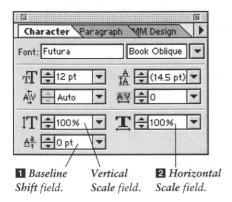

1 *Baseline Shift* field. *Vertical Scale* field. **2** *Horizontal Scale* field.

Type on a Path

3 *Characters on a path, baseline shifted downward.*

Alicia

4 *The "A" baseline shifted 9 points downward.*

5 DANIELLE

Normal type (no scaling).

DANIELLE

75% horizontal scale.

DANIELLE

125% horizontal scale.

IMPOSTER

You can stylize any typeface using a scale command, but a Multiple Master typeface or a typeface that has been extended or condensed by its designer (i.e. Univers Extended or Helvetica Narrow) will look much better, because its weight, proportions, and counters (interior spaces) are adjusted specifically for that typeface.

The Baseline Shift command repositions characters above or below the baseline. You can use this command to offset curved path type from its path or to create superscript or subscript characters (there is no superscript or subscript type style in Illustrator).

To baseline shift type:

1. Highlight the type you want to modify.

2. In the Baseline Shift field on the Character palette (choose Show Options from the palette menu if the field isn't visible), enter a positive number to baseline shift characters upward or a negative number to baseline shift characters downward, then press Return/Enter to apply **1**, **3**–**4**. Or choose a preset amount from the drop-down menu or click the up or down arrow.

or

Option-Shift-press/Alt-Shift-press the up arrow to shift highlighted characters upward, or the down arrow to shift characters downward. The amount type shifts each time you press an arrow is specified in the Baseline Shift field in File menu > Preferences > Type & Auto Tracing.

The Horizontal Scale option extends (widens) or condenses (narrows) type. The Vertical Scale option makes type taller or shorter. The default scale is 100%.

To horizontally/vertically scale type:

1. Select the type you want to modify.

2. Enter a higher or lower percentage in the Horizontal or Vertical Scale field on the Character palette, then press Return/Enter or Tab to apply **2** and **5**. Or choose a preset amount from the drop-down menu or click the up or down arrow.

TIP To scale point or path type manually, select it using the Selection tool, then drag a midpoint handle of its bounding box. To scale a selected type block, double-click the Scale tool and change the Non-Uniform: Horizontal or Vertical value.

Baseline Shift; Horizontal/Vertical Scale

Alignment and indent values affect whole paragraphs. To create a new paragraph (hard return) in a text block, press **Return/Enter**. Type preceding a return is part of one paragraph; type following a return is part of the next paragraph. Type that wraps automatically is part of the same paragraph. To create a line break (soft return) within a paragraph in non-tabular text, press **Shift-Return/Shift-Enter**.

To change paragraph alignment:

1. Choose a type tool, then click in a paragraph or drag through a series of paragraphs.
   or
   Choose a selection tool and select a type object.

2. On the Paragraph palette, click the Align Left, Align Center, Align Right, Justify Full Lines, or Justify All Lines alignment button **1**–**2**.
   or
   Use one of the keyboard shortcuts listed at right.

TIP Don't apply Justify Full Lines or Justify All Lines alignment to path type or to point type (type that's not in an object or in a block), because there are no container edges to justify the type against.

PARAGRAPH ALIGNMENT SHORTCUTS	
Left	Command-Shift-L/Ctrl-Shift-L
Center	Command-Shift-C/Ctrl-Shift-C
Right Justify	Command-Shift-R/Ctrl-Shift-R
Justify Full Lines	Command-Shift-J/Ctrl-Shift-J
Justify All Lines	Command-Shift-F/Ctrl-Shift-F

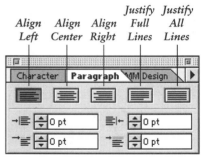

1 *The five* **Alignment** *buttons on the* **Paragraph** *palette.*

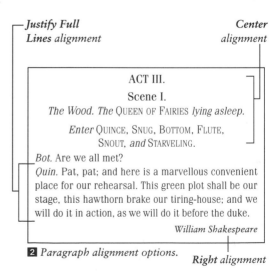

2 *Paragraph alignment options.*

HOW TO SELECT PARAGRAPHS FOR MODIFICATION

If you want to change paragraph attributes for *all* the text in a type object or on a path, select the object or path with the Selection tool. To isolate a paragraph or series of paragraphs, select just those paragraphs with a type tool.

Left Indent   *Right Indent*

First Line Left Indent

1 *The Indent fields on the Paragraph palette. If you forget which one is which, rest the mouse over an icon—the tool tip will remind you.*

Left and Right Indent values affect area type; only a Left Indent value will affect point type.

To change paragraph indentation:

1. Choose a type tool, then select the paragraph(s) you want to modify or click an insertion point in a single paragraph.
   or
   Choose a selection tool, then select a type object.

2. *On the Paragraph palette:*
   Enter a new number in the Left or Right Indent field, then press Return/Enter or Tab to apply **1**–**2**.
   or
   Click the up or down arrow.
   or
   To indent only the first line of each paragraph, enter a number in the First Line Left Indent field.

TIP You can enter a negative value in the Left Indent, First Line Left Indent, or Right Indent field to expand the measure of each line. The type will be pushed outside its object, but it will still display and print **3**.

ACT II.

Scene I.

A Wood near Athens.

Enter a FAIRY *at one door, and* PUCK *at another.*
Puck. How now, spirit! whither wander you?
Fai.   Over hill, over dale,
        Thorough bush, thorough brier,
        Over park, over pale,
        Thorough flood, thorough fire,
        I do wander everywhere,
        Swifter than the moon's sphere;

2 *Left Indentation.*

ACT III.

Scene I.

The Wood. The QUEEN OF FAIRIES *lying asleep.*

   Enter QUINCE, SNUG, BOTTOM, FLUTE,
          SNOUT, *and* STARVELING.

Bot.   Are we all met?
Quin. Pat, pat; and here is a marvellous convenient place for our rehearsal. This green plot shall be our stage, this hawthorn brake our tiring-house; and we will do it in action, as we will do it before the duke.

William Shakespeare

3 *To create a* **hanging indent,** *as in the last paragraph in this illustration, enter a number in the* **Left Indent** *field and the same number with a minus sign in front of it in the* **First Line Left Indent** *field.*

Use the Space Before Paragraph field on the Paragraph palette to add or subtract space *between* paragraphs in area type. Point type isn't modified by this feature. (To adjust the spacing between lines of type *within* a paragraph (leading), see page 191.)

To adjust inter-paragraph spacing:

1. Select the type you want to modify. To modify the space before only one paragraph in a type block, select the paragraph with a type tool. To change all the type in an object, select the object with the Selection tool.

2. In the Space Before Paragraph field on the Paragraph palette **1**, enter a positive value to move paragraphs apart or a negative value to move them closer together, then press Return/Enter or Tab to apply **2**.
   or
   Click the up or down arrow.

   TIP To create a new paragraph (hard return), press Return/Enter. To create a line break within a paragraph (soft return), press Shift-Return/Shift-Enter.

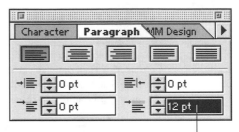

1 *The Space Before Paragraph field on the Paragraph palette.*

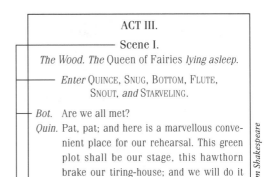

ACT III.

Scene I.

The Wood. The Queen of Fairies lying asleep.

Enter QUINCE, SNUG, BOTTOM, FLUTE, SNOUT, *and* STARVELING.

Bot. Are we all met?

Quin. Pat, pat; and here is a marvellous convenient place for our rehearsal. This green plot shall be our stage, this hawthorn brake our tiring-house; and we will do it in action, as we will do it before the duke.

William Shakespeare

2 *Higher Space Before Paragraph values were applied to these paragraphs to enlarge the space above them.*

WORD AND LETTER SPACING

To change the horizontal word or letter spacing for justified paragraphs, change the percentage in the Minimum, Desired, or Maximum Word Spacing or Letter Spacing fields on the Paragraph palette **3**–**5** (choose Show Options from the Paragraph palette menu if these options aren't visible). Non-justified type is only affected by the Desired value. Headlines are usually improved by reduced word spacing.

Ocean

Body more immaculate than a wave, salt washing away its own line, and the brilliant bird flying without ground roots.

Pablo Neruda

3 *Normal word and letter spacing.*

Ocean

Body more immaculate than a wave, salt washing away its own line, and the brilliant bird flying without ground roots.

4 *Loose letter spacing.*

Ocean

Body more immaculate than a wave, salt washing away its own line, and the brilliant bird flying without ground roots.

5 *Tight word spacing.*

Use the Find/Change command to search for and replace characters.

To find and replace text:

1. *Optional:* Click with a type tool to create an insertion point from which to start the search. If you don't do this, the search will begin from the most recently created object.

2. Choose Type menu > Find/Change.

3. Enter a word or phrase to search for in the "Find what" field **1**.

4. Enter a replacement word or phrase in the "Change to" field **2**. Leave the "Change to" field blank to delete instances of the "Find what" text altogether.

5. *Do any of these optional steps:*

Check the Whole Word box to find the "Find what" letters only if they appear as a complete word—not as part of a larger word.

Check the Case Sensitive box to find only those instances that match the exact uppercase/lowercase configuration of the "Find what" text.

Check the Wrap Around box to search the whole file from the current cursor position to the end of the text object or string of linked objects and then continue the search from the most recently created object. With Wrap Around unchecked, the search will proceed only from the current cursor position forward to the end of that text object; you'll have to click Find Next to resume the search.

Check the Search Backward box to search backward from the current cursor position.

6. Click **Find Next** to search for the first instance of the "Find what" word or phrase or to skip over a word **3**.

7. Click **Change** to replace only the currently found instance of the "Find what" text.
or
Click **Change All** to replace all instances at once **4**.
or
Click **Change/Find** to replace the current instance and search for the next instance.

8. Click Done.

TIP Bug alert: The corrected word will take on the styling of the text preceding it and lose its original styling.

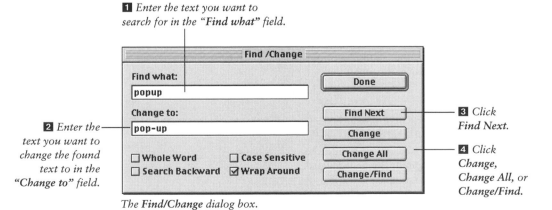

1 *Enter the text you want to search for in the "Find what" field.*

2 *Enter the text you want to change the found text to in the "Change to" field.*

3 *Click Find Next.*

4 *Click Change, Change All, or Change/Find.*

The Find/Change dialog box.

Find and Replace Text

The Check Spelling command checks spelling in an entire document using a built-in dictionary. You can also create and edit your own word list.

To check spelling:

1. Choose Type menu > Check Spelling. Any words not found in the application or user dictionary will appear on the Misspelled Words list **1**.

2. Leave the currently highlighted Misspelled Word selected or click a different word on the list. The selected misspelled word will be highlighted in your illustration.

3. *Optional:* Check the Case Sensitive box to display the Misspelled Word both ways if it appears in both upper and lower case (such as *Spelle* and *spelle*).

4. If the correctly spelled word appears on the **Suggested Corrections** list, double-click it **2**. Or to change all instances of the misspelled word instead, click the correctly spelled word, then click **Change All**. The next misspelled word will now become highlighted.
    or
    If the correct word doesn't appear on the list, or no words appear at all (because there are no similar words in Illustrator's dictionary), type the correctly spelled word in the entry field at the bottom of the dialog box. Then click **Change** to change only the first instance of the highlighted Misspelled Word to the currently highlighted Suggested Correction, or click **Change All** to change all instances of the Misspelled Word.

    For any word, you can click **Skip** to leave the current instance of the Misspelled Word as is or click **Skip All** to leave all instances of the Misspelled Word as is.

5. *Optional:* Click Add to List to add the currently highlighted Misspelled Word or Words to the Learned Words list (which is in Plug-ins > Text Filters > AI User Dictionary).

6. If you spell-check all the Misspelled Words, a prompt will appear. Click OK,

CHECK SPELLING IN DUTCH?

Click Language in the Check Spelling dialog box, locate and highlight the dictionary you want to use in Adobe Illustrator 8 folder > Plug-ins > Text Filters, then click Select.

Note: The Check Spelling command can only be used with Roman fonts, not with Chinese, Japanese, or Korean fonts.

1 *Misspelled words.*

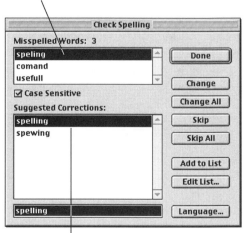

2 *Correctly spelled replacement words.*

*Click **Done** when you're finished.*

Click a Misspelled Word.

*Click **Change** or **Change All**.*

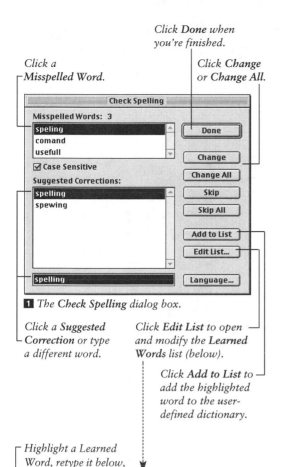

1 *The Check Spelling dialog box.*

Click a Suggested Correction or type a different word.

*Click **Edit List** to open and modify the **Learned Words** list (below).*

*Click **Add to List** to add the highlighted word to the user-defined dictionary.*

*Highlight a Learned Word, retype it below, then click **Change**.*

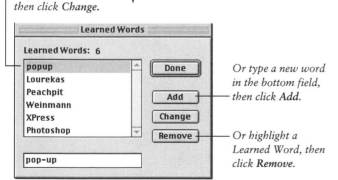

*Or type a new word in the bottom field, then click **Add**.*

*Or highlight a Learned Word, then click **Remove**.*

2 *Create your own word list using the **Learned Words** dialog box.*

then click Done. You can also click Done at any time to stop spell-checking.

TIP Bug alert: The corrected word will take on the styling of the text preceding it and lose its original styling.

To edit the user-defined dictionary:

1. If the Check Spelling dialog box isn't open, choose Type menu > Check Spelling **1**.

2. Click Edit List to open the Learned Words list dialog box **2**.

3. Click on a word in the list, correct it in the field at the bottom of the dialog box, then click **Change**.
   or
   Click on a word, then click **Remove**.
   or
   Type a completely new word, then click **Add**. Hyphenated words—like "pop-up" —are permitted.

Use the Export command to save Illustrator text in a format that can be imported into another application.

To export text:

1. Select the text you want to export with a type tool or a selection tool.

2. Choose File menu > Export.

3. Choose a location in which to save the text file 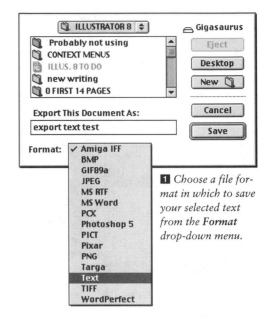.

4. Enter a name for the new file in the Export This Document As field.

5. Choose a file format from the Format drop-down menu (Macintosh) or Save as Type drop-down menu (Windows).

6. Click Save.

7. If another dialog box opens, choose further options, and then click OK.

1 *Choose a file format in which to save your selected text from the* **Format** *drop-down menu.*

The Find Font command can be used to generate a list of the fonts currently being used in an illustration. Or it can be used to actually replace fonts. The type color, kerning/tracking, and other attributes are retained.

To find and replace a font:

1. Choose Type menu > Find Font.

2. Check any of the following Include in List boxes to selectively display only fonts of those types on the scroll lists: Multiple Master, Standard, Type 1, Roman, TrueType, or CID. For Multiple Master fonts, you must also check the Type 1 box.

3. To have the replacement font list display only fonts of the types checked in step 2 that are currently being used in your document, leave the Replace Font From menu option on Document.

   or

   Choose System from the Replace Font From drop-down menu to display on the replacement font list all the fonts currently available in your system.

4. Click a font to search for on the Fonts in Document scroll list **2**. The first instance of that font will be highlighted in your document.

5. Click a replacement font on the replacement font list.

6. Click **Change** to change only the current instance of the currently highlighted font.
or
Click **Change All** to change all instances of the currently highlighted font. Once all the instances of a font are replaced, that font is removed from the Fonts in Document list.
or
Click **Find Next** to search for the next instance of the currently highlighted font.
or
Click **Skip** to leave the current instance of the font unchanged and move on to the next instance of the font in your document.

7. *Optional:* To save a list of the fonts currently being used in the illustration as a text document, click Save List, enter a name, choose a location in which to save the file, then click Save. The text document can later be opened directly from the Desktop (Mac) or it can be imported into a text editing or layout application.

Click Done (Return/Enter).

*Choose **System** from the **Replace Font From** drop-down menu to display on the replacement font list all available fonts of the types checked, or choose **Document** to list only the fonts currently being used in your illustration.*

2 *Click on a font to search for on the **Fonts in Document** scroll list.*

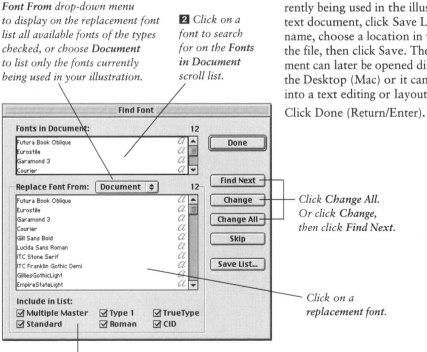

*Click **Change All.** Or click **Change,** then click **Find Next.***

Click on a replacement font.

Uncheck font types to narrow the selection of replacement fonts.

Find and Replace Fonts

To arrange text in linked rows and columns:

1. Select one text object with the Selection tool or select a series of linked text objects.

2. Choose Type menu > Rows & Columns.

3. Check the Preview box to apply changes immediately 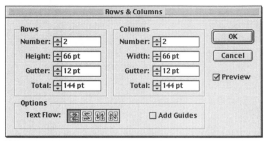.

4. Click the up or down arrow or enter values in the fields to choose:

   The total Number of Rows and Columns to be produced.
   and
   The Height of each Row and the Width of each Column.
   and
   The Gutter (space) between each Row and each Column.
   and
   The Total width and Total height of the entire block of Rows and Columns. If you change the Total values, the height or width of the boxes will change, but the gutter values will remain constant.

5. Click a different Text Flow button to control the direction of the text flow.

6. *Optional:* Check the Add Guides box to make guides appear around the text blocks. Make sure the ruler origin is in the correct location.

7. Click OK (Return/Enter) **2**–**3**.

TIP If you select the entire block of rows and columns with the Selection tool and then reopen the Rows & Columns dialog box, the current settings for that block will be displayed.

1 *The Rows & Columns dialog box.*

Hey! diddle, diddle,
The cat and the Fiddle,
The cow jumped over the moon;
The little dog laugh'd
To see such sport,
And the dish ran away with the spoon.

2 *One text object...*

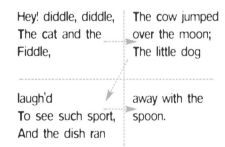

3 *...converted into two rows and two columns.*

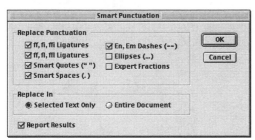

1 *Check* **Replace Punctuation** *options in the* **Smart Punctuation** *dialog box.*

Dialog box option	*Keyboard*	*Smart punctuation*
ff, fi, ffi Ligatures	ff, fi, ffi	ff, fi, ffi
ff, fl, ffl Ligatures	ff, fi, ffl	ff, fi, ffl
Smart Quotes	' "	' " " '
Smart Spaces (one space after a period)	. T	. T
En [dashes]	--	—
Em Dashes	---	—
Ellipses	...	...
Expert Fractions	1/2	½

The Smart Punctuation command converts keyboard punctuation into professional typesetter's marks.

To create smart punctuation:

1. *Optional:* Select text with the Type tool to smart-punctuate that text only. Otherwise, the command will affect the entire document.

2. Choose Type menu > Smart Punctuation.

3. Check any of the Replace Punctuation boxes **1**.

4. Click Replace In: Selected Text Only if you selected text for step 1, otherwise click Entire Document.

5. *Optional:* Check Report Results to display a list of your changes.

6. Click OK (Return/Enter) **2**–**3**.

TIP To apply Ligatures and Expert Fractions, the Adobe Expert font set for the font you are using must be available in your system.

Smart Punctuation

He supposed Miss Petiigrew might have leaned over the sugar bowl and said, "Mayor," which Daddy said was all she ever called him any-more, "I'd be pleased to have a chimpanzee." And Daddy supposed the mayor frumped him-self up a little and muddied his expression and said, "Sister darling, your chimpanzee is just around the corner."

    "Louis!" Momma said. Daddy was hardly ever a very big hit with Momma.

2 *Dumb punctuation: Straight quotes and two spaces after each period.*

He supposed Miss Petiigrew might have leaned over the sugar bowl and said, "Mayor," which Daddy said was all she ever called him any-more, "I'd be pleased to have a chimpanzee." And Daddy supposed the mayor frumped him-self up a little and muddied his expression and said, "Sister darling, your chimpanzee is just around the corner."

    "Louis!" Momma said. Daddy was hardly ever a very big hit with Momma.

T.R. Pearson

3 *Smart punctuation: Curly quotes and one space after each period.*

To turn on auto hyphenation:

1. Auto hyphenation affects only currently selected or subsequently created text. If you want to hyphenate existing text, select it with a type tool now.

2. Check the Options: Auto Hyphenate box on the Paragraph palette **1**. (If this option isn't visible, choose Show Options from the palette menu.)

3. To choose hyphenation options, choose Hyphenation from the Paragraph palette menu.

4. In the "Hyphenate [ ] letters from beginning" field, enter the minimum number of characters to precede any hyphen **2**. Fewer than three letters before or after a hyphen can impair readability.

5. In the "Hyphenate [ ] letters from end" field, enter the minimum number of characters to carry over onto the next line following a hyphen **3**.

6. In the "Limit consecutive hyphens to" field, enter the maximum allowable number of hyphens in a row **4**. More than two hyphens in a row impairs readability and looks unsightly.

7. Click OK (Return/Enter).

TIP To hyphenate using rules of a different language for selected text in the current document only, choose Show Multilingual from the Character palette menu, then choose from the Language drop-down menu. You can change the hyphenation language for the application in File menu > Preferences > Hyphenation Options. You can also enter hyphenation exceptions or specify how particular words are to be hyphenated in that dialog box.

TIP To hyphenate a word manually: Command-Shift--(hyphen)/Ctrl-Shift--.

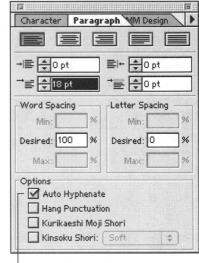

1 Check the **Auto Hyphenate** box on the **Paragraph** palette.

AN
OVER-
ABUN-
DANCE
OF
HYP-
HENS
MAKES
FOR
TIR-
ING
READ-
ING
(SIC).

2 Minimum number of characters preceding a hyphen.

3 Minimum number of characters after a hyphen.

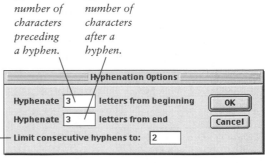

4 Maximum number of hyphens in a row.

Auto Hyphenation

OUT OF HIDING

To show the tab characters that are hidden in your text, along with other non-printing characters like spaces and line breaks, choose Type menu > Show Hidden Characters. Tab characters display as right-pointing arrows. Choose the command again to turn it off.

The Tab Ruler palette is used to set custom left-, center-, right-, and decimal-justified tabs in horizontal type, and top-, center-, bottom-, and decimal-justified tabs in vertical type. Default tab stops are half an inch apart.

To insert tabs into text:

Press Tab as you input copy before typing each new column. The cursor will jump to the next tab stop.

or

To add a tab to already inputted text, click just to the left of the text that is to start a new column, then press Tab.

Basic Plaid Country Club			
	Front 9	**Back 9**	**Total**
Tiger	34	36	70
Jack	38	44	82
Lee	42	48	90
Hubie	34	35	69

Text aligned using custom tab stops.

To set or modify custom tab stops:

1. Choose the Selection tool, then select a text object that contains tab characters.
   or
   Choose a type tool and select text that contains tab characters.

2. Choose Type menu > Tab Ruler (Command-Shift-T/Ctrl-Shift-T).

3. Click in the tab ruler where you want the tab stop to occur (text will align to the new stop immediately) **1**, then click a tab alignment button in the top left corner of the palette. Or Option-click/Alt-click a tab stop to cycle through the alignment types. Repeat for other stops.

TIP To delete a tab stop, drag the tab marker up and out of the ruler. As you drag it, the word *delete* will display on the palette. Shift-drag to delete a marker and all markers to its right.

TIP To move a tab stop, drag the marker to the left or the right. Shift-drag a marker to move all the markers to the right of it along with it.

*Check the **Snap** box to have a tab marker snap to the nearest ruler tick mark as you insert it or drag it. Or to temporarily turn on the Snap feature when the Snap box is unchecked, hold down **Command/Ctrl** as you drag a marker.*

The location of the currently selected tab marker. Tab Ruler measurements display in the currently chosen Artboard Units (File menu > Document Setup).

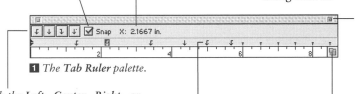

1 *The **Tab Ruler** palette.*

*Click the **Left-**, **Center-**, **Right-**, or **Decimal-Justified** tab button (or Top- or Bottom-Justified button for vertical type).*

*A **left-justified** tab marker.*

*Drag the **Extend Tab ruler** box to the right to widen the ruler.*

*Click the **Alignment** box to realign the tab ruler with the left margin of the selected text for horizontal type or the top margin for vertical type.*

The Change Case command changes selected text to all UPPER CASE, all lower case, or Mixed Case (initial capitals).

To change case:

1. Highlight the text you want to modify with a type tool.

2. Choose Type menu > Change Case.

3. Click Upper Case (ABC); Lower Case (abc); or Mixed Case (Abc), in which the initial cap in every word is uppercase 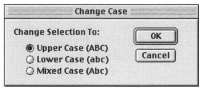.

4. Click OK (Return/Enter).

1 *Click an option in the Change Case dialog box.*

Use hanging punctuation to make the edge of your paragraphs look more uniform. This option works only with area type. It affects the period, comma, quotation mark, apostrophe, hyphen, dash, colon, and semicolon.

To hang punctuation:

1. Select a paragraph with a type tool.
    or
    Select a type object with a selection tool.

2. Check the Hang Punctuation box on the Paragraph palette. If this option isn't visible, choose Show Options from the palette menu.

Hanging punctuation

> 'Lo! all these trophies of affections hot,
> Of pensiv'd and subdued desires the tender,
> Nature hath charg'd me that I hoard them not,
> But yield them up where I myself must render,
> That is, to you, my origin and ender:
> For these, of force, must your oblations be,
> Since I their altar, you enpatron me.

William Shakespeare

2 *Let it hang out.*

1 *Eyedropper tool.*

The more things change, the more they remain the same.

The more things change, the more they, remain the same.

Select the type object whose attributes you want to change.

2 *Then click with the Eyedropper on the attributes you want to copy.*

The more things change, the more they remain the same.

The more things change, the more they remain the same.

3 *The attributes are copied to the selected type.*

drag drag

4 *Drag across the characters to which you want to apply the newly sampled attributes.*

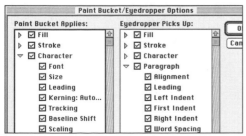

Paint Bucket/Eyedropper Options

Paint Bucket Applies:	Eyedropper Picks Up:
▷ ☑ Fill	▷ ☑ Fill
▷ ☑ Stroke	▷ ☑ Stroke
▽ ☑ Character	▷ ☑ Character
☑ Font	▽ ☑ Paragraph
☑ Size	☑ Alignment
☑ Leading	☑ Leading
☑ Kerning: Auto...	☑ Left Indent
☑ Tracking	☑ First Indent
☑ Baseline Shift	☑ Right Indent
☑ Scaling	☑ Word Spacing

5 *Choose which attributes the **Paint Bucket Applies** or the **Eyedropper Picks Up**.*

When you click on a type object with the Eyedropper tool, it samples the type's character, paragraph, fill, and stroke attributes, copies them to the Character, Paragraph, Color, and Stroke palettes, and applies them to any currently selected text—essentially creating a temporary "style sheet" on the fly.

To copy type attributes using the Eyedropper or Paint Bucket:

1. Select the type object or objects whose attributes you want to change using the Selection tool, or select type characters with a type tool.

2. Choose the Eyedropper **1** tool (**don't** use the "I" shortcut if type is selected!).

3. Click on any selected or unselected type in any open document window that contains the desired attributes **2** (a small "t" will appear next to the pointer). The type attributes will be copied to the Character, Paragraph, Color, and Stroke palettes and to the selected type **3**.

4. *Optional:* Hold down Option/Alt (or choose the Paint Bucket tool) and click on or drag across any other type object to apply the newly sampled paint and type attributes **4**.

By default, all the attributes are checked on.

To change the attributes that the Eyedropper picks up or the Paint Bucket applies:

1. Double-click the Eyedropper or Paint Bucket tool.

2. Click a triangle to expand the Fill, Stroke, Character, or Paragraph list, then check any individual attributes on or off **5**.
   or
   Check or uncheck the Fill, Stroke, Character, or Paragraph box to turn all the attributes in that category on or off.

3. Click OK (Return/Enter).

Eyedropper and Paint Bucket for Type

207

To wrap type around an object:

1. Create area type inside an object.
2. Choose the Selection tool.
3. Select the object the type is to wrap around **1**. It can even be a placed image with a clipping path from Photoshop.
4. Choose Object menu > Arrange > Bring To Front.
5. Drag a marquee around both objects.
6. Choose Type menu > Wrap > Make **2**.

TIP Use the Direct-selection tool to move the object the type is wrapping around. To move multiple objects, first Shift-click them.

TIP To move the type away from the edge of the wrap object, enter values in the Left or Right Indentation fields on the Paragraph palette for the type.

TIP To undo the type wrap, select both objects using the Selection tool, then choose Type menu > Wrap > Release.

TIP To wrap type around part of a placed image or any vector object, create an object with the desired shape for the wrap with a stroke and fill of None, apply the Wrap command to that object and the type object, and then bring the placed image to the front. To tweak the wrap, move or adjust the object's anchor points using the Direct-selection tool.

To create type with a shadow:

1. Create point type (see page 174) **3**.
2. *Optional:* Select the type with the Type tool, then track the characters out (Option/Alt right arrow).
3. Choose the Selection tool, then click on the type block.
4. Apply a dark fill color and a stroke of None.
5. Option-drag/Alt-drag the type block slightly to the right and downward. Release the mouse, then Option/Alt.
6. With the copy of the type block still selected, lighten its shade.

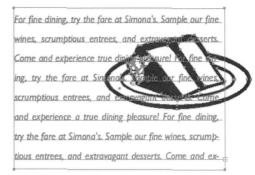

1 *Select a type object and the object the type is going to wrap around.*

For fine dining, try the fare at Simona's. Sample our fine wines, scrumptious entrees, and extravagant desserts. Come and experience true dining pleasure! For fine dining, try the fare at Simona's. Sample our fine wines, scrumptious entrees, and extravagant desserts. Come and experience a true dining pleasure! For fine dining,

2 *The* type *wraps around the cake.*

Shadow

3 *The original type.*

Wrap Type; Shadow Type

Shadow

4 *The shadow is created and sent to the back.*

 5 *Scale tool*

Shadow

6 *The shadow is shortened using the Scale tool.*

 7 *Shear tool*

Shadow

8 *The shadow is slanted using the Shear tool.*

Shadow

9 *The type is reflected using the Reflect tool.*

7. *Optional:* Choose Object menu > Arrange > Send To Back **4**.

8. Reposition either type block—press any arrow key to move it in small increments.

TIP With the Type Area Select option on in File > Preferences > Type & Auto Tracing, it may be hard to select the type block that's in the back. Turn on Smart Guides with Object Highlighting, move the pointer near the type you want to select, and click when the type highlights.

To *slant the shadow:*

1. Choose the Selection tool.

2. Click on the baseline or anchor point of the shadow type (see the last tip on this page).

3. Double-click the Scale tool **5**.

4. Click Non-uniform, enter 100 in the Horizontal field, enter 60 in the Vertical field, then click OK **6**.

5. With the shadow type still selected, double-click the Shear tool **7**.

6. Enter 45 in the Shear Angle field, click Axis: Horizontal, then click OK.

7. Use the arrow keys to move the baseline of the shadow text so it aligns with the baseline of the original text **8**. You might also need to move it to the right.

TIP You can also use the Free Transform tool to vertically scale and shear a type block. Move the top center handle.

To *reflect the shadow:*

1. Choose the Selection tool.

2. Click on the shadow type.

3. Double-click the Reflect tool.

4. Click Axis: Horizontal, then click OK (Return/Enter).

5. Move the two blocks of type together so their baselines meet **9**.

TIP If you're having trouble selecting the shadow type layer in the back, select the original type first, press the up arrow to move it upward, then click on the baseline or anchor point of the shadow type.

Shadow Type

To slant a block of type:

1. Choose the Rectangle tool (M or Shift-M), then draw a rectangle.

2. Choose the Area Type tool (T or Shift-T).

3. Click on the edge of the rectangle, then enter type **3**.

4. With the rectangle still selected, double-click the Rotation tool.

5. Enter 30 in the Angle field, then click OK (Return/Enter). **4**.

6. Make sure Smart Guides is turned on (Command-U/Ctrl-U) with Object Highlighting (File menu > Preferences > Smart Guides).

7. Choose the Direct-selection tool (A or Shift-A), then Shift-drag the top segment diagonally to the right until the side segments are vertical **5**–**6**.

8. *Optional:* Drag the right segment of the rectangle a little to the right to enlarge the object and reflow the type.

USE THE SHEARS

You can use the Shear tool to slant a block of type **1**–**2**.

SHEARING

1 *The original type block.*

2 *Select the type, click with the **Shear** tool on the center of the type, then drag upward or downward from the edge of the type block. (Hold down Shift to constrain vertically or horizontally.)*

3 *The original type object.*

4 *Rotate the type 30°.*

5 *Drag the top segment diagonally to the right.*

6 *The reshaped type object (Preview view).*

LAYERS 14

In this chapter you will learn to group and ungroup objects and to restack objects. Using the Layers palette, you will learn to create standard and template layers; select, restack, duplicate, and delete layers; move an object to a different layer; and hide/show, lock/unlock, print, merge, and flatten layers.

Each new object you draw in an illustration is automatically positioned on top of the previous object. This positioning is called the stacking order. All new objects are stacked on a single, default layer which is created automatically when you create a new illustration. Using the Layers palette, you can add additional layers to an illustration, each of which can contain a stack of objects . You can change the stacking order of objects within a layer, and you can change the order of whole layers. You can also group objects together onto the same layer so they can be moved as a unit. If you place objects on separate layers, you can selectively display/hide, lock, and print them.

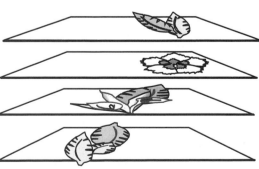

1 *Imagine your illustration is built on transparent modular shelves. You can rearrange (restack) objects within the same shelf (layer), move an object to a different shelf, or rearrange the order of the shelves (layers).*

If you group objects together, you can easily select, cut, copy, paste, transform, recolor, or move them as a unit. When you group objects, they are automatically placed on the same layer (the layer of the frontmost object in the group). If you then change any of the Layers palette hide/show, lock/unlock, preview, or print options, those options will affect the whole group.

To group objects:

1. Choose the Selection tool (V).

2. Shift-click on each of the objects to be grouped.
   or
   Position the pointer outside all the objects, then drag a marquee diagonally across them 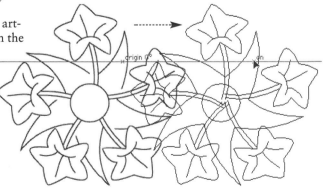.

3. Choose Object menu > Group (Command-G/Ctrl-G).
   or
   Control-click/Right-click on the artboard and choose Group from the context menu **2**–**3**.

TIP You can group multiple groups into a larger parent group.

To ungroup objects:

1. Choose the Selection tool.

2. Click on a group.

3. Choose Object menu > Ungroup (Command-Shift-G/Ctrl-Shift-G).
   or
   Control-click/Right-click on the artboard and choose Ungroup from the context menu.

1 *Drawing a* **marquee** *around the objects to be grouped.*

2 *All the objects are* **selected.** *Control-click/Right-click on the artboard and choose* **Group** *from the context menu.*

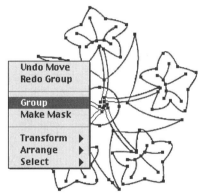

3 *Moving* the **group** *using the selection tool. All the objects in the group move in concert.*

Group; Ungroup

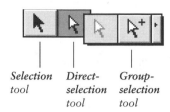

Selection
tool

Direct-
selection
tool

Group-
selection
tool

1 *Illustrator's **selection** tools.*

2 *Click once with the **Group-selection** tool to select an object in a group.*

To select grouped objects:

To select an entire group, click on any item in the group with the Selection tool (V) **1**.
or
To select individual anchor points or segments of an object within a group, use the Direct-selection tool (A or Shift-A).
or
To select multiple groups that are nested in a larger group, use the Group-selection tool (A or Shift-A). Click once to select an object in a group **2**; click again on the same object to select the whole group that object is part of **3**; click again on the same object to select the next group that was added to the larger group **4**, and so on.

TIP Hold down Option/Alt to quickly access the Group-selection tool when the Direct-selection tool is chosen.

3 *Click again to select the remaining objects in the same group.*

4 *Keep clicking to select other groups that are nested inside the same, larger group.*

Select Grouped Objects

213

Use the Bring To Front or Send To Back command to move an object or a group to the front or the back of its stack within its layer. If you restack an object within a group, it will move to the frontmost or backmost position in the same group.

To place an object on the bottom or top of its stack:

1. Choose the Selection tool (V).

2. Click on the object or group.

3. Choose Object menu > Arrange > Send To Back (Command-Shift-[/Ctrl-Shift-[ ) or > Bring To Front (Command-Shift-]/ Ctrl-Shift-]). The selected object or group will be placed on the bottom or top of its stack within the *same* layer.
   or
   Control-click/Right-click and choose Arrange > Bring To Front or Send To Back from the context menu 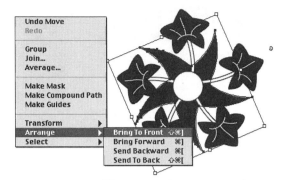–.

TIP If you select only part of a path (a point or a segment) and then change its stacking position, the entire object will move.

To move an object forward or backward within its stack:

1. Select an object.

2. Choose Object menu > Arrange > Bring Forward (Command-]/Ctrl-]) or Send Backward (Command-[/Ctrl-[) to shift the object one level at a time in its stacking order within the *same* layer .
   or
   Control-click/Right-click and choose Arrange > Bring Forward or Send Backward from the context menu.

1 *Select an object or group, then* ***Control-click/Right-click*** *and choose from the* ***Arrange*** *submenu on the context menu. (The star shape is selected in this illustration.)*

2 *The star shape is now in the* ***front***.

3 *The star shape is sent* ***backward*** *(compare with figure* **1***).*

1 *Select the object you want to restack, then choose Edit menu > **Cut**.*

2 *Select the object that you want to paste just in front of or just behind.*

3 *Choose Edit menu > **Paste In Front** or **Paste in Back**. (In this case, Paste in Back was chosen.)*

The Paste In Front and Paste In Back commands paste the Clipboard contents just in front of or just behind the currently selected object within the selected object's layer, in the same horizontal and vertical *(x,y)* position from which it was cut. You can also use either command to paste from one document to another.

To restack an object in front of or behind another object:

1. Choose the Selection tool (V).
2. Click on an object **1**.
3. Choose Edit menu > Cut (Command-X/ Ctrl-X) to place the object on the Clipboard.
4. Click on the object that you want to paste just in front of or just behind **2**. It can be in the same document or a different document.
5. Choose Edit menu > Paste In Front (Command-F/Ctrl-F).
   or
   Choose Edit menu > Paste In Back (Command-B/Ctrl-B) **3**.

TIP If you cut an object, use the Direct-selection tool to select an item in a group, and then choose Paste In Front or Paste In Back, the pasted object will be added to the group.

TIP If no object is selected when you choose Paste In Front or Paste In Back, the object on the Clipboard will paste to the front or back, respectively, of the stack within the currently active layer (the highlighted layer on the Layers palette).

TIP You can use the Paste In Front or Paste In Back command to stack type outlines. For example, you can copy and Paste In Back a type outline with a stroke color and a fill of None, and then apply a wider stroke of a different color to the copy to create a two-tone stroke.

Restack an Object

215

The first layer, Layer 1, is created automatically when you create a new document. You can create as many additional layers as you like. To activate an individual layer to work on, simply click its name on the Layers palette ◼. You can also reorder layers and lock, hide, or print individual layers. Any new object you create will be placed on the currently highlighted layer.

To create a new layer:

1. On the Layers palette, click on the layer above which you want the new layer to appear.

2. To create a new layer without choosing options for it, click the New Layer button. Illustrator will assign to the new layer the next available color from the Color drop-down menu in the Layer Options dialog box.
   or
   To create a new layer and choose options, follow the remaining steps.

3. Option-click/Alt-click the New Layer button ◼.
   or
   Choose New Layer from the Layers palette menu.

4. Enter a name for the new layer ◼.

5. *Optional:* Choose a different selection color for items on that layer from the Color drop-down menu. Selection colors help to make it easier to tell which layer an object is on. The default order of colors, as they are assigned to new layers, is the order of colors as they appear on the Color drop-down menu.

6. *Optional:* Choose other layer options (see page 220).

7. Click OK (Return/Enter).

TIP To insert a new layer in the topmost layer position, Command-click/Ctrl-click the New Layer button.

*Layer for **currently** selected object*

*Currently **active** layer*

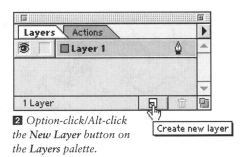

Show/ Hide   Lock/ Unlock   New Layer   Delete Layer

◼ *The Layers palette.*

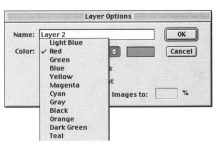

◼ *Option-click/Alt-click the **New Layer** button on the **Layers** palette.*

◼ *In the **Layer Options** dialog box, type a **Name** and choose a **Color**.*

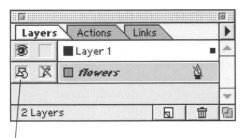

1 A *template layer* icon. The template layer name is in italics.

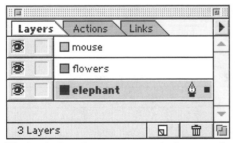

2 *Drag a layer name upward or downward, and release the mouse when the dark bar is in the desired position.*

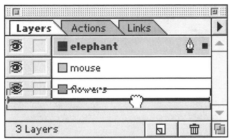

3 *The elephant layer is now on the bottom; objects on that layer are now in the back of the illustration.*

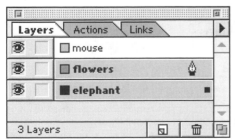

4 *Two layers are selected at the same time.*

A template layer is locked and nonprintable. Use a template layer if you want to trace over an object or a placed image (more about tracing on pages 99–102).

To create a template layer:

1. Double-click an existing layer name.
   or
   To create a new layer, Option-click/ Alt-click the New Layer button on the Layers palette.

2. Click Template. Change the Dim Images to: percentage for placed images or rasterized objects on that layer, if desired.

3. Click OK (Return/Enter) **1**.

   Note: You can also make an existing, active layer into a template by choosing Template from the Layers palette menu.

   TIP To show/hide all template layers, use this shortcut: Command-Shift-W/Ctrl-Shift-W.

   TIP Template layers always stay in Preview view, even if the illustration is in Artwork view.

The order of names on the Layers palette matches the front-to-back order of layers in the illustration.

To restack layers:

Drag a layer name upward or downward (the pointer will turn into a fist icon). Release the mouse when the dark bar is in the desired position **2**–**3**. The illustration will redraw.

To select multiple layers:

Click a layer, then Shift-click another layer on the list **4**. The layers you clicked on and all layers in between will be selected.
or
Command-click/Ctrl-click non-contiguous layer names. Only the layers you click on will be selected.

TIP Command-click/Ctrl-click to deselect an individual layer when more than one layer is selected.

Template Layer; Restack Layers; Select Multiple Layers

Duplicate a layer to copy that layer with all its layer options and all the objects contained on that layer.

Note: A mask that masks objects from more than one layer will duplicate as an object if its layer is duplicated, but the copy won't behave as a mask, and it will be assigned a stroke and fill of None.

To duplicate a layer:

1. Click on the layer you want to duplicate.

2. Choose Duplicate Layer from the Layers palette menu.
or
Drag the layer name over the New Layer button **1**–**2**. A new layer will be created and the word "copy" will be added to the layer name. Objects from the original layer will appear in their same *x-y* location on the duplicate.

Note: If you delete a layer, all the objects on that layer will be removed from the file.

To delete a layer:

1. Click the name of the layer you want to delete.

2. Choose Delete "[layer name]" from the Layers palette menu or click the palette Delete button. If there were any objects on the deleted layer, a warning prompt will appear. Click Yes (Return/Enter).
or
Drag the layer name onto the palette Delete button **3**.

TIP To retrieve the deleted layer and the objects on it, choose Edit menu > Undo Layer Deletion immediately.

QUICK-SELECT OBJECTS

Option-click/Alt-click a layer name to select all the objects on that layer. Or Option-click/Alt-click on or drag through a series of consecutive layer names to select all the objects on those layers (the layer names won't highlight).

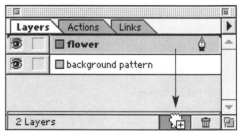

1 *To duplicate a layer, drag it over the New Layer button.*

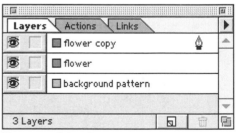

2 *A copy of the "flower" layer is made.*

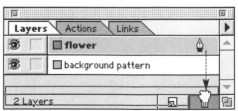

3 *Click on the name of the layer you want to delete, then drag it to the trash button or click the Delete button.*

The tiny colored square indicates which layer the currently selected object is on.

Layers \ Links \ Swatches

Plants & Juniper

holly & yew

sweet chestnut

horse chestnut

4 Layers

1 *Move the little square for the selected object. Release the mouse when the temporary square is at the desired layer. Note: If you move to another layer an object that's part of a group or a mask, the object will be released from the group or mask.*

To move an object to a different layer using the Layers palette:

1. Choose any selection tool, then click on the object or group you want to move. The object's current layer will be highlighted on the Layers palette.

2. Drag the tiny colored square located to the right of the highlighted layer name upward or downward (the pointer will turn into a pointing hand icon) **1**, then release the mouse when the square outline is at the desired layer name (it's okay if that layer is hidden). The illustration will redraw with the object in its new layer. *Note:* Option-drag/Alt-drag the square to *copy* the object to another layer.

To move an object to a different layer using the Clipboard:

1. Choose the Selection tool (V), then click on the object you want to move.

2. Choose Edit menu > Cut (Command-X/ Ctrl-X).

3. Click on the name of the layer on the Layers palette to which you want the object to move. (Or select an object or a group that's on that layer. If you select an object in a group using the Direct-selection or Group-selection tool, the pasted object will then become part of that group.)

4. Choose Edit menu > Paste (Command-V/ Ctrl-V). The object will be placed at the top of the stack within the active layer.
   or
   If an object is selected, choose Edit menu > Paste in Front (or Paste in Back) to paste it in its original *x,y* location, stacked in front of (or behind) the selected object.

   Note: If the object moves to the top of its stack rather than to a different layer, choose Paste Remembers Layers from the Layers palette menu to uncheck this option, or turn this option off in File menu > Preferences > General.

Move an Object to a Different Layer

The following options affect all the objects on the currently highlighted layer.

To choose layer options:

1. Double-click a layer name on the Layers palette.
   or
   Click a layer name on the Layers palette, then choose "Options for [layer name]" from the palette menu.

2. Do any of the following :

   Rename the layer.

   Choose a different **Color** for the selection of objects on the layer.

   Check **Show** to display objects on the layer; uncheck to hide objects on the layer. Hidden layers don't print.

   Check **Preview** to display the layer in Preview view; uncheck to display the layer in Artwork view. (To switch views for a layer without opening the Layer Options dialog box, see "To change the view for a layer" on page 222.)

   Check **Lock** to prevent all the objects on that layer from being edited; uncheck to allow objects to be edited.

   Note: Choosing the Layers palette Lock option will not cause the Object menu > Lock command to be turned on, and vice versa.

   Check **Print** to make the layer printable; uncheck to prevent all the objects on that layer from printing. The names of non-printing layers appear in italics. Hidden layers don't print either.

   Check **Dim Images to** to dim any placed images or rasterized objects on that layer (useful for tracing) and specify a percentage by which you want those images dimmed; uncheck this option to display placed images normally.

1 *In the **Layer Options** dialog box, check the **Show, Preview, Lock, Print**, or **Dim Images to** box on or off.*

MAXED OUT?

Choose Small Palette Rows from the Layers palette command menu to shrink the layer listings. More listings can then be displayed on the palette **2**–**3**.

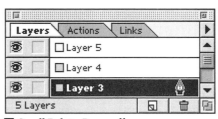

2 *Small Palette Rows off.*

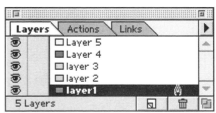

3 *Small Palette Rows on.*

Layer Options

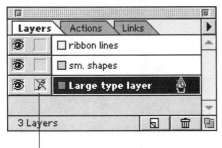

1 *Click in the **edit** column to lock a layer and make this icon appear. Locked layers are **uneditable**.*

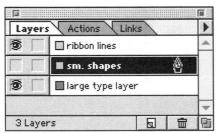

2 *Click the **eye** icon to **hide** a layer. Click again to show a layer. In this illustration, the "sm.shapes" layer is hidden and uneditable.*

If there is a crossed-out pencil icon next to a layer name, objects on that layer are currently locked (not editable). Locked layers stay locked, even if you close and reopen the file.

To lock a layer or layers:

Click the edit column next to the layer name **1**. Now objects in that layer cannot be selected or edited. To unlock the layer, click on the crossed-out pencil icon.
or
To lock multiple layers, drag upward or downward in the edit icon column.
or
Option-click/Alt-click in the edit column to lock or unlock all other layers except the one you click on.

Why would you want to hide a layer? To speed screen redraw or to make it easier to focus on other components of your artwork.

To hide a layer or layers:

Click the eye icon next to the layer name **2**. All objects on that layer will be hidden, whether or not they are selected. To redisplay the layer, click where the eye icon was.
or
To hide multiple, consecutive layers, drag upward or downward in the eye column.
or
Option-click/Alt-click in the eye column to hide/show all other layers except the one you click on.

Note: Hidden layers don't print. To make a visible layer non-printable, uncheck the Print box in the Layer Options dialog box.

TIP To display all layers, choose Show All Layers from the Layers palette menu.

TIP To lock or hide one item at a time, choose Object menu > Lock or Hide Selection. You can't unlock or show individual items via the Object menu. Choosing Unlock All or Show All will affect all objects that were locked or hidden using the Object menu command (if the objects are on a locked or hidden layer, you must unlock or show the layer first).

Lock Layers; Hide Layers

221

To change the view for a layer:

To display a layer in Artwork view, regardless of the current view for the illustration, Command-click/Ctrl-click on the eye icon next to the layer name 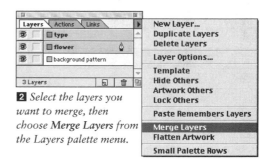. To redisplay the layer in Preview view, Command-click/Ctrl-click the eye icon again.

or

Command-Option-click/Ctrl-Alt-click an eye icon to display all layers except that one in Artwork view.

If your illustration contains more than one layer, you can select two or more of them and merge them into one to reduce the file's storage size. The Merge Layers command doesn't change the stacking order of objects, and **hidden layers don't merge.**

Note: Before applying the Merge Layers command, if you think there's a chance you'll want to work with the individual layers again, you should save a copy of the layered illustration using Save As.

To merge layers:

1. Select the layers you want to merge.

2. Choose Merge Layers from the Layers palette menu **2**–**3**. The layers will merge into the currently active layer (the layer that has the pen tip icon).

TIP Let's say you have a mask on one layer that is masking objects on two or more other layers. If you then merge the layers that contain the mask and the masked objects into any layer except the bottommost layer of the objects being masked, the mask will be released.

The Flatten Artwork command merges all the currently visible layers into the bottommost layer and **discards hidden layers.**

To flatten artwork:

1. Make sure there are no hidden layers that you want to keep.

2. Choose Flatten Artwork from the Layers palette menu.

Preview view   *Artwork view*
(dark eye)   *(hollow eye)*

1 *Command/Ctrl click the eye icon to toggle a layer between* **Artwork** *and* **Preview** *views.*

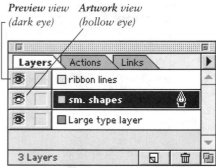

2 *Select the layers you want to merge, then choose* **Merge Layers** *from the Layers palette menu.*

3 *The two layers are* **merged** *into the active layer.*

COMBINE PATHS 15

The compound path command joins two or more objects into one object—until or unless the compound path is released. Where the original objects overlapped, a transparent hole is created, through which shapes or patterns behind the object are revealed. In this chapter, you will learn to create a compound path using the Make Compound Paths command or the Minus Front command, to release a compound path, and to recolor parts of a compound path.

You will also learn about the Pathfinder commands, which are applied via the Pathfinder palette. The Pathfinders create a new, closed object by uniting, splitting, cropping, intersecting, etc.

The gray bar behind shows through the transparent areas in the compound path.

Daniel Pelavin

Regardless of their original paint attributes, all the objects in a compound path are painted with the attributes of the *backmost* object, and they're also grouped.

To create a compound path:

1. Arrange the objects you want to see through in front of a larger shape .

2. Choose the Selection tool.

3. Marquee or Shift-click all the objects.

4. Choose Object menu > Compound Paths > Make (Command-8/Ctrl-8).
   or
   If the objects aren't grouped, you can Control-click/Right-click on the artboard and choose Make Compound Path from the context menu **2**.

   The frontmost objects will cut through the backmost object like a cookie cutter **3**–**4**. Any areas where the frontmost objects originally overlapped each other or any parts of the frontmost objects that originally extended beyond the edge of the backmost object will be painted with the color of the backmost object.

   Note: Use the Selection tool to select or move a whole compound path; use the Direct-selection tool to select or move part of a compound path. Only one fill color can be applied to a compound path at a time.

TIP Regardless of the layers the objects were on originally, the compound path will be placed on the frontmost object's layer.

TIP Don't overdo it. Too many compound paths in the same illustration or a compound path that is made up of very complex shapes could cause a printing error.

To add an object to a compound path:

1. Choose the Selection tool.

2. Select both the compound path and the object you want to add to it.

3. Choose Object menu > Compound Paths > Make.

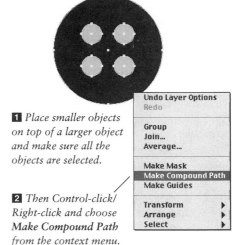

1 *Place smaller objects on top of a larger object and make sure all the objects are selected.*

2 *Then Control-click/ Right-click and choose Make Compound Path from the context menu.*

3 *The objects are converted into a compound path.*

4 *A background object is placed behind the compound path (and a white stroke is applied).*

1 *Click on the compound path.*

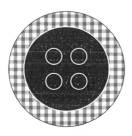

2 *Choose Release Compound Path from the context menu.*

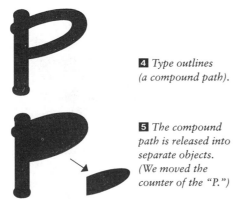

3 *The compound path is released. The buttonholes are no longer transparent.*

4 *Type outlines (a compound path).*

5 *The compound path is released into separate objects. (We moved the counter of the "P.")*

You can convert a compound path back into its individual objects at any time.

To release a compound path:

1. Choose the Selection tool.

2. Click on the compound path **1**.

3. Choose Object menu > Compound Paths > Release (Command-Option-8/ Ctrl-Alt-8) **2**.
   or
   Control-click/Right-click on the artboard and choose Release Compound Path from the context menu.

   All the objects will be selected and they will be painted with the attributes from the compound path **3**.

TIP If you release a type outline compound path that has a counter (interior shape), the counter will become a separate shape with the same paint attributes as the outer part of the letterform **4**–**5**.

TIP To remove an object from a compound path without releasing the whole compound, select the object with the Direct-selection tool, then press Delete/Backspace. Or cut and paste the object if you want to save it (and then move or recolor it).

TIP All objects released from a compound path will have the same stroke and fill, not their original, pre-compound colors. It may be difficult to distinguish overlapping objects if your illustration is in Preview view; they will be easier to distinguish in Artwork view. The objects will also stay on the same layer, regardless of which layer they were on before being assembled into a compound.

Release a Compound Path

You can remove the fill color of any shape in a compound and make the object transparent, or vice versa, by flicking the Reverse Path Direction switch on the Attributes palette.

To reverse an object's fill in a compound path:

1. Choose the Direct-selection tool.

2. Click on the object in the compound path whose color you want to reverse **1**.

3. Display the Attributes palette (Window menu > Show Attributes).

4. Click the Reverse Path Direction On button **2** or the Reverse Path Direction Off button **3**–**4**, whichever button isn't currently highlighted.

TIP If neither of the Reverse Path Direction buttons is highlighted, you have selected the whole compound path. Select only one path in the compound instead.

1 *Click on an object in the compound path.*

3 *Reverse Path Direction Off button*   **2** *Reverse Path Direction On button*

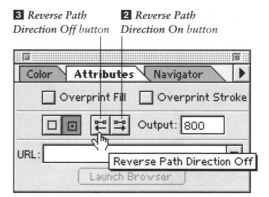

4 *The color of two of the buttonholes is reversed.*

Reverse the Fill of an Object in a Compound Path

Unite   Intersect   Exclude   Minus Front   Minus Back

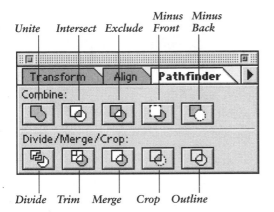

Divide   Trim   Merge   Crop   Outline

The Pathfinder palette.

The Pathfinders

The Pathfinder commands on the Pathfinder palette are among Illustrator's most powerful and useful features. They create a new, closed path or paths or a compound path (a group of two or more closed shapes) from two or more selected and overlapping objects by joining, splitting, or cropping them. The Pathfinder commands fall into four general categories: combining, dividing, color mixing and trapping. They are applied via the Pathfinder palette (shown at left).

Notes: For the best results, apply Pathfinders to filled, closed paths. If a Pathfinder command is applied to an open path, Illustrator closes the path before performing the command. If you want to control how a path is closed, apply Object menu > Path > Outline Path before applying a Pathfinder. The Pathfinders cannot be applied to a gradient mesh or pattern fill. To use type as path shapes, make it into outlines first. If an object has a brushstroke, apply the Object menu > Expand command (only the Stroke or Object option checked) first.

To **repeat** the last-applied Pathfinder command, choose Repeat [command name] from the Pathfinder palette menu (Command-4/ Ctrl-4).

Combining commands

Unite: Joins the outer edges of selected objects into one compound path object. Interior objects are deleted. The paint attributes of the frontmost object, including any stroke, are applied to the new object **1**–**2** (see also page 90).

Intersect: Deletes any non-overlapping areas from overlapping, selected objects. The paint attributes of the frontmost object are applied to the new object **3**–**4**. The selected objects must partially—not completely—overlap to apply this command.

Exclude: Areas where an even number of selected objects overlap become transparent; areas where an odd number of objects overlap are filled. The paint attributes of the frontmost object, including any stroke, are applied to the new object **5**–**6**.

1 *The original objects.*   **2** *Unite.*

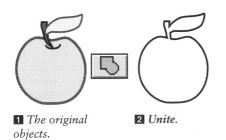

3 *The original objects.*   **4** *Intersect.*

5 *The original objects.*   **6** *Exclude.*

Unite; Intersect; Exclude

Minus Front: Subtracts the frontmost selected objects from the backmost object. The paint attributes of the backmost object, including any stroke, are preserved. This command works like the Make Compound Paths command if the original frontmost objects do not extend beyond the edge of the backmost object **1**–**2**.

Note: If you want the backmost object to be divided into separate objects and *not* become a compound path, make sure the edges of the frontmost objects extend beyond the edge of the backmost object before clicking Minus Front **3**–**4**. Overhanging areas will be deleted.

Minus Back: Subtracts the backmost selected objects from the frontmost object. Parts of objects that overlap the frontmost object are deleted. The paint attributes of the frontmost object, including any stroke, are applied to the new path **5**–**6**. The selected objects must at least partially overlap for this command to produce an effect.

Dividing commands

These commands divide overlapping areas of selected paths into separate, non-overlapping closed paths or lines.

Note: If the "Divide & Outline will remove unpainted artwork" box is checked in the Pathfinder Options dialog box (open from the palette menu), any non-overlapping areas of paths that originally had a fill of None will be deleted after the Divide or Outline command is applied.

Divide: The new objects will keep their original fill and stroke colors **7**–**8**.

TIP After applying the Divide command, click away from all objects to deselect them, choose the Direct-selection tool, click on any of the objects, and apply new fill colors or apply a fill of None to make an object appear transparent. Or remove individual objects to create cutouts.

1 *The frontmost object doesn't extend beyond the edge of the black square.*

2 *Minus Front. The box is a compound path.*

3 *The lines extend beyond the box.*

4 *After clicking **Minus Front**, the box is divided into three separate, grouped objects. It doesn't become a compound path.*

5 *The original objects.*

6 *Minus Back.*

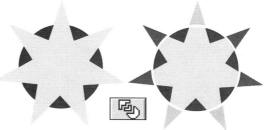

7 *The original objects.*

8 *Divide. The resulting shapes were moved and/or recolored.*

1 *The original objects.*

2 *Trim (pulled apart for emphasis).*

3 *The original objects.*

4 *Merge (pulled apart for emphasis).*

5 *The original objects.*

6 *Crop.*

7 *The original objects.*

8 *Outline (pulled apart for emphasis).*

Trim: The frontmost object shape is preserved; parts of objects that are behind it and overlap it are deleted. Adjacent or overlapping objects of the same color or shade remain separate (unlike the Merge command). Objects retain their original solid or gradient fill colors; stroke colors are deleted **1**–**2**.

Merge: The frontmost object shape is preserved; adjacent or overlapping objects of the same color or shade are combined. Objects retain their original solid or gradient fill colors; stroke colors are deleted **3**–**4**.

Crop: The frontmost object "trims" away areas of selected objects that extend beyond its borders. The remaining non-overlapping objects retain only their fill colors; stroke colors are removed. The frontmost object is also removed **5**–**6**. Unlike a mask, the original objects can't be restored, unless you Undo immediately.

Outline: Objects turn into stroked lines **7**–**8**. The fill colors of the original objects become the stroke colors, and fill colors are removed. Use this command to create strokes on individual sides of objects that originally had a stroke of None.

Trim; Merge; Crop; Outline

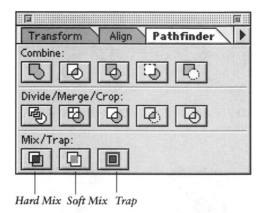

Color mixing commands

The color mixing commands convert areas where objects overlap into separate objects. The new fill colors are a mixture of the overlapping colors, and stroke colors are removed.

Note: If the color mixing commands aren't displayed on the Pathfinder palette, choose Show Options from the palette menu.

Hard Mix: Simulates overprinting. The highest C, M, Y, and K values from each of the original objects are mixed in areas where they overlap. The resulting effect is most noticeable where colors differed most between the original objects **1**–**2**.

Soft Mix: Creates an illusion of transparency. The higher the Mixing Rate you enter in the Pathfinder Soft Mix dialog box, the more transparent and altered the frontmost object will become **3**–**5**. To create a painterly effect, layer three color objects, then apply Soft Mix at about 75%. Or, to lighten the underlying colors, place an object with a white fill across other filled objects and enter a Mixing Rate between 75% and 100%.

To choose Pathfinder options:

1. Choose Pathfinder Options from the Pathfinder palette menu.

2. Change any of the following **6**:

   The higher the Calculate Precision value, the more precisely a Pathfinder command is applied, but the longer that application takes.

   With Remove Redundant Points checked, any anchor points that have a duplicate in the exact same location are deleted when the Pathfinder command is applied.

   With "Divide & Outline will remove unpainted artwork" checked, any overlapping portions of objects that originally had a fill of None will be deleted by the Divide or Outline command.

3. Click OK (Return/Enter).

Hard Mix   Soft Mix   Trap

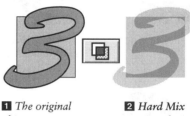

1 *The original objects.*

2 *Hard Mix command.*

3 *The original objects.*

4 *Soft Mix command (90%).*

5 *Enter a Mixing Rate for the Soft Mix command.*

6

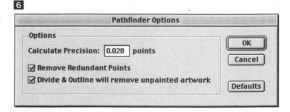

A gradient fill is a gradual blend between two or more colors. In this chapter you will learn how to fill an object or objects with a gradient, how to create two-color and multicolor gradients, how to change the angle of a gradient using the Gradient tool, and how to edit a gradient using the Gradient palette.

You will also learn how to use the Gradient Mesh tool and the Gradient Mesh command to create painterly gradient mesh objects, and how to modify mesh objects by adding, moving, deleting, or recoloring mesh points and lines.

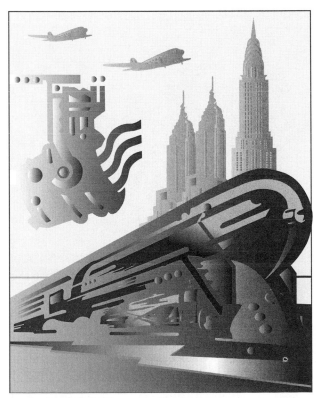

Chris Spollen, **New York Retro**

Gradient basics

The simplest gradient fill consists of a starting color and an ending color, with the point where the colors are equally mixed together located midway between them. A gradient can be **linear** (side-to-side) or **radial** (out-from-center). You can apply a gradient fill to one object or across several objects. A set of predefined gradients is supplied with Illustrator, but you can also create your own gradients using the **Gradient palette**.

Once an object is filled with a gradient, you can use the **Gradient tool** to modify how the fill is distributed within the object. You can change the direction of the gradient or change how quickly one color blends into another. You can also change the placement of the center of a radial gradient fill.

Note: Open the Color, Gradient, and Swatches palettes for the instructions in this chapter.

Follow these instructions to apply an existing gradient to an object. You can use a gradient that's supplied with Illustrator or a gradient that you have created. To create your own gradient, follow the instructions that start on the next page.

To fill an object with a gradient:

1. Select an object.

2. On the Swatches palette, click a Gradient swatch **1**.

or

To apply the last-selected gradient, click the Gradient Fill box on the Gradient palette **2** or click the Gradient button on the Toolbox (".").

3. *Optional:* On the Gradient palette, enter a different Angle for a linear gradient.

TIP Here are two other ways to apply a gradient: Drag a gradient swatch or the Gradient Fill box over a selected or unselected object. Or choose a gradient, and then click on an object with the Paint Bucket tool.

TIP To apply a gradient to a stroke, first apply Object menu > Path > Outline Path to convert the stroke into a closed object (see page 97).

TIP To fill type with a gradient, you must first convert it into outlines (Type menu > Create Outlines).

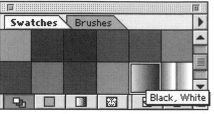

1 *A gradient is selected on the Swatches palette.*

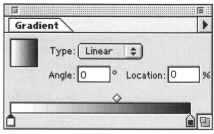

2 *The same selected gradient is displayed on the Gradient palette.*

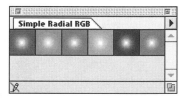

MORE GRADIENTS

The Simple Radial RGB gradient library displayed above is one of several libraries of predefined gradients that are supplied with Illustrator. To open one of these libraries, choose Window menu > Swatch Libraries > Other Library, open the Illustrator 8 folder > Other Libraries > Gradients, highlight the library you want to open, then click Select. Finally, drag swatches from the library palette into your document's Swatches palette.

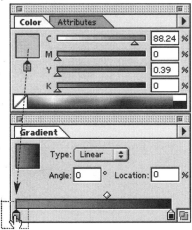

1 *Drag a color from the* **Color** *palette to the far left side of the* **Gradient slider** *to define it as the starting color. When you release the mouse, the slider's color squares will display.*

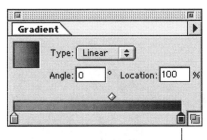

2 *Next, click the Color box on the Color palette, and mix a color for the right side of the Gradient slider (the ending color).*

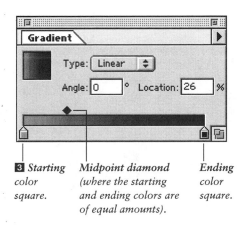

3 *Starting* ..... *Midpoint diamond* ..... *Ending*
color ..... *(where the starting* ..... *color*
square. ..... *and ending colors are* ..... *square.*
..... *of equal amounts).*

A gradient can be composed of CMYK and/or RGB process colors, tints of the same spot color, or multiple spot colors. When a gradient containing a mixture of color models is color separated, by default, all the colors are converted to CMYK process color.

To create and save a two-color gradient:

1. Display the full Gradient palette, with its options panel.

2. Click the Black/White gradient swatch on the Swatches palette.

3. Click the Color box on the Color palette, use the palette to mix what will be the starting color of the gradient, then drag that color from the Color box over the starting color square at the far left side of the Gradient slider on the Gradient palette **1**.

   or

   Drag a swatch from the Swatches palette over the starting color square at the far left side of the Gradient slider on the Gradient palette.

   or

   Click the starting color square on the Gradient palette, then Option-click/Alt-click a swatch on the Swatches palette.

4. Repeat the previous step to mix a different color for the ending color square on the far right side of the Gradient slider **2**.

5. On the Gradient palette, choose Type: Linear or Radial.

6. *Optional:* Move the midpoint diamond (above the Gradient slider) to the right to produce more of the starting color than the ending color, or to the left to produce more of the ending color than the starting color (**3** on this page and **4**–**5** on the next page).

7. Selecting any other object or swatch now will cause the current gradient to be lost—unless you save it. To save the gradient, drag the Fill box from the Gradient palette or the Toolbox onto the Swatches palette.

   or

(Continued on the following page)

Create a Two-Color Gradient

Click the New Swatch button on the Swatches palette.

or

To type a name for the gradient as you save it, Option-click/Alt-click the New Swatch button, type a name for the gradient, then click OK.

TIP To swap the starting and ending colors or any other two colors, Option-drag/ Alt-drag one square on top of the other.

TIP To delete a gradient swatch that's been saved, drag it over the Delete button on the Swatches palette.

TIP Ask your service bureau for advice if you're color separating a gradient that contains more than one spot color. You can assign a different screen angle to each color using File menu > Separation Setup (uncheck the Convert to Process box). See page 330. You can also convert each spot color to process by clicking the spot color square on the Gradient slider and then choosing a process color model from the Color palette menu.

TIP To color separate a gradient that changes from a spot color to white on one piece of film (one plate), create a gradient with the spot color as the starting color and 0% tint of the same color as the ending color.

To edit colors in an existing gradient:

1. Choose the Selection tool and click on an object that contains the gradient that you want to edit.

   or

   Click the gradient swatch on the Swatches palette that you want to edit.

2. On the Gradient palette, click the square below the Gradient slider for the color you want to change, then choose a color from the Color palette.

   or

   Drag a swatch from the Swatches palette right on top of a color square.

TIP To copy a gradient color square, Option-drag/Alt-drag the square.

4 *A gradient fill with the **midpoint** diamond in the **center** of the slider.*

5 *The same gradient fill with the **midpoint** diamond moved to the **right**.*

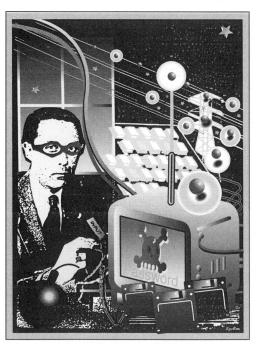

Chris Spollen, **Internet Theft**

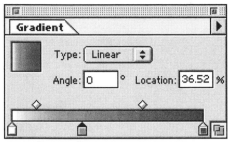

1 *To add a color to a gradient, click under the Gradient slider to add a new square, then mix a process color on the Color palette or Option/Alt click a swatch on the Swatches palette.*

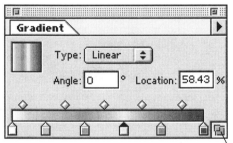

2 *Four new shades of gray were added to this gradient.*

Drag the resize box to widen the palette when creating a gradient with a lot of colors.

A gradient can contain up to 32 colors. The colors can be changed and the number of squares can be adjusted at any time.

To create a multicolor gradient:

1. Follow the steps on the previous two pages to produce a two-color gradient.
   or
   On the Swatches palette, click an existing gradient swatch.

2. Click on the bottom of the Gradient slider where you want the new color to appear, then use the Color palette to mix the new color.
   or
   Click the Color palette Color box, mix a color using the Color palette, then drag from the Color palette to the Gradient slider on the Gradient palette. A new color square will appear **1**.
   or
   Drag a swatch from the Swatches palette to the Gradient slider.

3. Do any of the following optional steps:

   Move the new square to the left or to the right to change its location.

   Move the midpoint diamond located above the Gradient slider to the left or right of the new color to change the location where the new color is equally mixed with either of the colors adjacent to it.

   Repeat step 2 to add more colors **2**–**3**.

   Note: If you modify a gradient that's been saved as a swatch, the original gradient swatch won't change. If you want to keep the modified gradient, save it as a new swatch.

TIP To produce a sharp transition between colors, drag the midpoint diamond close to a color square or move the color squares close together.

TIP To remove a color square, drag it downward out of the Gradient palette.

3 *Multi-color gradients.*

Multicolor Gradient

Gradient Tool

Once an object is filled with a gradient, you can use the Gradient tool to manually change the direction of a linear fill or the location of the center of a radial gradient fill. You can also use this tool to apply a gradient across a series of objects (see the next page).

To use the Gradient tool:

1. Apply a gradient fill to an object, and keep the object selected.

2. Choose the Gradient tool (G) .

3. To modify a linear gradient fill, you can drag across the object in a new direction (right-to-left or diagonally) **2**–**3**. To blend the colors abruptly, drag a short distance; to blend the colors more gradually across a wider span, drag a longer distance.

   To modify a radial gradient fill, position the pointer where you want the center of the fill to be, then click or drag **4**–**5**.

   If you're not happy with the results, drag in a different direction. Drag in the opposite direction to reverse the order of the fill colors.

   Note: If you start to drag or finish dragging outside the edge of an object with the Gradient tool, the colors at the beginning or end of the gradient fill won't appear in the object.

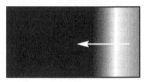

1 *Gradient* tool.

2 *A linear gradient fill applied using the Gradient or Swatches palette only.*

3 *The* **Gradient tool** *dragged a short distance from right to left across the same gradient.*

4 *A radial gradient fill before using the Gradient tool.*

5 *After dragging the* **Gradient tool** *across the same radial gradient.*

To spread a gradient across multiple objects:

1. Select several objects, and fill them with the same gradient **1**.

2. Choose the Gradient tool (G).

3. Drag across all the objects **2**. Hold down Shift while dragging to constrain the angle to a multiple of 45°.

TIP Once multiple objects are filled with the same gradient, they shouldn't be combined into a compound path. The resulting object may be too complex to print.

1 *A gradient fill applied using the Swatches palette only. Each type outline is filled with its own gradient.*

2 *The gradient adjusted using the **Gradient tool**. The arrow shows the direction the mouse was dragged. A single gradient blends across all the type outlines.*

What is a gradient mesh?

A gradient mesh is an object that contains multiple gradients in various directions with seamless transitions between them **1**. Using the gradient mesh features, you'll be able to easily render and modify photorealistic or painterly objects and complex modeled surfaces, such as skin tones, objects of nature, machinery, etc.

Both the **Gradient Mesh tool** and the **Create Gradient Mesh command** convert a standard object into a mesh object with lines and intersecting points. A gradient mesh can be produced from any path object or bitmapped image, even a radial or linear blend, but not from a compound path, a text object, or a placed EPS file.

After you create a mesh object, you'll assign colors to mesh points or mesh patches. Then you'll manipulate the points and lines to push colors around in the object—sharpen or soften color transitions, or add or delete gradient colors. It's like a watercolor or airbrush drawing with a flexible armature above it. Reconfigure the armature, and the colors beneath the armature will shift right along with it.

Mesh building blocks

A mesh object consists of anchor points, mesh points, mesh lines, and mesh patches **2**. A gradient mesh can be reshaped by manipulating its anchor or mesh points or mesh lines.

- **Anchor points** appear as square points in the mesh. They are the standard Illustrator anchor points that can be added, deleted, or moved in order to reshape the overall object.

- **Mesh points** are diamond-shaped, and like anchor points, they can be added, deleted, or moved. Their purpose, however, is for assigning colors to the gradients.

- **Mesh lines** crisscross the object to connect the mesh points. They act as guides for placing and moving points.

- A **mesh patch** is an area that is defined by four mesh points.

1 *Illustrator's gradient mesh features are ideal for rendering natural forms.*

Anchor point (square-shaped)

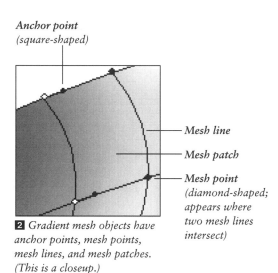

Mesh line

Mesh patch

Mesh point (diamond-shaped; appears where two mesh lines intersect)

2 *Gradient mesh objects have anchor points, mesh points, mesh lines, and mesh patches. (This is a closeup.)*

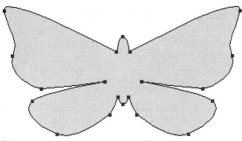

1 *Select an object that has a fill.*

2 *Gradient Mesh tool.*

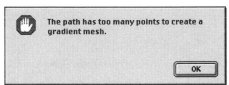

3 *Click on the object—it will convert immediately into a gradient mesh object.*

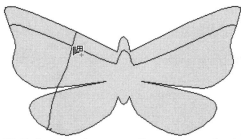

The path has too many points to create a gradient mesh.

OK

4

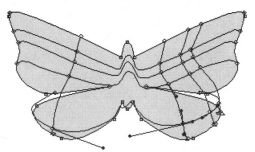

5 *Continue to click to create additional sets of mesh lines.*

Note: If you're converting a complex object into a gradient mesh, it's best to use the Create Gradient Mesh command. If you're converting a simple objects, on the other hand, you can use either the Create Gradient Mesh command or the Gradient Mesh tool, whichever you prefer. The Gradient Mesh command creates more regularly-spaced mesh points and lines than the Gradient Mesh tool does.

Beware: A mesh object cannot be converted back to a path object.

To convert an object into a gradient mesh using the Gradient Mesh tool:

1. Select a simple object that has a fill **1**. Copy the object if you want to preserve a non-gradient mesh version of it.

2. Choose the Gradient Mesh tool (U) **2**.

3. Click on the object to place a mesh point. The object will convert immediately to a mesh object, with the minimum number of mesh lines **3**.

If you get an alert box **4**, it means you must remove points from the path before you can convert it into a gradient mesh. You can do this using the Delete-anchor-point tool or the Smooth tool.

4. Click to create other sets of mesh lines **5**. Now proceed to page 241 to learn how to apply colors to the mesh.

Note: Complex gradient meshes increase file size and require a significant amount of computation, so keep them as simple as possible. You'll be less likely to get a printing error if you build a drawing from a few mesh objects than from one large, complex one.

To convert an object into a gradient mesh using a command:

1. Choose the Selection tool, then select a filled object.

2. Choose Object menu > Create Gradient Mesh.

3. Click the Preview box **1**.

4. Enter the number of horizontal Rows and Vertical columns for the grid.

5. From the Appearance drop-down menu, choose Flat for a uniform surface with no highlight; To Center for a highlight at the center of the object; or To Edge for a highlight at the object's edges.

6. If you chose the To Center or To Edge Appearance option, enter an intensity percentage for the white Highlight.

7. Click OK (Return/Enter) **2**–**4**. Now recolor the gradient mesh by following the instructions on the next page.

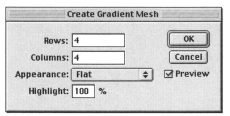

1 The **Create Gradient Mesh** *dialog box.*

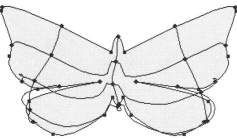

2 **Create Gradient Mesh** *command, Appearance:* **Flat.**

3 *Create Gradient Mesh command, Appearance:* **To Center.**

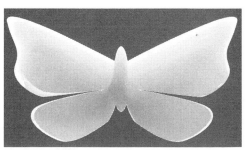

3 *Create Gradient Mesh command, Appearance:* **To Edge** *(shown here on a dark background so you can see the highlight on the edge).*

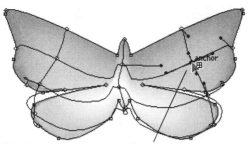

1 *Click on an existing mesh point.*

2 *The point is recolored.*

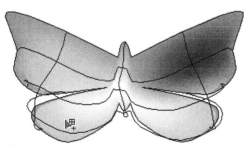

3 *Or click inside a mesh patch.*

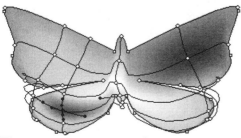

4 *A new mesh point is created.*

Each mesh point or mesh patch can be assigned a different color, which will blend into the surrounding area. Click on a mesh point to assign a color to a small area; click on a mesh patch to assign a color to a wider area. In either case, pause to allow the screen to redraw after clicking.

To recolor a gradient mesh:

1. Zoom in on the mesh object—but so you can still see the entire object in the document window, and deselect it.

2. Choose the Gradient Mesh tool (U) 🔲 or the Direct-selection tool, click on a **mesh point 1**–**2**, then choose a fill color from the Color or Swatches palette. You can use Smart Guides (Command-U/Ctrl-U to help you locate mesh points.

   or

   Choose a fill color from the Color or Swatches palette, choose the Gradient Mesh tool, then click inside a **mesh patch 3**–**4**. A **new** point with connecting mesh lines will be created in the current fill color.

   or

   Choose the Direct-selection tool, click on a **mesh patch**, then choose a fill color from the Color or Swatches palette. The Direct-selection tool will not create a new point, but all four mesh points that encircle the patch will be colored with the current fill color.

   or

   Make sure the mesh object isn't selected, choose the **Paint Bucket** tool, choose a fill color from the Color or Swatches palette, position the very tip of the black spill of the bucket pointer on a mesh point or inside a mesh patch, then **click**. The Paint Bucket doesn't create new mesh points or lines.

   or

   Choose the Direct-selection tool, select the mesh object, then **drag** a color from the Color or Swatches palette over a mesh point or mesh patch.

   TIP Read more about recoloring a mesh object on the following page.

To add mesh points or lines:

1. Choose the Gradient Mesh tool (U).

2. Click anywhere on the mesh object. A new point and connecting mesh lines will appear, and the current fill color will be applied to that point.

   or

   Shift-click on a mesh line to add a mesh point without applying the current fill color.

   or

   Click on an existing mesh line to add a new line perpendicular to it **1**–**2**.

TIP To recolor the new mesh point with a color of another mesh area in the object, keep the new point still selected, choose the Eyedropper tool (I), then click on the desired color elsewhere in the mesh.

TIP You can also recolor a gradient mesh using Filter menu > Colors > Adjust Colors, Convert to CMYK, Convert to RGB, Invert, or Saturate.

Follow these instructions to add or remove square-shaped (not diamond-shaped) anchor points from a mesh object. These points are used to reshape the overall mesh object—not to push colors around on the mesh. To add diamond-shaped mesh points with their connecting mesh lines, follow the previous set of instructions instead.

To add or remove square points:

1. Select the object to display its existing anchor points.

2. To add an anchor point, choose the Add-anchor-point tool from the Pen tool pop-out menu, then click on the outer edge of the mesh object or on a mesh line **3**. You can use Smart Guides (Command-U/Ctrl-U) to help you locate points.

   or

   To delete an anchor point, choose the Delete-anchor-point tool, then click on the anchor point you want to delete **4**.

MORE COLOR CONTROLS

To select and recolor multiple instances of the same color, choose the Direct-selection tool, click on a patch that contains the color you want to change, choose Edit menu > Select > Same Fill Color, then choose a new color from the Color palette or the Swatches palette.

To make a color area smaller, add more mesh lines around it in a different color. To spread a color, delete mesh points around it or assign the same color to adjacent mesh points.

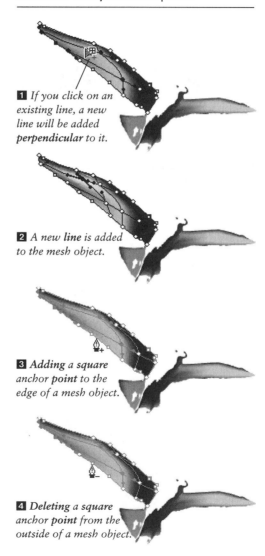

1 *If you click on an existing line, a new line will be added **perpendicular** to it.*

2 *A new **line** is added to the mesh object.*

3 *Adding a square anchor **point** to the edge of a mesh object.*

4 *Deleting a square anchor **point** from the outside of a mesh object.*

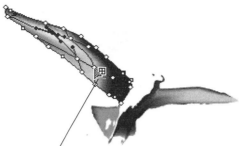

1 *Option-click/Alt-click a mesh point to delete it.*

2 *The point is deleted.*

3 *Drag a direction line.*

To delete a mesh point:

1. Choose the Gradient Mesh tool (U).

2. Option-click/Alt-click on the point you want to delete (a minus sign will appear next to the pointer). The mesh lines that cross through that point will be deleted as well **1**–**2**.

To reshape mesh lines:

1. Choose the Direct-selection tool, then click on the gradient mesh object to select it.

2. Click on a mesh point or anchor point.

3. Lengthen or rotate either of the point's direction lines to reshape its adjacent mesh lines **3**. Shift-drag a direction line to constrain the angle of the line to a multiple of 45°.

or

Choose the Convert-direction-point tool, click on a point, then drag a direction line to convert the point into a corner with direction lines that move independently of each other.

or

Drag a mesh point **4**. You can drag a point outside the object.

or

Drag a mesh patch **5**. You can drag a patch outside the object.

TIP You can use a transformation tool, the Twirl tool, or Filter menu > Distort > Twirl on a gradient mesh object.

4 *Drag a mesh point.*

5 *Drag a mesh patch.*

Delete Mesh Points; Reshape Mesh Lines

To expand a standard gradient into separate objects:

1. Select the object that contains the gradient (not a mesh object) **1**.

2. Choose Object menu > Expand.

3. Click Expand Gradient To: Specify, then enter the desired number of objects to be created **2**. If you want to keep the gradient color effect, you'll need to enter a number that's high enough to produce smooth color transitions.

4. Click OK (Return/Enter) **3**.

   Note: The resulting number of objects may not match the specified number of objects if there were minimal color changes in the original gradient.

TIP You could also apply this command to simplify a gradient fill that won't print.

To expand a radial or linear gradient into a gradient mesh:

1. Select an object that contains a radial or linear gradient **1**.

2. Choose Object menu > Expand.

3. Click Expand Gradient To: Gradient Mesh.

4. Click OK (Return/Enter) **4**. The resulting expanded objects can be a little confusing. You'll have a mask object that limits the gradient color area, with the gradient mesh object on top of it. Use the Direct-selection tool to select either object separately.

TIP Chose the Selection tool and marquee the expanded objects. Then group them so you can move them as a unit.

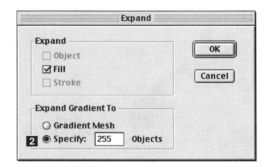

1 *The original object containing a linear gradient.*

Bird by Diane Margolin

2 *(Expand dialog box)*

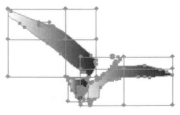

3 *After applying the Expand command, the gradient is converted into a series of separate rectangles grouped with a mask. Each rectangle is a different shade.*

4 *This is figure 1 after expanding it into a gradient mesh.*

Illustrator's object-reshaping and raster image-enhancing filters are powerful, but easy to use. This chapter includes a how-to section for applying filters, instructions for applying a few of the vector filters, a section on applying filters to bitmap images, a compendium of all the raster filters, and instructions for applying the two Pen and Ink filters (Hatch Effects and Photo Crosshatch).

Hatch lines created using Illustrator's Hatch Effects filter.

Diane Margolin

The last-used filter (Command-E/Ctrl-E). Choose this command to reapply the filter using the same settings.

SPEED TIP

*The last-used filter dialog box (Command-Option-E/ Ctrl-Alt-E). Choose this command to reapply the filter with **new** settings.*

Filter	
Apply Crystallize	⌘E
Crystallize...	⌥⌘E
Colors	▶
Create	▶
Distort	▶
Pen and Ink	▶
Stylize	▶
Artistic	▶
Blur	▶
Brush Strokes	▶
Distort	▶
Pixelate	▶
Sharpen	▶
Sketch	▶
Stylize	▶
Texture	▶
Video	▶

Vector filters for path objects (except Photo Crosshatch).

Raster filters for placed images or RGB color mode bitmap objects.

1 *The Filter menu.*

Filter basics

Some of Illustrator's filters are designed primarily for use with path objects, and they are grouped in five submenu categories: Color, Create, Distort, Pen and Ink, and Stylize **1**. Several of these filters are discussed in the pages that follow.

Other Illustrator filters are designed for use with bitmap images or rasterized objects, and they are grouped in 10 submenu categories at the bottom of the Filter menu: Artistic, Blur, Brush Strokes, Distort, Pixelate, Sharpen, Sketch, Stylize, Texture, and Video. If you're a Photoshop user, you may already be familiar with these. The raster filters are discussed and illustrated in the latter part of this chapter. *Note:* Some raster filters work only on RGB or Grayscale images, not on CMYK or 1-bit Bitmap images.

You can also apply Photoshop-compatible filters to placed images and to objects that are rasterized in Illustrator. To make them accessible in Illustrator, copy the filters (or aliases of the filters) into the Photoshop Filters folder inside Illustrator's Plug-ins folder, then re-launch Illustrator.

Some filters are applied simply by selecting the filter name from a submenu. Other filters are applied via a dialog box in which special options are chosen. You'll probably also want to memorize the two keyboard shortcuts shown in the illustration at left.

(Continued on the following page)

Filter Basics

Some filters are memory-intensive, but using lower or different settings in a filter dialog box can help speed things up.

Vector filter dialog boxes have a Preview box **2**. Check it to preview the filter effect in your illustration while the dialog box is open. Press Tab to preview after entering a new amount in a field.

Raster filter dialog boxes have a preview window **3**. You can drag in most preview windows to move the image inside it. With some filter dialog boxes open, the pointer becomes a square when it's passed over a raster image, in which case you can click to preview that area of the image.

Click the + button to zoom in on the image in the preview window, or click the – button to zoom out.

A flashing line below the preview percentage indicates the filter effect is taking a moment to render in the preview window.

TIP In a raster filter dialog box, you can hold down Option/Alt and click Reset to reset the slider settings to what they were when the dialog box was opened.

Note: Some Illustrator filters are covered in other chapters. Look up the filter name in the index for page locations.

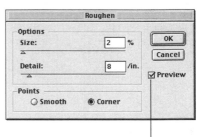

2 *Some filter dialogs have a **Preview box**.*

3 *Other filter dialogs have a preview window.*

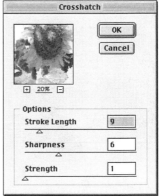

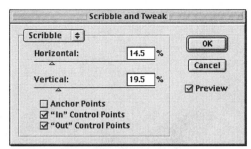

1 *The Scribble and Tweak dialog box.*

2 *The original object.*

3 *After applying the* **Scribble** *filter (Horizontal 14.5, Vertical 19.5, "In" and "Out" boxes checked).*

A few vector filters

To scribble or tweak:

1. Select a path object or objects.

2. Choose Filter menu > Distort > Scribble and Tweak.

3. Check the Preview box **1**.

4. Choose Scribble or Tweak from the drop-down menu. Scribble moves points randomly away from the object, Tweak moves points randomly along the object by the percentages you specify.

5. Choose Horizontal and Vertical percentages to control how much anchor points can be moved in either direction.

6. Check the Anchor Points box if you want anchor points to move, and check the "In" Control Points or "Out" Control Points boxes to change the segments that extend to and from anchor points.

7. Click OK (Return/Enter) **2**–**3**. Corner points will automatically be converted into points with direction lines. How direction lines are moved depends on whether you chose either or both of the "In" or "Out" options.

TIP The greater the number of anchor points on the path, the greater the Scribble or Tweak effect. To intensify the filter's effect, apply Object menu > Path > Add Anchor Points before applying the filter.

Scribble and Tweak Filter

The Roughen filter makes an object look more hand drawn by adding anchor points and then moving them.

To rough up a shape:

1. Select a path object or objects, and choose View menu > Hide Edges (Command-H/Ctrl-H), if you like, to make previewing easier.

2. Choose Filter menu > Distort > Roughen.

3. Check the Preview box **1**.

4. Choose a Size percentage to specify how far points can be moved. Try a low number first.

5. Choose a Detail amount for the number of points to be added to each inch of the path segments.

6. Click Smooth to produce soft edges or click Corner to produce pointy edges.

7. Click OK (Return/Enter) **2**–**3**.

To twirl path points around an object's center (dialog box method):

1. Select a path object or objects **4**. If two or more objects are selected, they will be twirled together.

2. Choose Filter menu > Distort > Twirl (in the upper part of the menu).

3. Enter an Angle between -3600 and 3600. Enter a positive number to twirl the paths clockwise; enter a negative number to twirl them counterclockwise.

4. Click OK (Return/Enter) **5**–**6**. Now try using the Twirl tool for comparison (instructions on the next page).

TIP To add points to a path and heighten the Twirl filter effect, choose Object menu > Path > Add Anchor Points before applying the Twirl filter.

1 *The Roughen dialog box.*

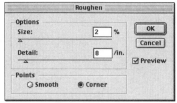

2 *The original object.*

3 *After applying the Roughen filter (or seeing a dog).*

4 *The original objects.*

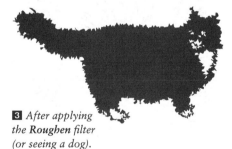

5 *The objects twirled together, Angle 1000°.*

6 *The Twirl filter applied to **5**, Angle 3000°.*

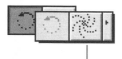

1 *The Twirl tool.*

2 *The original objects.*   **3** *After twirling.*

4 *The original objects (type outlines).*

5 *After applying the Punk filter.*

6 *The original object.*

7 *After applying the Bloat filter.*

Like the Twirl filter, the Twirl tool twirls points around an object's center, but its effect is usually more subtle.

To twirl points around an object's center (mouse method):

1. Select a path object.

2. Choose the Twirl tool (R or Shift-R) **1**.

3. *Optional:* Click to establish a different location for the center of the twirl than the object's center.

4. Move the mouse slightly away from the center point (if one was established), then drag clockwise or counterclockwise. Repeat to intensify the twirl effect **2**–**3**.

TIP To open the Twirl dialog box to enter an angle, Option/Alt click in the document window with the Twirl tool.

TIP Neither the Twirl tool nor the Twirl filter will affect a pattern or a gradient fill—they will twirl only the object's outer shape. To twirl a pattern or gradient fill, apply the Object menu > Expand command to the object first (use a low number of objects), and select all the shapes before twirling. Beware: This monster may not print easily.

TIP To tighten the twirl, keep dragging several times around the object.

To punk or bloat an object:

1. Select an object or objects **4** and **6**.

2. Choose Filter menu > Distort > Punk & Bloat.

3. Check the Preview box.

4. Move the slider to the left to Punk (anchor points move outward and curve segments move inward) **5**, or move the slider to the right to Bloat (anchor points move inward and curve segments move outward) **7**.

5. Click OK.

TIP To add points to the path and intensify the Punk or Bloat effect, choose Object menu > Path > Add Anchor Points before applying the filter. See also Figures 1–3 on page 86.

Twirl Tool; Punk & Bloat Filter

The separate drop shadow objects that the Drop Shadow filter creates are colored in a darker shade of the object's fill and stroke colors. (To produce a shadow by copying an object, see pages 208–209.)

To create a drop shadow:

1. Select one or more objects ◼1. The Drop Shadow filter can be applied to type—it doesn't have to be converted into outlines.

2. Choose Filter menu > Stylize > Drop Shadow.

3. Enter a number in the X Offset field (the horizontal distance between the object and the shadow) and a number in the Y Offset field (the vertical distance) ◼2.

4. In the Darkness field, enter the percentage of black to be added to the object's fill color to produce the shadow color. 100% will produce solid black.

5. *Optional:* Check the Group Shadows box to group each object with its shadow. If this option is checked, each shadow will be stacked directly below its matching object ◼3. If this option is unchecked, all the shadow objects will be placed below all the selected objects ◼4.

6. Click OK (Return/Enter). You can recolor the shadow.

TIP If you apply the Drop Shadow filter to ungrouped type outlines with the Group Shadows box checked, each character will be grouped individually with its shadow. If you prefer, you can group the type outlines together first, leave the Group Shadows box unchecked when you apply the Drop Shadow filter, and then group the shadow characters together afterwards.

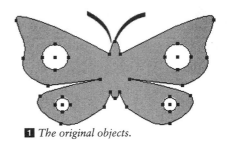

◼1 *The original objects.*

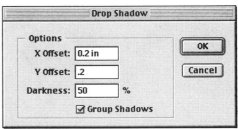

◼2 *The **Drop Shadow** dialog box.*

◼3 *After applying the **Drop Shadow** filter with the **Group Shadows** box **checked**. Each shadow appears directly below its matching object.*

◼4 *After applying the **Drop Shadow** filter, with the **Group Shadows** box **unchecked**. All the shadow objects appear below all the selected objects (some are hidden).*

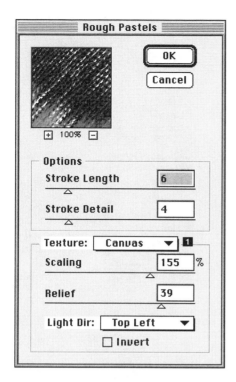

2 *Rough Pastels filter, Burlap **Texture**.*

Applying filters to raster images

All the raster filters are available for a rasterized object or a placed bitmap image in RGB or Grayscale color mode; only the Blur, Sharpen, and Pixelate filters are available for an image in CMYK color mode; no raster filters are available for an image in Bitmap color mode. Some of these filters introduce an element of randomness or distortion that would be difficult to achieve by hand. Others, like the Artistic, Brush Strokes, Sketch, and Texture filters, are designed to make an image look a little less machine-made, more hand-rendered.

When a raster filter is applied to a large, high resolution bitmap image, a progress bar displays while the filter is processing. Click Stop or press Return/Enter to cancel a filter in progress.

In some filter dialog boxes, like Rough Pastels or Grain, there is a Texture or Grain Type option. To use this option, choose a texture type from the Texture or Grain Type drop-down menu **1**–**2**, move the Scaling slider to enlarge or reduce the size of the texture pattern, and move the Relief slider, if there is one, to adjust the depth and prominence of the texture on the image's surface. In some dialog boxes you'll also have the option to load in a bitmap image saved in Photoshop format (files with the ".psd" extension) to use instead of a preset texture. To do this, choose Load Texture from the Texture drop-down menu, highlight the name of the bitmap file you want to use, then click Open.

In addition to the raster filters, other filters you can apply to a raster image include Colors submenu > Adjust Colors, Convert to CMYK, Convert to Grayscale, Convert to RGB, Invert Colors, and Saturate and the Photo Crosshatch filter under the Pen and Ink submenu.

Raster Filters

Rasterize an Object

Note: Before proceeding with any of the raster filters themselves, you should learn about Illustrator's Rasterize command, which converts a vector-based path object into a pixel-based image. You can apply any raster (bitmap) filter to a rasterized object.

To rasterize a path object:

1. Select a path object or objects.

2. Choose Object menu > Rasterize.

3. Choose a Color Model for the image: RGB for video or on-screen display (all raster filters available); CMYK for print output (only the Blur, Sharpen, and Pixelate raster filters available); Grayscale for shades of black and white (all raster filters available); or Bitmap for only black-and-white (no raster filters available) **1**.

4. Click a Resolution setting or enter a resolution value in the Other field.

5. *Optional:* Check the Anti-Alias box to have Illustrator softly fade the edge of the rasterized shape.

6. *Optional:* Check the Create Mask box to include a mask with the image that follows the contours of the object.

7. Click OK (Return/Enter). A bounding box will surround the path object **2–5**.

TIP If you rasterize an object that contains a pattern fill, the pattern color and line weight may change somewhat (especially if the Anti-Alias option is turned on). If the original object had a pattern fill with a transparent background, the transparent background will turn solid white, except if you use the Bitmap Color Model. Rasterizing an object that contains a pattern fill using the Bitmap Color Model can produce interesting results. If you rasterize an object using the Bitmap Color Model with the Create Mask box unchecked, you can then apply a fill color to the bitmap pattern via the Color palette.

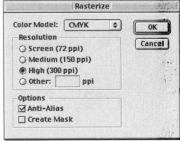

1 *Choose a **Color Model** and a Resolution in the **Rasterize** dialog box.*

2 *A rasterized object with a **mask** after applying **the** Glass filter. **The** mask limits the effect to the **object** shape.*

3 *A rasterized object without **a** mask after applying the Glass **filter.** The effect extends beyond the object's original edge.*

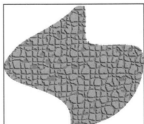

4 *A rasterized object with a **mask** after applying **the** Mosaic Tile **filter.** The mask limits the effect to **the** object shape.*

5 *A rasterized object without **a** mask after applying the Mosaic Tile filter. The effect extends beyond the object's original edge.*

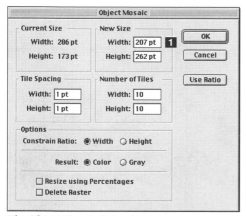

The Object Mosaic dialog box.

2 *The original image.*

3 *The Object Mosaic filter applied.*

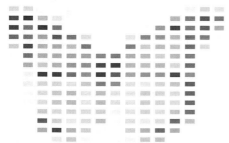

4 *The Object Mosaic filter applied to the original image with spacing between the tiles.*

The Object Mosaic filter breaks up a raster image into a grid of little squares. Each of the squares is a separate object that can be moved or recolored individually.

To apply the Object Mosaic filter:

1. Click on a rasterized object, or on a PICT, TIFF, or parsed (non-linked) EPS bitmap image. The image must be embedded (not linked).

2. Choose Filter menu > Create > Object Mosaic.

3. *Optional:*
   The Current Size field displays the width and height of the image in points. Enter new numbers in the New Size: Width and/or Height fields **1**. (If you want to enter the dimensions in percentages relative to the original, first check the Resize using Percentages box.)
   or
   Enter a New Size: Width (or Height), click Constrain Ratio: Width (or Height) to lock in that dimension, then click Use Ratio (right side of the dialog box) to have Illustrator automatically calculate the opposite dimension proportionate to the object's original dimensions.

4. Enter the Number of Tiles to fill the width and height dimensions. The tiles will be square. If you clicked Use Ratio, the Number of Tiles will be calculated automatically.

5. *Optional:* To add space between each tile, enter numbers in the Tile Spacing: Width and Height fields.

6. *Optional:* When it's applied to a bitmap image, the Object Mosaic filter affects a copy of the image that's made automatically, and the original is left unchanged. Check the Delete Raster box if you want the original image to be deleted.

7. Click Result: Color or Gray.

8. Click OK (Return/Enter) **2**–**4**.

Object Mosaic Filter

253

The raster filters illustrated
Artistic filters

Original image

Colored Pencil

Cutout

Dry Brush

Film Grain

Fresco

Neon Glow

Paint Daubs

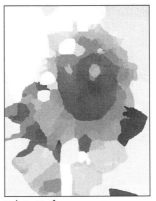
Palette Knife

Artistic Filters

Artistic filters

Original image

Plastic Wrap

Poster Edges

Rough Pastels

Smudge Stick

Sponge

Underpainting

Watercolor

Artistic Filters

255

Blur filters

Original image

Radial Blur

Gaussian Blur

Brush Strokes filters

Original image

Accented Edges

Angled Strokes

Crosshatch

Dark Strokes

Ink Outlines

Brush Strokes filters

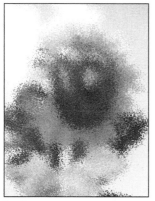

Spatter

Sprayed Strokes

Sumi-e

Distort filters

Original image

Diffuse Glow

Glass (Blocks)

Ocean Ripple

Pixelate filters

Original image

Color Halftone

Crystallize

Mezzotint (Short Strokes)

Mezzotint (Medium Dots)

Pointillize

For the Unsharp Mask filter, see our Visual QuickStart Guide on Photoshop!

Stylize filter

Original image

Glowing Edges

Sketch filters

Original image

Bas Relief

Chalk & Charcoal

Charcoal

Chrome

Conté Crayon

Graphic Pen

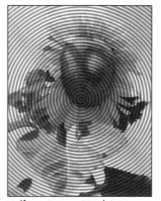

Halftone Pattern (Circle)

Halftone Pattern (Dot)

Sketch filters

Original image

Note Paper

Photocopy

Plaster

Reticulation

Stamp

Torn Edges

Water Paper

Sketch Filters

Texture filters

Original image

Craquelure

Grain (Enlarged)

Grain (Horizontal)

Mosaic Tiles

Patchwork

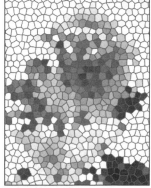

Stained Glass

Texturizer

Texture Filters

The Pen & Ink filters

In this section, we discuss the Hatch Effects filter and the Photo Crosshatch filter. The Hatch Effects filter creates an amazing assortment of line work patterns by turning a path object into a mask and then creating a fill of linework shapes behind the mask. You can choose from 26 preset pen patterns—called hatch styles—that you can use as is or further modify using a wide variety of options. You can also create a new hatch from scratch from an Illustrator object.

To apply the Pen and Ink filter:

1. Select an object.

2. Choose Filter menu > Pen and Ink > Hatch Effects.

3. Check the Preview box or leave it unchecked to speed processing.

4. Choose a predefined effect from the Hatch Effect drop-down menu **1**.

   If you're satisfied with the pattern, click OK. To further modify it, follow any of the remaining steps.

5. Choose another predefined hatch from the Hatch drop-down menu to use with the current effect.

6. Move the **Density** slider to adjust the number of hatch shapes in the fill. Or to adjust the density a different way, click a different gray on the vertical grayscale bar next to the preview window **2**.

7. For any of the following options, choose a setting other than None from the drop-down menu on the right side (read the sidebar on the next page), and move one or both of the sliders.

   Dispersion controls the spacing between hatch shapes.

   Thickness controls the line thickness of the hatch shapes. This property is available only for hatch styles that are composed of lines (Cross, Vertical lines, Crosshatch 1, and Worm).

   Scale controls the size of the hatch shapes.

   Rotation controls the angle of the hatch shapes.

Pen and Ink fills can be quite complex, and their direction lines and line endpoints may extend way beyond the edge of the original object. To prevent inadvertent selection of a Pen and Ink fill, put the Pen and Ink object on its own layer and then lock that layer.

If your Pen and Ink fill doesn't print, try reducing the object's Output resolution (see page 312). Also, don't apply the Pen and Ink filter to an object that already contains a Pen and Ink fill—it will demand too much from your output device.

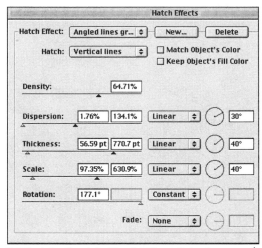

1 *The left side of the* **Hatch Effects** *dialog box.*

2 *The right side of the* **Hatch** *Effects dialog box.*

Pen and Ink Filter

HATCH EFFECT DROP-DOWN MENU OPTIONS

None: No effect.

Constant: Effect repeats without changing across the entire shape.

Linear: Effect intensifies in a progression from one side of the fill shape to the other.

Reflect: Effect varies from the center of the fill shape outward.

Symmetric: Like Linear, but more proportionate and even. Hatch shading looks like shading on a cylindrical object.

Random: Effect changes in a random, haphazard fashion across the fill shape.

The Linear, Reflect, Symmetric, and Random options have two sliders each, and their position controls the range of choices for that option. The wider the distance between a pair of sliders, the wider the range of possibilities for that option. Enter a value in the Angle box or drag the angle dial to specify an axis for the change. Press Tab to preview an Angle change.

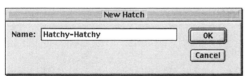

1 *Enter a name for the new hatch. Note: In Windows, this dialog box is called "New Settings."*

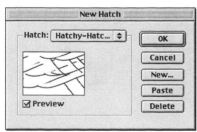

2 *The new hatch previews.*

8. Check the **Match Object's Color** box to make the hatch match the object's fill color. Check the **Keep Object's Fill Color** box to make the hatch black and leave the object color unchanged.

9. From the **Fade** drop-down menu, choose whether the hatch style will fade To White or To Black across the fill shape. If the object's fill was a gradient, choose Use Gradient to color the hatch shapes with the gradient. If you like, you can enter an angle for the axis along which the fade will occur.

10. Click OK (Return/Enter).

TIP To **save** any current property option changes to a custom Hatch Effect variation, click New at the top of the dialog box, enter a Name, then click OK.

TIP To **delete** the current Hatch Effect variation, click Delete, then click Yes. *Warning:* This can't be undone by pressing Cancel in the Hatch Effects dialog box or by using the Undo command.

TIP Click **Update** to save the current property options to the current Hatch Effect variant. *Warning:* Update overwrites the existing Hatch Effect variant. Click **Reset** to remove any property variations from the current Hatch Effect.

The hatch is the underlying pattern tile that is used by the Pen and Ink filter.

To create a new hatch pattern:

1. Create a small object or objects to use as the hatch pattern.

2. Select the object or objects.

3. Choose Filter menu > Pen and Ink > New Hatch.

4. Click New.

5. Type a Name for the hatch **1**, then click OK.

6. Check the Preview box to display the new pattern in the preview window **2**. Click OK (Return/Enter) to close the New Hatch dialog box. The hatch will be saved in the current open hatch library.

To modify an existing hatch:

1. Scroll to a blank area of the artboard, and deselect all objects.

2. Choose Filter menu > Pen and Ink > New Hatch.

3. Choose the pattern you want to edit from the Hatch drop-down menu.

4. Click Paste.

5. Click OK (Return/Enter). The hatch pattern objects will be selected.

6. Zoom in, and modify the hatch pattern.

7. Reselect the hatch pattern object(s).

8. Follow steps 3–6 in the previous set of instructions.

TIP Click Delete to remove the currently chosen hatch style from the Hatch drop-down menu. This can't be undone.

The default Hatch Sets library opens automatically when Illustrator is launched.

To save a hatch library:

1. Create your own custom Hatch Effect variations.

2. Choose Filter menu > Pen and Ink > Library Save As.

3. Enter a new name for the library, open the Adobe Illustrator 8 > Plug-ins > Illustrator Filters > Pen and Ink folder, where the default Hatch Sets library is located, then click Save. *Note:* If you don't change the file name from the default name, and you then click Save, you will be asked to cancel or replace the existing file. Click Replace if you want to edit the default library.

To open a hatch library:

1. Choose Filter menu > Pen and Ink > Library Open.

2. Locate and highlight the name of a pre-saved library, then click Select.

TIP A handful of custom hatch set libraries are supplied with the application. They are located in the Adobe Illustrator 8 > Sample Files > Hatch Sets folder.

Fanya, Diane Margolin.

Taj Mahal, Diane Margolin.

1 *The original grayscale photo.*

2 *The **Photo Crosshatch** filter applied using these settings: Two Layers, Density 3.5, Dispersion Noise 0, Thickness .4, Max. Line Length 24, Rotation Noise 2°, Rotation Variance 100°, Top angle 40°. The image below is a close-up.*

The Photo Crosshatch filter translates a rasterized, photographic image into a crosshatch pattern. When it's applied at the appropriate density, the crosshatches create an appearance of hand-drawn shading—like an artist's pen drawing.

To convert a continuous-tone image into a crosshatch image:

1. Place a photographic image into an Illustrator document **1**. Don't link an EPS image—the filter won't be available.
or
Select an image in your illustration, then choose Object menu > Rasterize.

2. Choose Filter menu > Pen and Ink > Photo Crosshatch.

3. Choose the number of Hatch Layers (1–8). This is similar to choosing levels of posterization. The greater the number of hatch layers, the more levels of shading will be produced in the image. (Don't get confused here. The layers will not appear as separate layers in the document.)

4. *Optional:* Move the sliders under the histogram to determine how different lightness levels in the original image will be rendered by line patterns. Move the rightmost slider to the right to create more line patterning in the image highlights and lessen areas of absolute white, or move the rightmost slider to the left to decrease line patterning in the highlights and increase areas of absolute white. Move the middle slider to increase or decrease line patterning in the midtones. Move the leftmost slider to the right to decrease line patterning in the shadows.

5. Move the sliders on the left side of the dialog box to control the hatch lines (**3**, next page):

The **Density** slider controls the number of hatch lines used. A low Density will produce a very dense collection of hatch lines. A high image resolution may affect the density of the hatch lines.

(Continued on the following page)

Photo Crosshatch Filter

Photo Crosshatch Filter

The **Dispersion Noise** slider controls the spacing between hatch line segments. 0% Dispersion Noise produces line segments that align perfectly end to end to form a long, straight-line texture. A value greater than 0% produces line segments that don't align end to end, and thus no long straight lines. A low Dispersion Noise produces a hand-done look; a high Dispersion Noise produces more obvious patterning and less obvious shading.

The **Thickness** slider controls the stroke weight of the line segments.

The **Max. Line Length** slider controls the length of the line segments.

The **Rotation Noise** slider controls the amount of arbitrary rotation given to individual line segments on each hatch layer. The higher the Rotation Noise setting, the more obvious the patterning and the less obvious the shading.

The **Rotation Variance** slider controls how much each hatch layer is rotated relative to the previous layer. High values distinguish each layer more, but make shading less smooth.

The **Top Angle** is the angle along which hatch lines are drawn in the topmost hatch layer.

6. Click OK (Return/Enter) (**2**, previous page, and **4**, this page). To produce shading, hatch lines start on the edge of an image's highlights and continue into the midtones or all the way into the shadows, while other hatch lines start in the midtones and continue into the shadows. Still other hatch lines are drawn only in the shadows.

TIP The Photo Crosshatch filter converts the original rasterized image. Make a copy of it first if you want the original image to be unchanged.

TIP To darken selected areas in the resulting crosshatch, Shift-select line segments using the Direct-selection tool, and then increase their stroke weight.

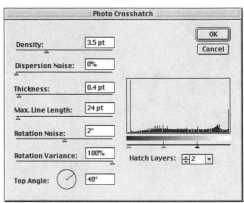

3 *The Photo Crosshatch dialog box.*

4 *The Photo Crosshatch filter applied to the original image on the previous page using these settings: Two Layers, Density 3.5, Dispersion Noise 15%, Thickness .5, Max. Line Length 24, Rotation Noise 18°, Rotation Variance 90%, Top angle 40°. In this image, the higher Dispersion Noise, Rotation Noise, and Rotation Variance values create a more hand-drawn look, as compared with the image on the previous page. The image below is a close-up.*

MASKS 18

In Illustrator, a mask works like a picture frame or mat. While it is in effect, it hides parts of an illustration that fall outside its borders. Only parts of objects that are within the confines of the masking object will show. Masked objects can be moved, restacked, reshaped, or repainted. In this chapter you will learn how to mask objects; how to restack, select, or add masked objects; how to lock or release a mask; and how to unmask one object.

Daniel Pelavin (icon appears courtesy of DFS Group, Ltd.)

Masking object.   *Masked* object.

The same image in artwork view.

Note: To use a group of objects as one masking object, you must first convert them into a compound path (choose Object menu > Compound Paths > Make).

To mask objects:

1. *Optional:* Follow the instructions on the next page to place the masking object and the objects to be masked on one layer before you create the mask so you can easily reposition them using the Layers palette.

2. Arrange the objects to be masked **1**. The masking object can be an open or closed path. A brushstroke or gradient mesh object can be masked, but it cannot be used as the masking object. You can use type as a masking object. You don't need to convert it to outlines.

3. Select the masking object using the Selection tool, then choose Object menu > Arrange > Bring to Front (Command-Shift-]/Ctrl-Shift-]). Or bring the object to the top layer by moving the tiny square upward on the Layers palette.

4. Choose the Selection tool (V).

5. Select all the objects, including the masking object.

6. Choose Object menu > Masks > Make (Command-7/Ctrl-7) **2**. The masking object will now have a stroke and fill of None and all the objects will be selected. You can move a masked object individually using the Selection or Direct-selection tool. If the masking object was made from a compound, use the Direct-selection tool to move individual objects within the compound.

TIP If the mask is too complex, it may not print. Don't make a mask out of a complex shape that contains hundreds of points or out of an intricate compound path. And don't use more than a dozen type characters as one masking object.

TIP To copy only a masked object, drag it with Option/Alt held down. The copy will also be masked.

1 *Place the masking object in front of the object or objects to be masked, and make sure all the objects are selected.*

2 *The type is masking part of the gradient.*

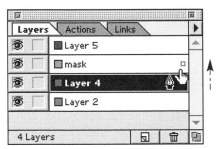

1 *The current selection square from Layer 4 being moved up to the layer called "mask."*

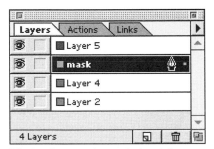

2 *The objects to be masked and the masking object are now on the same layer.*

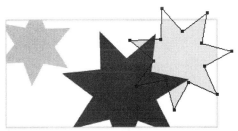

3 *A masked object is selected.*

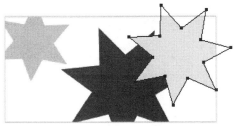

4 *The object is brought forward.*

If the masking object-to-be and the objects to be masked are on more than one layer, any unselected object between the backmost object to be masked and the masking object will also be masked. Follow these steps to move the objects you want to mask to their own layer, which will prevent other objects from being masked inadvertently.

To position the objects to be masked on one layer:

1. On the Layers palette, Option/Alt click the New Layer button, enter a Name (e.g., "Mask"), then click OK.

2. Choose the Selection tool (V).

3. Shift-click on the masking object and the objects to be masked.
   or
   Drag a marquee over the masking object and all the objects to be masked.

4. On the Layers palette, drag the current selection square up or down to the new layer **1**–**2**.
   or
   Choose Item menu > Group (Command-G/Ctrl-G).

5. Follow the instructions on the previous page to create a mask.

Stacking is explained in Chapter 14.

To restack a masked object:

1. Choose the Selection tool (V).

2. Select the object to be restacked **3**.

3. Choose Object menu > Arrange > Bring Forward (Command-]/Ctrl-]) or Send Backward (Command-[/Ctrl-[) **4**.
   or
   Control-click/Right-click and choose from the Arrange submenu on the context menu.
   or
   Choose Edit menu > Cut, select another masked object, then choose Edit menu > Paste In Front (Command-F/Ctrl-F) or Paste In Back (Command-B/Ctrl-B).

Re-Layer or Restack Mask Objects

To select mask objects:

To select the masking object *and* the masked objects, choose the Group-selection tool (or hold down Option/Alt with the Direct-selection tool), then double-click on any of the objects.

To select *one or more* individual masked objects, use the Selection tool.

If you haven't applied a fill or stroke color to the masking object, it will be invisible in Preview view. To select *only* the masking object when your illustration is in Preview view, choose the Selection tool, and turn on Smart Guides (Command-U/Ctrl-U). The edge of the masking object will display as a Smart Guide (Object Highlighting) when the pointer is over it. If your illustration is in Artwork view, choose the Selection tool, then click on the edge of the masking object.

To select *all* the masking objects in your illustration, deselect all objects, then choose Edit menu > Select > Masks. Shift-click with the Selection tool on the edge of any masking object you don't want selected.

TIP To convert a gradient or a pattern into a grouped set of masked objects, select an object that contains a gradient or pattern fill, then use Object menu > Expand.

TIP To find out whether an object is acting as a mask, select the object, choose File menu > Selection Info, then choose Objects from the Info drop-down menu. If the Masks entry has the number 1 after it, then the object is a masking object.

To add an object to a mask:

1. Choose the Selection tool (V).

2. Select the object to be added.

3. Move the object over the mask **1**.

4. Choose Edit menu > Cut (Command-X/Ctrl-X).

5. Click on a masked object (not the masking object).

6. Choose Edit menu > Paste In Front (Command-F/Ctrl-F) or Paste In Back (Command-B/Ctrl-B) **2**.

1 *The object to be added (the star) is moved over the masking object (the banner shape).*

2 *The object is now being masked.*

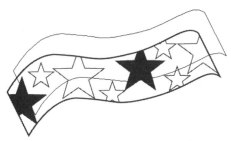

1 *If you move an **unlocked** masking object (the banner shape)...*

2 *...only that object will move.*

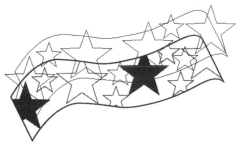

3 *If you move a **locked** masking object, the masked objects will move along with it.*

4 *The mask is **released**.*

TIP To change the stacking position of the newly pasted object, follow the instructions on page 269.

If a masking object is locked, you can then click on any visible part of it with a Selection tool and move it as a unit—the masked objects will move along with it.

To lock a mask:

1. Choose the Direct-selection tool.
2. Click on the masking object.
3. Choose Object menu > Masks > Lock **1**–**3**. (Choose Unlock from the same submenu to unlock the mask.)

When you release a mask, the complete objects are displayed again. If no fill or stroke was applied to the masking object, that object will not display in Preview view. It will display as a Smart Guide object when the pointer is over it.

To release a mask:

1. Choose the Group-selection tool (A or Shift-A).
2. Double-click a masked object or click on the masking object.
3. Choose Object menu > Masks > Release (Command-Option-7/Ctrl-Alt-7) **4**.

Lock a Mask; Release a Mask

271

To unmask one object:

1. Choose the Selection tool (V).

2. Click on the object you want to unmask 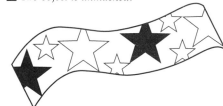.

3. Choose Edit menu > Cut (Command-X/Ctrl-X).

4. *Optional:* If the masking object and the masked objects are on different layers, highlight a layer on the Layers palette that is above or below those layers.

5. Choose Edit menu > Paste (Command-V/Ctrl-V). The pasted object will now be independent of the mask. Move it, if you like **2**.

TIP To unmask an object another way, select the object, then, on the Layers palette, drag the little current selection square to a different layer.

TIP To unmask an object and delete it from the illustration, select it, then press Delete/Backspace.

Note: To **recolor** a masking object **3**–**6**, select it with the Selection tool and apply color as you would to any single object. The fill and stroke belong to one object (they're not separate objects, as in previous application versions).

Unmask One Object

1 *Select the object you want to unmask.*

2 *The object is **unmasked**.*

3 *The original mask.*

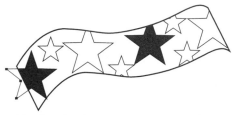

4 *A black fill was applied to the masking object. The masked objects were also **recolored**.*

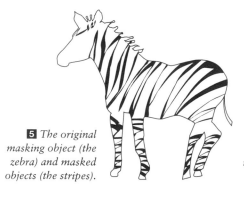

5 *The original masking object (the zebra) and masked objects (the stripes).*

6 *The recolored masking object and masked objects.*

GRAPHS | 19

Nine different graph styles can be created in Illustrator: column, stacked column, bar, stacked bar, line, area, scatter, pie, and radar. Explaining Illustrator's elaborate graphing features in depth is beyond the scope of this book. However, this chapter contains learn-by-example instructions for creating a simple grouped column graph and then customizing the graph design. Also included are general guidelines for creating other types of graphs. Alternate design and graph style variations are discussed in the Tips.

See the Illustrator User Guide for more information about creating graphs. Also, check out the files in the Adobe Illustrator 8 > Sample Files > Graphs & Graph Designs folder, which contain graph examples and artwork for custom graph designs.

The nine **graph** tools.

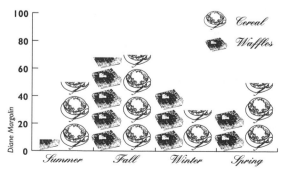

Seasonal Breakfast Favorites

Diane Margolin

The basic graph-making steps

1) Define the graph **area**
2) Enter graph **data** and **labels**
3) Choose **graph style** options
4) Add custom **design** elements

A graph created in Illustrator is a group of objects. As long as a graph remains grouped, its data and style remain associated. As with any group, individual elements in a graph can be selected using the Direct-selection or Group-selection tool and then modified without having to ungroup the whole graph.

To define the graph area:

Choose a graph tool **1**, then drag diagonally.

or

Choose a graph tool, click on your page, enter overall Width and Height values for the graph, then click OK **2**. The Graph Data palette will open automatically.

TIP You can use the Scale tool to resize the whole graph later on.

The Graph Data palette is like a worksheet, with rows and columns for entering numbers and labels. Most graphs are created in an x/y axis formation. The y-axis (vertical) is numerical and shows the data in quantities. The x-axis (horizontal) represents information categories.

To enter graph data:

1. For this exercise, enter the data shown in **3** into the cells on the Graph Data palette. (*For other graphs:* If you enter dates in the first column, be sure the dates are inside quotation marks. If you enter any letters with the numbers, no quotes are needed. You can click the Import button to import a tab-delineated text file or a file from a spreadsheet application.)

   Click a cell, type the entry, then:

   Press Tab to move across a row.

   or

   Press Return to move down a column.

   or

   Click on any row or column cell.

   or

   Press an arrow key.

2. On the top row of the palette, enter the labels. These will appear next to the legend boxes in the graph.

3. Click the close box, then click Save.

TIP If you make a mistake when entering data, click on the cell that contains the incorrect data, correct the error in the highlighted entry line, then press Tab or Return/Enter to accept the correction.

1 *The* **graph tools.**

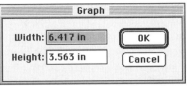

2 *Enter* **Width** *and* **Height** *dimensions for a new graph in the* **Graph** *dialog box.*

Do not enter any data in this first cell for a Column graph.

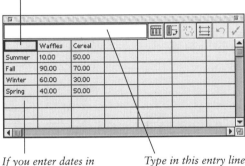

If you enter dates in this column, put them inside quotation marks.

Type in this entry line to fill the currently highlighted cell.

3 *The* **Graph Data** *palette.*

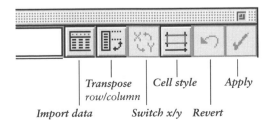

Transpose row/column   *Cell style*   *Apply*

Import data   *Switch x/y*   *Revert*

The buttons on the **Graph Data** *palette.*

1 *Drag a vertical line to the right to widen a column.*

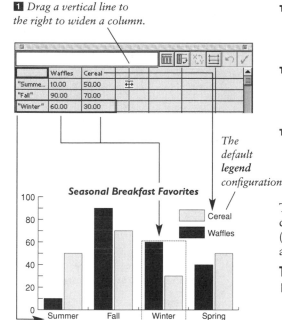

*The default **legend** configuration*

This illustration shows the relationship between the graph data palette and parts of the graph.

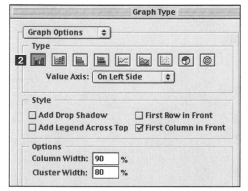

*The **Graph Type** dialog box with **Graph Options** displayed. Note: If you want the legend to appear in its default configuration (as in figure **1** on this page), don't check the Add Legend Across Top box.*

TIP To widen a column to accommodate a long label name, drag the vertical column line to the right **1** (you'll see a two-headed arrow pointer).

TIP To make a legend name appear on two lines, enter "|", which you get with this keystroke: Shift-\ (backslash), on the line where you want the name to break.

TIP To preview the new graph while the Graph Data palette is open, click the Apply (check mark) button. Move the palette to the side if you need to.

The Graph Type dialog box contains three different option screens: Graph Options (graph choices), Value Axis (vertical axis), and Category Axis (horizontal axis).

To restyle the graph:

1. Choose the Selection tool, marquee the whole graph, then choose Object menu > Graphs > Type (or double-click the current graph tool).

2. For this exercise, click the Column (first) button **2**. This graph type is a good choice if you want to compare two or three entities over several time periods.

3. Enter 90 in the Options: Column Width field to make the individual columns narrower. Enter a Cluster Width percentage of 80. The two column objects will now spread across only 80% of the horizontal area allotted for each x-axis category.

4. For this exercise, choose On Left Side from the Value Axis drop-down menu. The Value Axis options affect how and where the x/y axis appears.

5. To style the vertical axis, choose Value Axis from the topmost drop-down menu (**3**, next page). For this exercise, leave the Override Calculated Values box unchecked (this is the default). Illustrator will scale the y-axis automatically based on the largest and smallest numbers entered on the worksheet. (Check this box to enter your own minimum and

(Continued on the following page)

Restyle the Graph

maximum values and the number of divisions for the *y*-axis.)

6. The middle part of the dialog box is used for styling the vertical axis tick lines (the small lines perpendicular to the axis lines). For this exercise, choose Short from the Length drop-down menu and enter 2 in the "Draw...tick marks per division" field. This will add an extra tick mark between each *y*-axis number.

7. Click OK (Return/Enter) 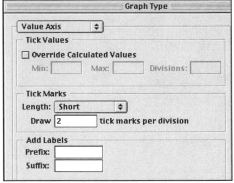.

3 The **Graph Type** *dialog box with Value Axis options displayed.*

To customize the graph

To move, transform, or modify the fill or stroke of an individual object in a graph, select it first with the Group-selection tool.

TIP To restack part of a graph, select a whole group (e.g., the bars and their legend or an axis and its tick marks) with the Group-selection tool, then choose Object menu > Arrange > Bring To Front or Send To Back.

To recolor the columns/legend:

1. Choose the Group-selection tool (A or Shift-A).

2. Double-click on a legend rectangle to select the legend and its four related columns.

3. Change the fill and/or stroke. Both the legend rectangle and its related column objects will change **5**. Repeat for the other legend rectangle.

TIP You can also click on a column with the Group-selection tool to select it, click a second time to add its related columns to the selection, then click a third time to add its legend to the selection. Or use the Direct-selection tool with Option/Alt held down instead of choosing the Group-selection tool.

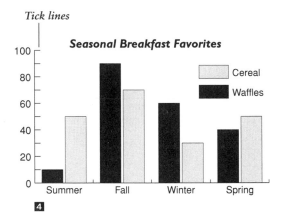

4

5 *To restyle this column graph, new fill patterns were applied to the legend rectangles and their related columns, a heavier stroke weight was applied to the axes, and the typefaces were changed.*

Customize a Graph

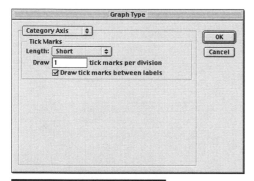

DON'T FORGET YOUR X

This is the Graph Type dialog box with its Category Axis options displayed. Here you can choose a Length option and enter a value for the number of tick marks for the x-axis (horizontal axis).

2 *Click on the line (not the square marker) to select the legend and its line bar.*

1 *The **Column style** and **Line style** are combined in this graph. A new legend name and a column of new data was entered in the third column on the Graph Data palette. The new legend box and its bars were selected, and then the Line button was clicked in the Graph Type dialog box. Finally, the new line and the legend were selected with the Group-selection tool (two clicks) and Object menu > Arrange > Bring to Front was chosen.*

To change the type in a graph:

1. Choose the Group-selection tool.

2. Click once on the baseline of a type block to select just that block.
   or
   Click twice to select all the type in the legends or all the labels.
   or
   Click three times to select all the type in the graph.

3. Modify the type as usual.

TIP To switch the row and column data, choose Object menu > Graphs > Data, then click the Transpose row/column (second) button.

TIP Turn on Smart Guides to help you select the type baseline.

To combine more than one style in a graph:

1. Choose the Group-selection tool.

2. Click twice on the legend box for the category you want to change to a new style.

3. Choose Object menu > Graphs > Type.

4. Click a new Graph type button, and then choose options for that type. For this exercise, click the Line graph (fifth) button.

5. Choose On Left Side from the Value Axis drop-down menu.

6. Check Options: Draw Filled Lines box and enter 6 in the Line Width field.

7. Click OK (Return/Enter) **1**.

TIP To select and modify the line bar in the graph, click twice with the Group-selection tool on the small line bar in the legend (not on the small square marker) **2**, or click on the actual line bar segments in the graph. To modify the marker squares (the points on the line), double-click the square marker in the legend.

(Continued on the following page)

Customize a Graph

You can replace the rectangles in a graph with graphic objects.

To create a custom graph design:

1. Create a graphic object (not a blend or a brushstroke, unless it's expanded). Draw a rectangle around the object, and apply a fill and stroke of None to the rectangle (unless you want it to display in the graph). With the rectangle selected, choose Object menu > Arrange > Send To Back.

2. Choose the Selection tool (V), then marquee the rectangle and the graphic object. Group the objects, if desired, and leave them selected.

3. Choose Object menu > Graphs > Design.

4. Click New Design ■.

5. Click Rename, enter a name for the graphic object, then click OK twice.

6. Click twice on a legend box with the Group-selection tool (the legend and its bars should be selected).

7. Choose Object menu > Graphs > Column.

8. Choose the new column design, and choose from the Column Type drop-down menu ■. The selected type will preview as a thumbnail. For our graph ■, we chose Repeating to create a stacked column of objects, and we unchecked the Rotate Legend Design box. We also chose the Chop Design option from the For Fractions drop-down menu. To prevent the design object from shrinking too much, use a higher Each Design Represents value. You can also use the Scale tool to resize a selected object.

    Choose Uniformly Scaled to maintain the design object's proportions.

    Choose Vertically Scaled to stretch the entire design object.

    Choose Sliding to stretch the design object across a section that you'll designate. (See page 317 of the Adobe Illustrator User Guide.)

9. Click OK (Return/Enter).

An object that was created for our graph.

Diane Margolin

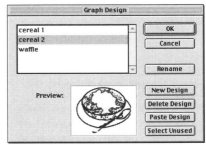

1 The *Graph Design* dialog box.

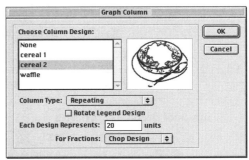

2 The *Graph Column* dialog box.

Seasonal Breakfast Favorites

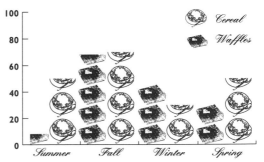

3 *Custom design elements used in a column graph (Graph Column, Column type: Repeating). In the Graph Type dialog box, we decreased the Column width value to narrow the food designs (we chose 75%).*

PRECISION TOOLS 20

There are many tools you can use to position or move objects more precisely. In this chapter you will learn how to use rulers, guides, and grids to align and position objects. How to move an object a specified distance via the Move dialog box. How to use the Measure tool to calculate distances between objects. How to use the Transform palette to reposition, resize, rotate, or shear an object. And how to use the Align palette to align or distribute objects.

Smart Guides are precision tools, too, but they're so helpful and so easy to use, we discussed them early in the book. See pages 76 and 303.

Move the Ruler Origin

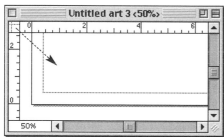

1 *Drag diagonally away from the intersection of the rulers.*

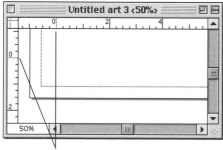

2 *Note the new position of the zeros on the rulers after you change the **ruler origin.***

The rulers are located on the top and left edges of the document window. All measurements are read from the ruler origin, which is the point where the zero is on each ruler. By default, the ruler origin is positioned at the lower left corner of the page, but it can be moved to a different location in any individual document.

To move the ruler origin:

1. Make sure the rulers are displayed. To do this, choose View menu > Show Rulers; or use the Command-R/Ctrl-R shortcut; or Control-click/Right-click on the artboard and choose Show Rulers from the context menu.

2. Drag the square where the two rulers intersect to a new position **1**–**2**.

   Note: To restore the ruler origin to its default position, double-click where the two rulers intersect at the upper left corner of the document window.

TIP If you move the ruler origin, the position of a pattern fill in any existing objects may change.

For most purposes, Smart Guides work adequately for arranging objects (see page 76). If you need guides that stay on the screen, however, you'll need to create them using either method described on this page. Ruler guides don't print. If View menu > **Snap to Point** is turned on, as you drag an object near a guide, the black pointer will turn white and the part of the object that's under the pointer will snap to the guide.

To create a ruler guide:

1. *Optional:* Create a new layer expressly for the guides.

2. If the rulers are not displayed, choose View menu > Show Rulers.

3. Drag a guide from the horizontal or vertical ruler onto your page 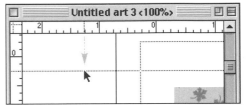. If **Snap to Grid** is on, as you create or move the guide, it will snap to the nearest ruler tick mark. The newly created guide will be locked.

   Note: Choose View menu > Hide Guides or Show Guides (Command-;/Ctrl-;) to hide or display guides. To clear all guides, choose View menu > Clear Guides.

TIP Control-click/Right-click either ruler to open a context menu from which you can choose a different unit of measure. This setting will supercede the units setting in File menu > Preferences > Units & Undo.

To turn an object into a guide:

1. Select an object or a group of objects .

2. Choose View menu > Make Guides (Command-5/Ctrl-5).
   or
   Control-click/Right-click and choose Make Guides from the context menu 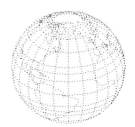.

TIP You can transform a guide object, as long as it isn't locked.

To turn a guide back into an object:

1. If guides are locked, Control-click/Right-click and choose Lock Guides from the context menu to uncheck that option.

2. Choose the Selection tool (V).

1 *Drag a guide from the horizontal or vertical ruler.*

2 *An object is selected.*

3 *Make Guides is chosen from the context menu.*

4 *The object is now a guide.*

Create Ruler Guide; Object into Guide

CONSTRAIN YOURSELF

Choose File menu > Preferences > General, then enter a new number in the Tool Behavior: Constrain Angle field (0° is the default). Any *new* object that you draw in a new or existing document will rest on the new axes, and any new object that you move or transform with Shift held down will snap to the new axes. This tool also affects text objects; the Rectangle, Ellipse, and Graph tools; the transformation tools (Scale, Reflect, Rotate, and Shear, but not Blend) the Gradient tool when used with Shift held down; the arrow keys; the grid; and Info palette readouts.

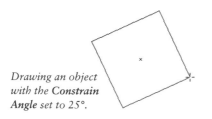

*Drawing an object with the **Constrain Angle** set to 25°.*

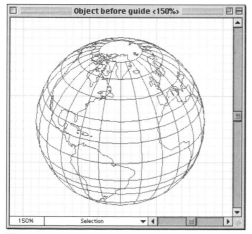

1 *The **Grid** displayed.*

3. Select one guide or marquee or Shift-click multiple guides.

4. Choose View menu > Release Guides (Command-Option-5/Ctrl-Alt-5).
or
Control-click/Right-click and choose Release Guides from the context menu. The guide will revert to an object, with its former fill and stroke.

To select or move guides, they must first be unlocked. By default, the Lock Guides command is turned on. *Note:* To lock *one* guide, unlock all guides, click on the guide, then choose Object menu > Lock.

To lock or unlock all guides:

Choose View menu > Lock Guides (Command-Option-;/Ctrl-Alt-;) to check or uncheck the command.
or
Control-click/Right-click on the artboard and choose Lock Guides from the context menu.

To remove one guide:

I. Make sure guides are unlocked (instructions above).

2. Choose the Selection tool (V), and select the guide.

3. *Macintosh:* Press Delete. *Windows:* Press Backspace or Del.

The grid is like non-printing graph paper. You can use it to help you arrange objects. To change the grid style (lines or dots), color, or spacing, see page 302. To force objects to snap to the grid, choose View menu > **Snap to Grid** (Command-Shift-"/Ctrl-Shift-"). This snap function works even when the grid isn't displayed.

To hide/show the grid:

Choose View menu > Show Grid (Command-"/Ctrl-") **1** or Hide Grid.
or
Control-click/Right-click and choose Show Grid or Hide Grid from the context menu.

Unlock Guides; Remove a Guide; Show Grid

To place guides around an object or create evenly spaced guides:

1. Choose the Selection tool (V), then select an existing rectangle. Make sure the rectangle is on the printable page. *Warning:* If you use a non-rectangular shape, the shape will revert to a rectangle!
   or
   Choose the Rectangle tool, then drag a rectangle to define the guide area .

2. Make sure the ruler origin is in the default location.

3. Choose Type menu > Rows & Columns.

4. Make sure the Preview box is checked 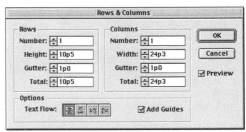, and check the Add Guides box.

5. To encircle the object with guides without dividing it, leave both the Columns and Rows Numbers as 1. To create a set of evenly spaced guides, enter a Rows: Number, Height, and Gutter width and a Columns: Number, Width, and Gutter width.

6. Click OK (Return/Enter) 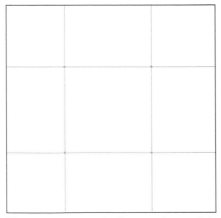.

7. With the Selection tool, Shift-click on the rectangle or rectangles to deselect them so they are not affected by the next step.

8. Choose View menu > Make Guides (Command-5/Ctrl-5) 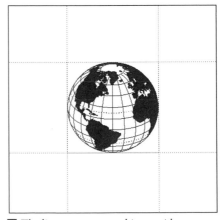. If you like, you can now delete the rectangles that were used to create the guides.

1 *A rectangle is drawn around the globe to define the guide area.*

2 *The Rows & Columns dialog box.*

3 *Lines are automatically created around the rectangle.*

4 *The lines are converted into guides.*

SHIFTING PATTERNS

If you move an object that contains a pattern fill manually or using the Move dialog box and the Patterns box is unchecked in the Move dialog box, the pattern will shift its position within the object. If the Patterns box is checked but the Objects box is not and you use the Move command, only the pattern position will shift—not the object.

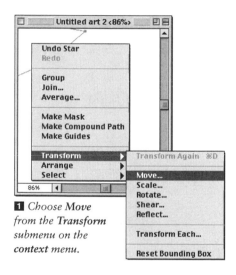

1 *Choose* Move *from the* Transform *submenu on the context menu.*

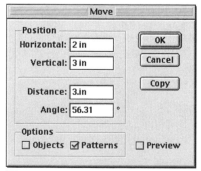

2 *In the* Move *dialog box, enter numbers in the* Horizontal *and* Vertical *fields or enter the* Distance *and* Angle *you want the object to move.*

You can precisely reposition an object by entering values in the Move dialog box. Move dialog box settings remain the same until you change them, move an object using the mouse, or use the Measure tool, so you can repeat the same move as many times as you like using the Transform Again shortcut (Command-D/Ctrl-D).

To move an object a specified distance:

1. Choose a low view percentage for your illustration so the object won't disappear from view when it's moved.

2. Choose the Selection tool (V).

3. Select the object you want to move.

4. Control-click/Right-click and choose Move from the Transform submenu on the context menu **1**.
   or
   Choose Object menu > Transform > Move.
   or
   Double-click the Selection tool.

5. Enter a positive number in the Horizontal and/or Vertical field to move the object to the right or upward, respectively. Enter a negative number to move the object to the left or downward **2**. Enter 0 in either field to prevent the object from moving along that axis. You can use any of these units of measure: "p," "pt," "in," "mm," "q," or "cm".
   or
   Enter a positive Distance and a positive Angle between 0 and 180 to move the object upward. Enter a positive Distance and a negative Angle between 0 and –180 to move the object downward. The other fields will change automatically.

6. Check the Preview box. If Preview was already checked, uncheck and recheck it.

7. *Optional:* Click Copy to close the dialog box and move a copy of the object (not the object itself).

8. Click OK (Return/Enter).

You can use the Measure tool to calculate the distance and/or angle between two points in an illustration. When you use the Measure tool, the amounts it calculates are displayed on the Info palette, which opens automatically.

The distances calculated using the Measure tool, as displayed on the Info palette, also become the current values in the Move dialog box, so you can use the Measure tool as a guide to judge how far to move a selected object first, then open the Move dialog box and click OK.

To measure a distance using the Measure tool:

1. Choose the Measure tool on the Hand tool pop-out menu (H or Shift-H) .

2. Click the starting and ending points spanning the distance or angle you want to measure –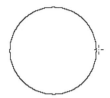.

   or

   Drag from the first point to the second point.

   Measurements will be displayed in the "D:" area on the Info palette .

TIP Hold down Shift while clicking or dragging with the Measure tool to constrain the measurement to a multiple of 45°.

1 *Measure tool.*

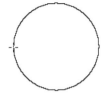
2 *Click a starting point. The **Info** palette will open.*

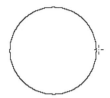
3 *Click an **ending** point. The distance between clicks will display on the **Info** palette.*

*Vertical distance from the **starting point**.*

*Horizontal distance from the **x** axis.*

*Horizontal distance from the **starting point**.*

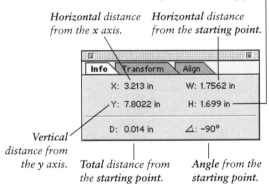

X: 3.213 in   W: 1.7562 in
Y: 7.8022 in   H: 1.699 in
D: 0.014 in   ∠: -90°

*Vertical distance from the **y** axis.*

*Total distance from the **starting point**.*

*Angle from the **starting point**.*

4 *The Info palette after clicking a starting and ending point with the **Measure** tool. The x and y positions are measured from the ruler origin.*

Measure a Distance

LET THE PALETTE DO THE MATH

In the W or H field on the Transform palette, you can perform simple math to resize an object. Type an asterisk, then a percentage value. For example, to reduce the current size value by half, click to the right of the current value, then type "*50%" (i.e., 4p becomes 2p). Or replace the entire field with "50%". Or type "75%" or "*.75" to reduce the W or H to three-quarters of its current value (i.e., 4p becomes 3p). Or enter a positive or negative number to the right of the current number, like "+2" or "-2", to increase or decrease, respectively, the current value by that amount. Press Tab to apply the math and advance to the next field, or press Return/Enter to exit the palette.

Use the Transform palette to reposition, resize, rotate, or shear an object or objects based on exact values or percentages.

To reposition, resize, rotate, or shear an object using the Transform palette:

1. If the Transform palette isn't open, choose Window menu > Show Transform.

2. Select an object or objects.

3. Choose the reference point from which you want the transformation to be measured by clicking a handle on the Reference Point button on the left side of the palette **1**.

4. Press Return (to exit the palette) or press Tab (to highlight the next field) to apply any of these new values:

    To **move** the object horizontally, enter a new value in the X field. (Enter a higher value to move the object to the right.)

    To **move** the object vertically, enter a new value in the Y field. (Enter a higher value to move the object upward.)

    To change the **width** and/or **height** of the object, enter new values in the W (width) and/or H (height) fields.

    To **rotate** the object counterclockwise, enter or choose a positive Rotate value. Enter or choose a negative value to rotate it clockwise.

    To **shear** an object to the right, enter or choose a positive Shear value. To shear an object to the left, enter or choose a negative Shear value.

    Note: If the **Scale Stroke Weight** option is turned on in File menu > Preferences > General or on the Transform palette menu and you change an object's width or height, the object's stroke will also resize proportionately.

    If the **Add Stroke Weight** box is checked in File menu > Preferences > General, the full dimensions of an object, including its stroke, will be reflected in the Width and Height fields on the Transform palette.

The x and y axes location of the currently selected reference point. Enter new values to move the object.

The selected object's Height.

The selected object's Width.

Transform	Align	Pathfinder
X: 10p2		W: 24p9
Y: 55p11.5		H: 10p5
⊿: 0°		∠: 0°

1 *The Reference Point (the part of the object from which the Transform palette values are calculated).*

The Rotate field for rotating the object.

The Shear field for shearing the object.

Transform Palette

To align or distribute objects:

1. To align, select two or more objects . To distribute, select three or more objects.

2. On the Align palette, click an Align Objects button –.
   and/or
   Click a Distribute Objects or Distribute Spacing button. Objects will distribute evenly between the two objects that are farthest apart.

TIP If you'd like to apply a different align or distribute option, first use the Undo command to undo the last one.

1 *The original objects.*

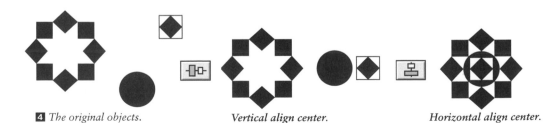

2 *Horizontal distribute space.*

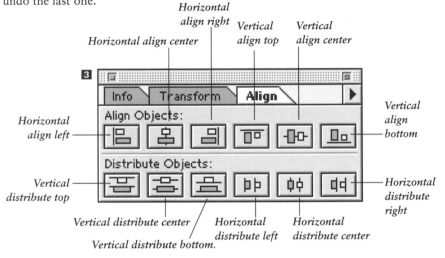

Horizontal align center
Horizontal align right
Vertical align top
Vertical align center
Vertical align bottom
Horizontal align left
Vertical distribute top
Vertical distribute center
Vertical distribute bottom.
Horizontal distribute left
Horizontal distribute center
Horizontal distribute right

*Note: To display this bottom panel, choose **Show Options** from the palette menu or double-click the Align tab twice.*

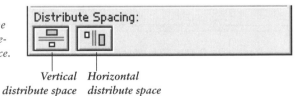

Vertical distribute space *Horizontal distribute space*

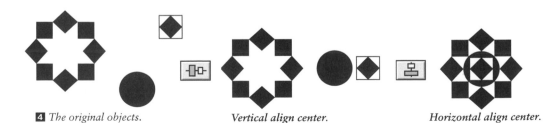

4 *The original objects.*   *Vertical align center.*   *Horizontal align center.*

In this chapter you will learn how to record a sequence of edits in an action, edit the action using various methods, and replay the action on one document or a batch of documents.

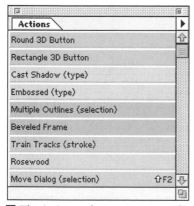

Actions
Round 3D Button
Rectangle 3D Button
Cast Shadow (type)
Embossed (type)
Multiple Outlines (selection)
Beveled Frame
Train Tracks (stroke)
Rosewood
Move Dialog (selection)   ⇧F2

1 *The Actions palette in Button mode.*

An actions set

Expand/
collapse
list

Toggle
item
on/off

Toggle
dialog
pause
on/off

✓	▢	▷ ☐	Default Actions
✓	▢	▽ ☐	Pathgrinders
✓		▷	Bulge
✓		▷	Outline
✓		▷	Fan
✓		▷	BrushBrush
✓		▷	OutlineUnite
✓	▢	▽	RoughenBrush
✓	▢	▷	Scribble and Tweak

— *A recorded action*

— *A recorded command*

2 *The Actions palette in List mode.*

Stop   Record   Play   Create
                          New Set
Create New   Delete
Action *or*
Command

Actions and the Actions palette

An action is a recorded sequence of tool and menu events. When an action is replayed, the same series of commands is executed in exactly the same sequence in which it was recorded. Actions can be simple (as short as a single command) or complex—whatever your work demands. And they can be replayed on any document. What's more, actions can be edited, reorganized, included in other actions, and traded around among Illustrator 8 users.

Actions are recorded, played back, edited, saved, and deleted using the Actions palette. The Actions palette has two modes: Button and List. **Button mode** is used only for playback, since in this mode only the action name is listed **1**. Actions can be assigned keyboard shortcuts for fast access in Button mode. To turn Button mode on or off, choose Button Mode from the Actions palette menu.

In **List mode** (Button mode turned off), the actual commands that the action contains are displayed in sequential order on the palette. This mode is used to record, play, edit, save, and load actions **2**.

Actions Palette

Actions are organized in sets, which are represented as folder icons on the Actions palette.

To create a new actions set:

1. Click the Create New Set button at the bottom of the Actions palette **1**.
   or
   Choose New Set from the Actions palette menu.

2. Enter a Set Name **2**.

3. Click OK (Return/Enter). A new folder icon and set name will appear on the palette **3**. (To save the set, see page 295.)

Note: Until you become familiar with using actions, you should practice recording on a duplicate file. Figure out beforehand what the action is supposed to accomplish, and run through the command sequence a few times before you actually record it.

To record an action:

1. Open an existing file or create a new one.

2. On the Actions palette, click the name of the action set you want the new action to belong to. (To create a new set, follow the previous set of instructions on this page).

3. Click the Create New Action button at the bottom of the Actions palette **4**.

4. Enter a name for the action **5**.

5. *Optional:* Assign a keyboard shortcut to the action from the Function Key drop-down menu and the Shift or Command box. Choose a color in which to display the action in Button mode from the Color drop-down menu.

6. Click Record.

7. Create and edit objects as you normally would. Any tool and menu commands that are recordable will appear on the action command list.

8. Click the Stop button to end recording **6**.

TIP You can record small actions and then combine part of an action or an entire action with another one (see page 294).

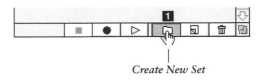

Create New Set

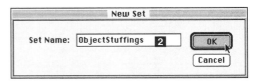

3 *A new set folder appears on the Actions palette.*

Create New Action

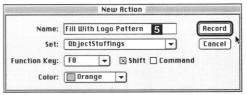

You can assign a keyboard shortcut or button display color in this dialog. The color will only be displayed when the palette is in Button mode.

Stop

New Actions Set; Record an Action

WHAT'S RECORDABLE/WHAT ISN'T

NO   **YES**

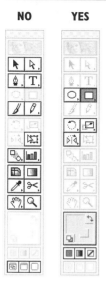

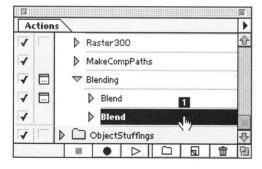

You may find that an action needs to be enhanced or modified from its original recorded version. There are several techniques you can use to edit actions.

To insert a menu item into an action's command list:

1. Put the Actions palette in List mode (Button Mode option turned off).

2. If the list for the action into which you want to insert the menu item isn't expanded, click the right-pointing triangle.

3. To add a menu command to an action, click the command on the action list after which you want the new command to follow **1**.

4. Choose Insert Menu Item from the Actions palette menu.

5. Choose the desired menu command from the menu bar (the command name will appear in the Find field) **2**.
   or
   Type the command name into the Find Field, then click the Find button.

6. Click OK (Return/Enter). When the action is played back, a pause will occur at any menu command that includes a dialog box.

If you insert a stop into an action, the action will pause during playback to allow you to perform a manual operation, like entering type or selecting an object. When you're finished with the manual operation, you can easily resume the action playback.

To insert a stop in an existing action:

1. Put the Actions palette in List mode, and expand the action into which you want to insert a stop.

2. Select the command after which you want the stop to be inserted **1**.

3. Choose Insert Stop from the Actions palette menu.

4. Enter an instructional message in the Record Stop dialog box to tell the user which operations to perform during the stop and to instruct the user to click the Play button on the Actions palette when they're ready to resume playback **2**–**3**.

5. *Optional:* Check the Allow Continue box to give the user the option to bypass the pause.

6. Click OK (Return/Enter).

TIP To insert a pause while you're recording an action, choose Insert Stop from the Actions palette menu, follow steps 4–6 on this page, then click the Play button to continue recording.

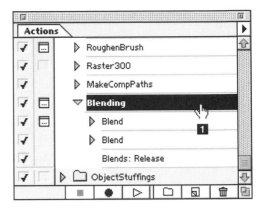

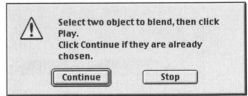

3 *In this example of a **pause** dialog box, the user is instructed to press **Stop** and then select two objects for blending. To resume the action playback, the user clicks the Play button on the Actions palette. If the two objects were already selected, the user can click **Continue** instead of Stop.*

Insert Stop

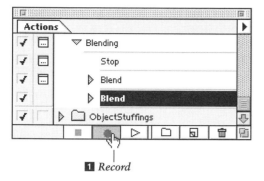

1 *Record*

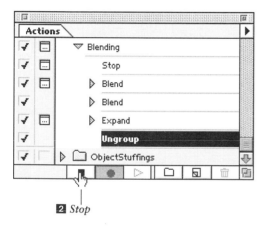

2 *Stop*

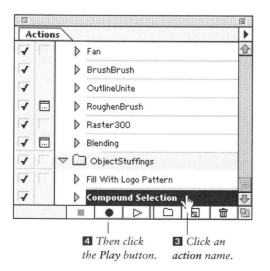

4 *Then click the **Play** button.*   **3** *Click an action name.*

In much the same manner as you would insert a menu command, you can record additional commands into an existing action.

To record commands into an existing action:

1. Put the Actions palette in List mode, and expand the action into which you want to insert a command or commands.

2. Choose the command after which you want the new command(s) to follow.

3. Click the Record button **1**.

4. Make modifications to the file as you would normally, using the commands you want inserted in the action. Any recordable tool (see the sidebar on page 289) or menu command that you use now will be added to the action.

5. Click the square Stop button to end recording **2**. The command(s) you just recorded will be listed below the chosen insertion point on the Actions palette.

Note: The first time you play back an action, do it on a duplicate file or on a file that you don't care about.

To replay an action on an image:

1. Open the Illustrator file on which you want to play the action, and select any objects, if necessary.

2. If the palette is in List mode, make sure the check mark is present for the action you want to play back. Click an action name on the Actions palette **3**, then click the Play button at the bottom of the palette **4**.
   or
   If the palette is in Button mode, just click an action name. If the action name is dark (unavailable), go back to List mode and make sure a check mark is present for the action you want to play back.

Add to an Action; Replay an Action

If you find that you've got the right action for the job, but it contains more commands than you need, you can temporarily exclude the ones you don't need from playback.

To exclude or include a command from a playback:

1. Put the Actions palette into List mode.

2. Click the right-pointing triangle to expand the command list of the action you want to play back **1**.

3. Click the check mark (√) in the leftmost column to disable that command **2** or click in the blank spot to restore the check mark and enable that command.

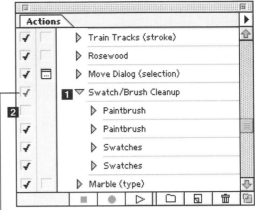

*A **red check mark** signifies that at least one of the commands in that action is turned off.*

For any command or tool that uses a dialog box that requires pressing Return/Enter (also known as a "modal control"), you can insert a pause to enable the user to change any of the dialog settings during playback. To insert this type of pause, you simply click a button on the Actions palette.

To turn on a command's dialog pause:

If a recorded command has a dialog box associated with it, it will have either a pause icon **3** or a blank space in the same spot for toggling the icon on **4**. Click the icon to disable the dialog pause and use the pre-recorded input instead. Or click the blank space to enable the command's dialog pause and allow user input.

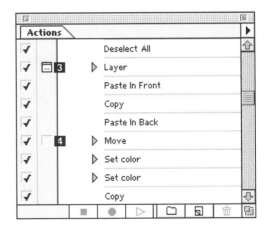

To rerecord a dialog:

1. Put the Actions palette into List mode.

2. Click the right-pointing triangle to expand the action's command list **1**.

3. Double-click a command with a dialog box icon (or blank space) you want to rerecord **5**.

4. Change any of the dialog settings. The next time this action is played back, the new parameters will be used.

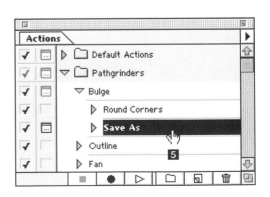

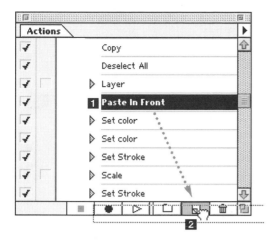

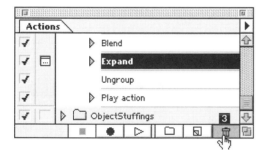

Note: Before you go ahead and wreck all the good work you've done so far, save the actions set you're working on! (See page 295.)

To move a command from one action to another:

Click on the action command you want to move, then drag it into another action list. It will appear at the bottom of that list.

To copy a command from one action to another:

1. Click on the action command you want to copy ▮.
2. Option-drag/Alt-drag the command into another action list.
   or
   Drag the command name over the Create New Action button at the bottom of the Actions palette ▮, then drag the duplicate command into another action list. It will appear at the bottom of that list.

Follow these instructions if you want to include an action in more than one set.

To copy an action from one set to another:

1. Click on the action you want to duplicate.
2. Drag the action over the New Action button.
   or
   Choose Duplicate from the Actions palette menu.
3. Drag the duplicate action to another set.
4. *Optional:* To rename the new action, double-click it.

To delete an action or a command:

Select the action or command you want to delete, click the Delete button at the bottom of the Actions palette ▮, then click Yes.
or
To bypass the prompt, drag the action or command over the Delete button.

Move or Copy a Command; Copy or Delete an Action

Another way to combine actions is to prompt an action from one set to play back from within another set. You can build a complex action from simpler, smaller actions this way, without having to actually duplicate and move them.

To include one action in another action:

1. If you want to insert a Play Action command as you're recording an action, skip to step 3.

   or

   If you want to insert a Play Action command into an existing, completed action, click on the command after which you want the Play Action to occur, then click the Record button **1**.

2. Click the action you want to include **2**.

3. Click the Play button **3**. The secondary action will play through. When it has completed, it will be listed on the action's command action list as "Play Action."

4. If you're in the middle of recording an action, continue recording.

   or

   If you're inserting the Play Action into an existing action, click Stop to finish.

   Note: If you expand the Play Action command list, you'll see the name of the secondary action to be played and the name of the set that that action belongs to **4**.

TIP If the action or set that the Play Action is calling for has been deleted or if its name has been changed, an alert dialog will appear during playback **5**.

TIP Create a set of simple utility actions that you can use when you construct larger actions, and save them into a utility set. Remember to supply the utility set along with the main action. Instructions for saving and loading actions are on the next page.

TIP Watch out for any commands in a Play Action that could conflict with the main action. For example, a Deselect command in the Play Action could have an adverse effect on the main action playback.

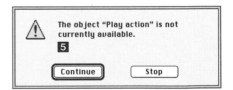

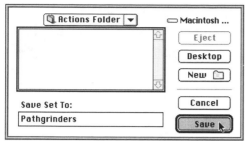

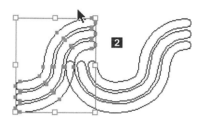

1 *Enter a name in the Save Set To field. Note: In Windows, the actions set file name must have the ".aia" extension.*

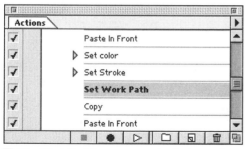

3 *"Set Work Path" appears on the Actions palette.*

One of the handiest things about actions is that you can share them with other Illustrator users. To do this, you must save them as sets. Try to keep your actions and sets well organized—and back up frequently!

To save an actions set:

1. Click on the actions set you want to save.
2. Choose Save Actions from the Actions palette menu.
3. Enter a name in the Save Set To field **1**, and choose a location in which to save the set. You can save it in the Action Sets folder inside the Illustrator 8 folder.
4. Click Save (Return/Enter).

To load an actions set:

1. Choose Load Actions from the Actions palette menu.
2. Locate and select the actions set file you want to load, then click Select. The action will appear on the palette.

If you want a path shape or text path to be part of an action, it has to be inserted as a pre-drawn path.

To record paths for insertion:

1. Have the path(s) you want to insert into the action ready to be selected.
2. Start recording an action.
   or
   To insert the path(s) into an existing action, choose the command after which you want it to appear.
3. Select the paths you want to insert **2**. You can use up to ten paths at a time. You can't use a path that's masked or that's part of a group, blend, or compound.
4. Choose Insert Select Path from the Actions palette menu. "Set Work Path" will appear on the action's command list **3**. It cannot be renamed.

TIP If you want specific stroke and fill attributes to be applied to an inserted path, you'll need to record those steps separately.

Workarounds for non-recordable tools

The sidebar on page 289 shows which tools are recordable and which aren't. For some tools that aren't recordable, their menu equivalents can be recorded as commands in an action.

For example, to make a blend part of an action, use the Blends submenu commands instead of the Blend tool. Start recording an action, select the two objects you want to blend, choose Object menu > Blends > Blend Options, choose a Spacing value , and click OK. Then choose Object menu > Blends > Make. The two separate blend steps will appear with the same name on the action's command list, but if you expand the command lists, you'll see the differences between the two steps 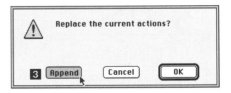. Continue recording the action, or stop recording.

Important note: Back up all your actions sets using the Save Actions command before performing any of the remaining instructions.

To reset actions to the default set:

1. Choose Reset Actions from the Actions palette menu.

2. If you want the default set to **replace all** the actions on the palette, click OK.
   or
   If you want to **append** the original default set to the current actions set list , click Append, then rename the appended set.

To clear all actions sets from the palette:

Choose Clear Actions from the Actions palette menu, then click Yes.

To replace all current actions sets:

1. Choose Replace Actions from the Actions palette menu.

2. Locate and highlight the replacement actions set 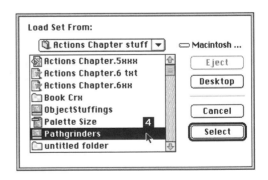.

3. Click Select.

(Sidebar, rotated text on left margin:) Reset Actions; Clear Actions; Replace Actions

PREFERENCES 22

In this chapter you will learn to choose default settings for features, tools, and palettes. You will learn how to create a startup file containing colors, patterns, gradients, and document settings that you work with regularly so they will automatically be part of any new document you create. Using the File menu > Preferences submenu dialog boxes, you can set tool behavior, keyboard increments, units, undos, guides, grid, hyphenation, scratch disk, and many other preferences for current and future documents.

1 *The Adobe Illustrator **Startup** file.*

To create a custom startup file:

1. Duplicate the existing Adobe Illustrator Startup file (Macintosh) or Startup.ai file (Windows) (in the Plug-ins folder in the Illustrator 8 application folder), and move the copy to a different folder.

2. Double-click the default Adobe Illustrator Startup file **1**.

3. Do any of the following:

   Create new colors, patterns, or gradients, and add these new items to the Swatches palette. For a visual reminder, apply swatches to separate objects in the file.

   Copy swatches from other swatch libraries to the Swatches palette—spot color libraries or files from the Other Libraries folder in the Illustrator folder.

   Create custom brushes.

   Choose Document Setup or Page Setup options.

   Choose ruler and page origins.

   Choose a view size, document window size, and scroll positions.

   Create new view settings.

4. Delete any elements you *don't* want in the startup file, such as brushes from the Brushes palette or swatches from the Swatches palette you don't need.

5. Save the file in the Plug-ins folder using the same name as listed in step 1.

Custom Startup File

297

General Preferences

Choose File menu > Preferences > General

Keyboard Increment

Cursor Key
The distance a selected object moves when an arrow is pressed on the keyboard.

Tool Behavior

Constrain Angle
The angle for the x and y axes. The default setting is 0° (parallel to the edges of the document window). Tool and dialog box measurements are calculated relative to the current Constrain Angle (see page 281).

Corner Radius
The amount of curvature in the corners of objects drawn with the Rounded Rectangle tool. 0 produces a right angle. Changing this number updates the same value in the Rectangle dialog box, and vice versa.

General Options

Use Bounding Box
Turns on display of the bounding box for selected objects.

Use Area Select
When checked, clicking with a selection tool on an object's fill when your illustration is in Preview view will select the whole object.

Use Precise Cursors
The drawing and editing tool pointers display as a crosshair icon.

Paste Remembers Layers
When checked, an object that is cut or copied to the Clipboard can be pasted back only onto its current layer. When this option is unchecked, an object can be pasted onto other layers. Paste Remembers Layers can also be turned on or off from the Layers palette menu.

(Continued on the following page)

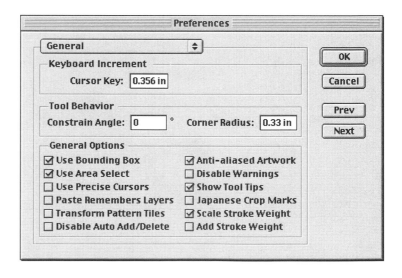

FAST TRACK TO THE PREFERENCES

Use the shortcut that opens the General Preferences dialog box (Command-K/Ctrl-K), then choose the desired preferences dialog box from the drop-down menu.

Transform Pattern Tiles

When checked, if you use a transformation tool on an object that contains a pattern fill, the pattern will also transform. You can also turn this option on or off for an individual transformation tool in its own dialog box or in the Move dialog box.

Disable Auto Add/Delete

Disables the Pen tool's ability to change to the Add-anchor-point tool when the pointer passes over a path segment or to the Delete-anchor point-tool when the pointer passes over an anchor point.

Anti-aliased Artwork

Smooths the edges of existing and subsequently created objects.

Disable Warnings

Check this box to prevent Illustrator from displaying an alert dialog box when a tool is used incorrectly.

Show Tool Tips

Check this box to see an on-screen display of the name of the tool or button currently under the pointer.

Japanese Crop Marks

Check this box to use Japanese style crop-marks when printing separations. Preview this style in the Separation Setup dialog box.

Scale Stroke Weight

Check this box to scale an object's stroke weight when you use the bounding box or the Scale or Free Transform tool. This option can also be turned on or off in the Scale dialog box.

Add Stroke Weight

Includes an object's stroke weight when an object's height and width dimensions are calculated.

Type & Auto Tracing Preferences

*Choose File menu > Preferences > Type &
Auto Tracing*

Type Options

Size/Leading, Baseline Shift, Tracking
The increment by which selected text is
altered each time a keyboard shortcut is
executed for the respective command.

Greeking
The point size at or below which type displays on the screen as gray bars rather than
as readable characters. Greeking speeds
up screen redraw. It has no effect on how a
document prints.

Type Area Select
When checked, you can select type by clicking with a selection tool anywhere within a
type character.

Show Font Names in English
When checked, two-byte font names display
in English on the font pop-up menu. When
unchecked, these font names display in a
two-byte script.

Auto Trace Options

Auto Trace Tolerance
The value (0–10) that controls how many
anchor points will be created when you autotrace a placed image using the Auto Trace
tool. 1 will produce many points on a path;
10 will produce fewer points.

Tracing Gap
The exactness with which the Auto Trace
tool traces the contour of a bitmap image
(0–2). The lower the gap, the more closely
an image will be traced, and the more anchor
points will be created.

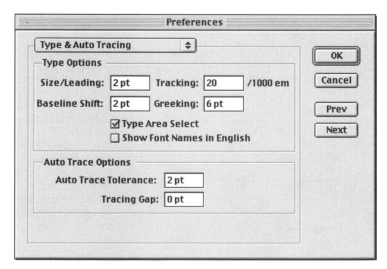

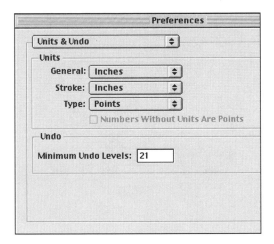

Units & Undo Preferences

Choose File menu > Preferences > Units & Undo

Units

General

The unit of measure for the rulers and all dialog boxes for the current document and all new documents. If you choose different Units in the Document Setup dialog box, those new Units will override the Units & Undo setting for the current document only (see page 23).

Stroke

The unit of measure used on the Stroke palette.

Type

The unit of measure used on the Character and Paragraph palettes.

Undo

Minimum Undo Levels

Normally, you can undo/redo up to 200 operations, depending on available memory. If additional RAM is required to perform illustration edits, the number of undos will be reduced to this specified minimum.

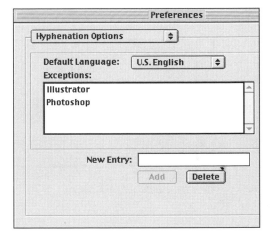

Hyphenation Options Preferences

Choose File menu > Preferences > Hyphenation Options

Default Language

Choose the language dictionary Illustrator will use when inserting hyphen breaks. You can choose a different hyphenation language dictionary for the current document only from the Language drop-down menu on the Character palette.

Exceptions

Enter words that you want to be hyphenated in a particular way. Type the word in the New Entry field, inserting hyphens where you would want them to appear. Enter a word with no hyphens to prevent Illustrator from hyphenating it. Click Add. To remove a word from the list, highlight it, then click Delete.

Guides & Grid Preferences

Choose File menu > Preferences > Guides & Grid

Guides

Color

The guide color. Choose from the Color drop-down menu. Or choose Other from this menu or double-click the color square to open the System color picker and mix your own color.

Style

The guide Style. To help differentiate between guide lines and grid lines, choose the Dots style for guides.

Grid

Color

The grid color. Choose from the Color drop-down menu. Or choose Other from this menu or double-click the color square to open the System color picker and mix your own color.

Style

The grid style. Subdivision lines won't display if the Dot style is chosen.

Gridline every

The distance between the more prominent grid lines.

Subdivision

The number of subdivision lines to be drawn between the major grid lines when the Line Style is chosen for the grid.

Grids in Back

Check the Grids In Back box to have the grid display behind all objects. With the grid in back, you can easily tell which objects have a fill of None, because the grid will be visible underneath them.

TIP Guides will snap to grid lines if View menu > Snap to Grid is turned on.

TIP If Snap to Grid and Snap to Point are both turned on, it can be hard to tell whether an object is snapping to the grid or to a guide, particularly if the grid isn't displayed.

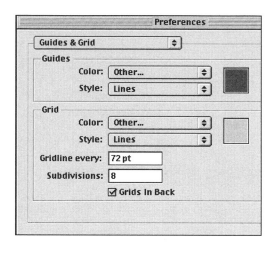

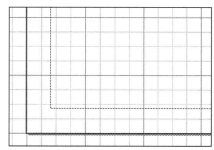

Grid lines with four subdivisions.

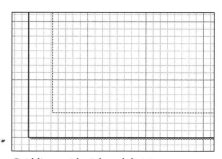

Grid lines with eight subdivisions.

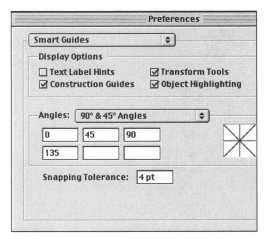

Smart Guides Preferences

Choose File menu > Preferences > Smart Guides

Note: To turn on smart guides, choose View menu > Smart Guides (Command-U/Ctrl-U).

Display Options

Text Label Hints
Display terms show as you pass the pointer over an object, an anchor point, etc.

Construction Guides
As you draw an object, angle lines will display temporarily between the current pointer position and any existing anchor points that you've recently moved the pointer over **1**. Choose or create an angle set in the Angles area of the dialog box.

Transform Tools
Angle lines display as you transform an object using an individual transformation tool (but not the Free Transform tool) **2**. Choose or create an angle set in the Angles area of the dialog box.

Object Highlighting
An object's path displays as you pass the pointer over it **3**. This is helpful for locating unpainted paths (like masks) or paths that are hidden behind other paths.

Angles

When Smart Guides are turned on, angle lines will temporarily display relative to other objects in the illustration as you drag an object or move the pointer. You can choose a preset angle set from the Angles drop-down menu or enter your own angles in any of the text fields. If you enter custom angles, "Custom Angles" will appear on the drop-down menu. If you switch from Custom Angles to a predefined set and then later switch back to Custom Angles, the last-used custom settings will reappear in the text fields.

Snapping Tolerance
The Snapping Tolerance is the distance within which the pointer must be from an object for Smart Guides to display.

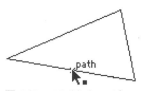

1 *Construction guide.*

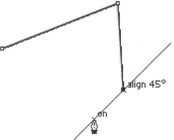

2 *Transform tool guide.*

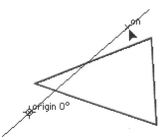

3 *Object Highlight guide.*

Plug-ins & Scratch Disk Preferences

*Choose File menu > Preferences > Plug-ins &
Scratch Disk*

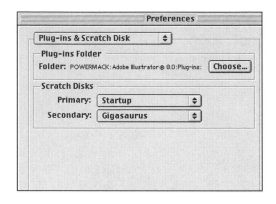

Plug-ins folder

Note: For changes made in this dialog box to
take effect, you must quit/exit and re-launch
Illustrator.

Folder

Illustrator contains core and add-on plug-in
files that provide additional functionality
to the main application. These plug-in files
are placed in the Plug-ins folder in the
Illustrator folder. If for some reason you
need to move the Plug-ins folder, you must
use this Preferences dialog box to tell
Illustrator the new location of the folder.

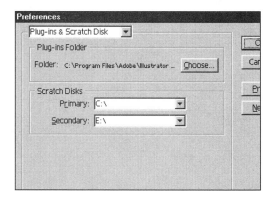

The current Plug-ins folder location is listed
after the word "Folder." To change the
plug-ins location, click Choose, locate and
highlight the desired folder name, then click
the "Select [folder name]" button at the bottom of the dialog box. The new location will
now be listed.

Scratch Disks

Primary

The primary (and optional Secondary)
Scratch Disk is used when available RAM is
insufficient for image processing. Choose an
available hard drive, preferably your largest
and fastest, from the Primary drop-down
menu. Startup (Mac) or C:\ (Windows) is the
default.

Secondary

As an optional step, choose an alternate
Secondary hard drive to be used as extra
work space, when needed. If you have only
one hard drive, of course you'll only have
one scratch disk.

TIP To see how much of Illustrator's memory
allotment is currently available, choose
Free Memory from the status line
pop-up menu at the bottom of the docu-
ment/program window and look at the
readout there.

OUTPUT 23

Illustrator objects are described and stored as mathematical commands. But when they are printed, they are rendered as dots. The higher the resolution of the output device, the finer and sharper the rendering of lines, curves, gradients, and continuous-tone images. In this chapter you will learn to print an illustration on a PostScript black-and-white or composite color printer, to create crop or trim marks, to print an oversized illustration, to troubleshoot printing problems, to lower an object's output resolution to facilitate printing, and to produce smooth blends. You'll also learn how to save a file in a variety of formats for export to other applications, and how to prepare a file for the World Wide Web. To produce color separations, read the next chapter.

Charles, *Nancy Stahl*

Norah, *Nancy Stahl*

To print on a black-and-white or color PostScript printer:

1. *Mac:* Open the Chooser (Apple menu), select the desired printer name, then close the Chooser.

2. *Mac:* Choose File menu > Page Setup (Command-Shift-P).

   Win: Choose File menu > Print Setup (Ctrl-Shift-P), select a printer.

3. Choose a size from the Paper drop-down menu 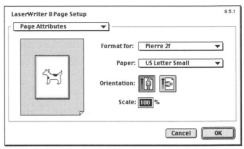.
   and
   Make sure the correct Orientation icon is selected (to print vertically or horizontally on the paper), then click OK.

4. Choose File menu > Print (Command-P/Ctrl-P).

5. *Mac:* Choose Adobe Illustrator 8.0 from the drop-down menu 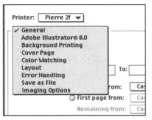.

   Mac and Win: Choose PostScript®: Level 2 or 3 (depending on your printer and printer driver) 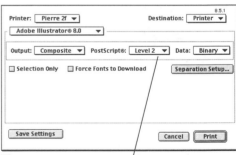. Use Level 1 only when necessary.

6. *Mac:* Choose Color Matching from the menu. Choose Print Color: Color/Grayscale. For a color printer, choose the appropriate color options.

   Win: Accept the default setting for your printer. If necessary, click the Properties button, click the Page Setup tab, then choose a Color Appearance. For a color printer, choose the appropriate color options.

7. *Mac:* Choose General from the menu. *Mac and Win:* Enter the desired number of Copies .

8. To print a single full page document or a Tile imageable areas document, *Mac:* leave the Pages: All button selected; *Win:* leave the Print Range: All button selected.
   or
   To print select tiled pages, enter starting and ending page numbers in the From and To fields.

9. *Mac:* Click Print. *Win:* Click OK.

1 *In the* **Page Setup** *dialog box for a* **black-and-white** *printer, choose a paper size from the* **Paper** *pop-up menu.*

2 *On Macintosh, choose* **Adobe Illustrator 8.0.**

3 *Choose PostScript®:* **Level 2** *or* **Level 3.**

4 *In the* **Print** *dialog box, enter a number of* **Copies** *and the* **Pages** *you want to print.*

1 *Rectangle tool.*

2 *A rectangle is drawn.*

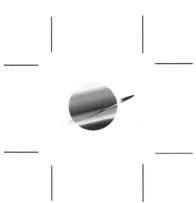

3 *After choosing the Make Crop Marks command.*

Crop marks are short perpendicular lines around the edge of a page that a print shop uses as guides to trim the paper. Illustrator's Crop Marks command creates crop marks around a rectangle that you draw, and they become part of your illustration.

To create crop marks:

1. Choose the Rectangle tool (M or Shift-M) **1**.

2. Carefully draw a rectangle to encompass some or all of the objects in the illustration **2**.

3. With the rectangle still selected, choose Object menu > Crop Marks > Make. The rectangle will disappear, and crop marks will appear where the corners of the rectangle were **3**.

TIP If you don't create a rectangle before choosing Object menu > Crop Marks > Make, crop marks will be placed around the full page. If Tile full pages is selected in File menu > Document Setup, crop marks will be created for only one page.

TIP Only one set of crops can be created per illustration using the Crop Marks command. If you apply Object menu > Crop Marks > Make a second time, new marks will replace the existing ones. To create more than one set of crop marks in an illustration, use the Trim Marks filter (see the next page).

To remove crop marks created with the Crop Marks command:

Choose Object menu > Crop Marks > Release. The selected rectangle will reappear, with a fill and stroke of None. Toggle to Artwork view to locate it. You can repaint it or delete it.

TIP If crop marks were created for the entire page, the released rectangle will have the same dimensions as the printable page (and also the same size as the artboard, if the dimensions of the artboard match the dimensions of the printable page).

Create or Remove Crop Marks

The Trim Marks filter places eight trim marks around a selected object or objects. You can create more than one set of Trim Marks in an illustration.

To create trim marks:

I. Select the object or objects to be trimmed.

2. Choose Filter menu > Create > Trim Marks. Trim marks will surround the smallest rectangle that could be drawn around the object or objects 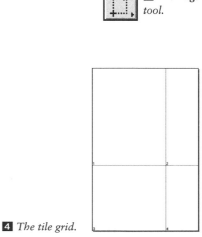.

TIP Group the trim marks with the objects they surround so you can move them as a unit.

TIP To move or delete trim marks, select them first with the Selection tool.

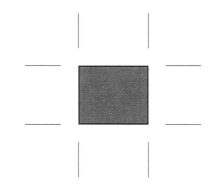

1 *After applying the* **Trim Marks** *filter.*

To print (tile) an illustration that is larger than the paper size:

I. Choose File menu > Document Setup (Option-Shift-P/Alt-Shift-P).

2. For the illustration's Artboard dimensions, choose a preset size from the Size drop-down menu, or choose a unit of measure from the Units drop-down menu and enter custom Width and Height dimensions 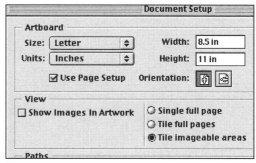.

3. Click "Tile imageable areas."

4. *Optional:* Click Page Setup/Print Setup, and then change the Orientation to change the orientation of the tiles.

5. Click OK (Return/Enter).

6. Double-click the Hand tool to display the entire artboard.

7. *Optional:* Choose the Page tool (Shift-H) **3**, then drag the tile grid so it divides the illustration into better tiling breaks. The grid will redraw **4**.

8. Follow steps 4–9 on page 306 to print.

TIP On a document that's set to Tile imageable areas, only tile pages with objects on them will print. If a direction line from a curved anchor point extends onto a blank tile, that page will print.

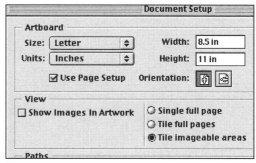

2 *In File menu >* **Document Setup,** *choose or enter the appropriate* **Artboard** *dimensions and turn on* **Tile imageable areas.**

3 *The Page tool.*

4 *The tile grid.*

Trim Marks; Oversized Documents

Windows: Using File menu > Send, you can send the current illustration file directly to a specific system device (i.e., Microsoft Mail).

1 *Delete-anchor-point tool.*

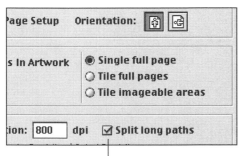

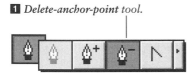

2 *Check the Split long paths box in File menu > Document Setup.*

Solving printing problems

If things don't go as smoothly as you'd like...

Patterns

■ By default, patterns preview and print. If a document containing patterns doesn't print, place the objects that contain patterns on a new layer, uncheck the Print option for that layer, and then try printing again. If the document prints, the patterns were the likely culprit.

■ Try to limit the number of pattern fills in an illustration.

■ Make the original bounding rectangle for the pattern tile no larger than one-inch square (see page 144).

■ Use a PostScript Level 2 or Level 3 printer when printing elaborate patterns.

■ Don't use a blend, or gradient fill, or type as a pattern fill on a compound path.

Complex paths

Sometimes a file containing complex paths with many anchor points won't print—a limitcheck or VM error message will appear in the print progress window. To help prevent a limitcheck error, limit the number of complex objects in your illustration. If you do get such a message, first manually delete excess anchor points from long paths using the Delete-anchor-point tool **1** and try printing again.

If that doesn't work, check the "Split long paths" box in File menu > Document Setup **2** and try printing again. Complex paths will be split into two or more separate paths, but their overall path shapes won't change. The "Split long paths" option does not affect stroked paths, compound paths, or masks. You can also split a stroked path manually using the Scissors tool. (To preserve a copy of a document with its non-split paths, before checking the "Split long paths" box, save the document under a new name using File menu > Save As.) To rejoin split paths, select them and then click the Unite button on the Pathfinder palette.

(Continued on the following page)

Solving Printing Problems

More troubleshooting tips

- Masks may cause printing problems, particularly if they're produced from compound paths. A file containing multiple masks may not print at all. For a complex mask, consider using the Knife tool to cut all the shapes in half—including the mask object itself—before you create the mask. Select and mask each half separately, then move them together.

- Choose Object menu > Path > Cleanup to delete any Stray Points (inadvertent clicks on the artboard with the Pen tool), Unpainted Objects, or Empty Text Paths 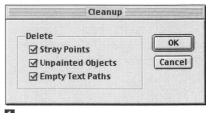.

- If you get a VM error, try reducing the number of fonts used in the file or convert large type into outlines (Type menu > Create Outlines) so fewer fonts need to be downloaded.

- Use a Pathfinder command—like Divide or Minus Front—to produce the same effect as a compound.

- To improve gradient fill printing on a PostScript Level 1 imagesetter and some PostScript clone printers, check the "Compatible gradient and gradient mesh printing" box in File menu > Document Setup, then re-save the file. Don't check this option if your gradients are printing well, as it may slow printing, or if you're using a PostScript Level 2 or 3 imagesetter.

- If you're using complex elements like compounds, masks, or patterns in a document and the *document* doesn't print, place a complex object on its own layer, uncheck the print option for that layer, and try printing again. And by the same token, if an *object* doesn't print, double-click the name of the layer the object is on and make sure the Print box *is* checked.

- If a pattern doesn't print, simplify it.

- As a last resort you can lower the output resolution of individual objects to facilitate printing (see page 312).

Troubleshoot Printing Problems

SMOOTHER HALFTONES

If your printer has halftone enhancing software:

Macintosh: Choose File menu > Print, choose Imaging Options from the drop-down menu, click On for PhotoGrade and/or FinePrint, then click OK.

Windows: Choose File menu > Print Setup, choose Properties, turn on the enhancement option under the Graphics tab or the Device Options tab (on NT, click the Advanced tab), then click OK.

Next, make sure the Use printer's default screen option is checked in File menu > Document Setup (this is the default setting) to enable the printer's halftone method and disable Illustrator's built-in halftone method.

Smoother blends

When printing gradients and blends, consider the relationship between the printer's lines per inch setting and the number of gray levels the printer is capable of producing. The higher the lines per inch (also known as screen frequency), the fewer the printable levels of gray. For the smoothest printing of gradients and blends, use a printer that's capable of outputting 256 levels of gray.

If you—and not the print shop—are supervising the color separation process, first ask your print shop what screen frequency (lpi) you will need to specify when imagesetting your file and what resolution (dpi) to use for imagesetting. Some imagesetters can achieve resolutions above 3000 dpi.

The blend or gradient length

To ensure that a gradient fill or a blend does not band into visible color strips:

- Use the correct lines per inch setting for the printer to output with 256 levels of gray.
- Make sure at least one color component (R, G, or B or C, M, Y, or K) in the starting color of the gradient or blend differs in percentage by at least 50% from the same component in the ending color.
- Keep the blend length to a maximum of 7½ inches. If you need a longer blend, create it in Photoshop and place it in Illustrator.

Illustrator determines the number of steps in a gradient or a blend based on the largest difference in percentage between the gradient color components. The greater the percentage difference, the greater the potential number of steps, and thus the longer the blend can be. At 256 steps, for example, the blend can be up to 7½ inches long. Here's the formula for calculating the optimal number of blend steps:

Number of steps = Number of gray levels from the printer X The largest color percentage difference

Use the chart on page 349 of the Adobe Illustrator 8.0 User Guide to calculate the maximum blend length based on the number of blend steps.

Smoother Blends

The precision with which Illustrator renders an object is determined by the object's output resolution. Different objects in the same illustration can be rendered at different resolutions. If a complex object doesn't print, try lowering its output resolution and then print the document again. But first, read the sidebar at right.

To lower an object's output resolution to facilitate printing:

1. Choose any selection tool, then click on the object that did not print, or you anticipate may not print.

2. Show the Attributes palette.

3. Enter a lower number in the Output field 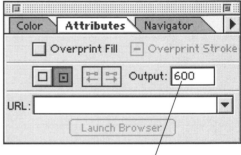, then try printing the file again. If the object prints, but with noticeable jaggedness on its curve segments, its output resolution is too low. Raise the Output value, and try printing again.

TIP To reset the Output resolution for all future objects in the same document, choose File menu > Document Setup, then change the number in the Output resolution field. 800 dpi is the default Output resolution for path objects.

THE FLATNESS EQUATION

The Output resolution controls the degree of flatness in an object's curve segments. Flatness equals the printing device resolution divided by the object's output resolution. For any given printer, lowering the output resolution raises the flatness value. The lower the output resolution (or the higher flatness value), the less precisely an object's curve segments will print.

1 *Change the* **Output** *resolution for an individual object using the* **Attributes** *palette.*

Potential gray levels at various output resolutions and screen frequencies

	Output Resolution (DPI)	Screen Frequency (LPI)					
		60	**85**	**100**	**133**	**150**	**180**
Laser printers	**300**	26	13				
	600	101	51	37	21		
Image-setters	**1270**	256	224	162	92	72	
	2540		256	256	256	256	
	3000			256	256	256	256

Object Output Resolution

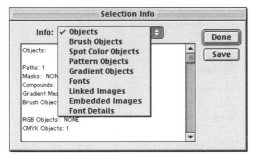

1 *The* Selection Info *dialog box opens when an object is selected in the illustration.*

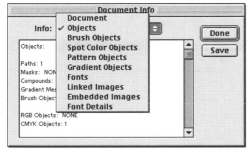

2 *The* Document Info *dialog box when no objects are selected.*

Selection Info and Document Info

To display information about a selected object (or objects), choose File menu > **Selection Info.** With Objects chosen from the Info drop-down menu, the Selection Info dialog box lists the number of paths, masks, compounds, gradient meshes, brush objects, color objects, patterns, gradients, fonts, linked images, and embedded images in the object. To view more detailed information about some of these elements, choose a category from the Info drop-down menu **1**. Click Done when you're finished.

To display information about the entire illustration, make sure no objects are selected, then choose File menu > **Document Info.** Choose Info: Document to display the current Document Setup dialog box settings **2**. You can also choose to display information about all Objects, all Spot Colors, etc.

Click Save to save Document or Selection Info as a text document. Choose a location in which to save the text file, rename the file, if desired, then click Save. Use the system's default text editor to open the text document. You can print this file and refer to it when you prepare your document for imagesetting.

An Illustrator file can be saved in a variety of file formats for export into other applications. Some of these formats are discussed on the following four pages.

To export a file:

1. With the file open, choose File menu > Export.

2. Enter a new name in the Export This Document As field *(Mac)* or File Name field *(Windows)* if you don't want to store over the original file.

3. Choose from the Format drop-down menu *(Mac)* 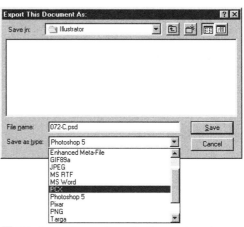 or Save as Type drop-down menu *(Win)* 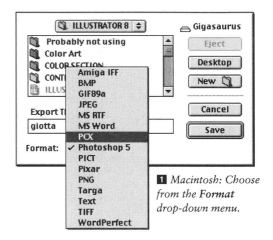.

4. Choose a location in which to save the new version.

   To create a new folder for the file:
   Mac: Click New, enter a name, then click Create.

   Win: Click Create New Folder, enter a name, then click Create.

5. Click Save (Return/Enter). Choose the desired settings from the secondary dialog box, then click OK 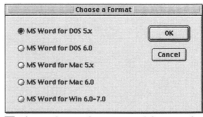. Some of these dialogs are discussed on pages 315–318.

TIP The text formats (MS RTF, MS Word, Text, WordPerfect) save only text objects (text in a box, text on a path, or point text). Each text object will become a separate paragraph when it's imported. The original paragraph groups, text styling, and color are preserved.

TIP *Windows:* When saving a file, Illustrator automatically appends the proper file extension to the name (i.e., .ai, .eps, .tif, etc.) based on the chosen Save as Type format.

TIP If you don't change the name of the file in the Export dialog box and you click Save, you'll get a warning prompt. Click Replace to save over the original file or click Cancel to return to the Export dialog box.

1 *Macintosh: Choose from the **Format** drop-down menu.*

2 *Windows: Choose from the **Save as type** drop-down menu.*

3 *If you choose the MS Word format, this dialog box will open. Other dialogs are discussed on the following four pages.*

Export a File

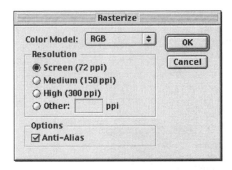

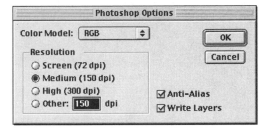

LAYERS AND LAYERS

If you keep layers intact when you export files to Photoshop, you'll then have the opportunity to apply Photoshop filters to those individual layers. You can also drop a native Photoshop PSD file containing Illustrator layers into Adobe's ImageReady application, where you can convert the layers to animations. ImageReady is designed specifically for creating and optimizing raster graphics, roll-over elements, and animations for the Web.

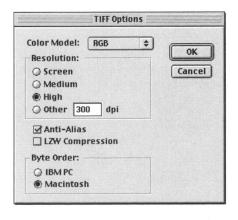

Secondary export dialog boxes

Raster

If you choose a raster (bitmap) file format, such as Amiga IFF, BMP, PCX, Pixar, PNG, or Targa, the Rasterize dialog box will open. Choose a Color Model for the resulting file color. For file Resolution, choose Screen (72 dpi), Medium (150 dpi), or High (300 dpi), or enter a custom resolution (Other). Check the Anti-Alias box to smooth the edges of objects (pixels will be added along objects' edges).

Photoshop 5

If you choose the Photoshop 5 file format, the Photoshop Options dialog box will open. Choose a Color Model, a Resolution (preset or custom), and turn the Anti-Alias option on or off. To export Illustrator layers to Photoshop, check the Write Layers box. If this option is unchecked, Illustrator will flatten layers and the illustration will appear as one layer in Photoshop. You must use the Photoshop 5 format to place an illustration that contains gradient mesh objects into Photoshop. (Neither Copy/Paste nor drag-and-drop will correctly import a gradient mesh object.)

TIFF

If you choose the TIFF file format, the TIFF Options dialog box will open. Choose a Color Model. Choose a Resolution: Screen (72 dpi), Medium (150 dpi), or High (300 dpi), or type in a custom resolution. And turn the Anti-Alias option on or off. Check the LZW Compression box to compress the file. This type of compression is lossless, which means it doesn't cause loss or degradation of image data. Choose your target operating platform in the Byte Order area.

JPEG

JPEG format is a good choice if you want to compress files that contain placed, continuous-tone, bitmap images, or objects with gradient fills. JPEG is also used for viewing 24-bit images via the Web. (The JPEG format is also discussed on pages 320 and 322).

(Continued on the following page)

Raster; Photoshop 5; TIFF; JPEG

When you choose an Image Quality, keep in mind that there's a tradeoff between image quality and the amount of compression. The greater the compression, the greater the loss of image data and the lower the image quality. To experiment, export multiple copies of a file and use a different compression setting for each copy, and then view the results in the target application. Or use Adobe's ImageReady program to preview different compression settings (see page 322).

If you choose the JPEG file format the JPEG Options dialog box will open.

1. Choose an Image Quality. Enter a numerical value (0–10); or move the slider; or choose Low, Medium, High, or Maximum from the drop-down menu.

2. Choose a Color model: RGB, CMYK or Grayscale.

3. Choose a Format Method: Baseline ("Standard"); Baseline Optimized, which lets you adjust the color quality of the image; or Progressive. A Progressive JPEG displays at increasingly higher resolutions as the file downloads from the Web. Choose the number of scans (iterations) you want displayed before the final image is available. (This type of JPEG is not supported by all Web browsers and requires more RAM to view.)

4. Choose a Resolution Depth: Screen, Medium, or High. Or choose Custom and enter a Custom resolution (dpi).

5. In the Options section:

   Check the Anti-Alias box if you want your image to have smooth edges.

   If you have linked objects in your file to URLs, check Imagemap and choose Client-side or Server-side. For Client-side, Illustrator saves the JPEG file with an accompanying HTML file that holds the link information; both files are required by your Web-creation application in order to interpret the links correctly. For Server-side, Illustrator saves the file for use on a Web server.

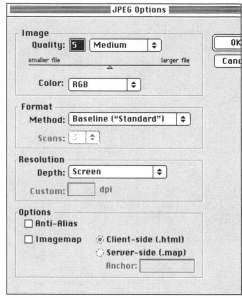

*The **JPEG Options** export dialog lets you tailor your image for a number of uses, whether it's optimizing it for fast downloading on the Web or preserving enough resolution to output a crisp print.*

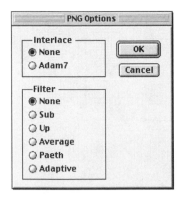

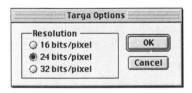

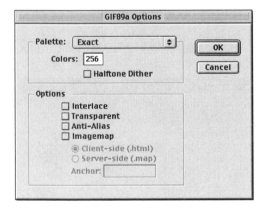

PNG

Choose the PNG format to compress 24-bit color images for viewing in Web browsers. This format supports alpha channels of 256 levels of gray that can be used to define areas of graduated transparency. If you choose the PNG file format and then click OK in the Rasterize dialog box, the PNG Options dialog box will open. Choose an Interlace method and a Filter option for the file compression method. If you choose Filter: Adaptive, Illustrator will choose the compression filter that best suits the illustration.

Targa

If you choose the Targa file format and then click OK in the Rasterize dialog box, the Targa Options dialog box will open. Choose a Resolution (bit depth) for the amount of color/shade information each pixel is capable of storing.

GIF

GIF is the standard format used on the Web. It's an 8-bit format and it's capable of reducing a file to a maximum of only 256 colors. This format makes Web images suitable for viewing on an 8-bit monitor (which displays a maximum of 256 colors). Use GIF for images that contain flat color areas and shapes with well-defined edges, like type. GIF compresses a file's storage size, but with a small reduction in image quality. Smaller files download faster, and the drop in image quality usually isn't too obvious (see page 320).

GIF89a

I. Choose a palette from the drop-down menu in the GIF89a Options dialog box:

Exact if the image contains 256 or fewer colors. No colors will be eliminated.

System (Macintosh or Windows) if you're going to export the file to an application that accepts only the Macintosh or Windows default palette. The color table (palette) for the exported file will derive from the chosen operating system.

Web if the image is intended for Web viewing. This option limits the file's color table to the colors available in the most

(Continued on the following page)

commonly used Web browsers. This is also a good choice if you want to display more than one image per page. All the images will have the same default color palette.

Adaptive for the best color substitution. Use this option when the Exact option is not available.

Custom to choose an existing custom palette. Locate a custom palette file, then click Open.

2. Check any of the following options:

Halftone Dither to dither gradients and placed images in a horizontal/vertical scheme.

Interlace to display the image in progressively greater detail as it downloads to the Web page.

Transparent to have unpainted areas in the file become transparent in a Web browser. This is a good choice for displaying an image with a non-uniform background pattern on a Web page.

Anti-Alias if you want the edges of shapes to be smoothed using added pixels.

Imagemap to have objects, to which you have assigned URLs via the Attributes palette, become clickable buttons on a Web page to link a viewer to the specified URL. Choose Client-side when you will be placing the two resulting files into an HTML-code page or into a Web-page-design application like PageMill, Fusion, or CyberStudio for the purpose of creating a Web page. Illustrator will save the objects to a GIF file and produce the appropriate HTML file with the link information for the imagemap.

The two resulting files must be saved in the same location to be read correctly by the HTML code and the Web browser. You must designate an Anchor name for the imagemap to differentiate it from other imagemaps within the same HTML code.

Choose Server-side if the artwork file will be uploaded to a Web server. Consult with your Internet service provider when using this option.

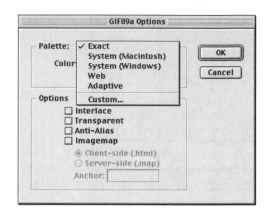

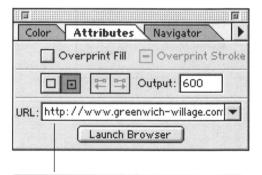

ATTACH A URL LINK TO AN OBJECT

Select an object or objects in Illustrator, and then type a URL address in the URL field on the Attributes palette.

GIF89a

ILLUSTRATOR TO MACROMEDIA DIRECTOR

In Illustrator, choose Edit menu > Copy to place a selected object on the Clipboard. The object will be rasterized. In Director, click on a Cast Member window on the Cast palette and choose Edit menu > Paste Bitmap. You can copy an object containing a gradient or a pattern fill or a small object that was rasterized in Illustrator this way into Director.

TIP Create Illustrator objects in RGB color mode to prevent possible color substitution and dithering when they appear in Director.

TIP Illustrator type can be copied into Director. If you discover that type edges in Director have white halos around them, choose Illustrator's Preferences > General, uncheck Anti-aliased Artwork, then copy the type. If Illustrator type is copied first into Photoshop, use Photoshop's Edit menu > Paste and be sure to uncheck the Anti-Alias option in the Paste dialog box to prevent white halos from eventually appearing in Director.

Copying objects between applications

You can use the Clipboard (Copy and Paste commands) to copy objects from Illustrator to any other Adobe program. If you paste into Photoshop 5, you'll be prompted to choose whether to paste the objects as pixels or as paths 1.

If you drag-and-drop a path object from Illustrator into Photoshop, it will appear as pixels on its own layer. Hold down Command/Ctrl when dragging to keep the path object as a path in Photoshop 5.

TIP To match colors between Illustrator and other applications, see page 140.

Illustrator to the World Wide Web

The basic formula for outputting an image for on-line viewing may seem straightforward: Design the image in RGB color mode and export it in GIF or JPEG format, which is the file format used by Web browsers (the applications that combine text, images, and HTML code into a viewable page on the World Wide Web). However, when you load and view an image via a Web browser, you may be disappointed to find that not all colors or blends display well on the Web, and an illustration with a large, placed image may take an unacceptably long time to download and render, due to its large storage size. If an image looks overly dithered (grainy and dotty), or was subject to unexpected color substitutions, or takes too long to view on a Web page, it means your design is not outputting well. Some of the key issues that you'll need to address for on-line output are discussed on the remaining pages of this chapter.

Illustration size

In order to calculate the appropriate dimensions for your illustration, you must know beforehand what your intended viewers' monitor size and modem speed are. In most cases, you should design your image for a 14- or 15-inch monitor (the most common monitor sizes) and a 28.8 kbps or 56 kbps modem.

(Continued on the following page)

The largest Web page that can be viewed on such monitors is between 480 pixels high by 640 pixels wide or 600 x 800 pixels. Two different sets of pixel values are suggested because different monitor resolutions can be chosen. Since the Web browser window toolbar will display within the monitor size, your Web page can't occupy the entire browser window. It has to fit within the available space.

Saving a file in the GIF or JPEG file format will result in a smaller than normal file size due to the compression schemes built into these formats. The degree to which a GIF or JPEG file format compresses depends on how compressible the image is. Both formats cause a small reduction in image quality, but it's worth the size reduction tradeoff, because your image will download faster on the Web.

A file size of about 50K will download in about 30 seconds on a 28.8 kbps modem or 15 seconds on a 56 kbps modem. A document with a flat background color and a few flat color shapes will compress a great deal (expect a file size in the range of 20 to 50K). A large document (over 100K) with many color areas, a placed bitmap image, or gradients won't compress nearly as much.

Exporting gradients and placed images from Illustrator

A placed continuous-tone image will become posterized and dithered in Illustrator's GIF89a format, regardless of whether you use the Adaptive or Web palette. This posterization will be visible when you reopen the GIF file in Illustrator or in the browser. If you want to combine Illustrator paths with continuous-tone images, we recommend you place the illustration into Photoshop and use Photoshop's File menu > Export > GIF89a Export command. The resulting Web image will be truer to the original bitmap image's colors. If you want to export only paths, then Illustrator's GIF89a format option in the File menu > Export dialog box command will work fine.

TIPS FOR CREATING WEB IMAGES

■ Let the nature of the image content—whether it's flat color or continuous-tone—determine which file format you use.

■ Use as small an illustration size as is practical, balancing the file size, which affects download speed, with aesthetics.

■ Remember this fail-safe option for coloring objects for viewing on both Macintosh and Windows browsers: Copy swatches from the Web Swatch library into the document's Swatches palette, and choose your colors from there.

■ Reduce the resolution of any placed images to 72 ppi.

■ View the image through a Web browser on someone else's computer so you can see how quickly it actually downloads and how good (or bad) it looks.

World Wide Web

Macintosh: To determine a file's actual storage size, highlight the file name in the Finder, then choose File > Get Info. This is a more accurate measure of a file's storage size than the View by Name readout in the Finder.

Windows: To determine a file's actual storage size, highlight the file name in the Explorer, then right-click on the file name and choose Properties. This is a more accurate measure of a file's storage size than the View > Details readout in the Explorer.

SMOOTHIE

Here's a way to produce a smoother gradient image in the browser. Rasterize the gradient mesh object in Illustrator, place or paste the raster object into Photoshop, and then export it using Photoshop's GIF89a option.

JPEG is the better format choice for illustrations that contain placed, photographic-type images that were exported from Illustrator.

GIF: A compromise

GIF is an 8-bit file format, which means a GIF image can contain a maximum of 256 colors. Since a lot of Web users have 8-bit monitors, which can display a maximum of 256 colors (not the thousands or millions of colors that make images look pleasing to the eye), GIF is the standard format to use. It's a good choice for images that contain flat color areas and shapes with well-defined edges, like type.

To prepare an image for the GIF format and to see how the image will look when viewed via the browser, set your monitor's resolution to 256 colors (not Thousands or Millions). This technique is only worthwhile if changing monitor resolution is convenient. Otherwise use a program like ImageReady to preview images.

Your color choices for a GIF image should be based on the display capabilities of the Web browser palette. Most browser palettes are 8-bit, which means they can display only 256 colors. Macintosh and Windows browsers share only 216 colors out of the possible 256 colors on an 8-bit palette, so working with a Web palette is essential. Colors that aren't on the palette are simulated by dithering, a display technique that intermixes color pixels to simulate other colors. To prevent unexpected color substitutions or dithering, make sure you use the Web palette when creating or exporting your illustration as a GIF. Color substitutions are particularly noticeable in flat color areas. (See also page 317.)

Illustrator's Web palette

Illustrator provides two places for accessing the Web palette. You can open the Web Swatch library and copy the color swatches into the document's Swatches palette. Or you can choose the Web palette option in the GIF89a dialog box, which is accessed via File menu > Export. Use the Web Swatch library

World Wide Web

for coloring objects; use the GIF89a Web palette for making colors in placed images conform to the standard Web browser palette. *Note:* using Illustrator's Web or Adaptive palette option for exporting a GIF will cause gradients and placed imagery to become posterized and dithered.

JPEG: The sometimes solution

The JPEG format is a better choice for preserving color fidelity if your illustration contains gradients and placed images and if it's intended for viewing on a 24-bit monitor, which can display millions of colors.

A JPEG plus: it can compress a 24-bit image to a file as small as GIF's compression can create from an 8-bit image.

JPEG's shortcomings: First, a JPEG file has to be decompressed when it's downloaded for viewing on a Web page, which takes time. Secondly, JPEG is not a good choice for flat-color images or type, because its compression methods tend to produce artifacts along the well-defined edges of those types of images. And third, not all Web viewers use 24-bit monitors, and a JPEG image will be dithered on an 8-bit monitor. You can lower your monitor's setting to 256 Colors to preview what the image will look like in an 8-bit setting.

If you choose JPEG as your output format, you can experiment by creating and saving several versions of an illustration using varying degrees of compression. Open the JPEG versions of the illustration in Illustrator and view them at 100% or a more magnified view. Decide which degree of compression is acceptable by weighing the file size versus the diminished image quality.

Each time an image is re-saved as a JPEG, some original image data is destroyed, and the more the image is degraded. The greater the degree of compression, the greater the data loss. To prevent this data loss, edit your illustration in Illustrator format and then save a JPEG copy when the illustration is finished.

DRESS DOWN YOUR BITMAPS

Use an image editing program such as Photoshop to reduce the number of pixels and lessen the color complexity in a bitmap image before placing it. And lower the image resolution to 72 ppi.

You can also use Illustrator's Rasterize command to reduce the pixel resolution of a placed image (check the Anti-Alias option).

To reduce color complexity, try posterizing a continuous-tone image down to somewhere between four and eight levels in the image editing program and then place the image. The resulting file size will be similar to that of a flat-color image, but you will have lost the smooth, continuous-color transitions in the bargain.

IMAGEREADY

Using the LiveView window in Adobe's ImageReady program, which is used to prepare graphics for optimal Web viewing, you can instantly preview various file formats and compression methods on an image.

SEPARATIONS 24

You can produce color separations directly from Illustrator. This chapter contains a brief introduction to Illustrator's Separation Setup dialog box and an introduction to trapping, which helps to compensate for color misregistration on press.

Si Huynh

Trapping and color separations are usually handled by a prepress provider—either a service bureau or a print shop. Talk with your print shop before producing color separations or building traps. They'll tell you what settings to use. Don't guess—this isn't the time to "wing it."

What are color separations?

To print an illustration on press, unless your print shop uses direct-to-plate technology, you need to supply them with or have them produce film output (color separations) from your Illustrator file—one sheet per process or spot color. Your print shop will use the film separations to produce plates to use on the press—one plate for each color.

In **process color** printing, four ink colors, Cyan (C), Magenta (M), Yellow (Y), and Black (K), are used to produce a multitude of colors. A document that contains color photographs or other continuous-tone images must be output as a four-color process job.

In **spot color** printing, a separate plate is produced for each spot color. Pantone inks are the most commonly used spot color inks. Using Illustrator's Separation Setup, you can control which spot colors are converted into process colors and which will remain as spot colors, and you can specify which colors will output.

Managing color in Illustrator

Colors in digital images can vary dramatically from one device to the next. For example, an apple in your illustration of a fruit basket may be the perfect shade of red when you see it on your monitor, but when it's printed, it may end up looking more like an orange, or even a banana!

Taking a few minutes to calibrate your monitor and to learn how to use ICC profiles can help you achieve a closer match between colors on your screen and those produced by your printer or another monitor.

ICC profiles are standard cross-platform profiles established by the International Color Consortium (www.icc.org). They describe the color spaces of images and output devices and help you maintain accurate colors from one device to the next, as well as across different platforms and other applications that support ICC profiles.

An image you import can have an attached ICC profile that will ensure your computer displays the colors accurately. In addition, you can attach, or "tag," files you save in Illustrator with an ICC profile that will remain with it.

Calibration

The first step toward achieving color consistency is to calibrate your monitor. In this 10-minute procedure, you will define the RGB color space your monitor can display using the Adobe Gamma control panel, which is installed automatically with Illustrator and some other Adobe applications. You will adjust the contrast and brightness, gamma, color balance, and white point of your monitor. The Adobe Gamma Control Panel creates an ICC profile, which Illustrator uses to display the colors in your artwork accurately.

Note: It is necessary to calibrate your monitor and save the settings as an ICC profile only once for all applications.

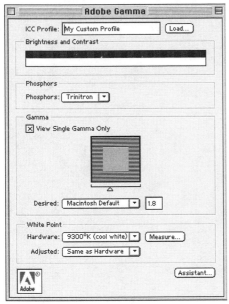

1 *The Adobe Gamma dialog box.*

To calibrate your monitor:

1. Give the monitor 30 minutes to warm up so the display is stabilized, and establish a level of room lighting that will remain constant.

2. Set the desktop pattern to light gray.

3. *Macintosh:* Choose Apple menu > Control Panels > Adobe Gamma.

   Windows: Choose Program Files > Common Files > Adobe > Calibration > Adobe Gamma.

4. Click Step by Step (Assistant), which will walk you through the process.
   or
   Click Control Panel to choose settings from a single dialog box with no explanation **1**. (If the Adobe Gamma dialog opens directly, you can skip this step.)

   Note: Click Next. If you're using the Assistant, click Next between dialogs.

5. Leave the default monitor ICC profile.
   or
   Click Load and select a profile that more closely matches your monitor.

6. Turn up your monitor's brightness and contrast settings; leave the contrast at maximum; and adjust the brightness to make the alternating gray squares in the top bar as dark as possible, but not black, while keeping the lower bar bright white.

7. For Phosphors, choose your monitor type or choose Custom and enter the Red, Green and Blue chromaticity coordinates specified by your monitor manufacturer.

   The gray square represents a combined grayscale reading of your monitor. Adjust the gamma using this slider until the smaller solid-color box matches the outer, stripey box. It helps to squint. You might find it easier to deselect the View Single Gamma Only box and make separate adjustments based on the readings for Red, Green, and Blue.

(Continued on the following page)

Calibrate Your Monitor

For Desired, select the default for your system: 1.8 (Mac) or 2.2 (Windows), if this option is available.

For Hardware, select the white point the monitor manufacturer specifies, or click Measure and follow the instructions.

For Adjusted, choose Same as Hardware. Or if you know the color temperature at which your image will ultimately be viewed, you can choose it from the drop-down menu or choose Custom and enter it. *Note:* This option is not available for all monitors.

8. Close the Adobe Gamma window and save the settings. You're done!

Note: If you change your monitor's brightness and contrast settings or change the room lighting, you should recalibrate your monitor. Also keep in mind that this procedure is just a beginning. Professional calibration requires more precise monitor measurement using expensive hardware devices such as colorimeters and spectrophotometers.

Color management modules

Illustrator uses a Color Management Module, or CMM, to interpret ICC profiles, and there are several from which you can choose: Adobe CMS; the Kodak Digital Science Color Management System; or a system-level CMM that comes with your operating system (Apple's ColorSync for Macs, Microsoft's ICM for Windows).

We recommend using Illustrator's default CMM, Adobe CMS. It works best in most circumstances. The CMM file, called RB2Connection.mac (Macintosh)/ RB2Connection.win (Windows), is automatically installed in the Adobe Illustrator folder. Illustrator also requires the Color Conversion and Color Conversion Utilities plug-ins, which are installed in the Adobe Illustrator > Plug-ins > Extensions folder.

TIP To un-install color management in Illustrator, remove the Color Conversion and Color Conversion Utilities plug-ins.

CMMs

USING PHOTOSHOP RGB COLOR SPACES AS RGB PROFILES IN ILLUSTRATOR 8

On the Illustrator 8 CD-ROM, in the Adobe Technical Info > Photoshop RGB Color Profiles folder, is a set of RGB ICC color profiles that match the working RGB color space options accessible in Photoshop 5. Copy these profiles to the appropriate system folder location. Once installed, these profiles can help maintain color consistency between RGB images generated in Photoshop 5 and imported into Illustrator 8.

These Photoshop color space profiles are accessed when a profile is chosen from the Monitor (RGB) drop-down menu (step 2, at right). Choose the same profile that was used when the image was created in Photoshop 5.

In Illustrator 8, the SMPTE-240M profile in Photoshop is called "Adobe RGB (1998).icm" and the sRGB profile in Photoshop is called "sRGB Color Space Profile.icm".

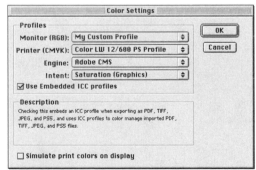

1 *The Color Settings dialog box when color management system software is installed.*

The Color Settings dialog box is where you can customize Illustrator's color management features.

To enter Color Settings:

1. Choose File menu > Color Settings.

2. From the Monitor (RGB) drop-down menu, choose the profile you created when you calibrated your monitor **1** or choose the built-in profile for your monitor. *Note:* The Adobe Illustrator Monitor Default profile does not support color management.

3. From the Printer (CMYK) drop-down menu, choose the profile that matches your final, CMYK output printer.

4. Leave the Engine setting on Adobe CMS—the default.

5. You have several options for determining how Illustrator converts colors from the RGB color space to the CMYK color space for printing purposes. Base your decision on how you plan to use the artwork, and experiment with the settings to achieve the best results for your artwork. These are the Intent options:

   Default, which uses the source file's rendering intent when converting from RGB to CMYK.

   Perceptual (Images), which may alter the color values but maintains the relationship between colors. This mode is suitable for continuous-tone images.

   Saturation (Graphics), which converts out-of-gamut colors to colors with the same saturation that fall just within the printable gamut. This mode is useful for business graphics and other circumstances in which color saturation and vividness are top priorities.

   Relative Colorimetric, which converts out-of-gamut colors to those with the same lightness that fall just within the printable gamut. This mode is useful in instances when maintaining color exactitude is a high priority.

(Continued on the following page)

Color Settings

Absolute Colorimetric, which converts colors without matching white points. This mode is the most accurate but it may produce artifacts or banding and so is not recommended.

6. Check the Use Embedded ICC profiles box. This tells Illustrator to read and apply the ICC profile information accompanying files you import from other ICC-supporting applications. It works only with JPEG, PDF, Photoshop 5, and TIFF file formats.

Checking the Use Embedded ICC profiles box will also tell Illustrator to tag with an ICC profile the artwork you create and save in JPEG, PDF, Photoshop 5, or TIFF format. If you open one of these files in another ICC-supporting application, this information will be used to display the colors accurately.

Illustrator cannot tag images in its native vector format or the EPS format with an ICC profile. If you want to move an Illustrator file to another operating system and continue editing there while maintaining color management, you must save the file as a PDF document with an embedded profile. However, PDF offers only limited editing capabilities.

7. Check the "Simulate print colors on display" box if you want Illustrator to display a simulation of how your colors will look when printed.

8. Click OK (Return/Enter).

To manage colors in artwork imported from or exported to other ICC-supporting applications:

1. Make sure the aforementioned CMM file and Color Conversion Utilities plug-ins have been installed in the Illustrator folder.

2. Set the exporting application's color-management settings to use ICC profiles and the same CMM you use in Illustrator, which may require that you select one of the other CMM options in Illustrator.

WHAT IS OVERPRINTING?

Normally, Illustrator automatically knocks out any color under an object so the object color won't mix with the color beneath it. If you check the Overprint Fill or Overprint Stroke box on the Attributes palette, the fill or stroke color will overprint colors underneath it. Where colors overlap, a combination color will be produced. Turn on this Overprint option if you're building traps. Colors will overprint on a printing press, but not on a PostScript color composite printer. You can simulate the mixing of overlapping colors by applying the Pathfinder palette's Hard Mix command.

(Consult the exporting application's documentation for directions.)

3. Export the artwork in JPEG, PDF, Photoshop 5, or TIFF format and open it in Illustrator.

To prepare a file for separations:

1. Calibrate your monitor (see pages 325–326).

2. Decide which colors in the illustration you want to overprint (see the sidebar at left).

3. Create traps, if needed (see pages 334–338).

4. Place any objects that you don't want to appear on the color separations on a separate layer and uncheck the Print option for that layer, or hide the layer altogether.

5. Create cropmarks, if you need them (see page 307).

Now proceed with the instructions on the next page.

Prepare a File for Separations

To use Separation Setup:

1. Choose File menu > Separation Setup.

2. You'll see a file preview window on the left and separation settings on the right. The dialog box will be grayed out until a PPD file is opened (the next step).

3. To open or change the current PPD file, click Open PPD on the right side of the dialog box, locate and highlight the PPD file specified by your service bureau for your target printer or imagesetter, then click Open 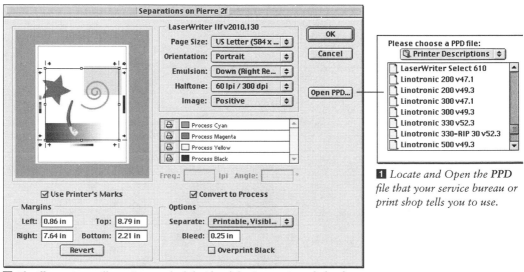1. The PPD files should be located in the Printer Descriptions folder in the Macintosh Systems folder > Extensions folder (Mac)/Windows > System subdirectory (Win). If they're not there, look in the Utilities folder in the Illustrator 8 application folder.

4. *Optional:* The white (or black) area in the preview window represents the page size. Separation Setup will automatically choose the default page size for the chosen printer definition. Choose a new size from the Page Size drop-down menu if your print shop requests that you do so.

For steps 5–8, ask your print shop for advice.

5. From the Orientation drop-down menu, choose Portrait to position the image vertically inside the imageable area of the separation **2**.
   or
   Choose Landscape to position the image horizontally inside the imageable area of the separation. The orientation of the image on the page will change; the orientation of the page on the film will not.

6. Choose Up (Right Reading) or Down (Right Reading) from the Emulsion drop-down menu.

7. Choose a combined Halftone screen ruling (lpi)/Device resolution (dpi) from the Halftone drop-down menu.

8. Choose Positive or Negative from the Image drop-down menu.

9. You can click OK at any time to save the current Separation Setup settings and you can reopen the dialog box at a later time to make further changes. When you save your document, the separation settings will save with the document. Continue with the instructions on pages 331–333.

1 *Locate and Open the PPD file that your service bureau or print shop tells you to use.*

2 *The illustration will preview on the left side of the **Separations** dialog box. Choose the settings your print shop specifies from the right side of the dialog box.*

By default, Illustrator will create and print a separation for each process and spot color used in an illustration. Using the Separation Setup dialog box, you can turn printing on or off for individual colors or convert individual spot colors into process colors.

Choosing colors to print and/or convert to process

1. Choose File menu > Separation Setup if that dialog box isn't already open.

2. In the scroll window, you will see a listing for each color used in the illustration. For each process color you do not want to print, click the printer icon next to the color name to hide the icon. (Click again to show the icon.)

3. Check the Convert to Process box to convert all spot colors in the document into process colors. This is the default setting.
   or

   Uncheck the Convert to Process box **1**, then:

   Click in the box next to the spot color name until a four-color process icon appears for each spot color you want to convert into a process color and print.
   or
   Keep clicking until a printer icon appears to keep the color as a spot color and print it.
   or
   Keep clicking until the printer icon disappears to prevent a spot color from printing.

TIP Don't change the Freq. (Frequency) or Angle settings unless you're advised to do so by your service bureau.

TIP Check the Overprint Black box if you want black fills and strokes to overprint background colors. You don't need to mix a process black (a black made from a mixture of C, M, Y, and K) to use this option.

(Continued on the following page)

Four-color process icon: This spot color will convert to process and print. *Printer icon: This color will print as a separate plate.*

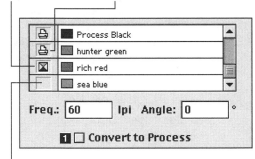

A blank space (no icon): This color won't print.

Separation Setup

Creating crop marks for separations

If you haven't created crop marks for your document in Illustrator, the Separation Setup feature will, by default, create crop marks at the edge of the illustration's bounding box, which is the smallest rectangle that can encompass all the objects and direction lines in the illustration. It displays as a black rectangle in the preview window. Adobe recommends setting crop marks in Illustrator using Object menu > Crop Marks > Make rather than using Separation Setup to set crop marks so you can control more precisely the exact printable area of your illustration.

Separation Setup regards crop marks created using the Trim Marks filter as artwork. If your document contains Trim Marks, you can uncheck Use Printer's Marks to remove the default cropmarks. Unfortunately, this will also remove all printer's marks (crop and registration marks and color bars). Check this box to restore printer's marks.

The bounding box defines the printable area around which Separation Setup places crop marks. You can resize the bounding box in the preview window so it surrounds a different part of the illustration, though it usually does not need to be adjusted. If you move or resize the bounding box, Separation Setup crop marks will move with the bounding box. You might need to move the image and/or resize the bounding box if the illustration contains objects that are outside the artboard and there are no Illustrator-generated crop marks, because Separation Setup will include off-the-page objects as part of the image to be printed. Follow the instructions below if you want to resize the bounding box (and thus re-crop the illustration).

Re-cropping the illustration in the bounding box

In the Separation Setup dialog box:

To move the illustration relative to the bounding box, position the pointer over the image in the preview window, then drag **1**.

or

There are several reasons to proof your computer artwork before it's printed. First, the RGB colors that you see on your computer screen won't match the printed CMYK colors unless your monitor is properly calibrated. Obtaining a proof will give you an opportunity to correct the color balance or brightness of a picture, or to catch output problems like banding in a gradient. And most print shops need a proof to refer to so they know what the printed piece is supposed to look like. Digital (direct-from-disk) color proofs—like IRIS or 3M prints—are inexpensive, but they're not perfectly reliable. An advantage of using an IRIS print, though, is that you can color correct your original electronic file and run another IRIS print before you order film.

A more accurate but more expensive proof is a Chromalin or Matchprint, which is produced from the actual film (color separations). Matchprint colors may be slightly more saturated than final print colors, though. The most reliable color proof—and the most expensive—is a press proof, which is produced in the print shop from your film negatives on the final paper stock.

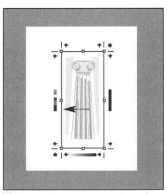

1 *Move the image in its bounding box.*

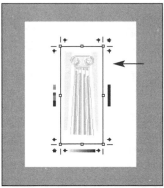

2 *Drag any part of the line except a handle to move the bounding box and the illustration together.*

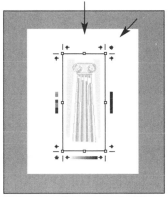

3 *Drag a side or corner handle to reshape the bounding box.*

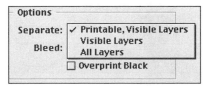

4 *The Separate drop-down menu in the Separation Setup dialog box.*

To move the black line bounding box and the image, position the pointer over any non-handle part of the line and drag the box **2**.

or

To resize the black line bounding box, drag any of its four corner or side handles **3**.

TIP To restore the default bounding box, click Revert. The original values will be reentered into the Left, Right, Top, and Bottom fields.

Specifying which layers in the illustration will separate

Choose one of these options from the Separate drop-down menu in the Separation Setup dialog box to control which layers will be color separated **4**:

Printable, Visible Layers to separate only those visible layers for which the Print option was turned on. To use this option effectively, place any objects you don't want separated on a special non-printing layer. Separation Setup will place the crop marks correctly.

Visible Layers to separate only those layers that aren't hidden.

All Layers to separate all layers.

Separation Setup

What is trapping?

Trapping is the slight enlargement of a color area so it overlaps another color. The purpose of trapping is to compensate for gaps that might appear between colors due to misregistration on press.

There are two basic kinds of traps. A **spread** trap extends a lighter-color object over a darker background color **1**. A **choke** trap extends a lighter background color over a darker-color object **2**. In either case, the extending color overprints the object or background color, and a combination color is produced where they overlap.

In Illustrator, you can build traps automatically or manually by specifying your own stroke-width percentages. To turn on automatic trapping, see page 337.

Note: Ask your print shop for advice before building traps into your illustration.

To create a spread trap manually:

1. Select the lighter-color foreground object.

2. Apply a stroke in the same color as the object's fill. The stroke weight should be **twice** the trap width that your print shop recommends for this object.

3. Open the Attributes palette, and check the Overprint Stroke box **3**. The foreground object will overlap the background object by half the thickness of the new stroke. The new stroke will blend with the background color via the Overprint option, and it will extend halfway inside and halfway outside the edge of the object. *Note:* You'll see this only on high-end output.

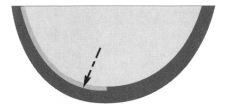

1 *Spread a lighter-color foreground object.*

2 *Choke a darker-color foreground object.*

The trap shrinks the darker-color object.

3 *Overprint Stroke*

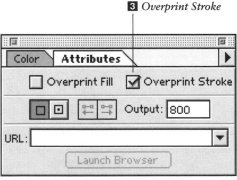

*The **Attributes** palette.*

TRAP AFTER SCALING

If you apply automatic trapping and then change an object's size, the trap width will change. You should apply trapping *after* you finalize the size of the objects.

STROKES WHERE YOU NEED 'EM

You can use the Outline command to create trap strokes only where they're needed. To do this, create a new layer, then select the objects to be trapped. On the Layers palette, Option-drag/Alt-drag the small square (to the right of the Layer name) up to the new layer to copy the objects to the exact same location on the new layer. Hide the original layer. Select the copied objects, click the Outline button on the Pathfinder palette to create strokes from those objects, then set the resulting strokes to overprint. Finally, using the Direct-selection tool, select and delete any stroke segments that you don't need, such as any strokes on a blank, white background, and apply a stroke weight that's twice the trap amount your print shop specifies.

To create a choke trap manually:

1. Select the darker-colored foreground object.

2. Apply a stroke in the same color as the lighter background object's fill, in a weight that's twice the trap width your print shop recommends for this object.

3. Check the Overprint Stroke box on the Attributes palette. The lighter background color will now overlap the dark foreground object by half the width of the new stroke.

TIP A choke trap reduces the area of the darker object by half the stroke weight. Be careful if you choke small type!

To trap a line manually:

1. Apply a stroke color and weight.

2. Choose Object menu > Path > Outline Path. The line will become a filled object, the same width as the original stroke.

3. Apply a stroke to the modified line. If the line is lighter than the background color, apply the same color as the fill of the line. Otherwise, apply the lighter background color. Choose a stroke weight that is twice the trap width your print shop recommends for this object.

4. Check the Overprint Stroke box on the Attributes palette. The line will now overlap the background color by half the width of the new stroke ■. The stroke will blend with the background color when it overprints.

TIP If you're going to apply a choke trap to the line (where the stroke created in step 3 takes on the background color), the original outlined path will be reduced by the stroke weight. The stroke will reduce the path by half the stroke weight on each side of the path. To counteract this, create a stroked line (step 1) in a weight that is equal to the desired line weight plus the needed trap weight. For example, you have a 1 pt. line that needs a .2 pt. trap. Create a line with a 1.2 pt. weight stroke for step 1.

Before using this feature, read the sidebar at right and consult with your print shop.

To overprint a specified percentage of black:

1. Select an object or objects that contain black.

2. Choose Filter menu > Colors > Overprint Black.

3. Choose Add Black from the drop-down menu to turn the Overprint option on for the specified percentage you will enter 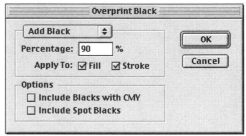.

   or

   Choose Remove Black to turn the Overprint option off for the specified percentage entered.

4. Enter a Percentage value. Objects containing this black percentage will overprint or not overprint depending on your choice for step 3.

5. Check Apply To: Fill to overprint black fills; check Stroke to overprint black strokes.

6. Check the Include Blacks with CMY box to have any CMYK mixture containing the specified percentage of black overprint.

7. Check the Include Spot Blacks box to have any custom color containing the specified percentage of black overprint.

   Note: To overprint a spot color, you must check both options boxes.

8. Click OK (Return/Enter).

TIP If you select more than one black object and then apply the Overprint Black filter, the filter will affect only those objects containing the specified percentage of black. The objects that are affected will remain selected after the filter is applied.

WHY THE OVERPRINT BLACK FILTER?

Normally, in PostScript color separations, objects on top knock out the color of objects underneath them so their ink colors don't intermix on press. When a color overprints, on the other hand, it prints right on top of the color beneath it and mixes with that color. Black is sometimes printed this way to eliminate the need for trapping. Using the Overprint Black filter, you can turn on overprinting or prevent overprinting in individual objects by exact percentages of black. (Using the Separation Setup dialog box to specify overprinting instead would cause all black areas to overprint.)

1 *The Overprint Black dialog box.*

Trapping

ADJUST TRAP HEIGHT AND WIDTH

Using the Trap command, you can adjust a trap to compensate for horizontal or vertical stretching of the paper on press. Enter a Height/ Width percentage above 100% to widen the trap thickness for horizontal lines, or enter a Height/ Width percentage below 100% to narrow the trap thickness for horizontal lines. Leave the percentage at 100 to have the same trap width apply to both horizontals and verticals.

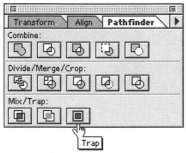

1 *Click the* **Trap** *button on the* **Pathfinder** *palette.*

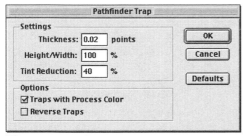

2 *Choose the trap* **Thickness** *and other options in the* **Pathfinder Trap** *dialog box.*

The Trap command creates traps automatically by determining which color object is lighter, and then spreading that color into the darker object. *Note:* The Trap command won't trap a placed image or any object that contains a gradient or pattern fill.

To create traps automatically:

1. Select two or more objects.

2. Click the Trap button on the Pathfinder palette **1**. If this button isn't visible, choose Show Options from the palette menu.

3. Enter the Thickness amount your print shop specifies for the trap **2**.

Ask your print shop about optional steps 4–7.

4. Enter a Height/Width percentage to compensate for paper stretch on press (see the sidebar).

5. Enter a Tint Reduction percentage to prevent trap areas between light colors from printing too darkly.

6. Check the Traps with Process Color box to convert spot color traps in the selected objects into process colors, and thus prevent the creation of a separate plate just for traps.

7. Check the Reverse Traps box to trap darker colors into lighter colors.

8. Click OK (Return/Enter).

Trapping

The Trap filter doesn't always account for the stroke color of a selected object. To overcome this limitation, convert the stroke into a filled object.

To create a trap on top of a fill and a stroke (a workaround):

1. Choose the Selection tool, then click on an object that contains a fill and stroke.

2. Choose Object menu > Path > Outline Path.

3. Deselect both objects, choose the Direct-selection tool, then click on the outermost object (the "stroke").

4. Click the Unite button on the Pathfinder palette to remove any excess points from the outline path object (the "stroke").

5. Apply the Trap command (instructions on the previous page).

AVOID TRAPPING ALTOGETHER?

Make sure all your colors share at least one component color in common (Cyan, Magenta, Yellow, or Black).

TRAPPING TYPE

Try not to use process colors on small type. Any misregistration on press will make the small type difficult to read. To trap type, make a copy of the type, choose Paste in Back, create a stroke for the copy, and set the stroke to overprint. Type can also be converted into outlines. The resulting outline objects can be trapped like any other object.

Trapping

KEYBOARD SHORTCUTS

Files	**Macintosh**	**Windows**
New dialog box	Command-N	Ctrl-N
Open dialog box	Command-O	Ctrl-O
Close	Command-W	Ctrl-W
Save	Command-S	Ctrl-S
Save As dialog box	Command-Shift-S	Ctrl-Shift-S
Save a Copy dialog box	Command-Option-S	Ctrl-Alt-S
Document Setup dialog box	Command-Option-P	Ctrl-Alt-P
Page/Print Setup dialog box	Command-Shift-P	Ctrl-Shift-P
General Preferences dialog box	Command-K	Ctrl-K
Print dialog box	Command-P	Ctrl-P
Quit/Exit Illustrator	Command-Q	Ctrl-Q

Dialog boxes

Highlight next field/option	Tab	Tab
Highlight previous field/option	Shift Tab	Shift Tab
Cancel	Command . (period key) or Esc	Esc
OK	Return	Enter

Open/Save dialog boxes

Desktop	Command-D	
Up one folder level	Command-up arrow	
Open file	Double-click file name	Double-click file name

Palettes

Show/hide all palettes	Tab	Tab
Show/hide all palettes except Toolbox	Shift-Tab	Shift-Tab
Reset Toolbox to default settings	Command-Shift double-click any tool	Ctrl-Shift double-click any tool
Show/Hide Brushes	F-5	F-5
Show/Hide Color	Command-I or F-6	Ctrl-I or F-6
Show/Hide Layers	F-7	F-7
Show/Hide Info	F-8	F-8
Show/Hide Gradient	F-9	F-9
Show/Hide Stroke	F-10	F-10
Show/Hide Attributes	F-11	F-11
Show/Hide Character	Command-T	Ctrl-T

Keyboard Shortcuts

	Macintosh	**Windows**
Show/Hide Paragraph	Command-M	Ctrl-M
Apply value in palette field	Return	Enter
Apply value in field, keep field selected	Shift-Return	Shift-Enter
Highlight next field	Tab	Tab
Highlight previous field	Shift Tab	Shift Tab
Highlight field used in last-used palette (if there are no fields, whole palette highlights)	Command-~	Ctrl-~

Layers palette

Hide/show all other layers	Option-click eye icon	Alt-click eye icon
View a layer in Artwork/Preview view	Command-click eye icon	Ctrl-click eye icon
View all other layers in Artwork/ Preview view	Command-Option-click eye icon	Ctrl-Alt-click eye icon
Lock/unlock all other layers	Option-click blank box in second column	Alt-click blank box in second column
Delete a layer (no alert box)	Option-click palette trash button	Alt-click palette trash button
Create a new layer at the top of the list	Command-click New Layer button	Ctrl-click New Layer button
Create a new layer below the currently selected layer	Command-Option-click New Layer button	Ctrl-Alt-click New Layer button

Swatches palette

Quick-type to select a swatch name	Command-Option-click list, start typing name	Ctrl-Alt-click list, start typing name

Color palette

Change fill color if Stroke box on Toolbox is selected, or vice versa	Option-click or drag in color spectrum bar on Color palette	Alt-click or drag in color spectrum bar on Color palette
Cycle through color models	Shift-click color spectrum bar	Shift-click color spectrum bar

Undo/redo

Undo last operation	Command-Z	Ctrl-Z
Redo last undone operation	Command-Shift-Z	Ctrl-Shift-Z

Display

Preview/Artwork View toggle	Command-Y	Ctrl-Y
Preview Selection	Command-Shift-Y	Ctrl-Shift-Y
Use crosshair pointer (drawing tools)	Caps lock	Caps lock
Show/Hide Rulers	Command-R	Ctrl-R
Show/Hide Edges	Command-H	Ctrl-H
Display entire artboard	Double-click Hand tool	Double-click Hand tool
Fit in Window	Command-0	Ctrl-0

	Macintosh	**Windows**
Actual size (100%)	Double-click Zoom tool or Command-1	Double-click Zoom tool or Ctrl-1
Zoom out (Zoom tool selected)	Option-click	Alt-click
Zoom in (any tool selected)	Command-Spacebar-click or Command-+	Ctrl-Spacebar-click or Ctrl-+
Zoom out (any tool selected)	Command-Option-Spacebar-click or Command-– (minus)	Ctrl-Alt-Spacebar-click or Ctrl-– (minus)
Adjust Zoom marquee position	Drag with Zoom tool then hold Spacebar	Drag with Zoom tool then hold Spacebar
Zoom in on specific area of artboard	Drag Zoom tool or Command-drag in Navigator palette	Drag Zoom tool or Ctrl-drag in Navigator palette
Use Hand tool (any tool selected)	Spacebar	Spacebar
Hide a selected object	Command-3	Ctrl-3
Hide all unselected objects	Command-Option-Shift-3	Ctrl-Alt-Shift-3
Show All	Command-Option-3	Ctrl-Alt-3

Create objects

Create object from center using Rectangle, Rounded Rectangle, or Ellipse tool	Option-drag	Alt-drag
Create circle or square using Rectangle, Rounded Rectangle, or Ellipse tool	Shift-drag	Shift-drag

Polygon, Star, Spiral tools

Move object as you draw with Polygon, Star, or Spiral tool	Spacebar	Spacebar
Constrain orientation as you draw with Polygon, Star, or Spiral tool	Shift	Shift
Add or subtract sides as you draw with Polygon tool, points as you draw with the Star tool, or segments as you draw with the Spiral tool	Up or down arrow	Up or down arrow
Align shoulders as you draw with Star tool	Option	Alt
Increase or decrease outer radius as you draw with Star tool or decay as you draw with Spiral tool	Command	Ctrl

Select

Use the last-used selection tool (with any other tool chosen)	Command	Ctrl
Toggle between Selection tool and Direct-selection tool or Group-selection tool	Command-Tab	Ctrl-Tab
Toggle between Group-selection tool and Direct-selection tool	Option	Alt

Keyboard Shortcuts

	Macintosh	**Windows**
Selection marquee (any selection tool)	Drag	Drag
Select All	Command-A	Ctrl-A
Deselect All	Command-Shift-A	Ctrl-Shift-A
Select an object hidden behind another object	Command-Option-[	Ctrl-Alt-[

Move

Move dialog box	Double-click Selection tool	Double-click Selection tool
Drag a copy of object	Option-drag	Alt-drag
Move selected object in current Cursor key increments (Preferences > General)	Arrow keys	Arrow keys
Move selection in 10-pixel increments	Shift-arrow key	Shift-arrow key
Constrain movement to 45°, 90°, 135°, or 180°	Shift	Shift

Paths

Toggle between Add-anchor-point tool and Delete-anchor-point tool (either selected)	Option	Alt
Use Add-anchor-point tool (Scissors tool selected)	Option	Alt
Use Convert-direction-point tool (Pen tool selected)	Option	Alt
Constrain angle of direction line to 45°, 90°, 135°, or 180° (Direct-selection tool or Convert-direction-point tool selected)	Shift-drag	Shift-drag
Join two selected endpoints	Command-J	Ctrl-J
Average two selected points	Command-Option-J	Ctrl-Alt-J
Average and Join two selected endpoints	Command-Option-Shift-J	Ctrl-Alt-Shift-J
Close a path while drawing with the Pencil or Paintbrush tool	Drag tool and Option-click	Drag tool and Alt-click
Cut with Knife tool along a straight line	Option-drag tool	Alt-drag tool
Move mesh point along one of its lines	Shift-drag with Gradient Mesh tool	Shift-drag with Gradient Mesh tool
Add mesh point using current mesh color	Shift-click with Gradient Mesh tool	Shift-click with Gradient Mesh tool
Remove mesh point	Option-click with Gradient Mesh tool	Alt-click with Gradient Mesh tool

Paint

Toggle between Eyedropper tool and Paint Bucket tool (either one selected)	Option	Alt
Fill/Stroke box toggle (Toolbox and Color palette)	X	X
Apply last-used solid color	, (comma)	, (comma)

	Macintosh	**Windows**
Apply last-used gradient	. (period)	. (period)
Apply fill/stroke of None	/	/

Restack

Bring To Front	Command-Shift-]	Ctrl-Shift-]
Send To Back	Command-Shift-[	Ctrl-Shift-[
Bring Forward	Command-]	Ctrl-]
Send Backward	Command-[	Ctrl-[
Paste In Front	Command-F	Ctrl-F
Paste In Back	Command-B	Ctrl-B

Type

Use Area Type tool (Type tool selected, over open path)	Option	Alt
Use Path Type tool (Type tool selected, over closed path)	Option	Alt
Switch to vertical/horizontal type tool equivalent	Shift with any type tool	Shift with any type tool
Switch to Type tool when selecting type block	Double-click with any selection tool	Double-click with any selection tool
Select a word	Double-click	Double-click
Select a paragraph	Triple-click	Triple-click
Select all the type in a block	Command-A	Ctrl-A
Move insertion pointer left/right one word	Command-left/right arrow	Ctrl-left/right arrow
Move insertion pointer up/down one paragraph	Command-up/down arrow	Ctrl-up/down arrow
Hard Return	Return	Enter
Soft Return	Shift-Return	Shift-Enter
Align left	Command-Shift-L	Ctrl-Shift-L
Align center	Command-Shift-C	Ctrl-Shift-C
Align right	Command-Shift-R	Ctrl-Shift-R
Justify	Command-Shift-J	Ctrl-Shift-J
Justify last line	Command-Shift-F	Ctrl-Shift-F
Increase point size	Command-Shift->	Ctrl-Shift->
Decrease point size	Command-Shift-<	Ctrl-Shift-<
Increase leading	Option-down arrow	Alt-down arrow
Decrease leading	Option-up arrow	Alt-up arrow
Set leading to the current font size	Double-click leading button on Character palette	Double-click leading button on Character palette
Reset horizontal scale to 100%	Command-Shift-X	Ctrl-Shift-X
Reset tracking to 0	Command-Shift-Q	Ctrl-Shift-Q

Keyboard Shortcuts

	Macintosh	**Windows**
Select font field on Character palette	Command-Option-Shift-M	Ctrl-Alt-Shift-M
Increase kerning/tracking	Option-right arrow	Alt-right arrow
Decrease kerning/tracking	Option-left arrow	Alt-left arrow
Increase kerning/tracking 5x	Command-Option right arrow	Ctrl-Alt right arrow
Decrease kerning/tracking 5x	Command-Option left arrow	Ctrl-Alt left arrow
Increase baseline shift	Option-Shift up arrow	Alt-Shift up arrow
Decrease baseline shift	Option-Shift down arrow	Alt-Shift down arrow
Increase baseline shift 5x	Command-Option-Shift up arrow	Ctrl-Alt-Shift up arrow
Decrease baseline shift 5x	Command-Option-Shift down arrow	Ctrl-Alt-Shift down arrow
Force hyphenate a word	Command-Shift – (hyphen key)	Ctrl-Shift – (hyphen key)

Curly quotes

	Macintosh	**Windows**
'	Option Shift-]	Alt-146
'	Option-]	Alt-145
"	Option Shift-[	Alt-148
"	Option-[	Alt-147

Transform

	Macintosh	**Windows**
Transform tool dialog box (any transform tool except Free Transform)	Option-click	Alt-click
Transform object along multiple of 45° (Shear or Reflect tool)	Shift-drag	Shift-drag
Rotate object in 45° increments (Rotate tool)	Shift-drag	Shift-drag
Scale object uniformly (Scale tool)	Shift-drag	Shift-drag
Transform Again	Command-D	Ctrl-D
Transform pattern fill only (any transform tool)	~ drag	~ drag
Transform copy of object (any transform tool)	Option-drag	Alt-drag
Proportionally scale an object (Transform palette)	Modify W or H field, press Command-Return	Modify W or H field, press Ctrl-Enter
Transform copy of object (Transform palette)	Modify W or H field, press Option-Return	Modify W or H field, press Alt-Enter
Resize object proportionally using bounding box	Shift-drag a handle	Shift-drag a handle
Resize bounding box from center	Option-drag a handle	Alt-drag a handle

Free Transform tool

	Macintosh	**Windows**
Transform from center	Option-drag a handle	Alt-drag a handle

	Macintosh	**Windows**
Distort	Start dragging corner handle, then hold Command	Start dragging corner handle, then hold Ctrl
Shear	Start dragging side handle, then hold Command	Start dragging side handle, then hold Ctrl
Make Perspective	Start dragging corner handle, then hold Command-Option-Shift	Start dragging corner handle, then hold Ctrl-Alt-Shift

Compounds

Make compound path	Command-8	Ctrl-8
Release compound path	Command-Option-8	Ctrl-Alt-8

Clipboard

Cut	Command-X	Ctrl-X
Copy	Command-C	Ctrl-C
Paste	Command-V	Ctrl-V

Precision tools

Show/hide Guides	Command-;	Ctrl-;
Make Guides	Command-5	Ctrl-5
Release Guides	Command-Option-5	Ctrl-Alt-5
Release a guide	Command-Shift-double-click guide	Ctrl-Shift-double-click guide
Convert guide between horizontal/vertical orientation	Option-drag new guide	Alt-drag new guide
Lock/Unlock Guides	Command-Option-;	Ctrl-Alt-;
Show/Hide Grid	Command-"	Ctrl-"
Snap To Grid	Command-Shift-"	Ctrl-Shift-"
Snap To Point	Command-Option-"	Ctrl-Alt-"
Smart Guides	Command-U	Ctrl-U
Constrain Measure tool to multiple of 45°	Shift-drag with tool	Shift-drag with tool
Lock (selected object)	Command-2	Ctrl-2
Lock all unselected objects	Command-Option-Shift-2	Ctrl-Alt-Shift-2
Unlock All	Command-Option-2	Ctrl-Alt-2

Misc.

Group	Command-G	Ctrl-G
Ungroup	Command-Shift-G	Ctrl-Shift-G
Reapply last-used filter	Command-E	Ctrl-E
Open last-used filter dialog box	Command-Option-E	Ctrl-Alt-E
Repeat last-used Pathfinder command	Command-4	Ctrl-4

Keyboard Shortcuts

On-Screen help

The Help menu offers an on-screen help directory that functions like a digital stand-in for the Illustrator User Guide. To open it, choose Help menu > Contents. To access a topic, use one of these methods **1**–**2**.

■ Click the Contents tab, double-click a book name, then double-click a topic.

■ Click the Index tab, scroll through and double-click a name on the list or type in the full or partial name of the feature you are looking for to locate it on the list, then double-click the selected name.

■ Click the Find tab, type in a word or phrase to search for, then click Search.

You can quit the QuickHelp application completely or close the Help windows without quitting/exiting the Help application. If you don't quit QuickHelp, you can click in an open Illustrator window to get back to the program.

On-screen shortcuts

Mac & Windows: Choose Help menu > Quick Reference, then click a category **3**–**4**.

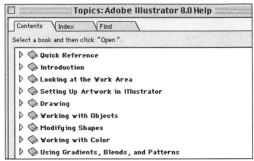

1 *Adobe Illustrator* **Help** *Contents (Macintosh). Each tab offers a different method for finding information.*

2 *Adobe Illustrator* **Help** *Contents (Windows).*

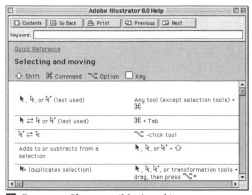

3 *On-screen Shortcuts (Macintosh).*

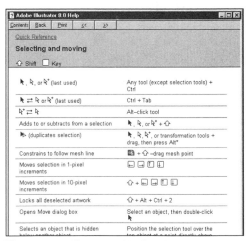

4 *On-screen Shortcuts (Windows).*

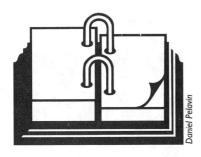
Daniel Pelavin

THE ARTISTS B

Ron Chan
Contact Jacqueline Dedell,
artists' representative
Voice 212-741-2539
ron@ronchan.com
http://www.ronchan.com
color section

Peter Fahrni
Voice 212-472-7126
100, 101

David Flaherty
1 Union Square West #712
New York, NY 10003
Voice 212-675-2038
Fax 212-675-4126
david@artarea.com
http://www.artarea.com
color section

Brad Hamann
80 Yerry Hill Road
Woodstock, NY 12498
Voice 914-679-4748
Fax 914-679-4699
brad@interport.net
http://www.darkdesign.com
color section

Si Huynh
Si Huynh Art and Design
5353 Dewar Road
Nanaimo, British Columbia
V9T5G1 Canada
Voice 1-250-758-2504
sihuynh@island.net
http://www.sihuynh.com
323, 348, color section

Diane Margolin
41 Perry Street
New York, NY 10014
Voice 212-691-9537
dimargolin@erols.com
60, 61, 63, 81, 86, 92, 94, 114,
139, 146, 148, 149, 152, 160,
161, 244, 245, 247, 264, 273, 278

Jose Ortega
Voice 212-228-2606
jose@joseortega.com
http://www.joseortega.com
color section

Daniel Pelavin
80 Varick Street
New York, NY 10013
Voice 212-941-7418
Fax 212-431-7138
daniel@pelavin.com
http://www.pelavin.com
iii, v, vii, ix, xi, xiii, xvi, 57, 63,
165, 223, 267, 347, color section

Carol Pulitzer
3311 Mandeville Canyon Road
Los Angeles, CA 90049
Voice 310-471-1805
Fax 310-440-0997
cpcooks@gte.net
http://www.theispot.com/
  artists/pulitzer
349, color section

Mike Quon
Designation, Inc.
53 Spring Street, 5th Floor
New York, NY 10012
Voice 212-226-6024
Fax 212-219-0331
mikequon@aol.com
http://www.mikequondesign.com
color section

Chris Spollen
Moonlight Press Studio
362 Cromwell Avenue
Ocean Breeze, NY 10305-2304
Voice 718-979-9695
Fax 718-979-8919
cjspollen@aol.com
http://www.inch.com/~cspollen/
1, 59, 121, 231, 234,
color section

Nancy Stahl
470 West End Avenue, 8G
New York, NY 10024
Voice 212-362-8779
Fax 212-362-7511
NStahl@aol.com
http://members.aol.com/nstahl/
  index.html
305, color section

Rich Stromwall
18600 Highland Avenue
Deephaven, MN 55391
Voice 612-473-5748
stromwal@bitstream.net
http://www2.bitstream.net/
  ~stromwal
color section

Special thanks to

All the artists listed on the previous page. Their contributions of artwork enliven this book, and they're certain to inspire our readers.

Nancy Aldrich-Ruenzel, Publisher, Peachpit Press; *Corbin Collins,* our editor; *Amy Changar,* production coordinator; *Gary-Paul Prince,* publicist; *Keasley Jones,* foreign rights manager; and the rest of the gang at Peachpit Press, for always being helpful and on the ball.

Victor Gavenda at Peachpit Press, for his patient and meticulous testing (and his sense of humor).

Rebecca Gulick, Senior Writer at eMediaweekly, San Francisco, *Jim Kingston,* of Kingston Design/New Media Productions, Macintosh guide and outfitter; and *Erle Grubb* of GrubbGraphics (New York City) for their writing contributions.

Adam Hausman, Macintosh systems specialist, for his layout services.

Jane Taylor Starwood (Mattituck, New York) and *Judy Susman* (New York City), for their proofreading services.

Emily Glossbrenner, of FireCrystal Communications, for her indexing services.

Cha-Rie Tang of Direct Imagination for sending us the wonderful Grammar of Ornament CD-ROM.

Christie Evans and *Dave Burkett* at Adobe Systems, Inc.

Si Huynh

INDEX

Carol Pulitzer

Index

Index

Index

Index

Index